Database Solutions

A step-by-step guide to building databases

D0217513

PEARSON Education

We work with leading authors to develop the
strongest educational materials in computing,
bringing cutting-edge thinking and best
learning practice to a global market.

Under a range of well-known imprints, including
Addison-Wesley, we craft high-quality print and
electronic publications which help readers to understand
and apply their content, whether studying or at work.

To find out more about the complete range of our
publishing, please visit us on the World Wide Web at:
www.pearsoned.co.uk

Database Solutions

A step-by-step guide to building databases

Second edition

Thomas M. Connolly

Carolyn E. Begg

PEARSON

Addison
Wesley

Harlow, England • London • New York • Boston • San Francisco • Toronto • Sydney • Singapore • Hong Kong
Tokyo • Seoul • Taipei • New Delhi • Cape Town • Madrid • Mexico City • Amsterdam • Munich • Paris • Milan

Pearson Education Limited
Edinburgh Gate
Harlow
Essex CM20 2JE
England

and Associated Companies throughout the world

Visit us on the World Wide Web at:
www.pearsoned.co.uk

First published 2000
Second edition published 2004

ISBN 0 321 17350 3

British Library Cataloguing-in-Publication Data
A catalogue record for this book is available from the British Library

Library of Congress Cataloging-in-Publication Data
A catalog record for this book is available from the Library of Congress

10 9 8 7 6 5 4 3 2 1
09 08 07 06 05 04

Typeset by 30
Printed and bound in Great Britain by Bell & Bain Ltd., Glasgow

The publisher's policy is to use paper manufactured from sustainable forests.

To   **Sheena,**

and to my three beautiful children **Kathryn, Michael,** and little **Stephen,** all of whom I owe so much to and love dearly.

To   **Carolyn,** for her friendship.

Thomas M. Connolly

To   **Neil,**

and to our sons **Calum** and **David.**

Carolyn E. Begg

Brief contents

Contents

Part 2   Database analysis and design techniques

Part 3 Logical database design

Part 4   Physical database design

Part 5 Second worked example

Part 6 Current and emerging trends

Appendices

Preface

Background

The database is now the underlying framework of the information system and has fundamentally changed the way many companies and individuals work. The developments in this technology over the last few years have produced database systems that are more powerful and more intuitive to use, and users are creating databases and applications without the necessary knowledge to produce an effective and efficient system. Looking at the literature, we found many excellent books that examine a part of the database system development lifecycle. However, we found very few that covered analysis, design, and implementation and described the development process in a simple-to-understand way that could be used by both technical and non-technical readers.

Our original concept therefore was to provide a book for both the academic and business community that explained as clearly as possible how to analyze, design, and implement a database. This would cover both simple databases consisting of a few tables and large databases containing tens to hundreds of tables. During the initial reviews that we carried out, it became clear that the book would also be useful for the academic community and provide a very simple and clear presentation of a database design methodology that would complement a more extensive recommended textbook, such as our own book *Database Systems*.

The methodology we present in this book for relational Database Management Systems (DBMSs) – the predominant system for business applications at present – has been tried and tested over the years in both industrial and academic environments. The methodology is divided into two phases:

■ a logical database design phase, in which we develop a model of what we're trying to represent while ignoring implementation details;

■ a physical database design phase, in which we decide how we're going to realize the implementation in the target DBMS, such as Microsoft Access, Microsoft SQL Server, Oracle, DB2, or Informix.

We present each phase as a series of simple-to-follow steps. For the inexperienced designer, we expect that the steps will be followed in the order described, and guidelines are provided throughout to help with this process. For the experienced designer, the methodology can be less prescriptive, acting more as a framework or checklist.

Helping to understand database design

To help you use the methodology and understand the important issues, we provide a comprehensive worked example that is integrated through the book based on a video rental company called *StayHome*. To reinforce the methodology we work through a second case study in Chapters 17 and 18 based on a veterinary clinic called *PerfectPets*.

To help you further, we have included additional database solutions in Appendix E (with corresponding SQL scripts included on the accompanying Website). Each solution has a small introduction, which you may like to read and then try to produce the database design yourself before looking at our sample solution.

Common data models

As well as providing you with additional experience of designing databases, Appendix E also provides you with many common data models that you may find useful. In fact, it has been estimated that one-third of a data model consists of common constructs that are applicable to most companies and the remaining two-thirds are either industry-specific or company-specific. Thus, most database design work consists of re-creating constructs that have already been produced many times before in other companies. The models featured may not represent your company exactly, but they may provide a starting point from which you can develop a more suitable model that matches your company's specific requirements. Some of the models we provide cover the following common business areas:

■ Customer Order Entry

■ Inventory Control

■ Asset Management

■ Project Management

- Course Management
- Human Resource Management
- Payroll Management.

UML (Unified Modeling Language)

Increasingly, companies are standardizing the way in which they model data by selecting a particular approach to data modeling and using it throughout their database development projects. A popular high-level data model used in logical database design, and the one we use in this book, is based on the concepts of the Entity–Relationship (ER) model. Currently there is no standard notation for an ER model. Most books that cover database design for relational DBMSs tend to use one of two conventional notations:

ER modeling covered in Chapter 7

- Chen's notation, consisting of rectangles representing entities and diamonds representing relationships, with lines linking the rectangles and diamonds;
- Crow's Feet notation, again consisting of rectangles representing entities and lines between entities representing relationships, with a crow's foot at the end of a line representing a one-to-many relationship.

Both notations are well supported by current CASE tools. However, they can be quite cumbersome to use and a bit difficult to explain. In this book, we instead use the class diagram notation from the latest object-oriented modeling language called **UML (Unified Modeling Language)**. UML is a notation that combines elements from the three major strands of object-oriented design: Rumbaugh's OMT modeling, Booch's Object-Oriented Analysis and Design, and Jacobson's Objectory. It is anticipated that UML will become a standard and the Object Management Group (OMG) has adopted UML as the standard notation for object methods.

We believe you will find this notation easier to understand and use.

What's new in the second edition

The first edition of the book has been revised to improve readability, to update or extend the coverage of existing material, and to include new material. The major changes in the second edition are as follows:

- New tutorial-style chapter on SQL (Structured Query Language) and QBE (Query-by-Example). SQL and QBE are the two main languages for relational DBMSs.
- New chapter on database administration and security.

■ Improvements to the database design methodology. In particular, the merging of user views during logical database design has been moved to an appendix to keep the basic methodology simple.

■ New chapter on current and emerging trends, discussing the requirements for advanced database applications and why current relational systems are not well suited to these requirements, and then providing an introduction to distributed DBMSs, data replication, object-oriented DBMSs, object-relational DBMSs, data warehousing, OnLine Analytical Processing (OLAP) and data mining, and approaches for integrating databases into the Web environment.

■ A more academic presentation with review questions at the end of most chapters and an accompanying Website with additional review questions, exercises, exam questions, transparencies, databases, and SQL scripts for the common data models in Appendix E.

Showing how to implement a design

We believe it is important to show you how to convert a database design into a physical implementation. In this book, we show how to implement the first case study (the video rental company called *StayHome*) in the Microsoft Access 2002 DBMS. In contrast, we show how to map the database design for the second case study (the veterinary clinic called *PerfectPets*) in the Oracle 9i DBMS.

Who should read this book?

Who should read this book? We have tried to write this book in a self-contained way. The exception to this is physical database design, where you need to have a good understanding of how the target DBMS operates. Our intended audience is anyone who needs to develop a database, including but not limited to the following:

■ information modelers and database designers;

■ database application designers and implementers;

■ database practitioners;

■ data and database administrators;

■ information systems, business IT, and computing science professors specializing in database design;

■ database students, namely undergraduate, advanced undergraduate, and graduate;

■ anyone wishing to design and develop a database system.

Structure of this book

We have divided the book into six parts and a set of five appendices:

■ Part 1 – Background. We provide an introduction to DBMSs, the relational model, and a tutorial-style chapter on SQL and QBE in Chapters 1, 2, and 3. We also provide an overview of the database system development lifecycle in Chapter 4 and a discussion of database administration and security in Chapter 5.

■ Part 2 – Database Analysis and Design Techniques. We discuss techniques for database analysis in Chapter 6 and show how to use some of these techniques to analyze the requirements for the video rental company *StayHome*. We show how to draw Entity–Relationship (ER) diagrams using UML in Chapter 7 and how to apply the rules of normalization in Chapter 8. ER models and normalization are important techniques that are used in the database design methodology we describe in Part 3.

■ Part 3 – Logical Database Design. We describe a step-by-step approach for logical database design. In Step 1 presented in Chapter 9, we create an ER model for the video rental company *StayHome*. In Step 2 presented in Chapter 10, we map the ER model to a set of database tables. To support the design of more complex databases, we present the main concepts associated with enhanced ER modeling in Chapter 11. Also in this chapter, we describe how such concepts are mapped to tables.

■ Part 4 – Physical Database Design. We describe a step-by-step approach for physical database design. In Step 3 presented in Chapter 12, we design a set of base tables for the target DBMS. In Step 4 presented in Chapter 13, we choose file organizations and indexes. In Steps 5 and 6 presented in Chapter 14, we consider the design of user views and the design of security mechanisms that will protect the data from unauthorized access. In Step 7 presented in Chapter 15, we describe how the introduction of controlled redundancy into a database can achieve improved performance. Finally, in Step 8 presented in Chapter 16, we monitor and tune the operational system. As we've just mentioned, we show you how to implement the design for the *StayHome* database system in Microsoft Access 2002.

■ Part 5 – Second Worked Example. In Chapters 17 and 18, we work through a second case study about the veterinary clinic *PerfectPets*. We show you how to implement the design for the *PerfectPets* database application in Oracle 9i.

■ Part 6 – Current and Emerging Trends. In Chapter 19, we discuss the requirements for advanced database applications and why current relational systems are not well suited to these requirements. We then provide an introduction to Distributed DBMSs (DDBMSs), data replication, Object-oriented DBMSs (OODBMSs), Object-relational DBMSs (ORDBMSs), data warehousing,

OnLine Analytical Processing (OLAP) and data mining, and approaches for integrating databases into the Web environment.

■ Appendices. Appendix A examines the two main alternative ER notations: Chen's notation and the Crow's Feet notation. Appendix B provides a summary of the methodology as a quick reference guide. Appendix C presents an extension to the basic logical database design methodology for database systems with multiple user views that have requirements which are managed using the view integration approach. Appendix D provides some background information on file organization and storage structures that may help you understand some aspects of the physical database design methodology presented in Part 3. Appendix E provides a set of 15 common data models.

Pedagogy

To make the book as readable as possible, we have adopted the following style and structure:

■ A set of objectives for each chapter, clearly highlighted at the start of the chapter.

■ A summary at the end of each chapter covering the main points introduced.

■ Review questions at the end of most chapters.

■ Each important concept that is introduced is clearly defined and highlighted by placing the definition in a box.

■ A series of notes and tips – you'll see these throughout the book with an adjacent icon to highlight them.

■ Diagrams liberally used throughout to support and clarify concepts.

■ A very practical orientation. Each chapter contains many worked examples to illustrate the points covered.

■ A glossary at the end of the book, which you may find useful as a quick reference guide. We also tend to use the margins to give you a reference to the section of the book that defines a concept we're discussing.

Accompanying Instructor's Guide and Website

A comprehensive supplement containing numerous instructional resources is available for this textbook, upon request to Pearson Education. The accompanying Instructor's Guide includes:

■ *Teaching suggestions* These include lecture suggestions, teaching hints, and student project ideas that make use of the chapter content.

- *Solutions* Sample answers are provided for all review questions.

- *Examination questions* Examination questions (similar to the questions at the end of each chapter), with solutions.

- *Transparency masters* (created using PowerPoint) containing the main points from each chapter, enlarged illustrations, and tables from the text are provided to help the instructor associate lectures and class discussion to the material in the textbook.

- An implementation of the *StayHome* database system in Microsoft Access 2002.

- An SQL script to create an implementation of the *PerfectPets* database system. This script can be used to create a database in many relational DBMSs, such as Oracle, Informix, and SQL Server.

- An SQL script for each common data model defined in Appendix E to create the corresponding set of base tables for the database system. Once again, these scripts can be used to create a database in many relational DBMSs.

Additional information about the Instructor's Guide and the book can be found on the Pearson Education Website at:

http://www.booksites.net/connbegg

Corrections and suggestions

As this type of textbook is so vulnerable to errors, disagreements, omissions, and confusion, your input is solicited for future reprints and editions. Comments, corrections, and constructive suggestions should be sent to Pearson Education, or by electronic mail to:

thomas.connolly@paisley.ac.uk

Acknowledgements

This book is the outcome of many years of work by the authors in industry, research, and academia. It is therefore difficult to name all the people who have directly or indirectly helped us in our efforts; an idea here and there may have appeared insignificant at the time but may have had a significant causal effect. For those people we are about to omit, we apologize now. However, special thanks and apologies must first go to our families, who over the years have been neglected, even ignored, while we have been writing our books.

We would first like to thank Kate Brewin, our editor, and Mary Lince, our desk editor. We should also like to thank the reviewers of this book, who contributed their comments, suggestions, and advice. In particular, we would like to mention Stuart Anderson and Andy Osborn, who reviewed the first edition, Aurélie Bechina and Nick Measor, who reviewed the second edition, and Willie Favero who reviewed both editions.

We should also like to thank our secretaries Lyndonne MacLeod and June Blackburn, for their help and support during the years.

Thomas M. Connolly
Carolyn E. Begg
Glasgow, May 2003

Part 1

Background

Background

Chapter 1

Introduction

In this chapter you will learn:

Some common uses of database systems. ◄

The meaning of the term database. ◄

The meaning of the term Database Management System (DBMS). ◄

The major components of the DBMS environment. ◄

The typical functions and services a DBMS should provide. ◄

The advantages and disadvantages of DBMSs. ◄

The database is now such an integral part of our day-to-day life that often we're not aware we are using one. To start our discussion of database systems, we briefly examine some of their applications. For the purposes of this discussion, we consider a **database** to be a collection of related data and the **Database Management System (DBMS)** to be the software that manages and controls access to the database. We also use the term **application program** to be a computer program that interacts with the database in some way and we use the more inclusive term *database system* to be the collection of application programs that interact with the database along with the DBMS and the database itself. We provide more accurate definitions in Section 1.2. Later in the chapter, we'll look at the typical functions of a modern DBMS and briefly review the main advantages and disadvantages of DBMSs.

1.1   Examples of the use of database systems

Purchases from the supermarket

When you purchase goods from your local supermarket, it's likely that a database is accessed. The checkout assistant uses a bar code reader to scan each of your purchases. This is linked to an application program that uses the bar code to find the price of the item from a product database. The program then reduces the number of such items in stock and displays the price on the cash register. If the reorder level falls below a specified threshold, the database system may automatically place an order to obtain more stocks of that item.

Purchases using your credit card

When you purchase goods using your credit card, the assistant normally checks that you have sufficient credit left to make the purchase. This check may be carried out by telephone or it may be done automatically by a card reader linked to a computer system. In either case, there is a database somewhere that contains information about the purchases that you've made using your credit card. To check your credit, there is a database application program that uses your credit card number to check that the price of the goods you wish to buy, together with the sum of the purchases you've already made this month, is within your credit limit. When the purchase is confirmed, the details of your purchase are added to this database. The application program also accesses the database to check that the credit card is not on the list of stolen or lost cards before authorizing the purchase. There are other database application programs to send out monthly statements to each cardholder and to credit accounts when payment is received.

Booking a holiday at the travel agents

When you make inquiries about a holiday, the travel agent may access several databases containing holiday and flight details. When you book your holiday, the database system has to make all the necessary booking arrangements. In this case, the system has to ensure that two different agents don't book the same holiday or overbook the seats on the flight. For example, if there is only one seat left on the flight from London to New York and two agents try to reserve the last seat at the same time, the system has to recognize this situation, allow one booking to proceed, and inform the other agent that there are now no seats available. The travel agent may have another, usually separate, database for invoicing.

Using the local library

Whenever you visit your local library, there is probably a database containing details of the books in the library, details of the readers, reservations, and so on. There will be a computerized index that allows readers to find a book based on its title, or its authors, or its subject area, or its ISBN. The database system handles reservations to allow a reader to reserve a book and to be informed by post when the book is available. The system also sends out reminders to borrowers who have failed to return books on the due date. Typically, the system will have a bar code reader, similar to that used by the supermarket described earlier, which is used to keep track of books coming in and going out of the library.

Renting a video

When you wish to rent a video from a video rental company, you will probably find that the company maintains a database consisting of the video titles that it stocks, details on the copies it has for each title, whether the copy is available for rent or whether it is currently on loan, details of its members (the renters) and which videos they are currently renting and date they are returned. The database may even store more detailed information on each video, such as its director and its actors. The company can use this information to monitor stock usage and predict future buying trends based on historic rental data. For example, Figure 1.1 shows some sample data for such a company.

Using the Internet

Many of the sites on the Internet are driven by database applications. For example, you may visit an online bookstore that allows you to browse and buy books, such as Amazon.com. The bookstore allows you to browse books in different categories, such as computing or management, or it may allow you to browse books by author name. In either case, there is a database on the organization's Web server that consists of book details, availability, shipping information, stock levels, and on-order information. Book details include book titles, ISBNs, authors, prices, sales histories, publishers, reviews, and in-depth descriptions. The database allows books to be cross-referenced: for example, a book may be listed under several categories, such as computing, programming languages, bestsellers, and recommended titles. The cross-referencing also allows Amazon to give you information on other books that are typically ordered along with the title you are interested in.

Figure 1.1

Sample data for a
video rental
company.

Video

catalogNo	title	category	dailyRental	price	directorNo
207132	Die Another Day	Action	5.00	21.99	D1001
902355	Harry Potter	Children	4.50	14.50	D7834
330553	Lord of the Rings	Fantasy	5.00	31.99	D4576
781132	Shrek	Children	4.00	18.50	D0078
445624	Men in Black II	Action	4.00	29.99	D5743
634817	Independence Day	Sci-Fi	4.50	32.99	D3765

Director

directorNo	directorName
D1001	Lee Tamahori
D7834	Chris Columbus
D4576	Peter Jackson
D0078	Andrew Adamson
D5743	Barry Sonnenfeld
D3765	Roland Emmerick

Actor

actorNo	actorName
A1002	Pierce Brosnan
A3006	Elijah Wood
A2019	Will Smith
A7525	Tommy Lee Jones
A4343	Mike Myers
A8401	Daniel Radcliffe

Role

actorNo	catalogNo	character
A1002	207132	James Bond
A3006	330553	Frodo Baggins
A3006	902355	Harry Potter
A2019	330553	Captain Steve Hiller
A2019	445624	Agent J
A7525	634817	Agent K
A4343	781132	Shrek

These are only a few of the applications for database systems, and you'll no doubt be aware of plenty of others. Although we take many of these applications for granted, behind them lies some highly complex technology. At the center of this technology is the database itself. For the system to support the applications that the end-users want, in as efficient a manner as possible, requires a suitably structured database. Producing this structure is known as *database design*, and it's this important activity that we're going to concentrate on in this book. Whether the database you wish to build is small, or large like the ones above, database design is a fundamental issue, and the methodology presented in this book will help you build your database correctly with relative ease. Having a well-designed database will allow you to produce a system that satisfies the requirements of the users and, at the same time, provides acceptable performance.

1.2 Database approach

In this section, we provide a more formal definition of the terms *database, Database Management System (DBMS),* and *application program* than we used in the last section.

1.2.1 The database

Database

A shared collection of logically related data (and a description of this data), designed to meet the information needs of an organization.

Let's examine the definition of a database in detail to understand this concept fully. The database is a single, possibly large repository of data, which can be used simultaneously by many departments and users. All data that is required by these users is integrated with a minimum amount of duplication. And importantly, the database is normally not owned by any one department or user but is a shared corporate resource.

As well as holding the organization's operational data, the database also holds a description of this data. For this reason, a database is also defined as a *self-describing collection of integrated records*. The description of the data, that is the **meta-data** – the 'data about data' – is known as the **system catalog** or **data dictionary**. It is the self-describing nature of a database that provides what's known as **data independence**. This means that if new data structures are added to the database or existing structures in the database are modified then the application programs that use the database are unaffected, provided they don't directly depend upon what has been modified. For example, if we add a new column to a record or create a new table, existing applications are unaffected. However, if we remove a column from a table that an application program uses, then that application program is affected by this change and must be modified accordingly.

The final term in the definition of a database that we should explain is 'logically related'. When we analyze the organization's information needs, we attempt to identify the important objects that need to be represented in the database and the *logical relationships* between these objects. The methodology we'll present for database design will give you guidelines for identifying these important objects and their logical relationships.

Methodology covered in Chapters 9 to 16

1.2.2   The Database Management System (DBMS)

> **DBMS**
>
> A software system that enables users to define, create, and maintain the database and also provides controlled access to this database.

The **DBMS** is the software that interacts with the users, application programs, and the database. Among other things, the DBMS allows users to insert, update, delete, and retrieve data from the database. Having a central repository for all data and data descriptions allows the DBMS to provide a general inquiry facility to this data, called a *query language*. The provision of a query language (such as SQL) alleviates the problems with earlier systems where the user has to work with a fixed set of queries or where there is a proliferation of programs, giving major software management problems. We'll discuss the typical functions and services of a DBMS in the next section.

SQL covered in Chapter 3

> The Structured Query Language (SQL – pronounced 'S-Q-L' or sometimes 'See-Quel') is the main query language for relational DBMSs, like Microsoft Access, Microsoft SQL Server, and Oracle.

1.2.3   (Database) application programs

> **Application program**
>
> A computer program that interacts with the database by issuing an appropriate request (typically an SQL statement) to the DBMS.

Users interact with the database through a number of **application programs** that are used to create and maintain the database and to generate information. These programs can be conventional batch applications or, more typically nowadays, they will be online applications. The application programs may be written in some programming language or in some higher-level fourth-generation language. Figure 1.2 illustrates the database approach. It shows the Sales and Stock Control Departments using their application programs to access the database through the DBMS. Each set of departmental application programs handles data entry, data maintenance, and the generation of reports. The physical structure and storage of the data are managed by the DBMS.

1.2.4   Views

With the functionality described above, the DBMS is an extremely powerful tool. However, as end-users are not too interested in how complex or easy a task

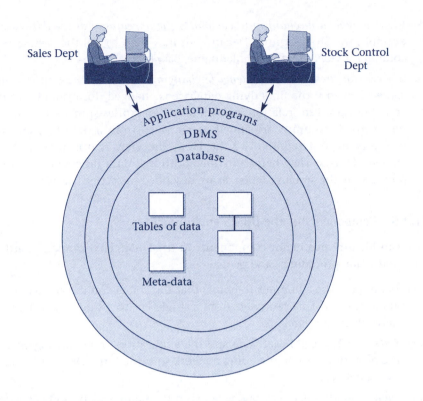

Figure 1.2

The database approach showing Sales and Stock Control Departments accessing the database through application programs and the DBMS.

is for the system, it could be argued that the DBMS has made things more complex because users may now see more data than they actually need, or want, to do their job. In recognition of this problem, a DBMS provides another facility known as a *view mechanism*, which allows each user to have his or her own customized view of the database, where a view is some subset of the database.

View

A *virtual table* that does not necessarily exist in the database but is generated by the DBMS from the underlying base tables whenever it's accessed.

A view is usually defined as a query that operates on the base tables to produce another *virtual table*. As well as reducing complexity by letting users see the data in the way they want to see it, views have several other benefits:

■ *Views provide a level of security*. Views can be set up to exclude data that some users should not see. For example, we could create a view that allows a branch manager and the Payroll Department to see all staff data, including salary details. However, we could create a second view that excludes salary details, which other staff use.

■ *Views provide a mechanism to customize the appearance of the database.* For example, the Stock Control Department may wish to call the Daily Rental Rate column for videos by the simpler name, Daily Rental.

■ *A view can present a consistent, unchanging picture of the structure of the database*, even if the underlying database is changed (for example, columns added or removed, relationships changed, data files split, restructured, or renamed). If columns are added or removed from a data file, and these columns are not required by the view, the view is not affected by this change. Thus, a view helps provide additional data independence to that provided by the system catalog, as we described in Section 1.2.1.

1.2.5   Components of the DBMS environment

We can identify five major components in the DBMS environment: hardware, software, data, procedures, and people:

(1) *Hardware*   The computer system(s) that the DBMS and the application programs run on. This can range from a single PC, to a single mainframe, to a network of computers.

(2) *Software*   The DBMS software and the application programs, together with the operating system, including network software if the DBMS is being used over a network.

(3) *Data*   The data acts as a bridge between the hardware and software components and the human components. As we've already said, the database contains both the operational data and the meta-data (the 'data about data').

(4) *Procedures*   The instructions and rules that govern the design and use of the database. This may include instructions on how to log on to the DBMS, make backup copies of the database, and how to handle hardware or software failures.

(5) *People*   This includes the database designers, database administrators (DBAs), application programmers, and the end-users.

1.2.6   DBMS architectures

Before the advent of the Web, generally a DBMS would be divided into two parts:

■ a **client** program that handles the main business and data processing logic and interfaces with the user;

■ a **server** program (sometimes called the **DBMS engine**) that manages and controls access to the database.

This is known as a **(two-tier) client–server architecture.** Figure 1.3 illustrates a simplified client–server architecture for a video rental company called *StayHome* that has offices throughout the US. It shows a centralized database and server located at the company's headquarters in Seattle and a number of clients located at some of the branches around the US.

In the mid-1990s, as applications became more complex and potentially could be deployed to hundreds or thousands of end-users, the client side of this architecture gave rise to two problems:

StayHome is used throughout this book and described in detail in Chapter 6

- A 'fat' client, requiring considerable resources on the client's computer to run effectively (resources include disk space, RAM, and CPU power).
- A significant client-side administration overhead.

By 1995, a new variation of the traditional two-tier client–server model appeared to solve these problems, called the **three-tier client–server architecture**.

Figure 1.3

Simplified two-tier client–server configuration for *StayHome*.

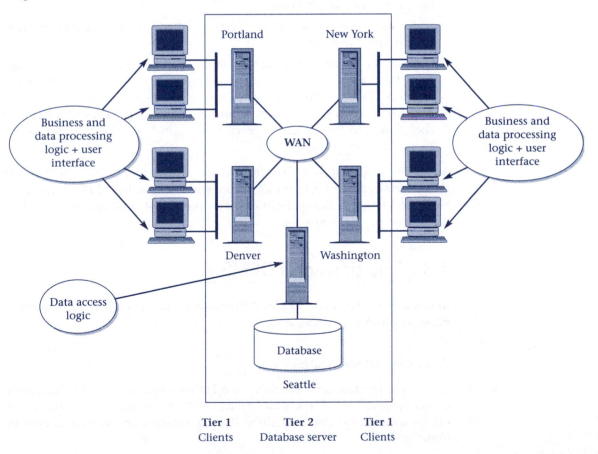

This new architecture proposed three layers, each potentially running on a different platform:

(1) The *user interface* layer, which runs on the end-user's computer (the *client*).

(2) The *business logic and data processing* layer. This middle tier runs on a server and is often called the application server. One **application server** is designed to serve multiple clients.

(3) A *DBMS*, which stores the data required by the middle tier. This tier may run on a separate server called the **database server.**

The three-tier design has many advantages over the traditional two-tier design, such as:

■ A 'thin' client, which requires less expensive hardware.

■ Simplified application maintenance, as a result of centralizing the business logic for many end-users into a single application server. This eliminates the concerns of software distribution that are problematic in the traditional two-tier client–server architecture.

■ Added modularity, which makes it easier to modify or replace one tier without affecting the other tiers.

■ Easier load balancing, again as a result of separating the core business logic from the database functions. For example, a **Transaction Processing Monitor (TPM)** can be used to reduce the number of connections to the database server. (A TPM is a program that controls data transfer between clients and servers in order to provide a consistent environment for Online Transaction Processing (OLTP).)

An additional advantage is that the three-tier architecture maps quite naturally to the Web environment, with a Web browser acting as the 'thin' client, and a Web server acting as the application server. The three-tier client–server architecture is illustrated in Figure 1.4.

1.3 Functions of a DBMS

In this section, we briefly look at the functions and services we would expect a full-scale DBMS to provide nowadays.

Data storage, retrieval, and update

This is the fundamental function of a DBMS. From our earlier discussion, clearly in providing this functionality the DBMS should hide the internal physical implementation details (such as file organization and storage structures) from the user.

Figure 1.4

Simplified three-tier client–server configuration for *StayHome*.

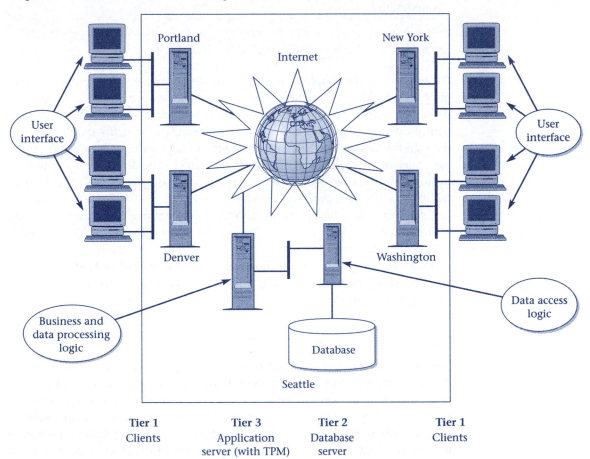

A user-accessible catalog

A key feature of a DBMS is the provision of an integrated *system catalog* to hold data about the structure of the database, users, applications, and so on. The catalog is expected to be accessible to users as well as to the DBMS. The amount of information and the way the information is used vary with the DBMS. Typically, the system catalog stores:

■ names, types, and sizes of data items;

■ integrity constraints on the data;

■ names of authorized users who have access to the data.

Transaction support

> **Transaction**
>
> An action, or series of actions, carried out by a single user or application program, which accesses or changes the contents of the database.

For example, some simple transactions for the *StayHome* video rental company might be to add a new member of staff to the database, to update the salary of a particular member of staff, or to delete a member from the register. A more complicated example might be to delete a manager from the database *and* to reassign the branch that he or she managed to another member of staff. In this case, there is more than one change to be made to the database. If the transaction fails during execution, perhaps because of a computer crash, the database will be in an *inconsistent* state: some changes will have been made and others not. For example, a branch is not allocated a new manager. Consequently, the changes that have been made will have to be undone to return the database to a consistent state again.

To overcome this, a DBMS should provide a mechanism that will ensure either that all the updates corresponding to a given transaction are made or that none of them are made.

Concurrency control services

One major objective in using a DBMS is to enable many users to access shared data concurrently; this is known as **concurrency control**. Concurrent access is relatively easy if all users are only reading data, as there is no way that they can interfere with one another. However, when two or more users are accessing the database simultaneously and at least one of them is updating data, there may be interference that can result in inconsistencies. For example, consider two transactions T_1 and T_2 that are executing concurrently as illustrated in Figure 1.5.

T_2 is withdrawing \$20 from a *StayHome* member's account (with a balance, bal_x, currently \$50) and T_1 is crediting \$5 to the same account. If these transactions were executed one after the other with no interleaving of operations, the final balance would be \$35 regardless of which was performed first. Transactions

Figure 1.5

The lost update problem.

Time	T_1	T_2	bal_x
t_1		read(bal_x)	50
t_2	read(bal_x)	$bal_x = bal_x - 20$	50
t_3	$bal_x = bal_x + 5$	write(bal_x)	30
t_4	write(bal_x)		55
t_5			

T_1 and T_2 start at nearly the same time and both read the balance as $50. T_2 decreases bal_x by $20 to $30 and stores the update in the database. Meanwhile, transaction T_1 increases its copy of bal_x by $5 to $55 and stores this value in the database, overwriting the previous update and thereby 'losing' $20.

When multiple users are accessing the database, the DBMS must ensure that interference like this cannot occur.

Recovery services

When discussing transaction support, we mentioned that if the transaction fails the database has to be returned to a consistent state; this is known as **recovery control**. This may be the result of a system crash, media failure, a hardware or software error causing the DBMS to stop, or it may be the result of the user detecting an error during the transaction and aborting the transaction before it completes. In all these cases, the DBMS must provide a mechanism to recover the database to a consistent state.

Authorization services

It's not difficult to envisage instances where we would want to protect some of the data stored in the database from being seen by all users. For example, we may want only branch managers and the Payroll Department to see salary-related information for staff and prevent all other users from seeing this data. Additionally, we may want to protect the database from unauthorized access. The term **security** refers to the protection of the database against unauthorized access, either intentional or accidental. We expect the DBMS to provide mechanisms to ensure the data is secure.

Security covered in Chapter 5 and Step 6 in Chapters 14 & 18

Support for data communication

Most users access the database from terminals. Sometimes, these terminals are connected directly to the computer hosting the DBMS. In other cases, the terminals are at remote locations and communicate with the computer hosting the DBMS over a network. In either case, the DBMS must be capable of integrating with networking/communication software. Even DBMSs for PCs should be capable of being run on a local area network (LAN) so that one centralized database can be established for users to share, rather than having a series of disparate databases, one for each user.

Integrity services

Database integrity refers to the correctness and consistency of stored data. It can be considered as another type of database protection. While it's related to security, it has wider implications; integrity is concerned with the quality of data itself. Integrity is usually expressed in terms of constraints, which are consistency rules that the database is not permitted to violate. For example, we may specify a constraint that no member of *StayHome* can rent more than 10 videos at the one time. Here, we want the DBMS to check when we assign a video to a member that this limit is not being exceeded and to prevent the rental from occurring if the limit has been reached.

Services to promote data independence

Data independence is normally achieved through a view mechanism, as we discussed in Section 1.2.4. There are usually several types of changes that can be made to the physical characteristics of the database without affecting the views, such as using different file organizations or modifying indexes. This is called *physical data independence*. However, complete *logical data independence* is more difficult to achieve. The addition of a new table or column can usually be accommodated, but not their removal. In some systems, any type of change to a table's structure is prohibited.

Utility services

Utility programs help the DBA to manage the database effectively. Some examples of utilities are:

- import facilities, to load the database from flat files, and export facilities, to unload the database to flat files;
- monitoring facilities, to monitor database usage and operation.

> The above discussion is general. The actual level of functionality offered by a DBMS differs from product to product. For example, a DBMS for a PC may not support concurrent shared access, and it may only provide limited security, integrity, and recovery control. However, modern, large multi-user DBMS products offer all the above functions and much more. Modern systems are extremely complex pieces of software consisting of millions of lines of code, with documentation comprising many volumes.

The above discussion is intentionally brief but should be sufficient to provide a general overview of DBMS functionality. For more information, the interested reader is referred to Connolly and Begg (2002).

1.4 Database design

Until now, we've taken it for granted that there is a structure to the data in the database. But how do we get this structure? The answer is quite simple: the structure of the database is determined during **database design**. However, carrying out database design can be extremely complex. To produce a system that will satisfy the organization's information needs requires a data-driven approach, which means we think of the data first and the applications second. For the system to be acceptable to the end-users, database design is crucial. A poorly designed database will generate errors that may lead to bad decisions being made, with potentially serious repercussions for the organization. On the other hand, a well-designed database produces a system that provides the correct information for the decision-making process to succeed, in an efficient way.

We devote several chapters to the presentation of a complete methodology for database design (see Chapters 9–16). We present it as a series of simple-to-follow steps, with guidelines provided throughout. In these chapters, we use a case study based on a video rental company called *StayHome*. To help reinforce the methodology, in Chapters 17 and 18 we go through a second case study, this time a veterinary clinic called *PerfectPets*. In addition, in Appendix E we provide a number of common business data models that you are likely to encounter in one form or another.

Unfortunately, database design methodologies are not very popular, which may be a major cause of failure in the development of database systems. Owing to the lack of structured approaches to database design, the time and resources required for a database project are typically underestimated, the databases developed are inadequate or inefficient in meeting the demands of users, documentation is limited, and maintenance is difficult.

We hope the methodology presented in this book will help change this attitude.

1.5 Advantages and disadvantages of DBMSs

The fact that you are reading this book probably means that you already know many of the advantages of DBMSs, such as:

- *Control of **data redundancy*** The database approach eliminates redundancy where possible. However, it does not eliminate redundancy entirely, but controls the amount of redundancy inherent in the database. For example, it's normally necessary to duplicate key data items to model relationships between data, and sometimes it's desirable to duplicate some data items to improve performance. The reasons for controlled duplication will become clearer when you read the chapters on database design.

■ *Data consistency* By eliminating or controlling redundancy, we're reducing the risk of inconsistencies occurring. If data is stored only once in the database, any update to its value has to be performed only once and the new value is immediately available to all users. If data is stored more than once and the system is aware of this, the system can ensure that all copies of the data are kept consistent. Unfortunately, many of today's DBMSs don't automatically ensure this type of consistency.

■ *Sharing of data* In a file-based approach (the predecessor to the DBMS approach), typically files are owned by the people or departments that use them. On the other hand, the database belongs to the entire organization and can be shared by all authorized users. In this way, more users share more of the data. Furthermore, new applications can build on the existing data in the database and add only data that is not currently stored, rather than having to define all data requirements again. The new applications can also rely on the functions provided by the DBMS, such as data definition and manipulation, and concurrency and recovery control, rather than having to provide these functions themselves.

■ *Improved data integrity* As we've already stated, database integrity is usually expressed in terms of **constraints**, which are consistency rules that the database is not permitted to violate. Constraints may apply to data within a single record or they may apply to relationships between records. Again, data integration allows users to define, and the DBMS to enforce, integrity constraints.

■ *Improved maintenance through data independence* Since a DBMS separates the data descriptions from the applications, it helps make applications immune to changes in the data descriptions. This is known as *data independence* and its provision simplifies database application maintenance.

Other advantages include: improved security, improved data accessibility and responsiveness, increased productivity, increased concurrency, and improved backup and recovery services. There are, however, some disadvantages of the database approach, such as:

■ *Complexity* As we've already mentioned, a DBMS is an extremely complex piece of software, and all users (database designers and developers, DBAs, and end-users) must understand the DBMS's functionality to take full advantage of it.

■ *Cost of DBMS* The cost of DBMSs varies significantly, depending on the environment and functionality provided. For example, a single-user DBMS for a PC may cost only $100. However, a large mainframe multi-user DBMS servicing hundreds of users can be extremely expensive, perhaps $100,000 to $1,000,000. There is also the recurrent annual maintenance cost, which is typically a percentage of the list price.

■ *Cost of conversion* In some situations, the cost of the DBMS and any extra hardware may be insignificant compared with the cost of converting existing applications to run on the new DBMS and hardware. This cost also includes the cost of training staff to use these new systems, and possibly the employment of specialist staff to help with the conversion and running of the system. This cost is one of the main reasons why some companies feel tied to their current systems and cannot switch to more modern database technology. The term **legacy system** is sometimes used to refer to an older, and usually inferior, system (such as file-based, hierarchical, or network systems).

■ *Performance* Typically, a file-based system is written for a specific application, such as invoicing. As a result, performance is generally very good. However, a DBMS is written to be more general, to cater for many applications rather than just one. The effect is that some applications may not run as fast using a DBMS as they did before.

■ *Higher impact of a failure* The centralization of resources increases the vulnerability of the system. Since all users and applications rely on the availability of the DBMS, the failure of any component can bring operations to a complete halt until the failure is repaired.

Chapter summary

✓ A **database** is a shared collection of logically related data (and a description of this data), designed to meet the information needs of an organization. A **DBMS** is a software system that enables users to define, create, and maintain the database, and also provides controlled access to this database. An **application program** is a computer program that interacts with the database by issuing an appropriate request (typically an SQL statement) to the DBMS. The more inclusive term **database system** is used to define a collection of application programs that interact with the database, along with the DBMS and the database itself.

✓ All access to the database is through the DBMS. The DBMS provides facilities that allow users to define the database, and to insert, update, delete, and retrieve data from the database.

✓ The DBMS environment consists of hardware (the computer), software (the DBMS, operating system, and applications programs), data, procedures, and people. The people include database administrators (DBAs), database designers, application programmers, and end-users.

✓ In the Web environment, the traditional two-tier client–server model has been replaced by a three-tier model, consisting of a user interface layer (the client), a business logic and data processing layer (the application server), and a DBMS (the database server), distributed over different machines.

✓ The DBMS provides controlled access to the database. It provides security, integrity, concurrency and recovery control, and a user-accessible catalog. It also provides a view mechanism to simplify the data that users have to deal with.

✓ Some advantages of the database approach include control of data redundancy, data consistency, sharing of data, and improved security and integrity. Some disadvantages include complexity, cost, reduced performance, and higher impact of a failure.

Review questions

1.1 List four examples of database systems other than those listed in Section 1.1.

1.2 Discuss the meaning of each of the following terms:
  (a) data;
  (b) database;
  (c) database management system;
  (d) application program;
  (e) data independence;
  (f) views.

1.3 Describe the main characteristics of the database approach.

1.4 Describe the five components of the DBMS environment and discuss how they relate to each other.

1.5 Describe the problems with the traditional two-tier client–server architecture and discuss how these problems were overcome with the three-tier client–server architecture.

1.6 Describe the functions that should be provided by a modern full-scale multi-user DBMS.

1.7 Of the functions described in your answer to Question 1.6, which ones do you think would not be needed in a standalone PC DBMS? Provide justification for your answer.

1.8 Discuss the advantages and disadvantages of DBMSs.

Chapter 2

The relational model

The Relational Database Management System (often called RDBMS for short) has become the dominant DBMS in use today, with estimated sales of approximately $15–$20 billion per year ($50 billion with tools sales included), and growing at a rate of about 25 percent per year. The RDBMS represents the second generation of DBMS and is based on the relational data model proposed by Dr E.F. Codd in his seminal paper 'A Relational Model of Data for Large Shared Data Banks' in 1970. In the relational model, all data is logically structured within *relations* (tables). A great strength of the relational model is this simple logical structure. Yet, behind this simple structure is a sound theoretical foundation that is lacking in the first generation of DBMSs (the network and hierarchical DBMSs typified by systems such as IDMS/R from Computer Associates and IMS from IBM).

The design methodology we present in this book is based on the relational data model, as this is the one most of you will be using. In this chapter, we discuss the basic principles of the relational data model. Let's start by first looking at what a data model is.

2.1   What is a data model?

Data model

An integrated collection of concepts for describing data, relationships between data, and constraints on the data used by an organization.

A model is a representation of 'real world' objects and events, and their associations. It concentrates on the essential, inherent aspects of an organization and ignores the accidental properties. A **data model** attempts to represent the data requirements of the organization, or the part of the organization, that you wish to model. It should provide the basic concepts and notations that will allow database designers and end-users to communicate their understanding of the organizational data unambiguously and accurately. A data model can be thought of as comprising three components:

(1) *a structural part*, consisting of a set of rules that define how the database is to be constructed;

(2) *a manipulative part*, defining the types of operations (transactions) that are allowed on the data (this includes the operations that are used for updating or retrieving data and for changing the structure of the database);

(3) possibly *a set of integrity rules*, which ensures that the data is accurate.

The purpose of a data model is to represent data and to make the data understandable. If it does this, then it can be easily used to design a database. In the remainder of this chapter, we examine one such data model: *the relational data model*.

2.2   Terminology

The relational model is based on the mathematical concept of a **relation**, which is physically represented as a **table**. Codd, a trained mathematician, used terminology taken from mathematics, principally set theory and predicate logic. In this section, we explain the terminology and structural concepts of the relational model. In Section 2.3, we'll discuss the integrity rules for the model and in Section 2.4 we'll examine the manipulative part of the model.

2.2.1   Relational data structure

Relation

A table with columns and rows.

A relational DBMS requires only that the database be perceived by the user as tables.

> Note that this perception applies only to the way we view the database; it does not apply to the physical structure of the database on disk, which we can implement using a variety of storage structures (such as a heap file or hash file).

Storage structures discussed in Appendix D

Attribute

A named column of a relation.

In the relational model, we use relations to hold information about the objects that we want to represent in the database. We represent a relation as a table in which the rows of the table correspond to individual records and the table columns correspond to **attributes**. Attributes can appear in any order and the relation will still be the same relation, and therefore convey the same meaning.

For example, in the *StayHome* video rental company, the information on branches is represented by the Branch relation, with columns for attributes branchNo (the branch number), street, city, state, zipCode, and mgrStaffNo (the staff number corresponding to the manager of the branch). Similarly, the information on staff is represented by the Staff relation, with columns for attributes staffNo (the staff number), name, position, salary, and branchNo (the number of the branch the staff member works at). Figure 2.1 shows instances of the Branch and Staff relations. As you can see from this figure, a column contains values for a single attribute; for example, the branchNo columns contain only numbers of branches.

StayHome is used throughout this book and discussed more fully in Chapter 6

Domain

The set of allowable values for one or more attributes.

Domains are an important feature of the relational model. Every attribute in a relational database is associated with a domain. Domains may be distinct for each attribute, or two or more attributes may be associated with the same domain. Figure 2.2 shows the domains for some of the attributes of the Branch and Staff relations.

> Note that, at any given time, typically there will be values in a domain that don't currently appear as values in the corresponding attribute. In other words, a domain describes *possible* values for an attribute.

Figure 2.1

An example of the Branch and Staff relations.

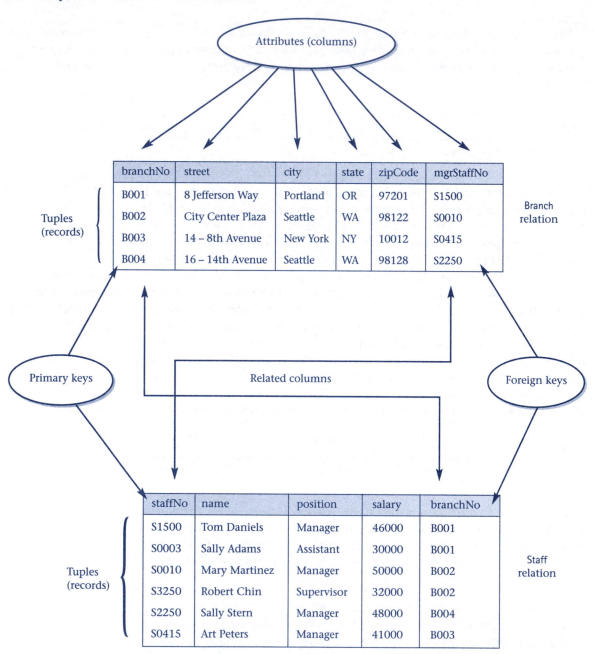

Figure 2.2

Domains for some attributes of the Branch and Staff relations.

Attribute	Domain name	Meaning	Domain definition
branchNo	Branch_Numbers	Set of all possible branch numbers.	Alphanumeric: size 4, range B001–B999
street	Street_Names	Set of all possible street names.	Alphanumeric: size 60
staffNo	Staff_Numbers	Set of all possible staff numbers.	Alphanumeric: size 5, range S0001–S9999
position	Staff_Positions	Set of all possible staff positions.	One of Director, Manager, Supervisor, Assistant, Buyer
salary	Staff_Salaries	Possible values of staff salaries.	Monetary: 8 digits, range $10,000.00–$100,000.00

The domain concept is important because it allows us to define the meaning and source of values that attributes can hold. As a result, more information is available to the system and it can (theoretically) reject operations that don't make sense. For example, it would not be sensible for us to compare a staff number with a branch number, even though the domain definitions for both these attributes are character strings. Unfortunately, you'll find that most RDBMSs don't currently support domains.

Tuple

A record of a relation.

The fundamental elements of a relation are the **tuples** or **records** in the table. In the Staff relation, each record contains five values, one for each attribute. As with attributes, tuples can appear in any order and the relation will still be the same relation, and therefore convey the same meaning.

Finally, we have the definition:

Relational database

A collection of normalized tables.

A **relational database** consists of tables that are appropriately structured. The appropriateness is obtained through the process of *normalization*, which we'll discuss in Chapter 8.

Alternative terminology

The terminology for the relational model can be quite confusing. In this chapter, we've introduced two sets of terms: (relation, attribute, tuple) and (table, column, record). Other terms that you may encounter are file for table, row for record, and field for column. You may also find various combinations of these terms, such as table, field, and row.

> From now on, we will tend to drop the formal terms of relation, tuple, and attribute, and instead use the more frequently used terms table, column, and record.

2.2.2   Properties of relational tables

A relational table has the following properties:

■ The table has a name that is distinct from all other tables in the database.

■ Each cell of the table contains exactly one value. (For example, it would be wrong to store several telephone numbers for a single branch in a single cell. In other words, tables don't contain repeating groups of data. A relational table that satisfies this property is said to be *normalized* or in *first normal form.*)

■ Each column has a distinct name.

■ The values of a column are all from the same domain.

■ The order of columns has no significance. In other words, provided a column name is moved along with the column values, we can interchange columns.

■ Each record is distinct; there are no duplicate records.

■ The order of records has no significance, theoretically. (However, in practice, the order may affect the efficiency of accessing records, as we'll see in Chapter 13.)

2.2.3   Relational keys

As we've just stated, each record in a table must be unique. This means that we need to be able to identify a column or combination of columns (called *relational keys*) that provides uniqueness. In this section, we explain the terminology used for relational keys.

> **Superkey**
>
> A column, or set of columns, that uniquely identifies a record within a table.

Since a **superkey** may contain additional columns that are not necessary for unique identification, we're interested in identifying superkeys that contain only the *minimum number* of columns necessary for unique identification.

Candidate key

A superkey that contains only the minimum number of columns necessary for unique identification.

A **candidate key** for a table has two properties:

■ *Uniqueness*   In each record, the values of the candidate key uniquely identify that record.

■ *Irreducibility*   No proper subset of the candidate key has the uniqueness property.

Consider the Branch table shown in Figure 2.1. For a given value of city, we would expect to be able to determine several branches (for example, Seattle has two branches). This column, therefore, cannot be selected as a candidate key. On the other hand, since *StayHome* allocates each branch a unique branch number, then for a given value of the branch number, branchNo, we can determine at most one record, so that branchNo is a candidate key. Similarly, as no two branches can be located in the same zip code, zipCode is also a candidate key for the Branch table.

There may be several candidate keys for a table. Consider, for example, a table called Role, which represents the characters played by actors in videos. The table comprises an actor number (actorNo), a catalog number (catalogNo), and the name of the character played (character), as shown in Figure 2.3. For a given actor number, actorNo, there may be several different videos the actor has starred in. Similarly, for a given catalog number, catalogNo, there may be several actors who have starred in this video. Therefore, actorNo by itself or catalogNo by

Role

actorNo	catalogNo	character
A1002	207132	James Bond
A3006	330553	Frodo Baggins
A8401	902355	Harry Potter
A2019	634817	Captain Steve Hiller
A2019	445624	Agent J
A7525	445624	Agent K
A4343	781132	Shrek

Figure 2.3

An example of the Role table.

itself cannot be selected as a candidate key. However, the combination of actorNo and catalogNo identifies at most one record. When a key consists of more than one column, we call it a **composite key**.

> **TIP**
>
> Be careful not to look at sample data and try to deduce the candidate key(s), unless you are certain the sample is representative of the data that will be stored in the table. Generally, an instance of a table cannot be used to prove that a column or combination of columns is a candidate key. The fact that there are no duplicates for the values that appear at a particular moment in time does not guarantee that duplicates are not possible. However, the presence of duplicates in an instance can be used to show that some column combination is not a candidate key. Identifying a candidate key requires that we know the 'real world' meaning of the column(s) involved so that we can decide whether duplicates are possible. Only by using this semantic information can we be certain that a column combination is a candidate key.
>
> For example, from the data presented in Figure 2.1, we may think that a suitable candidate key for the Staff table would be name, the employee's name. However, although there is only a single value of Tom Daniels in this table just now, a new member of staff with the same name could join the company, which would therefore prevent the choice of name as a candidate key.

Primary key

The candidate key that is selected to identify records uniquely within the table.

Since a table has no duplicate records, it's always possible to uniquely identify each record. This means that a table always has a **primary key**. In the worst case, the entire set of columns could serve as the primary key, but usually some smaller subset is sufficient to distinguish the records. The candidate keys that are not selected to be the primary key are called **alternate keys**. For the Branch table, if we choose branchNo as the primary key, zipCode would then be an alternate key. For the Role table, there is only one candidate key, comprising actorNo and catalogNo, so these columns would automatically form the primary key.

Foreign key

A column, or set of columns, within one table that matches the candidate key of some (possibly the same) table.

When a column appears in more than one table, its appearance usually represents a relationship between records of the two tables. For example, in Figure 2.1 the inclusion of branchNo in both the Branch and Staff tables is quite deliberate and links branches to the details of staff working there. In the Branch table, branchNo is the primary key. However, in the Staff table the branchNo column exists to match staff to the branch they work in. In the Staff table, branchNo is a **foreign key**. We say that the column branchNo in the Staff table *targets* or *references* the primary key column branchNo in the *home table*, Branch. In this situation, the Staff table is also known as the *child* table and the Branch table as the *parent* table.

> You may recall from Chapter 1 that one of the advantages of the DBMS approach was control of data redundancy. This is an example of 'controlled redundancy' – these common columns play an important role in modeling relationships, as we'll see in later chapters.

2.2.4 Representing relational databases

A relational database consists of one or more tables. The common convention for representing a description of a relational database is to give the name of each table, followed by the column names in parentheses. Normally, the primary key is underlined. The description of the relational database for the *StayHome* video rental company is:

Branch	(branchNo, street, city, state, zipCode, mgrStaffNo)
Staff	(staffNo, name, position, salary, branchNo)
Video	(catalogNo, title, category, dailyRental, price, directorNo)
Director	(directorNo, directorName)
Actor	(actorNo, actorName)
Role	(actorNo, catalogNo, character)
Member	(memberNo, fName, lName, address)
Registration	(branchNo, memberNo, staffNo, dateJoined)
RentalAgreement	(rentalNo, dateOut, dateReturn, memberNo, videoNo)
VideoForRent	(videoNo, available, catalogNo, branchNo)

Figure 2.4 shows an instance of the *StayHome* database.

Figure 2.4

An example of the *StayHome* video rental database.

Branch

branchNo	street	city	state	zipCode	mgrStaffNo
B001	8 Jefferson Way	Portland	OR	97201	S1500
B002	City Center Plaza	Seattle	WA	98122	S0010
B003	14 – 8th Avenue	New York	NY	10012	S0415
B004	16 – 14th Avenue	Seattle	WA	98128	S2250

Staff

staffNo	name	position	salary	branchNo
S1500	Tom Daniels	Manager	46000	B001
S0003	Sally Adams	Assistant	30000	B001
S0010	Mary Martinez	Manager	50000	B002
S3250	Robert Chin	Supervisor	32000	B002
S2250	Sally Stern	Manager	48000	B004
S0415	Art Peters	Manager	41000	B003

Video

catalogNo	title	category	dailyRental	price	directorNo
207132	Die Another Day	Action	5.00	21.99	D1001
902355	Harry Potter	Children	4.50	14.50	D7834
330553	Lord of the Rings	Fantasy	5.00	31.99	D4576
781132	Shrek	Children	4.00	18.50	D0078
445624	Men in Black II	Action	4.00	29.99	D5743
634817	Independence Day	Sci-Fi	4.50	32.99	D3765

Director

directorNo	directorName
D1001	Lee Tamahori
D7834	Chris Columbus
D4576	Peter Jackson
D0078	Andrew Adamson
D5743	Barry Sonnenfeld
D3765	Roland Emmerick

Actor

actorNo	actorName
A1002	Pierce Brosnan
A3006	Elijah Wood
A2019	Will Smith
A7525	Tommy Lee Jones
A4343	Mike Myers
A8401	Daniel Radcliffe

Role

actorNo	catalogNo	character
A1002	207132	James Bond
A3006	330553	Frodo Baggins
A3006	902355	Harry Potter
A2019	634817	Captain Steve Hiller
A2019	445624	Agent J
A7525	445624	Agent K
A4343	781132	Shrek

Member

memberNo	fName	lName	address
M250178	Bob	Adams	57 – 11th Avenue, Seattle, WA 98105
M166884	Art	Peters	89 Redmond Rd, Portland, OR 97117
M115656	Serena	Parker	22 W. Capital Way, Portland, OR 97201
M284354	Don	Nelson	123 Suffolk Lane, Seattle, WA 98117

Registration

branchNo	memberNo	staffNo	dateJoined
B002	M250178	S3250	1-Jul-01
B001	M166884	S0003	4-Sep-02
B001	M115656	S0003	12-May-00
B002	M284354	S3250	9-Oct-01

RentalAgreement

rentalNo	dateOut	dateReturn	memberNo	videoNo
R753461	4-Feb-03	6-Feb-03	M284354	245456
R753462	4-Feb-03	6-Feb-03	M284354	243431
R668256	5-Feb-03	7-Feb-03	M115656	199004
R668189	2-Feb-03		M115656	178643

VideoForRent

videoNo	available	catalogNo	branchNo
199004	Y	207132	B001
245456	Y	207132	B002
178643	N	634817	B001
243431	Y	634817	B002

Figure 2.4

Continued

2.3   Relational integrity

Domains defined
in Section 2.2.1

In the previous section, we discussed the structural part of the relational data model. As we mentioned in Section 2.1, a data model has two other parts: a manipulative part, defining the types of operations that are allowed on the data, and a set of integrity rules, which ensure that the data is accurate. In this section, we discuss the relational integrity rules and in the following section, we discuss the main relational manipulation languages.

Since every column has an associated domain, there are constraints (called *domain constraints*) in the form of restrictions on the set of values allowed for the columns of tables. In addition, there are two important integrity rules, which are constraints or restrictions that apply to all instances of the database. The two principal rules for the relational model are known as *entity integrity* and *referential integrity*. Before we define these terms, we need first to understand the concept of nulls.

2.3.1   Nulls

Null

Represents a value for a column that is currently unknown or is not applicable for this record.

A **null** can be taken to mean 'unknown'. It can also mean that a value is not applicable to a particular record, or it could just mean that no value has yet been supplied. Nulls are a way to deal with incomplete or exceptional data. However, a null is not the same as a zero numeric value or a text string filled with spaces; zeros and spaces are values, but a null represents the absence of a value. Therefore, nulls should be treated differently from other values.

For example, suppose it was possible for a branch to be temporarily without a manager, perhaps because the manager has recently left and a new manager has not yet been appointed. In this case, the value for the corresponding mgrStaffNo column would be undefined. Without nulls, it becomes necessary to introduce false data to represent this state or to add additional columns that may not be meaningful to the user. In this example, we may try to represent the absence of a manager with the value 'None at present'. Alternatively, we may add a new column 'currentManager?' to the Branch table, which contains a value Y (Yes), if there is a manager, and N (No), otherwise. Both these approaches can be confusing to anyone using the database.

Having defined nulls, we're now in a position to define the two relational integrity rules.

2.3.2 Entity integrity

The first integrity rule applies to the primary keys of base tables.

Entity integrity

In a base table, no column of a primary key can be null.

A **base table** is a named table whose records are physically stored in the database. This is in contrast to a view, which we mentioned in Section 1.2.4. A view is a 'virtual table' that does not actually exist in the database but is generated by the DBMS from the underlying base tables whenever it's accessed.

From an earlier definition, we know that a primary key is a minimal identifier that is used to identify records uniquely. This means that no subset of the primary key is sufficient to provide unique identification of records. If we allow a null for any part of a primary key, we're implying that not all the columns are needed to distinguish between records, which contradicts the definition of the primary key. For example, as branchNo is the primary key of the Branch table, we should not be able to insert a record into the Branch table with a null for the branchNo column.

2.3.3 Referential integrity

The second integrity rule applies to foreign keys.

Referential integrity

If a foreign key exists in a table, either the foreign key value must match a candidate key value of some record in its home table or the foreign key value must be wholly null.

In Figure 2.1, branchNo in the Staff table is a foreign key targeting the branchNo column in the home (parent) table, Branch. It should not be possible to create a staff record with branch number B300, for example, unless there is already a record for branch number B300 in the Branch table. However, we should be able to create a new staff record with a null in the branchNo column to allow for the situation where a new member of staff has joined the company but has not yet been assigned to a particular branch.

2.3.4 Other business rules

Business rules
Rules that define or constrain some aspect of the organization.

Examples of business rules include domains, which constrain the values that a particular column can have, and the relational integrity rules that we have just discussed. Another example is *multiplicity*, which defines the number of occurrences of one entity (such as a branch) that may relate to a single occurrence of an associated entity (such as a member of staff). It's also possible for users to specify additional constraints that the data must satisfy. For example, if *StayHome* has a rule that a member can only rent a maximum of 10 videos at any one time, then the user must be able to specify this rule and expect the DBMS to enforce it. In this case, it should not be possible for a member to rent a video if the number of videos the member currently has rented is 10.

Multiplicity will be discussed in Section 7.5

Unfortunately, the level of support for business rules varies from system to system. We'll discuss the implementation of business rules in Chapters 12 and 18.

2.4 Relational languages

In Section 2.1, we stated that one part of a data model is the manipulative part, which defines the types of operations that are allowed on the data. This includes the operations that are used for updating or retrieving data from the database, and for changing the structure of the database. The two main languages that have emerged for relational DBMSs are:

- SQL (Structured Query Language) and
- QBE (Query-by-Example).

SQL has been standardized by the International Organization for Standardization (ISO), making it both the formal and *de facto* standard language for defining and manipulating relational databases.

QBE is an alternative, graphical-based, 'point-and-click' way of querying the database, which is particularly suited for queries that are not too complex, and can be expressed in terms of a few tables. QBE has acquired the reputation of being one of the easiest ways for non-technical users to obtain information from the database. Unfortunately, unlike SQL, there is no official standard for QBE. However, the functionality provided by vendors is generally very similar and QBE is usually more intuitive to use than SQL. We'll provide a tutorial on SQL and QBE in the next chapter.

Chapter summary

✓ The RDBMS has become the dominant DBMS in use today. This software represents the second generation of DBMS and is based on the relational data model proposed by Dr E.F. Codd.

✓ Relations are physically represented as **tables**, with the records corresponding to individual tuples and the columns to attributes.

✓ Properties of relational tables are: each cell contains exactly one value, column names are distinct, column values come from the same domain, column order is immaterial, record order is immaterial, and there are no duplicate records.

✓ A **superkey** is a set of columns that identifies records of a table uniquely, while a **candidate key** is a minimal superkey. A **primary key** is the candidate key chosen for use in identification of records. A table must always have a primary key. A **foreign key** is a column, or set of columns, within one table that is the candidate key of another (possibly the same) table.

✓ A **null** represents a value for a column that is unknown at the present time or is not defined for this record.

✓ **Entity integrity** is a constraint that states that in a base table no column of a primary key can be null. **Referential integrity** states that foreign key values must match a candidate key value of some record in the home (parent) table or be wholly null.

✓ The two main languages for accessing relational databases are **SQL** (Structured Query Language) and **QBE** (Query-by-Example).

Review questions

2.1 Discuss each of the following concepts in the context of the relational data model:
   (a) relation;
   (b) attribute;
   (c) domain;
   (d) tuple ;
   (e) relational database.

2.2 Discuss the properties of a relational table.

2.3 Discuss the differences between the candidate keys and the primary key of a table. Explain what is meant by a foreign key. How do foreign keys of tables relate to candidate keys? Give examples to illustrate your answer.

2.4   What does a null represent?

2.5   Define the two principal integrity rules for the relational model. Discuss why it is desirable to enforce these rules.

Chapter 3

SQL and QBE

In this chapter you will learn:

The purpose and importance of SQL (Structured Query Language), the main language for querying relational databases. ◄

How to retrieve data from the database using the SELECT statement. ◄

How to insert data into the database using the INSERT statement. ◄

How to update data in the database using the UPDATE statement. ◄

How to delete data from the database using the DELETE statement. ◄

How to create a new table in the database using the CREATE TABLE statement. ◄

About another language for querying relational databases called QBE (Query–by–Example). ◄

In the previous chapter, we introduced the relational data model and noted that the two main languages that have emerged for relational DBMSs are:

- SQL (Structured Query Language)
- QBE (Query-by-Example).

QBE is essentially a graphical front-end to SQL that provides a potentially simpler method of querying relational databases than SQL. However, QBE will convert the query expressed graphically into a corresponding SQL statement that is then run on the database. In this chapter, we examine both these languages, although we concentrate primarily on SQL because of its importance. For a more complete discussion of SQL and QBE, the interested reader is referred to Connolly and Begg (2002).

3.1   Structured Query Language (SQL)

SQL is the most widely used commercial relational database language, designed to be used by professionals and non-professionals alike. It was originally developed in the SEQUEL and System-R projects at IBM's research laboratory in San Jose between 1974 and 1977. Today, many people still pronounce SQL as 'See-Quel', although the official pronunciation is 'S-Q-L'. Starting with Oracle in the late 1970s, there have been many commercial RDBMSs based on SQL, and with an ANSI (American National Standards Institute) and ISO (International Organization for Standardization) standard, it's now the formal and *de facto* language for defining and manipulating relational databases.

The main characteristics of SQL are:

■ It's relatively easy to learn.

■ It's a non-procedural language: you specify *what* information you require, rather than *how* to get it. In other words, SQL does not require you to specify the access methods to the data.

■ Like most modern languages, SQL is essentially free-format, which means that parts of statements don't have to be typed at particular locations on the screen.

■ The command structure consists of standard English words such as SELECT, INSERT, UPDATE, and DELETE.

■ It can be used by a range of users, including Database Administrators (DBAs), management personnel, application programmers, and many other types of end-users.

SQL is an important language for a number of reasons:

■ SQL is the first and, so far, only standard database language to gain wide acceptance. Nearly every major current vendor provides database products based on SQL or with an SQL interface, and most are represented on at least one of the standard-making bodies.

■ There is a huge investment in the SQL language both by vendors and by users. It has become part of application architectures such as IBM's Systems Application Architecture (SAA), and is the strategic choice of many large and influential organizations, for example the X/OPEN consortium for UNIX standards.

■ SQL has also become a Federal Information Processing Standard (FIPS), to which conformance is required for all sales of DBMSs to the US government.

■ SQL is used in other standards, and even influences the development of other standards as a definitional tool (for example, the ISO Remote Data Access (RDA) standard).

Before we go through some examples of SQL, let's first examine the objectives of SQL.

3.1.1 Objectives of SQL

Ideally, a database language should allow a user to:

■ create the database and table structures;

■ perform basic data management tasks, such as the insertion, modification, and deletion of data from the tables;

■ perform both simple and complex queries.

In addition, a database language must perform these tasks with minimal user effort, and its command structure and syntax must be relatively easy to learn. Finally, it must be portable: that is, it must conform to some recognized standard so that we can use the same command structure and syntax when we move from one DBMS to another. SQL is intended to satisfy these requirements.

SQL is an example of a *transform-oriented language*, or a language designed to transform input tables into required output tables. The ISO SQL standard has two major components:

■ a Data Definition Language (DDL) for defining the database structure and controlling access to the data;

■ a Data Manipulation Language (DML) for retrieving and updating data.

Until the most recent version of the ISO SQL standard released in 1999 (colloquially known as SQL3), SQL contained only these definitional and manipulative commands; it did not contain flow of control commands, such as IF . . . THEN . . . ELSE, GO TO, or DO . . . WHILE. These had to be implemented using a programming or job-control language, or interactively by the end-users. Due to this initial lack of *computational completeness*, SQL was used in two ways. The first is to use SQL *interactively* by entering the statements at a terminal. The second is to *embed* SQL statements in a procedural language. In this book, we only consider interactive SQL; for details on embedded SQL the interested reader is referred to Connolly and Begg (2002).

> **SQL conformance**: SQL3 has a set of features called Core SQL that a vendor must implement to claim conformance with the SQL3 standard. Many of the remaining features are divided into **packages**; for example, there are packages for object features and OLAP (OnLine Analytical Processing). Vendors tend to implement additional features, although this does affect portability.

3.1.2 Terminology

The ISO SQL standard does not use the formal terms of relations, attributes, and tuples, instead using the terms tables, columns, and rows. In our presentation of SQL we mostly use the ISO terminology. It should also be noted that SQL does not adhere strictly to the definition of the relational model described in Chapter 2. For example, SQL allows the table produced as the result of the SELECT operation to contain duplicate rows; it imposes an ordering on the columns; and it allows the user to order the rows of a table.

3.1.3 Writing SQL commands

In this section, we briefly describe the structure of an SQL statement and the notation we use to define the format of the various SQL constructs. An SQL statement consists of reserved words and user-defined words. **Reserved words** are a fixed part of the SQL language and have a fixed meaning. They must be spelled *exactly* as required and cannot be split across lines. **User-defined words** are made up by the user (according to certain syntax rules), and represent the names of various database objects such as tables, columns, views, indexes, and so on. Throughout this chapter, we use uppercase letters to represent reserved words and lowercase letters to represent user-defined words.

Most components of an SQL statement are **case insensitive**, which means that letters can be typed in either upper- or lowercase. The one important exception to this rule is that literal character data must be typed *exactly* as it appears in the database. For example, if we store a person's surname as 'SMITH' and then search for it using the string 'Smith', the row will not be found. The words in a statement are also built according to a set of syntax rules. Although the standard does not require it, many dialects of SQL require the use of a statement terminator to mark the end of each SQL statement (usually the semicolon ';' is used).

Throughout this chapter, we use the following extended form of the Backus Naur Form (BNF) notation to define SQL statements:

■ a vertical bar (|) indicates a **choice** among alternatives; for example, a | b | c;

■ curly brackets indicate a **required element**; for example, {a};

■ square brackets indicate an **optional element**; for example, [a];

■ an ellipsis (. . .) is used to indicate **optional repetition** of an item zero or more times.

For example:

{a | b} (, c . . .)

means either a or b followed by zero or more repetitions of c separated by commas.

In practice, the DDL statements are used to create the database structure (that is, the tables) and the access mechanisms (that is, what each user can legally access), and then the DML statements are used to populate and query the tables. However, in this book we concentrate on the DML statements to reflect their relative importance to the general user.

3.2 Data manipulation

In this section, we look at the SQL DML statements, namely:

■ SELECT to query data in the database;

■ INSERT to insert data into a table;

■ UPDATE to update data in a table;

■ DELETE to delete data from a table.

Due to the complexity of the SELECT statement and the relative simplicity of the other DML statements, we devote most of this section to the SELECT statement and its various formats. We begin by considering simple queries, and successively add more complexity to show how more complicated queries that use sorting, grouping, aggregates, and also queries on multiple tables can be generated. Thereafter, we consider the INSERT, UPDATE, and DELETE statements.

We illustrate the SQL statements using part of the instance of the *StayHome* case study shown in Figure 2.4 consisting of the following tables:

Staff	(staffNo, name, position, salary, branchNo)
Video	(catalogNo, title, category, dailyRental, price, directorNo)
Director	(directorNo, directorName)
Actor	(actorNo, actorName)
Role	(actorNo, catalogNo, character)
RentalAgreement	(rentalNo, dateOut, dateReturn, memberNo, videoNo)
VideoForRent	(videoNo, available, catalogNo, branchNo)

Literals

Before we discuss the SQL DML statements, it is necessary to understand the concept of **literals**. Literals are **constants** that are used in SQL statements. There are different forms of literals for every data type supported by SQL. However, for simplicity, we can distinguish between literals that are enclosed in single quotes and those that are not. All non-numeric data values must be enclosed in single quotes; all numeric data values must *not* be enclosed in single quotes. For example, we could use literals to insert data into a table:

INSERT INTO Video (catalogNo, title, category, dailyRental, price, directorNo)
VALUES ('207132', 'Die Another Day', 'Action', 5.00, 21.99, 'D1001');

The value in columns dailyRental and price are decimal literals; they are not enclosed in single quotes. All other columns are character strings and are enclosed in single quotes.

3.2.1 Simple queries

The purpose of the SELECT statement is to retrieve and display data from one or more database tables. It's an extremely powerful command and it's also the most frequently used SQL command. The SELECT statement has the following general form:

SELECT [**DISTINCT** | **ALL**] {* | [columnExpression [**AS** newName]] [, . . .]}
FROM TableName [alias] [, . . .]
[**WHERE** condition]
[**GROUP BY** columnList] [**HAVING** condition]
[**ORDER BY** columnList]

■ columnExpression represents a column name or an expression;

■ newName is a name you can give the column as a display heading;

■ TableName is the name of an existing database table or view that you have access to;

■ alias is an optional abbreviation for TableName.

The sequence of processing in a SELECT statement is:

FROM   specifies the table or tables to be used;
WHERE   filters the rows subject to some condition;
GROUP BY   forms groups of rows with the same column value;
HAVING   filters the groups subject to some condition;
SELECT   specifies which columns are to appear in the output;
ORDER BY   specifies the order of the output.

The order of the clauses in the SELECT statement *cannot* be changed. The only two mandatory clauses are the first two: SELECT and FROM; the remainder are optional. Every SELECT statement produces a query result table consisting of one or more columns and zero or more rows.

Query 3.1   Retrieve all columns, all rows

List the full details of all videos.

Since there are no restrictions specified in the query (that is, we want to list all rows in the Video table), no WHERE clause is required. We can express this query as:

SELECT catalogNo, title, category, dailyRental, price, directorNo
FROM Video;

When you want to list all columns of a table, you can use an asterisk (*) in place of the column names. Therefore, the above query can also be expressed more succinctly as:

SELECT *
FROM Video;

The result table in either case is shown in Table 3.1.

Table 3.1 Result table for Query 3.1.

catalogNo	title	category	dailyRental	price	directorNo
207132	Die Another Day	Action	5.00	21.99	D1001
902355	Harry Potter	Children	4.50	14.50	D7834
330553	Lord of the Rings	Fantasy	5.00	31.99	D4576
781132	Shrek	Children	4.00	18.50	D0078
445624	Men in Black II	Action	4.00	29.99	D5743
634817	Independence Day	Sci-Fi	4.50	32.99	D3765

Query 3.2 Retrieve specific columns, all rows

List the catalog number, title, and daily rental rate of all videos.

Once again, there are no restrictions specified in the query and so no WHERE clause is required. However, we only wish to list a subset of the columns, which we express as:

SELECT catalogNo, title, dailyRental
FROM Video;

The result table is shown in Table 3.2. Note that, unless specified, the rows in the result table may not be sorted. We describe how to sort the rows of a result table in the next section.

Table 3.2 Result table for Query 3.2.

catalogNo	title	dailyRental
207132	Die Another Day	5.00
902355	Harry Potter	4.50
330553	Lord of the Rings	5.00
781132	Shrek	4.00
445624	Men in Black II	4.00
634817	Independence Day	4.50

Query 3.3 Use of DISTINCT

List all video categories.

> **SELECT** category
> **FROM** Video;

The result table is shown in Table 3.3(a). Note that there are several duplicate values (by default, SELECT does not eliminate duplicate values). To eliminate duplicates, we use the **DISTINCT** keyword and by rewriting the above query as:

> **SELECT DISTINCT** category
> **FROM** Video;

we obtain the result table shown in Table 3.3(b).

Table 3.3(a) Result table for Query 3.3 with duplicates.

category
Action
Children
Fantasy
Children
Action
Sci-Fi

Table 3.3(b) Result table for Query 3.3 with duplicates eliminated.

category
Action
Children
Fantasy
Sci-Fi

Query 3.4 Calculated fields

List the rate for renting videos for three days.

> **SELECT** catalogNo, title, dailyRental * 3
> **FROM** Video;

This query is very similar to Query 3.2 with the exception that we're looking for the rental rate for three days rather than for just one day. In this case, we can obtain the three-day rate by multiplying the daily rate by 3, giving the result table shown in Table 3.4.

This is an example of the use of a **calculated field** (sometimes called a computed or derived field). In general, to use a calculated field, you specify an SQL expression in the **SELECT** list. An SQL expression can involve addition, subtraction, multiplication, and division, and you can use parentheses to build complex expressions. You can use more than one table column in a calculated column; however, the columns referenced in an arithmetic expression must be of a numeric type.

The third column of this result table has been displayed as col3. Normally, a column in the result table takes its name from the corresponding column of the database table from which it has been retrieved. However, in this case SQL does not know how to label the column. Some systems give the column a name corresponding to its position in the table (for example, col3); some may leave the column name blank or use the expression entered in the SELECT list. The SQL standard allows the column to be named using an **AS** clause. In the previous example, we could have written:

SELECT catalogNo, title, dailyRental * 3 **AS** threeDayRate
FROM Video;

In this case, the column heading in the result table would be threeDayRate rather than col3.

Table 3.4 Result table of Query 3.4.

catalogNo	title	col3
207132	Die Another Day	15.00
902355	Harry Potter	13.50
330553	Lord of the Rings	15.00
781132	Shrek	12.00
445624	Men in Black II	12.00
634817	Independence Day	13.50

3.2.2   Row selection (**WHERE** clause)

The above examples show the use of the SELECT statement to retrieve all rows from a table. However, we often need to restrict the rows that are retrieved. This can be achieved with the **WHERE** clause, which consists of the keyword WHERE followed by a search condition that specifies the rows to be retrieved. The five basic search conditions (or *predicates* using the ISO terminology) are as follows:

■ *Comparison*: compare the value of one expression to the value of another expression;

■ *Range*: test whether the value of an expression falls within a specified range of values;

Nulls defined in Section 2.3.1

■ *Set membership*: test whether the value of an expression equals one of a set of values;

■ *Pattern match*: test whether a string matches a specified pattern;

■ *Null*: test whether a column has a null (unknown) value.

We now present examples of some of these types of search conditions.

Query 3.5 Comparison search condition

List all staff with a salary greater than $40,000.

> **SELECT** staffNo, name, position, salary
> **FROM** Staff
> **WHERE** salary > 40000;

In this query, we have to restrict the rows in the Staff table to those where the value in the salary column is greater than $40,000. To do this, we specify a WHERE clause with the condition (*predicate*) 'salary > 40000'. The result table is shown in Table 3.5.

Table 3.5 Result table for Query 3.5.

staffNo	name	position	salary
S1500	Tom Daniels	Manager	46000
S0010	Mary Martinez	Manager	50000
S2250	Sally Stern	Manager	48000
S0415	Art Peters	Manager	41000

In SQL, the following simple comparison operators are available:

=	equals	< >	is not equal to
<	is less than	<=	is less than or equal to
>	is greater than	>=	is greater than or equal to

More complex predicates can be generated using the logical operators **AND**, **OR**, and **NOT**, with parentheses (if needed or desired) to show the order of evaluation. The rules for evaluating a conditional expression are:

■ an expression is evaluated left to right;

■ subexpressions in parentheses are evaluated first;

■ NOTs are evaluated before ANDs and ORs;

■ ANDs are evaluated before ORs.

The use of parentheses is always recommended to remove any possible ambiguities.

Query 3.6 Range search condition (BETWEEN/NOT BETWEEN)

List all staff with a salary between $45,000 and $50,000.

SELECT staffNo, name, position, salary
FROM Staff
WHERE salary >= 45000 **AND** salary <= 50000;

In this query, we use the logical operator AND in the WHERE clause to find the rows in the Staff table where the value in the salary column is between $45,000 and $50,000. The result table is shown in Table 3.6. SQL also provides the range test **BETWEEN** to test whether a data value lies between a pair of specified values. We could rewrite the previous query as:

SELECT staffNo, name, position, salary
FROM Staff
WHERE salary **BETWEEN** 45000 **AND** 50000;

The BETWEEN test includes the endpoints of the range, so any members of staff with a salary of $45,000 or $50,000 would be included in the result. There is also a negated version of the range test (**NOT BETWEEN**) that checks for values outside the range. The BETWEEN test does not add much to the expressive power of SQL because, as we have seen, it can be expressed equally well using two comparison tests.

Table 3.6 Result table for Query 3.6.

staffNo	name	position	salary
S1500	Tom Daniels	Manager	46000
S0010	Mary Martinez	Manager	50000
S2250	Sally Stern	Manager	48000

Query 3.7 Set membership search condition (IN/NOT IN)

List all videos in the Action or Children categories.

SELECT catalogNo, title, category
FROM Video
WHERE category = 'Action' **OR** category = 'Children';

As in the previous example, we can express this query using a compound search condition in the WHERE clause. The result table is shown in Table 3.7. However, SQL also provides the set membership keyword **IN** to test whether a value matches one of a list of values. We can rewrite this query using the IN test as:

SELECT catalogNo, title, category
FROM Video
WHERE category **IN** ('Action', 'Children');

There is a negated version (**NOT IN**) that can be used to check for data values that do not lie in a specific list of values. Like BETWEEN, the IN test does not add much to the expressive power of SQL. However, the IN test provides a more efficient way of expressing the search condition, particularly if the set contains many values.

Table 3.7 Result table for Query 3.7.

catalogNo	title	category
207132	Die Another Day	Action
902355	Harry Potter	Children
781132	Shrek	Children
445624	Men In Black II	Action

Query 3.8 Pattern match search condition (LIKE/NOT LIKE)

List all staff whose first name is 'Sally'.

SQL has two special pattern-matching symbols:

% percent character represents any sequence of zero or more characters (*wildcard*);

_ underscore character represents any single character.

All other characters in the pattern represent themselves. For example:

- name LIKE 'S%' means the first character must be *S*, but the rest of the string can be anything.
- name LIKE 'S_ _ _ _' means that there must be exactly four characters in the string, the first of which must be an *S*.
- name LIKE '%S' means any sequence of characters, of length at least 1, with the last character an *S*.
- name LIKE '%Sally%' means a sequence of characters of any length containing *Sally*.
- name NOT LIKE 'S%' means the first character cannot be an *S*.

If the search string can include the pattern-matching character itself, we can use an **escape character** to represent the pattern-matching character. For example, to check for the string '15%', we can use the predicate:

LIKE '15#%' ESCAPE '#'

Using the pattern-matching search condition of SQL, we can find all staff whose first name is 'Sally' using the following query:

SELECT staffNo, name, position, salary
FROM Staff
WHERE name **LIKE** 'Sally %';

The result table is shown in Table 3.8.

Table 3.8 Result table of Query 3.8.

staffNo	name	position	salary
S0003	Sally Adams	Assistant	30000
S2250	Sally Stern	Manager	48000

Note that some RDBMSs, such as Microsoft Access, use the wildcard characters * and ? instead of % and _.

Query 3.9 NULL search condition (IS NULL/IS NOT NULL)

List the video rentals that have not yet been returned.

The RentalAgreement table has a column dateReturn representing the date the video rental is returned. You may think that we can find such videos using the following search condition:

WHERE (dateReturn = ` ` **OR** dateReturn = 0)

Nulls defined in Section 2.3.1

However, neither of these conditions would work. A null dateReturn is considered to have an unknown value, so we cannot test whether it is equal or not equal to another value. If we tried to execute the SELECT statement using either of these compound conditions, we would get an empty result table. Instead, we have to test for null explicitly using the special keyword **IS NULL**:

SELECT dateOut, memberNo, videoNo
FROM RentalAgreement
WHERE dateReturn **IS NULL**;

The result table is shown in Table 3.9. The negated version (**IS NOT NULL**) can be used to test for values that are not null.

Table 3.9 Result table for Query 3.9.

dateOut	memberNo	videoNo
2-Feb-03	M115656	178643

3.2.3 Sorting results (ORDER BY clause)

In general, the rows of an SQL query result table are not arranged in any particular order (although some DBMSs may use a default ordering, for example, based on a primary key). However, we can ensure that the results of a query are sorted using the **ORDER BY** clause in the SELECT statement. The ORDER BY clause consists of a list of **column names** that the result is to be sorted on, separated by commas. The ORDER BY clause allows the retrieved rows to be ordered in ascending (**ASC**) or descending (**DESC**) order on any column or combination of columns, regardless of whether that column appears in the result. However, some dialects of SQL insist that the ORDER BY elements appear in the SELECT list. In either case, the ORDER BY clause must always be the last clause of the SELECT statement.

Query 3.10 Sorting results

List all videos sorted in descending order of price.

SELECT *
FROM Video
ORDER BY price **DESC**;

This is similar to Query 3.1 with the added requirement that the result table is to be sorted on the values in the price column. This is achieved by adding the ORDER BY clause to the end of the SELECT statement, specifying price as the column to be sorted, and DESC to indicate that the order is to be descending. In this case, we get the result table shown in Table 3.10.

If we had a number of values in the price column that were the same, we might then want to order the result first by price (the **major sort key**) and secondly in ascending order of title (the **minor sort key**). In this case, the ORDER BY clause would be:

ORDER BY price **DESC**, title **ASC**;

Table 3.10 Result table for Query 3.10.

catalogNo	title	category	dailyRental	price	directorNo
634817	Independence Day	Sci-Fi	4.50	32.99	D3765
330553	Lord of the Rings	Fantasy	5.00	31.99	D4576
445624	Men In Black II	Action	4.00	29.99	D5743
207132	Die Another Day	Action	5.00	21.99	D1001
781132	Shrek	Children	4.00	18.50	D0078
902355	Harry Potter	Children	4.50	14.50	D7834

3.2.4 Using the SQL aggregate functions

The ISO standard defines five **aggregate functions**:

COUNT	Returns the number of values in a specified column.
SUM	Returns the sum of the values in a specified column.
AVG	Returns the average of the values in a specified column.
MIN	Returns the minimum value in a specified column.
MAX	Returns the maximum value in a specified column.

These functions operate on a single column of a table and return a single value. COUNT, MIN, and MAX apply to both numeric and non-numeric fields, but SUM and AVG may be used on numeric fields only. Apart from COUNT(*), each function eliminates nulls first and operates only on the remaining non-null values. COUNT(*) is a special use of COUNT, which counts all the rows of a table, regardless of whether nulls or duplicate values occur.

If we want to eliminate duplicates before the function is applied, we use the keyword DISTINCT before the column name in the function. DISTINCT has no effect with the MIN and MAX functions. However, it may have an effect on the result of SUM or AVG, so consideration must be given to whether duplicates should be included or excluded in the computation. In addition, DISTINCT can be specified only once in a query.

HAVING and
GROUP BY
clauses discussed
in Section 3.2.5

> It is important to note that an aggregate function can be used only in the SELECT list and in the HAVING clause. It is incorrect to use it elsewhere. If the SELECT list includes an aggregate function and no GROUP BY clause is being used to group data together, then no item in the SELECT list can include any reference to a column unless that column is the argument to an aggregate function. For example, the following query is illegal:
>
> **SELECT** staffNo, **COUNT**(salary)
> **FROM** Staff;
>
> because the query does not have a GROUP BY clause and the column staffNo in the SELECT list is used outside an aggregate function.

Query 3.11 Use of COUNT and SUM

List the total number of staff with a salary greater than $40,000 and the sum of their salaries.

SELECT COUNT(staffNo) **AS** totalStaff, **SUM**(salary) **AS** totalSalary
FROM Staff
WHERE salary > 40000;

The WHERE clause is the same as in Query 3.5. However, in this case, we apply the COUNT function to count the number of rows satisfying the WHERE clause and we apply the SUM function to add together the salaries in these rows. The result table is shown in Table 3.11.

Table 3.11 Result table of Query 3.11.

totalStaff	totalSalary
4	185000

Query 3.12 Use of MIN, MAX, and AVG

List the minimum, maximum, and average staff salary.

> **SELECT MIN**(salary) **AS** minSalary, **MAX**(salary) **AS** maxSalary,
>   **AVG**(salary) **AS** avgSalary
> **FROM** Staff;

In this query, we wish to consider all staff rows and therefore do not require a WHERE clause. The required values can be calculated using the MIN, MAX, and AVG functions. The result table is shown in Table 3.12.

Table 3.12 Result table of Query 3.12.

minSalary	maxSalary	avgSalary
30000	50000	41166.67

3.2.5 Grouping results (GROUP BY clause)

The above summary queries are similar to the totals at the bottom of a report. They condense all the detailed data in the report into a single summary row of data. However, it is often useful to have subtotals in reports. We can use the **GROUP BY** clause of the SELECT statement to do this. A query that includes the GROUP BY clause is called a **grouped query**, because it groups the data from the SELECT table(s) and produces a single summary row for each group. The columns named in the GROUP BY clause are called the **grouping columns**. The ISO standard requires the SELECT clause and the GROUP BY clause to be closely integrated. When GROUP BY is used, each item in the SELECT list must be **single-valued per group.** Further, the SELECT clause may contain only:

- ▧ column names,
- ▧ aggregate functions,
- ▧ constants,
- ▧ an expression involving combinations of the above.

All column names in the SELECT list must appear in the GROUP BY clause unless the name is used only in an aggregate function. The contrary is not true: there may be column names in the GROUP BY clause that do not appear in the SELECT list. When the WHERE clause is used with GROUP BY, the WHERE clause is applied first, then groups are formed from the remaining rows that satisfy the search condition.

> The ISO standard considers two nulls to be equal for purposes of the GROUP BY clause. If two rows have nulls in the same grouping columns and identical values in all the non-null grouping columns, they are combined into the same group.

Query 3.13 Use of **GROUP BY**

Find the number of staff working in each branch and the sum of their salaries.

SELECT branchNo, **COUNT**(staffNo) **AS** totalStaff,
      SUM(salary) **AS** totalSalary
FROM Staff
GROUP BY branchNo
ORDER BY branchNo;

It is not necessary to include the column names staffNo and salary in the GROUP BY list because they appear only in the SELECT list within aggregate functions. On the other hand, branchNo is not associated with an aggregate function and so must appear in the GROUP BY list. The result table is shown in Table 3.13.

Conceptually, SQL performs the query as follows:

Table 3.13 Result table for Query 3.13.

(1)
SQL

branchNo	totalStaff	totalSalary
B001	2	76000
B002	2	82000
B003	1	41000
B004	1	48000

divides the staff into groups according to their respective branch numbers. Within each group, all staff have the same branch number. In this example, we get four groups:

branchNo	staffNo	salary		COUNT(staffNo)	SUM(salary)
B001	S1500	46000	→ 2		76000
B001	S0003	30000			
B002	S0010	50000	→ 2		82000
B002	S3250	32000			
B003	S0415	41000	→ 1		41000
B004	S2250	48000	→ 1		48000

(2)

For each group, SQL computes the number of staff members and calculates the sum of the values in the salary column to get the total of their salaries. SQL generates a single summary row in the query result for each group.

(3) Finally, the result is sorted in ascending order of branch number, branchNo.

Restricting groupings (**HAVING** clause)

The **HAVING** clause is designed for use with the GROUP BY clause to restrict the **groups** that appear in the final result table. Although similar in syntax, HAVING and WHERE serve different purposes. The WHERE clause filters **individual rows** going into the final result table, whereas HAVING filters **groups** going into the final result table. The ISO standard requires that column names used in the HAVING clause must also appear in the GROUP BY list or be contained within an aggregate function. In practice, the search condition in the HAVING clause always includes at least one aggregate function, otherwise the search condition could be moved to the WHERE clause and applied to individual rows. (Remember that aggregate functions cannot be used in the WHERE clause.)

The HAVING clause is not a necessary part of SQL – any query expressed using a HAVING clause can always be rewritten without the HAVING clause.

Query 3.14 Use of **HAVING**

For each branch office with more than one member of staff, find the number of staff working in each branch and the sum of their salaries.

```
SELECT      branchNo, COUNT(staffNo) AS totalStaff,
            SUM(salary) AS totalSalary
FROM        Staff
GROUP BY    branchNo
HAVING COUNT(staffNo) > 1
ORDER BY    branchNo;
```

This is similar to the previous example with the additional restriction that we want to consider only those groups (that is, branches) with more than one member of staff. This restriction applies to the groups and so the HAVING clause is used. The result table is shown in Table 3.14.

Table 3.14 Result table of Query 3.14.

branchNo	totalStaff	totalSalary
B001	2	76000
B002	2	82000

3.2.6 Subqueries

INSERT, UPDATE, and DELETE discussed in Section 3.2.8

In this section, we examine the use of a complete SELECT statement embedded within another SELECT statement. The results of this **inner** SELECT statement (or **subselect**) are used in the **outer** statement to help determine the contents of the final result. A subselect can be used in the WHERE and HAVING clauses of an outer SELECT statement, where it is called a **subquery** or **nested query**. Subselects may also appear in INSERT, UPDATE, and DELETE statements.

> **Query 3.15** Using a subquery

Find the staff who work in the branch at '8 Jefferson Way'.

```
SELECT staffNo, name, position
FROM Staff
WHERE branchNo = (SELECT branchNo
                  FROM Branch
                  WHERE street = '8 Jefferson Way');
```

The inner SELECT statement (SELECT branchNo FROM Branch . . .) finds the branch number that corresponds to the branch with street name '8 Jefferson Way' (there will be only one such branch number. Having obtained this branch number, the outer SELECT statement then retrieves the details of all staff who work at this branch. In other words, the inner SELECT returns a result table containing a single value 'B001', corresponding to the branch at '8 Jefferson Way', and the outer SELECT becomes:

```
SELECT staffNo, name, position
FROM Staff
WHERE branchNo = 'B001';
```

The result table is shown in Table 3.15.

Table 3.15 Result table of Query 3.15.

staffNo	name	position
S1500	Tom Daniels	Manager
S0003	Sally Adams	Assistant

We can think of the subquery as producing a temporary table with results that can be accessed and used by the outer statement. A subquery can be used immediately following a relational operator (that is, =, <, >, <=, >=, < >) in a WHERE clause or a HAVING clause. The subquery itself is always enclosed in parentheses.

Note, if the result of the inner query can result in more than one row, then you must use the set membership test IN rather than the equality test ('='). For example, if we wish to find staff who worked at a branch in Washington (WA), the WHERE clause would become:

WHERE branchNo **IN (SELECT** branchNo **FROM** Branch
WHERE state = 'WA');

Query 3.16 Using a subquery with an aggregate function

List all staff whose salary is greater than the average salary.

SELECT staffNo, name, position
FROM Staff
WHERE salary > (**SELECT AVG**(salary)
FROM Staff);

Recall from Section 3.2.4 that an aggregate function can be used only in the SELECT list and in the HAVING clause. It would be incorrect to write 'WHERE salary > AVG(salary)'. Instead, we use a subquery to find the average salary, and then use the outer SELECT statement to find those staff with a salary greater than this average. In other words, the subquery returns the average salary as $41,166.67. The outer query is reduced then to:

SELECT staffNo, name, position
FROM Staff
WHERE salary > 41166.67;

The result table is shown in Table 3.16.

Table 3.16 Result table of Query 3.16.

staffNo	name	position
S1500	Tom Daniels	Manager
S0010	Mary Martinez	Manager
S2250	Sally Stern	Manager

Note that the following rules apply to subqueries:

(1) The ORDER BY clause may not be used in a subquery (although it may be used in the outermost SELECT statement).

(2) The subquery SELECT list must consist of a single column name or expression (except for subqueries that use the keyword EXISTS – see Connolly and Begg (2002)).

(3) By default, column names in a subquery refer to the table name in the FROM clause of the subquery. It is possible to refer to a table in a FROM clause of an outer query by qualifying the column name.

(4) When a subquery is one of the two operands involved in a comparison, the subquery must appear on the right-hand side of the comparison. For example, it would be incorrect to express the last example as:

> **SELECT** staffNo, name, position
> **FROM** Staff
> **WHERE** (**SELECT AVG**(salary) **FROM** Staff) < salary;

because the subquery appears on the left-hand side of the comparison with salary.

3.2.7 Multi–table queries

All the examples we have considered so far have a major limitation: the columns that are to appear in the result table must all come from a single table. In many cases, this is not sufficient. To combine columns from several tables into a result table, we need to use a **join** operation. The SQL join operation combines information from two tables by forming pairs of related rows from the two tables. The row pairs that make up the joined table are those where the matching columns in each of the two tables have the same value.

If you need to obtain information from more than one table, the choice is between using a subquery and using a join. If the final result table is to contain columns from different tables, then you must use a join. To perform a join, you simply include more than one table name in the FROM clause, using a comma as a separator, and typically include a WHERE clause to specify the join column(s). It is also possible to use an **alias** for a table named in the FROM clause. In this case, the alias is separated from the table name with a space. An alias can be used to qualify a column name whenever there is ambiguity regarding the source of the column name. It can also be used as a shorthand notation for the table name. If an alias is provided it can be used anywhere in place of the table name.

Query 3.17 Simple join

List all videos along with the name of the director.

SELECT catalogNo, title, category, v.directorNo, directorName
FROM Video v, Director d
WHERE v.directorNo = d.directorNo;

We want to display details from both the Video table and the Director table, and so we have to use a join. The SELECT clause lists the columns to be displayed. To obtain the required rows, we include those rows from both tables that have identical values in the directorNo columns, using the search condition (v.directorNo = d.directorNo). We call these two columns the **matching columns** for the two tables. The result table is shown in Table 3.17.

Note that it is necessary to qualify the director number, directorNo, in the SELECT list: directorNo could come from either table, and we have to indicate which one. (We could equally well have chosen the directorNo column from the Director table.) The qualification is achieved by prefixing the column name with the appropriate table name (or its alias). In this case, we have used v as the alias for the Video table.

Table 3.17 Result table of Query 3.17.

catalogNo	title	category	v.directorNo	directorName
207132	Die Another Day	Action	D1001	Lee Tamahori
902355	Harry Potter	Children	D7834	Chris Columbus
330553	Lord of the Rings	Fantasy	D4576	Peter Jackson
781132	Shrek	Children	D0078	Andrew Adamson
445624	Men In Black II	Action	D5743	Barry Sonnenfeld
634817	Independence Day	Sci-Fi	D3765	Roland Emmerick

1:* relationships discussed in Section 7.5.2

The most common multi-table queries involve two tables that have a one-to-many (1:*) relationship. The previous query involving videos and directors is an example of such a query. Each director can direct one or more videos. In Section 2.2.5, we described how candidate keys and foreign keys model relationships in a relational database. To use a relationship in an SQL query, we specify a search condition that compares one of the candidate keys (normally the primary key) and the corresponding foreign key. In Query 3.16, we compared the foreign key in the Video table, v.directorNo, with the primary key in the Director table, d.directorNo.

The SQL standard provides the following alternative ways to specify this join:

FROM Video v **JOIN** Director d **ON** v.directorNo = d.directorNo;
FROM Video **JOIN** Director **USING** directorNo;
FROM Video **NATURAL JOIN** Director;

In each case, the FROM clause replaces the original FROM and WHERE clauses. However, the first alternative produces a table with two identical directorNo columns; the remaining two produce a table with a single directorNo column.

Query 3.18 Four-table join

List all videos along with the name of the director, the names of the actors, and their associated roles.

SELECT v.catalogNo, title, category, directorName, actorName, character
FROM Video v, Director d, Actor a, Role r
WHERE d.directorNo = v.directorNo **AND**
v.catalogNo = r.catalogNo **AND**
r.actorNo = a.actorNo;

In this example, we want to display details from the Video, Director, Actor, and Role tables, and so we have to use a join. The SELECT clause lists the columns to be displayed. To obtain the required rows, we need to join the tables based on the various matching columns (that is, the primary keys/foreign keys), as shown below:

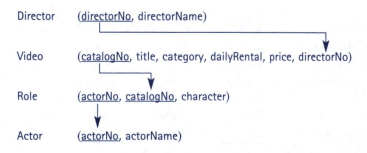

Director   (<u>directorNo</u>, directorName)

Video   (<u>catalogNo</u>, title, category, dailyRental, price, directorNo)

Role   (<u>actorNo</u>, <u>catalogNo</u>, character)

Actor   (<u>actorNo</u>, actorName)

The result table is shown in Table 3.18.

Table 3.18 Result table of Query 3.18.

catalogNo	title	category	directorName	actorName	character
207132	Die Another Day	Action	Lee Tamahori	Pierce Brosnan	James Bond
902355	Harry Potter	Children	Chris Columbus	Daniel Radcliffe	Harry Potter
330553	Lord of the Rings	Fantasy	Peter Jackson	Elijah Wood	Frodo Baggins
781132	Shrek	Children	Andrew Adamson	Mike Myers	Shrek
445624	Men In Black II	Action	Barry Sonnenfeld	Will Smith	Agent J
445624	Men In Black II	Action	Barry Sonnenfeld	Tommy Lee Jones	Agent K
634817	Independence Day	Sci-Fi	Roland Emmerick	Will Smith	Captain Steve Hiller

3.2.8 INSERT, UPDATE, and DELETE statements

SQL is a complete data manipulation language that can be used for modifying the data in the database as well as querying the database. The commands for modifying the database are not as complex as the SELECT statement. In this section, we describe the three SQL statements that are available to modify the contents of the tables in the database:

- **INSERT** adds new rows of data to a table;
- **UPDATE** modifies existing data in a table;
- **DELETE** removes rows of data from a table.

INSERT statement

The general format of the INSERT statement is:

> **INSERT INTO** TableName [(columnList)]
> **VALUES** (dataValueList)

TableName is the name of a base table and columnList represents a list of one or more column names separated by commas. The columnList is optional; if omitted, SQL assumes a list of all columns in their original CREATE TABLE order. If specified, then any columns that are omitted from the list must have been declared as NULL columns when the table was created, unless the DEFAULT option was used when creating the column (see Section 3.3.1). The *dataValueList* must match the columnList as follows:

- the number of items in each list must be the same;
- there must be a direct correspondence in the position of items in the two lists, so that the first item in *dataValueList* applies to the first item in columnList, the second item in *dataValueList* applies to the second item in columnList, and so on;
- the data type of each item in *dataValueList* must be compatible with the data type of the corresponding column.

Query 3.19 Insert a row into a table

Insert a row into the Video table.

INSERT INTO Video
VALUES ('207132', 'Die Another Day', 'Action' 5.00, 21.99, 'D1001');

CREATE
TABLE covered
in Section 3.3.1

In this particular example, we have supplied values for all columns in the order the columns were specified when the table was created (so we can omit the list of column names).

UPDATE statement

The format of the UPDATE statement is:

UPDATE TableName
SET columnName1 = dataValue1 [, columnName2 = dataValue2
                                    ...]
[**WHERE** searchCondition]

The SET clause specifies the names of one or more columns that are to be updated. The WHERE clause is optional; if omitted, the named columns are updated for *all rows* in the table. If a WHERE clause is specified, only those rows that satisfy the specified *searchCondition* are updated.

Query 3.20 Update rows in a table

Modify the daily rental rate of videos in the 'Thriller' category by 10 percent.

UPDATE Video
SET dailyRental = dailyRental * 1.1
WHERE action = 'Thriller';

DELETE statement

The format of the DELETE statement is:

DELETE FROM TableName
[**WHERE** searchCondition]

As with the UPDATE statement, the WHERE clause is optional; if omitted, *all rows* are deleted from the table. If a WHERE clause is specified, only those rows that satisfy the specified *searchCondition* are deleted.

Query 3.21 Delete rows in a table

Delete rental videos for catalog number 634817.

DELETE FROM VideoForRent
WHERE catalogNo = '634817';

3.3 Data definition

In this section, we briefly look at two of the SQL DDL statements, namely:

■ **CREATE TABLE**   to create a new table in the database;
■ **CREATE VIEW**   to create a new view from a base table.

3.3.1 CREATE TABLE

CREATE TABLE TableName
        {(columnName dataType [**NOT NULL**] [**UNIQUE**]
        [**DEFAULT** defaultOption] [, . . .]}
        [**PRIMARY KEY** (listOfColumns),]
        {[**UNIQUE** (listOfColumns),] [, . . .]}
        {[**FOREIGN KEY** (listOfForeignKeyColumns)
        REFERENCES ParentTableName [(listOfCandidateKeyColumns)],
                [[**ON UPDATE** referentialAction]
                [**ON DELETE** referentialAction]] [, . . .]})

The full version of the CREATE TABLE statement is rather complex and in this section we provide a simplified version of the statement to illustrate some of its main components. Figure 3.1 shows the CREATE TABLE statements to

Figure 3.1

CREATE TABLE statements for the Branch, Director, and Video tables

CREATE TABLE Branch (branchNo	**CHAR**(4)	**NOT NULL,**
street	**VARCHAR**(30)	**NOT NULL,**
city	**VARCHAR**(20)	**NOT NULL,**
state	**CHAR**(2)	**NOT NULL,**
zipCode	**CHAR**(5)	**NOT NULL UNIQUE,**
mgrStaffNo	**CHAR**(5)	**NOT NULL,**

    CONSTRAINT pk1 **PRIMARY KEY** (branchNo),

    CONSTRAINT fk1 **FOREIGN KEY** (mgrStaffNo) **REFERENCES** Staff

        ON UPDATE CASCADE ON DELETE NO ACTION);

CREATE TABLE Director (directorNo	**CHAR**(5)	**NOT NULL,**
directorName	**VARCHAR**(30)	**NOT NULL,**

    CONSTRAINT pk2 **PRIMARY KEY** (directorNo));

CREATE TABLE Video (catalogNo	**CHAR**(6)	**NOT NULL,**
title	**VARCHAR**(40)	**NOT NULL,**
category	**VARCHAR**(10)	**NOT NULL,**
dailyRental	**DECIMAL**(4, 2)	**NOT NULL DEFAULT** 5.00,
price	**DECIMAL**(4, 2),	
directorNo	**CHAR**(5)	**NOT NULL,**

    CONSTRAINT pk3 **PRIMARY KEY** (catalogNo),

    CONSTRAINT fk2 **FOREIGN KEY** (directorNo) **REFERENCES** Director

        ON UPDATE CASCADE ON DELETE NO ACTION);

create the Branch, Director, and Video tables. Each statement first defines each column of the table and then has one or two other clauses: one to define the primary key and one to define any foreign keys.

Defining a column

The basic format for defining a column of a table is as follows:

    columnName dataType [**NOT NULL**] [**UNIQUE**] [**DEFAULT** defaultOption]

where columnName is the name of the column and *dataType* defines the type of the column. The ISO standard supports the data types shown in Table 3.19. The most widely used data types are:

- **CHARACTER**(L): (usually abbreviated to CHAR) defines a string of fixed length L. If you enter a string with fewer characters than this length, the string is padded with blanks on the right to make up the required size.
- **CHARACTER VARYING**(L): (usually abbreviated to **VARCHAR**) defines a string of varying length L. If you enter a string with fewer characters than this length, only those characters entered are stored, thereby using less space.
- **DECIMAL**(precision, [scale]) or **NUMERIC**(precision, [scale]): defines a number with an exact representation. precision specifies the number of significant digits and scale specifies the number of digits after the decimal point. The difference between the types is that for NUMERIC the implementation must provide the precision requested but for DECIMAL the implementation may provide a precision that is greater than or equal to that requested. For example, DECIMAL(4) can represent numbers between −9999 and +9999; DECIMAL(4, 2) can represent numbers between −99.99 and +99.99.
- **INTEGER** and **SMALLINT**: define numbers where the representation of fractions is not required. Typically SMALLINT would be used to store numbers with a maximum absolute value of 32 767.
- **DATE**: stores date values in Julian date format as a combination of YEAR (4 digits), MONTH (2 digits), and DAY (2 digits).

In addition, you can define:

- whether the column cannot accept nulls (**NOT NULL**),
- whether each value within the column will be unique; that is, the column is a candidate key (**UNIQUE**),
- a default value for the column; this is a value that would be used if the value of the column is not specified (**DEFAULT**).

The full version of the ISO standard also allows other conditions to be specified but we refer the interested reader to Connolly and Begg (2002) for further details.

Table 3.19 ISO SQL data types.

Data type	Declarations			
boolean	BOOLEAN			
character	CHAR,	VARCHAR		
bit	BIT,	BIT VARYING		
exact numeric	NUMERIC,	DECIMAL,	INTEGER,	SMALLINT
approximate numeric	FLOAT,	REAL,	DOUBLE PRECISION	
datetime	DATE,	TIME,	TIMESTAMP	
interval	INTERVAL			
large objects	CHARACTER LARGE OBJECT		BINARY LARGE OBJECT	

PRIMARY KEY clause and entity integrity

Entity integrity
discussed in
Section 2.3.2

The primary key of a table must contain a unique, non-null value for each row. The ISO standard supports entity integrity with the **PRIMARY KEY** clause in the CREATE TABLE statement. For example, we can define the primary keys for the Video table and the Role table (which has a composite primary key) as follows:

> **CONSTRAINT** pk **PRIMARY KEY** (catalogNo)
> **CONSTRAINT** pk1 **PRIMARY KEY** (catalogNo, actorNo)

Note that the keyword CONSTRAINT followed by a name for the constraint is optional but allows the constraint to be dropped using the SQL statement ALTER TABLE.

FOREIGN KEY clause and referential integrity

Referential
integrity discussed
in Section 2.3.3

The ISO standard supports the definition of foreign keys with the **FOREIGN KEY** clause in the CREATE TABLE statement. The ISO standard supports referential integrity by rejecting any INSERT or UPDATE operation that attempts to create a foreign key value in a child table without a matching candidate key value in the parent table. The action SQL takes for any UPDATE or DELETE operation that attempts to update or delete a candidate key value in the parent table that has some matching rows in the child table is dependent on the **referential action** specified using the **ON UPDATE** and **ON DELETE** subclauses of the FOREIGN KEY clause:

■ **CASCADE**: Update/delete the row from the parent table and automatically update/delete the matching rows in the child table. Since these updated/deleted rows may themselves have a candidate key that is used as a foreign key in another table, the foreign key rules for these tables are triggered, and so on in a cascading manner.

■ **SET NULL**: Update/delete the row from the parent table and set the foreign key value(s) in the child table to NULL. This is valid only if the foreign key columns do not have the NOT NULL qualifier specified.

■ **SET DEFAULT**: Update/delete the row from the parent table and set each component of the foreign key in the child table to the specified default value. This is valid only if the foreign key columns have a DEFAULT value specified.

■ **NO ACTION**: Reject the update/delete operation from the parent table. This is the default setting if the ON UPDATE/ON DELETE rule is omitted.

3.3.2 CREATE VIEW

The (simplified) format of the CREATE VIEW statement is:

CREATE VIEW ViewName [(newColumnName [, . . .])]

AS subselect

A view is defined by specifying an SQL SELECT statement (known as the **defining query**). A name may optionally be assigned to each column in the view. If a list of column names is specified, it must have the same number of items as the number of columns produced by the *subselect*. If the list of column names is omitted, each column in the view takes the name of the corresponding column in the *subselect* statement. The list of column names must be specified if there is any ambiguity in the name for a column. This may occur if the *subselect* includes calculated columns and the AS subclause has not been used to name such columns, or it produces two columns with identical names as the result of a join.

For example, we could create a view of staff at branch B001 that excludes salary information as follows:

CREATE VIEW StaffBranch1
AS   **SELECT** staffNo, name, position
      FROM Staff
      WHERE branchNo = 'B001';

3.4 Query-by-Example (QBE)

QBE is an alternative, graphical-based, 'point-and-click' way of querying the database. QBE has acquired the reputation of being one of the easiest ways for non-technical users to obtain information from a database. QBE provides a visual means for querying the data through the use of templates. Querying the database is achieved by illustrating the query to be answered. The screen display is used instead of typing the SQL statement; however, you must indicate the columns (called **fields** in Microsoft Access) that you want to see and specify data values that you want to use to restrict the query. Languages like QBE can be a highly productive way to query or update the database interactively.

Like SQL, QBE was developed at IBM (in fact, QBE is an IBM trademark), but a number of other vendors, including Microsoft, sell QBE-like interfaces. Often vendors provide both SQL and QBE facilities, with QBE serving as a more intuitive interface for simple queries and the full power of SQL available for more complex queries.

Once you have read this section, you will see that the QBE version of the queries is usually more straightforward. For illustrative purposes, we use Microsoft Access 2002 and for each example we show the equivalent SQL statement for comparison.

Query 3.1 (Revisited) Retrieve all columns, all rows

List the full details of all videos.

The QBE grid for this query is shown in Figure 3.2(a). In the top part of the QBE grid, we display the table(s) that we wish to query. For each table displayed, Microsoft Access shows the list of fields in that particular table. We can then drag the fields we wish to see in the result table to the **Field** row in the bottom part of the QBE grid. In this particular example, we wish to display all rows of the Video table, so we drag the '*' field from the top part of the grid to the Field row. By default, Microsoft Access will tick the corresponding cell of the **Show** row to indicate that these fields are to be displayed in the result table.

Figure 3.2

(a) QBE corresponding to Query 3.1 – List the full details of all videos; (b) equivalent SQL statement.

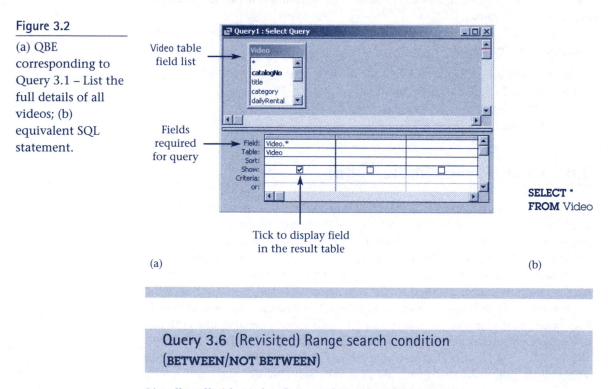

Video table field list

Fields required for query

Tick to display field in the result table

(a)

SELECT *
FROM Video

(b)

Query 3.6 (Revisited) Range search condition (BETWEEN/NOT BETWEEN)

List all staff with a salary between $45,000 and $50,000.

The QBE grid for this query is shown in Figure 3.3(a). In this example, we show the Staff table in the top part of the QBE grid and then drag the relevant fields to the Field row in the bottom part of the grid. In this particular case, we also have to specify the criteria to restrict the rows that will appear in the result table. The criteria are 'salary >=45000 AND salary <= 50000', so under the salary column we enter the criteria '>=45000 AND <= 50000' in the **Criteria** cell.

Note, if the criteria involved an OR condition, each part of the criteria would be entered on different rows, as illustrated in Figure 3.3(c) for the criteria (category = 'Action' **OR** category = 'Children').

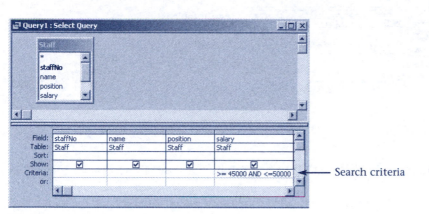

(a)

Figure 3.3

(a) QBE corresponding to Query 3.6 – List all staff with a salary between $45,000 and $50,000;
(b) equivalent SQL statement;
(c) example of how a criterion involving an OR condition would be entered.

SELECT staffNo, name, position, salary
FROM Staff
WHERE salary >= 45000 **AND** salary <= 50000;

(b)

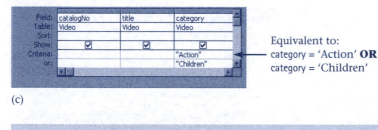

(c)

Query 3.10 (Revisited) Sorting results

List all videos sorted in descending order of price.

The QBE grid for this query is shown in Figure 3.4(a). In this particular example, we wish to sort the result table in descending order of price, which we achieve by selecting Descending from the drop down list in the **Sort** cell for the price field. Note in this case that the price field has not been ticked to be shown because the field has already been included in the result table via the use of '*' in the first Field cell.

Figure 3.4

(a) QBE corresponding to Query 3.10 – List all videos sorted in descending order of price; (b) equivalent SQL statement.

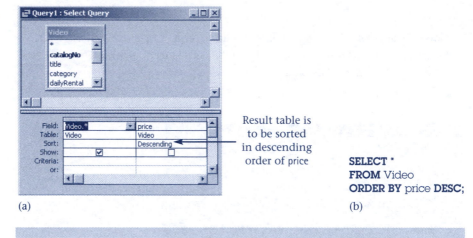

Result table is to be sorted in descending order of price

SELECT *
FROM Video
ORDER BY price **DESC;**

(a)

(b)

Query 3.11 (Revisited) Use of **COUNT** and **SUM**

List the total number of staff with a salary greater than $40,000 and the sum of their salaries.

The QBE grid for this query is shown in Figure 3.5(a). In this example, we wish to calculate the total number of staff and the sum of their salaries for a subset of staff (those with a salary greater than $40,000). To do this, we use the aggregate

Figure 3.5

QBE corresponding to Query 3.11 – List the total number of staff with a salary greater than $40,000 and the sum of their salaries; (b) equivalent SQL statement.

Field headings changed to totalStaff and totalSalary

Aggregate functions can be specified when query type is changed to Totals

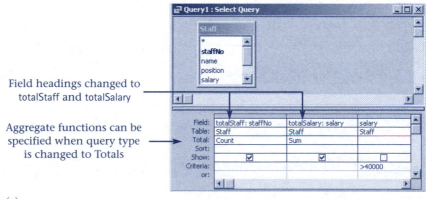

(a)

SELECT COUNT(staffNo) **AS** totalStaff, **SUM**(salary) **AS** totalSalary
FROM Staff
WHERE salary > 40000;

(b)

functions **COUNT** and **SUM**, which are accessed by changing the query type to **Totals**. This results in the display of an additional row called **Total** in the QBE grid with all fields that have been selected automatically set to GROUP BY. However, using the drop down list we can change the Total row for the staffNo field to **COUNT** and for the salary field to **SUM**. To make the output more meaningful, we change the name of the field headings in the resulting output to totalStaff and totalSalary, respectively. The condition '> 40000' is entered into the Criteria cell for the salary field.

Query 3.14 (Revisited) Use of **HAVING**

For each branch office with more than one member of staff, find the number of staff working in each branch and the sum of their salaries.

The QBE grid for this query is shown in Figure 3.6(a). As with the previous query, we change the query type to **Totals** and use the **COUNT** and **SUM** functions to calculate the required totals. However, in this particular example, we need to group the information based on the branch number (we're looking for totals for each branch), so the Total cell for the branchNo field has to be set to

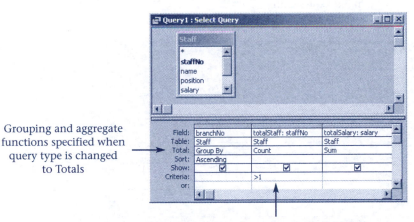

Grouping and aggregate functions specified when query type is changed to Totals →

Restriction of groups specified using the Criteria on the aggregate function, **Count**(staffNo)

Figure 3.6
(a) QBE corresponding to Query 3.14 – For each branch office with more than one member of staff, find the number of staff working in each branch and the sum of their salaries;
(b) equivalent SQL statement.

(a)

SELECT branchNo, **COUNT**(staffNo) **AS** totalStaff, **SUM**(salary) **AS** totalSalary
FROM Staff
GROUP BY branchNo
HAVING COUNT(staffNo) > 1
ORDER BY branchNo;

(b)

GROUP BY. Again, to make the output more meaningful, we change the name of the field headings to totalStaff and totalSalary, respectively. As we only wish to output this information for those branches with more than one member of staff, we enter the criteria '>1' for the COUNT(staffNo) field.

Query 3.17 (Revisited) Simple join

List all videos along with the name of their director.

The QBE grid for this query is shown in Figure 3.7(a). In the top part of the QBE grid, we display the tables that we wish to query, in this case the Video and Director tables. As before, we drag the columns we wish to be included in the output to the bottom part of the grid.

Note that in the SQL query we have to specify how to join the Director and Video tables. However, QBE does this automatically for us, making QBE significantly easier to use than SQL in this respect.

Figure 3.7

(a) QBE corresponding to Query 3.17 – List all videos along with the name of their director;
(b) equivalent SQL statement.

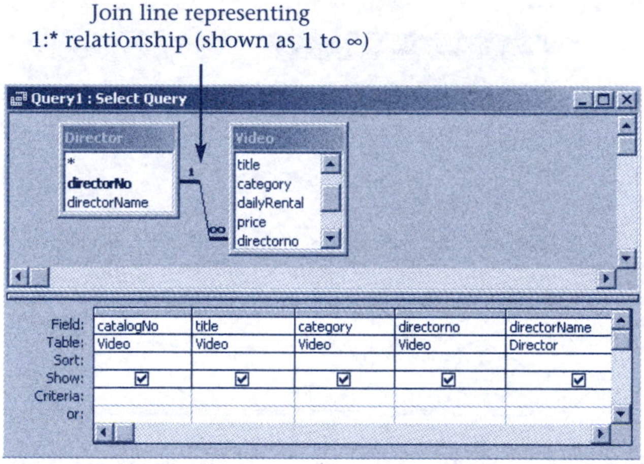

Join line representing
1:* relationship (shown as 1 to ∞)

(a)

SELECT catalogNo, title, category, v.directorNo, directorName
FROM Video v, Director d
WHERE v.directorNo = d.directorNo;

(b)

Query 3.18 (Revisited) Four-table join

List all videos along with the name of their director, the names of their actors, and associated roles.

The QBE grid for this query is shown in Figure 3.8(a). In the top part of the QBE grid, we display the four tables that we wish to query. As before, we drag the columns we wish to be included in the output to the bottom part of the grid. If the appropriate relationships have been established, QBE will automatically join the four tables on the join columns indicated in the top part of the grid.

Three joins – each representing a
1:* relationship (shown as 1 to ∞)

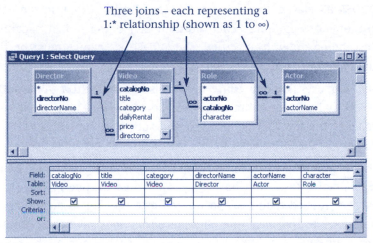

(a)

```
SELECT v.catalogNo, title, category, directorName, actorName, character
FROM Video v, Director d, Actor a, Role r
WHERE d.directorNo = v.directorNo AND
      v.catalogNo = r.catalogNo AND
      r.actorNo = a.actorNo;
```

(b)

Figure 3.8

(a) QBE corresponding to Query 3.18 – List all videos along with the name of their director, the names of their actors, and associated roles; (b) equivalent SQL statement.

Chapter summary

✓ SQL is a non-procedural language, consisting of standard English words such as **SELECT, INSERT, DELETE**, that can be used by professionals and non-professionals alike. It is both the formal and *de facto* standard language for defining and manipulating relational databases.

✓ The **SELECT** statement is the most important statement in the language and is used to express a query. Every SELECT statement produces a query result table consisting of one or more columns and zero or more rows.

✓ The **SELECT** clause identifies the columns and/or calculated data to appear in the result table. All column names that appear in the SELECT clause must have their corresponding tables or views listed in the FROM clause.

✓ The **WHERE** clause selects rows to be included in the result table by applying a search condition to the rows of the named table(s). The **ORDER BY** clause allows the result table to be sorted on the values in one or more columns. Each column can be sorted in ascending or descending order. If specified, the ORDER BY clause must be the last clause in the SELECT statement.

✓ SQL supports five aggregate functions (**COUNT**, **SUM**, **AVG**, **MIN**, and **MAX**) that take an entire column as an argument and compute a single value as the result. It is illegal to mix aggregate functions with column names in a SELECT clause, unless the GROUP BY clause is used.

✓ The **GROUP BY** clause allows summary information to be included in the result table. Rows that have the same value for one or more columns can be grouped together and treated as a unit for using the aggregate functions. In this case, the aggregate functions take each group as an argument and compute a single value for each group as the result. The **HAVING** clause acts as a WHERE clause for groups, restricting the groups that appear in the final result table. However, unlike the WHERE clause, the HAVING clause can include aggregate functions.

✓ A **subselect** is a complete SELECT statement embedded in another query. A subselect may appear within the WHERE or HAVING clauses of an outer SELECT statement, where it is called a **subquery** or **nested query**. Conceptually, a subquery produces a temporary table whose contents can be accessed by the outer query. A subquery can be embedded in another subquery.

✓ If the columns of the result table come from more than one table, a **join** must be used by specifying more than one table in the FROM clause and typically including a WHERE clause to specify the join column(s).

✓ As well as SELECT, the SQL DML includes the **INSERT** statement to insert a single row of data into a named table or to insert an arbitrary number of rows from another table using a **subselect**; the **UPDATE** statement to update one or more values in a specified column or columns of a named table; the **DELETE** statement to delete one or more rows from a named table.

 The ISO standard provides eight base data types: boolean, character, bit, exact numeric, approximate numeric, datetime, interval, and character/binary large objects.

 The SQL DDL statements allow database objects to be defined. The two DDL statements covered in this chapter were **CREATE TABLE** and **CREATE VIEW**.

 QBE is an alternative, graphical-based, 'point-and-click' way of querying the database. QBE has acquired the reputation of being one of the easiest ways for non-technical users to obtain information from a database.

Review questions

3.1 What are the two major components of SQL and what function do they serve?

3.2 Explain the function of each of the clauses in the SELECT statement. What restrictions are imposed on these clauses?

3.3 What restrictions apply to the use of the aggregate functions within the SELECT statement? How do nulls affect the aggregate functions?

3.4 Explain how the GROUP BY clause works. What is the difference between the WHERE and HAVING clauses?

3.5 What is the difference between a subquery and a join? Under what circumstances would you not be able to use a subquery?

3.6 What is QBE and what is the relationship between QBE and SQL?

Exercises

The following tables form part of a database held in a relational DBMS:

    Hotel   (hotelNo, hotelName, city)
    Room   (roomNo, hotelNo, type, price)
    Booking   (hotelNo, guestNo, dateFrom, dateTo, roomNo)
    Guest   (guestNo, guestName, guestAddress)

where   Hotel contains hotel details and hotelNo is the primary key;
        Room contains room details for each hotel and (roomNo, hotelNo) forms the primary key;
        Booking contains details of bookings and (guestNo, hotelNo, dateFrom) forms the primary key;
        Guest contains guest details and guestNo is the primary key.

Create tables

3.7 Create each of the above tables using SQL (create primary keys and foreign keys, where appropriate).

Populating tables

3.8 Insert rows into each of these tables.

3.9 Update the price of all rooms by 5 percent.

Simple queries

3.10 List full details of all hotels.

3.11 List full details of all hotels in Washington.

3.12 List the names and addresses of all guests living in Washington, alphabetically ordered by name.

3.13 List all double or family rooms with a price below $40.00 per night, in ascending order of price.

3.14 List the bookings for which no dateTo has been specified.

Aggregate functions

3.15 How many hotels are there?

3.16 What is the average price of a room?

3.17 What is the total revenue per night from all double rooms?

3.18 How many different guests have made bookings for August?

Subqueries and joins

3.19 List the price and type of all rooms at the Hilton Hotel.

3.20 List all guests currently staying at the Hilton Hotel.

3.21 List the details of all rooms at the Hilton Hotel, including the name of the guest staying in the room if the room is occupied.

3.22 What is the total income from bookings for the Hilton Hotel today?

3.23 List the rooms that are currently unoccupied at the Hilton Hotel.

3.24 What is the lost income from unoccupied rooms at the Hilton Hotel?

Grouping

3.25 List the number of rooms in each hotel.

3.26 List the number of rooms in each hotel in Washington.

3.27 What is the average number of bookings for each hotel in August?

3.28 What is the most commonly booked room type for each hotel in Washington?

3.29 What is the lost income from unoccupied rooms at each hotel today?

Chapter 4

The database system development lifecycle

In this chapter you will learn:

- ► How problems associated with software development led to the software crisis.

- ► How the software crisis led to a structured approach to software development called the information systems lifecycle.

- ► About the relationship between the information systems lifecycle and the database system development lifecycle.

- ► The stages of the database system development lifecycle.

- ► The activities associated with each stage of the database system development lifecycle.

This chapter begins by first explaining why there is a need for a structured approach to developing software applications. We introduce an example of such an approach called the information systems lifecycle and discuss the relationship between an information system and the database that supports it. We then focus on the database and introduce an example of a structured approach to developing database systems called the database system development lifecycle. Finally, we take you through the stages that make up the database system development lifecycle (DSDLC).

4.1 The software crisis

You are probably already aware that over the past few decades there has been a dramatic rise in the number of software applications being developed, ranging from small, relatively simple applications consisting of a few lines of code, to large, complex applications consisting of millions of lines of code. Once developed, many of these applications proved to be demanding, requiring constant mainte-nance. This maintenance involved correcting faults, implementing new user requirements, and modifying the software to run on new or upgraded platforms. With so much software around to support, the effort spent on maintenance began to absorb resources at an alarming rate. As a result, many major software projects were late, over budget, and the software produced was unreliable, difficult to main-tain, and performed poorly. This led to what has become known as the 'software crisis'. Although this term was first used in the late 1960s, more than 30 years later the crisis is still with us. As a result, some people now refer to the software crisis as the 'software depression'. As an indication of the software crisis, a study carried out in the UK by OASIG, a Special Interest Group concerned with the Organizational Aspects of IT, reached the following conclusions (OASIG, 1996):

■ 80–90 percent of systems do not meet their performance goals.

■ About 80 percent are delivered late and over budget.

■ Around 40 percent of developments fail or are abandoned.

■ Under 40 percent fully address training and skills requirements.

■ Less than 25 percent properly integrate business and technology objectives.

■ Just 10–20 percent meet all their success criteria.

There are several major reasons for the failure of software projects, including:

■ lack of a complete requirements specification;

■ lack of an appropriate development methodology;

■ poor decomposition of design into manageable components.

As a solution to these problems, a structured approach to the development of software was proposed and is commonly known as the *information systems (IS) lifecycle* or the *software development lifecycle (SDLC)*.

4.2 The information systems lifecycle

Information system

The resources that enable the collection, management, control, and dissemination of data/information throughout an organization.

An **information system** not only collects, manages, and controls data used and generated by an organization but enables the transformation of the data into information. An information system also provides the infrastructure to facili-tate the dissemination of information to those who make the decisions critical to the success of an organization. The essential component at the *heart* of an information system is the database that supports it.

Typically, the stages of the information systems lifecycle include: planning, requirements collection and analysis, design (including database design), prototyping, implementation, testing, conversion, and operational maintenance. Of course, in this book we're interested in the development of the database component of an information system. As a database is a fundamental component of the larger organization-wide information system, the database system development lifecycle is inherently linked with the information systems lifecycle.

4.3   The database system development lifecycle

Relational model discussed in Chapter 2

In this chapter, we describe the database system development lifecycle for relational DBMSs. An overview of the stages of the database system development lifecycle (DSDLC) is shown in Figure 4.1. Below the name of each stage is the section in this chapter that describes that stage. It's important to note that the stages of the database system development lifecycle are not strictly sequential, but involve some amount of repetition of previous stages through *feedback loops*. For example, problems encountered during database design may necessitate additional requirements collection and analysis. As there are feedback loops between most stages, we show only some of the more obvious ones in Figure 4.1.

For small database systems with a small number of users, the lifecycle need not be very complex. However, when designing a medium to large database system with tens to thousands of users, using hundreds of queries and application programs, the lifecycle can become extremely complex.

4.4   Database planning

Database planning

The management activities that allow the stages of the database system development lifecycle to be realized as efficiently and effectively as possible.

A starting point for establishing a database project is the creation of a mission statement and mission objectives for the database system. The *mission statement* defines the major aims of the database system, while each *mission objective* identifies a particular task that the database must support. Of course, as with any project, part of the database planning process should also involve some estimation of the work to be done, the resources with which to do it, and the money to pay for it all.

As we've already noted, a database often forms part of a larger organization-wide information system and therefore any database project should be integrated with the organization's overall IS strategy.

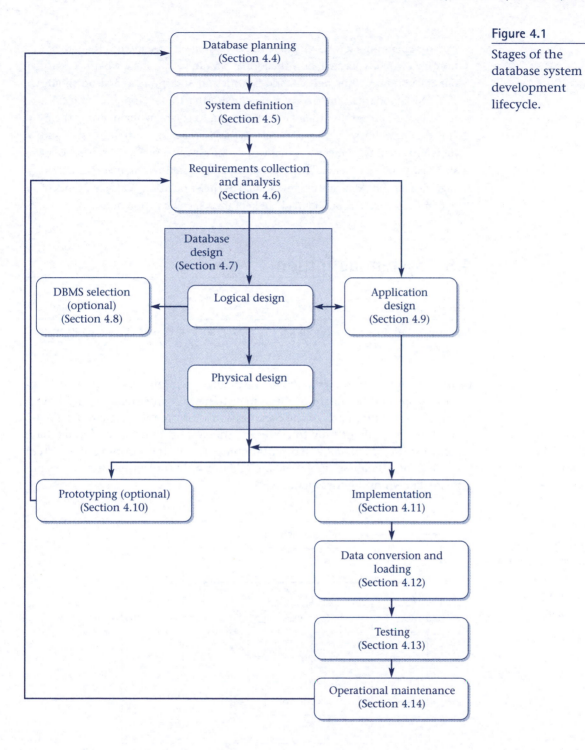

Figure 4.1

Stages of the database system development lifecycle.

Database planning may also include the development of standards that govern how data will be collected, how the format should be specified, what necessary documentation will be needed, and how design and implementation should proceed. Standards can be very time-consuming to develop and maintain, requiring resources to set them up initially and to continue maintaining them. However, a well-designed set of standards provides a basis for training staff and measuring quality, and ensures that work conforms to a pattern, irrespective of staff skills and experience. Any legal or organizational requirements concerning the data should be documented, such as the stipulation that some types of data must be treated confidentially or kept for a specific period of time.

4.5   System definition

System definition

Identification of the scope and boundary of the database system, including its major user views.

Before attempting to design a database system, it's essential that we first identify the scope and boundary of the system that we're investigating and how it interfaces with other parts of the organization's information system. Figure 4.2 shows one example of how to represent the system boundary of a database system for the *StayHome* video rental company. When defining the system boundary for a database system we include not only the current user views but also any known future user views.

StayHome video rental case study described in Section 6.4

Figure 4.2

Boundary of the database system for the *StayHome* video rental company.

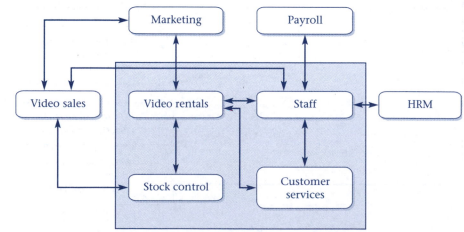

Database systems boundary

Note that this type of diagram can be drawn at any level of detail. A second example of this type of diagram (at a lower level) is shown in Figure 6.9.

4.5.1 User views

User view

Defines what is required of a database system from the perspective of a particular job (such as Manager or Supervisor) or business application area (such as marketing, personnel, or stock control).

A database system may have one or more user views. Identifying user views is an important aspect of developing a database system because it helps to ensure that no major users of the database are forgotten when developing the requirements for the new application. User views are also particularly helpful in the development of a relatively complex database system by allowing the requirements to be broken down into manageable pieces.

A user view defines what is required of a database system in terms of the data to be held and the transactions to be performed on the data (in other words, what the users will do with the data). The requirements of a user view may be distinct to that view or overlap with other views. Figure 4.3 is a diagrammatic representation of a database system with multiple user views (denoted user view 1 to 6). Note that while user views (1, 2, and 3) and (5 and 6) have overlapping requirements (shown as darker areas), user view 4 has distinct requirements.

4.6 Requirements collection and analysis

Requirements collection and analysis

The process of collecting and analyzing information about the organization to be supported by the database system, and using this information to identify the requirements for the new database system.

In this stage, we collect and analyze information about the organization, or the part of the organization, to be served by the database. There are many techniques for gathering this information, called fact-finding techniques, which we'll discuss in detail in Chapter 6.

We gather information for each major user view (that is, job role or business application area), including:

■ a description of the data used or generated,

■ the details of how data is to be used or generated,

■ any additional requirements for the new database system.

Figure 4.3

A diagram
representing a
database system
with multiple user
views: user view 4 is
distinct; the others
have some element
of overlap.

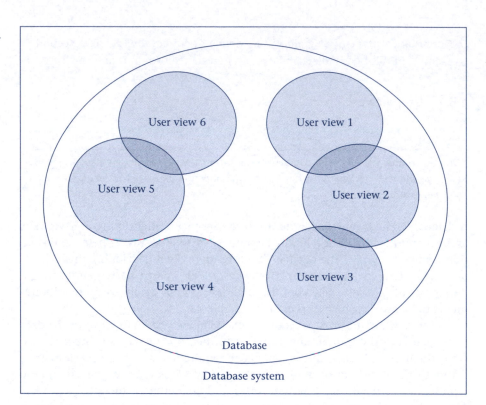

We then analyze this information to identify the requirements (or features) to be included in the new database system. These requirements are described in documents collectively referred to as *requirements specifications* for the new database system.

Another important activity associated with this stage is deciding how to deal with the situation where there is more than one user view. There are three approaches to dealing with multiple user views:

- the centralized approach,
- the view integration approach, and
- a combination of both approaches.

Centralized approach

Centralized approach
Requirements for each user view are merged into a single list of requirements for the new database system. A data model representing all user views is created during the database design stage.

The **centralized approach** involves collating the requirements for different user views into a single list of requirements. A data model representing all user views is created in the database design stage. A diagram representing the management of user views 1 to 3 using the centralized approach is shown in Figure 4.4. Generally, this approach is preferred when there is a significant overlap in requirements for each user view and the database system is not overly complex.

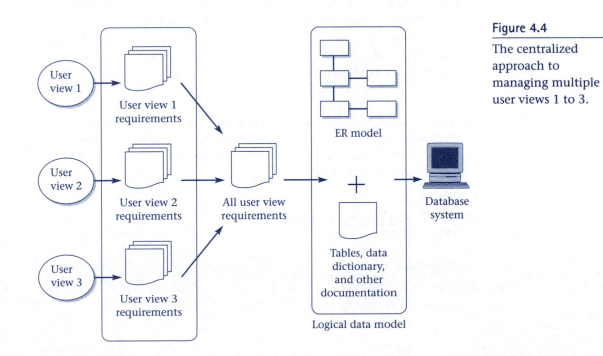

Figure 4.4

The centralized approach to managing multiple user views 1 to 3.

View integration approach

View integration approach

Requirements for each user view remain as separate lists. Data models representing each user view are created and then merged later during the database design stage.

The **view integration approach** involves leaving the requirements for each user view as separate lists of requirements. We create data models representing each user view. A data model that represents a single user view is called a **local logical data model**. We then merge the local data models to create a **global logical data model** representing all user views of the organization.

A diagram representing the management of user views 1 to 3 using the view integration approach is shown in Figure 4.5. Generally, this approach is preferred when there are significant differences between user views and the database system is sufficiently complex to justify dividing the work into more manageable parts.

TIP

For some complex database systems it may be appropriate to use a combination of both the centralized and view integration approaches to managing multiple user views. For example, the requirements for two or more user views may be first merged using the centralized approach and then used to create a **local logical data model**. (Therefore in this situation the local data model represents not just a single user view but the number of user views merged using the centralized approach.) The local data models representing one or more user views are then merged using the view integration approach to form the **global logical data model** representing all user views.

We'll discuss how to manage multiple user views in more detail in Section 6.4.4 and throughout this book we'll demonstrate how to build a database for the *StayHome* video rental case study using a combination of both the centralized and view integration approaches.

4.7   Database design

Database design

The process of creating a design that will support the organization's mission statement and mission objectives for the required database system.

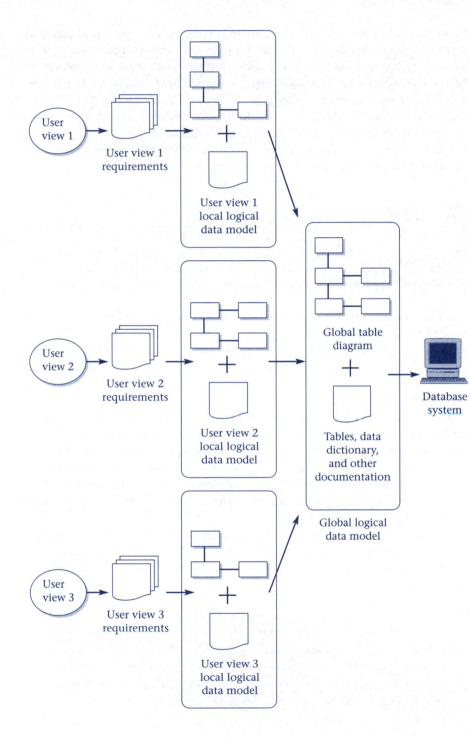

Figure 4.5

The view integration approach to managing multiple user views 1 to 3.

Global table diagram is described in Appendix C

Database design is made up of two main phases called logical and physical design. During logical database design, we try to identify the important objects that need to be represented in the database and the relationships between these objects. During physical database design, we decide how the logical design is to be physically implemented in the target DBMS. In Chapter 9, we'll discuss the two phases of database design in more detail and present an overview of a step-by-step methodology for logical and physical database design. The steps of the logical database design methodology will be described in detail in Chapters 9 and 10 and for physical database design in Chapters 12 to 16.

4.8 DBMS selection

DBMS selection

The selection of an appropriate DBMS to support the database system.

If no relational DBMS currently exists in the organization, an appropriate part of the lifecycle in which to make a selection is between the logical and physical database design phases. However, selection can be done at any time prior to logical design provided sufficient information is available regarding system requirements such as networking, performance, ease of restructuring, security, and integrity constraints.

Although DBMS selection may be infrequent, as business needs expand or existing systems are replaced, it may become necessary at times to evaluate new DBMS products. In such cases, the aim is to select a product that meets the current and future requirements of the organization, balanced against costs which include the purchase of the DBMS, any additional software/hardware required to support the database system, and the costs associated with changeover and staff training.

A simple approach to selection is to check off DBMS features against requirements. In selecting a new DBMS product, there is an opportunity to ensure that the selection process is well planned, and the system delivers real benefits to the organization.

Integrity constraints discussed in Section 1.3

TIP

Nowadays, the World Wide Web (WWW) is a great source of information and can be used to identify potential candidate DBMSs. Vendors' websites can provide valuable information on DBMS products. As a starting point, have a look at DBMS magazine's website called DBMS ONLINE (available at www.intelligententerprise.com) for a comprehensive index of DBMS products.

4.9   Application design

Application design

The design of the user interface and the application programs that use and process the database.

In Figure 4.1 shown earlier in this chapter, we observed that database and application design are parallel activities of the database system development lifecycle. In most cases, we cannot complete the application design until the design of the database itself has taken place. On the other hand, the database exists to support the applications, and so there must be a flow of information between application design and database design.

We must ensure that all the functionality stated in the requirements specifications is present in the application design for the database system. This involves designing the interaction between the user and the data, which we call *transaction design*. In addition to designing how the required functionality is to be achieved, we have to design an appropriate *user interface* to the database system.

4.9.1   Transaction design

Transaction

An action, or series of actions, carried out by a single user or application program that accesses or changes the content of the database.

Transactions represent 'real world' events such as the registering of a new member at a video rental company, the creation of a rental agreement for a member to rent a video, and the addition of a new member of staff. These transactions have to be applied to the database to ensure that the database remains current with the 'real world' and to support the information needs of the users.

The purpose of transaction design is to define and document the high-level characteristics of the transactions required on the database, including:

■ data to be used by the transaction;
■ functional characteristics of the transaction (what the transaction will do);
■ output of the transaction;
■ importance to the users;
■ expected rate of usage.

There are three main types of transactions:

- retrieval transactions;
- update transactions;
- mixed transactions.

Retrieval transactions are used to retrieve data for display on the screen (or as a report) or as input into another transaction. For example, the operation to search for and display the details of a video (given the video number) is a retrieval transaction. *Update transactions* are used to insert new records, delete old records, or modify existing records in the database. For example, the operation to insert the details of a new video into the database is an update transaction. *Mixed transactions* involve both the retrieval and updating of data. For example, the operation to search for and display the details of a video (given the video number) and then update the value of the daily rental rate is a mixed transaction.

4.9.2 User interface design

In addition to designing how the required functionality is to be achieved, we have to design an appropriate user interface for the database system. This interface should present the required information in a *user-friendly* way. The importance of user interface design is sometimes ignored or left until late in the design stages. However, it should be recognized that the interface might be one of the most important components of the system. If it's easy to learn, simple to use, straightforward, and forgiving, the users will be inclined to make good use of what information is presented. On the other hand, if the interface has none of these characteristics, the system will undoubtedly cause problems. For example, before implementing a form or report, it's essential that we first design the layout. Useful guidelines to follow when designing forms or reports are listed in Table 4.1 (Shneiderman, 1992).

4.10 Prototyping

At various points throughout the design process, we have the option either to fully implement the database system or to build a prototype.

Prototyping
Building a working model of a database system.

A prototype is a working model that does not normally have all the required features or provide all the functionality of the final system. The purpose of developing a prototype database system is to allow users to use the prototype to

Table 4.1 Guidelines for form/report design.

Meaningful title

Comprehensible instructions

Logical grouping and sequencing of fields

Visually appealing layout of the form/report

Familiar field labels

Consistent terminology and abbreviations

Consistent use of color

Visible space and boundaries for data-entry fields

Convenient cursor movement

Error correction for individual characters and entire fields

Error messages for unacceptable values

Optional fields marked clearly

Explanatory messages for fields

Completion signal

---

identify the features of the system that work well, or are inadequate, and if possible to suggest improvements or even new features for the database system. In this way, we can greatly clarify the requirements and evaluate the feasibility of a particular system design. Prototypes should have the major advantage of being relatively inexpensive and quick to build.

There are two prototyping strategies in common use today: requirements prototyping and evolutionary prototyping. *Requirements prototyping* uses a prototype to determine the requirements of a proposed database system and once the requirements are complete the prototype is discarded. While *evolutionary prototyping* is used for the same purposes, the important difference is that the prototype is not discarded but with further development becomes the working database system.

4.11 Implementation

Implementation

The physical realization of the database and application designs.

On completion of the design stages (which may or may not have involved prototyping), we're now in a position to implement the database and the application

DDL defined in
Section 2.4

programs. The database implementation is achieved using the *Data Definition Language (DDL)* of the selected DBMS or a graphical user interface (GUI), which provides the same functionality while hiding the low-level DDL statements. The DDL statements are used to create the database structures and empty database files. Any specified user views are also implemented at this stage.

DML defined in
Section 2.4

The application programs are implemented using the preferred **third or fourth generation language (3GL or 4GL)**. Parts of these application programs are the database transactions, which we implement using the *Data Manipulation Language (DML)* of the target DBMS, possibly embedded within a host programming language, such as Visual Basic (VB), VB.net, Python, Delphi, C, C++, C#, Java, COBOL, Fortran, Ada, or Pascal. We also implement the other components of the application design such as menu screens, data entry forms, and reports. Again, the target DBMS may have its own fourth generation tools that allow rapid development of applications through the provision of non-procedural query languages, reports generators, forms generators, and application generators.

SQL covered in
Chapter 3

Security and integrity controls for the application are also implemented. Some of these controls are implemented using the DDL, but others may need to be defined outside the DDL using, for example, the supplied DBMS utilities or operating system controls.

SQL (Structured Query Language) is both a DDL and a DML.

4.12 Data conversion and loading

Data conversion and loading

Transferring any existing data into the new database and converting any existing applications to run on the new database.

This stage is required only when a new database system is replacing an old system. Nowadays, it's common for a DBMS to have a utility that loads existing files into the new database. The utility usually requires the specification of the source file and the target database, and then automatically converts the data to the required format of the new database files. Where applicable, it may be possible for the developer to convert and use application programs from the old system for use by the new system. Whenever conversion and loading are required, the process should be properly planned to ensure a smooth transition to full operation.

4.13 Testing

> **Testing**
>
> The process of running the database system with the intent of finding programming errors.

Before going live, the newly developed database system should be thoroughly tested. This is achieved using carefully planned test strategies and realistic data so that the entire testing process is methodically and rigorously carried out. Note that in our definition of testing we have not used the commonly held view that testing is the process of demonstrating that faults are not present. In fact, testing cannot show the absence of faults; it can show only that software faults are present. If testing is conducted successfully, it will uncover errors in the application programs and possibly the database structure. As a secondary benefit, testing demonstrates that the database and the application programs *appear* to be working according to their specification and that performance requirements *appear* to be satisfied. In addition, metrics collected from the testing stage provide a measure of software reliability and software quality.

As with database design, the users of the new system should be involved in the testing process. The ideal situation for system testing is to have a test database on a separate hardware system, but often this is not available. If real data is to be used, it is essential to have backups taken in case of error.

Testing should also cover usability of the database system. Ideally, an evaluation should be conducted against a usability specification. Examples of criteria that can be used to conduct the evaluation include (Sommerville, 2000):

- Learnability – How long does it take a new user to become productive with the system?
- Performance – How well does the system response match the user's work practice?
- Robustness – How tolerant is the system of user error?
- Recoverability – How good is the system at recovering from user errors?
- Adaptability – How closely is the system tied to a single model of work?

Some of these criteria may be evaluated in other stages of the lifecycle. After testing is complete, the database system is ready to be 'signed off' and handed over to the users.

4.14 Operational maintenance

> **Operational maintenance**
>
> The process of monitoring and maintaining the database system following installation.

In this stage, the database system now moves into a maintenance stage, which involves the following activities:

■ Monitoring the performance of the database system. If the performance falls below an acceptable level, the database may need to be tuned or reorganized.

■ Maintaining and upgrading the database system (when required). New requirements are incorporated into the database system through the preceding stages of the lifecycle.

We'll examine this stage in more detail in Chapter 16.

Chapter summary

✓ An **information system** is the resources that enable the collection, management, control, and dissemination of data/information throughout an organization.

✓ The **database** is a fundamental component of an **information system**. The lifecycle of an information system is inherently linked to the lifecycle of the database that supports it.

✓ The stages of the **database system development lifecycle** include: database planning, system definition, requirements collection and analysis, database design, DBMS selection (optional), application design, prototyping (optional), implementation, data conversion and loading, testing, and operational maintenance.

✓ **Database planning** is the management activities that allow the stages of the database system development lifecycle to be realized as efficiently and effectively as possible.

✓ **System definition** involves identifying the scope and boundaries of the database system, including its major user views. A user view can represent a job role or business application area.

✓ **Requirements collection and analysis** is the process of collecting and analyzing information about the organization that is to be supported by the database system, and using this information to identify the requirements for the new system.

✓ There are three approaches to dealing with multiple user views, namely the centralized approach, the view integration approach, and a combination of both. The **centralized approach** involves collating the users' requirements for different user views into a single list of requirements. A data model representing all the user views is created during the database design stage. The **view integration approach** involves leaving the users' requirements for each user view as separate lists of requirements. Data models representing each user view are created and then merged at a later stage of database design.

✓ **Database design** is the process of creating a design that will support the organization's mission statement and mission objectives for the required database system. This stage includes the logical and physical design of the database.

✓ The aim of **DBMS selection** is to select a system that meets the current and future requirements of the organization, balanced against costs that include the purchase of the DBMS product and any additional software/hardware, and the costs associated with changeover and training.

✓ **Application design** involves designing the user interface and the application programs that use and process the database. This stage involves two main activities: transaction design and user interface design.

✓ **Prototyping** involves building a working model of the database system, which allows the designers or users to visualize and evaluate the system.

✓ **Implementation** is the physical realization of the database and application designs.

✓ **Data conversion and loading** involves transferring any existing data into the new database and converting any existing applications to run on the new database.

✓ **Testing** is the process of running the database system with the intent of finding programming errors.

✓ **Operational maintenance** is the process of monitoring and maintaining the system following installation.

Review questions

4.1 Describe what is meant by the term 'software crisis'.

4.2 Discuss the relationship between the information systems lifecycle and the database system development lifecycle.

4.3 Briefly describe the stages of the database system development lifecycle.

4.4 Describe the purpose of creating a mission statement and mission objectives for the required database during the database planning stage.

4.5 Discuss what a user view represents when designing a database system.

4.6 Compare and contrast the centralized approach and view integration approach to managing the design of a database system with multiple user views.

4.7 Explain why it is necessary to select the target DBMS before beginning the physical database design phase.

4.8 Discuss the two main activities associated with application design.

4.9 Describe the potential benefits of developing a prototype database system.

4.10 Discuss the main activities associated with the implementation stage.

4.11 Describe the purpose of the data conversion and loading stage.

4.12 Explain the purpose of testing the database system.

4.13 What are the main activities associated with the operational maintenance stage?

Chapter 5

Database administration and security

In this chapter you will learn:

- The distinction between *data* administration and *database* administration. ◀
- The purpose and tasks associated with data administration and database administration. ◀
- The scope of database security. ◀
- Why database security is a serious concern for an organization. ◀
- The type of threats that can affect a database system. ◀
- How to protect a database system using computer-based controls. ◀

In Chapter 4, we learned about the stages of the database system development lifecycle. In this chapter we discuss the roles played by the Data Administrator (DA) and Database Administrator (DBA) and the relationship between these roles and the stages of the database system development lifecycle. An important function of a DA and DBA is ensuring the security of the database. We discuss the potential threats to a database system and the types of computer-based countermeasures that can be applied to minimize such threats.

5.1 Data administration and database administration

The **Data Administrator (DA)** and **Database Administrator (DBA)** are responsible for managing and controlling the activities associated with the corporate data and the corporate database, respectively. The DA is more concerned with the early stages of the lifecycle, from planning through to logical database design. In contrast, the DBA is more concerned with the later stages, from application/physical database design to operational maintenance. Depending on the size and complexity of the organization and/or database system, the DA and DBA can be the responsibility of one or more people. We begin by discussing the purpose and tasks associated with the DA and DBA roles within an organization.

5.1.1 Data administration

Data administration

The management and control of the corporate data, including database planning, development and maintenance of standards, policies and procedures, and logical database design.

The DA is responsible for the corporate data, which includes non-computerized data, and in practice is often concerned with managing the shared data of users or business application areas of an organization. The DA has the primary responsibility of consulting with and advising senior managers, and ensuring that the application of database technologies continues to support corporate objectives. In some organizations, data administration is a distinct business area, in others it may be combined with database administration. The tasks associated with data administration are described in Table 5.1.

Table 5.1 Data administration tasks.

Selecting appropriate productivity tools

Assisting in the development of the corporate IT/IS and business strategies

Undertaking feasibility studies and planning for database development

Developing a corporate data model

Determining the organization's data requirements

Setting data collection standards and establishing data formats

Estimating volumes of data and likely growth

Determining patterns and frequencies of data usage

Table 5.1 *Continued*

Determining data access requirements and safeguards for both legal and corporate requirements

Undertaking logical database design

Liaising with database administration staff and application developers to ensure applications meet all stated requirements

Educating users on data standards and legal responsibilities

Keeping up to date with IT/IS and business developments

Ensuring documentation is complete, including the corporate data model, standards, policies, procedures, and controls on end-users

Managing the data dictionary

Liaising with end-users and database administration staff to determine new requirements and to resolve data access or performance problems

Developing a security policy

5.1.2   Database administration

Database administration

The management and control of the physical realization of the corporate database system, including physical database design and implementation, setting security and integrity controls, monitoring system performance, and reorganizing the database as necessary.

The DBA is more technically oriented than the DA, requiring knowledge of specific DBMSs and the operating system environment. The primary responsibilities of the DBA are centered on developing and maintaining systems using the DBMS software to its fullest extent. The tasks of database administration are described in Table 5.2.

5.1.3   Comparison of data and database administration

The preceding sections examined the purpose and tasks associated with data administration and database administration. A summary of the main task differences between data administration and database administration is shown in Table 5.3. Perhaps the most obvious difference lies in the nature of the work carried out. The work of DA staff tends to be much more managerial, whereas the work of DBA staff tends to be more technical.

Table 5.2 Database administration tasks.

Evaluating and selecting DBMS products

Undertaking physical database design

Implementing a physical database design using a target DBMS

Defining security and integrity constraints

Liaising with database system developers

Developing test strategies

Training users

Responsible for 'signing off' the implemented database system

Monitoring system performance and tuning the database, as appropriate

Performing backups routinely

Ensuring recovery mechanisms and procedures are in place

Ensuring documentation is complete, including in-house produced material

Keeping up to date with software and hardware developments and costs, and installing updates as necessary

Table 5.3 Data/Database administration – main task differences.

Data administration	Database administration
Involved in strategic IS planning	Evaluates new DBMSs
Determines long-term goals	Executes plans to achieve goals
Determines standards, policies, and procedures	Enforces standards, policies, and procedures
Determines data requirements	Implements data requirements
Develops logical database design	Develops physical database design
Develops and maintains corporate data model	Implements physical database design
Coordinates database development	Monitors and controls database use
Managerial orientation	Technical orientation
DBMS independent	DBMS dependent

5.2 Database security

In this section, we describe the scope of database security and discuss why organizations must take potential threats to their database systems seriously. We also identify the range of threats and their consequences on database systems.

Database security

The mechanisms that protect the database against intentional or accidental threats.

Security considerations do not only apply to the data held in a database. Breaches of security may affect other parts of the system, which may in turn affect the database. Consequently, database security encompasses hardware, software, people, and data. To implement security effectively requires appropriate controls, which are defined in specific mission objectives for the system. This need for security, while often having been neglected or overlooked in the past, is now increasingly recognized by organizations. The reason for this turnaround is due to the increasing amounts of crucial corporate data being stored on computer and the acceptance that any loss or unavailability of this data could be potentially disastrous.

A database represents an essential corporate resource that should be properly secured using appropriate controls. We consider database security in relation to the following outcomes:

■ theft and fraud;

■ loss of confidentiality (secrecy);

■ loss of privacy;

■ loss of integrity;

■ loss of availability.

These outcomes represent the areas where an organization should seek to reduce risk; that is, the possibility of incurring loss or damage. In some situations, these outcomes are closely related such that an activity that leads to loss in one situation may also lead to loss in another. In addition, outcomes such as fraud or loss of privacy may arise because of either intentional or unintentional acts, and do not necessarily result in any detectable changes to the database or the computer system.

Theft and fraud affect not only the database environment but also the entire organization. As it's people who perpetrate such activities, attention should focus on reducing the opportunities for this occurring. Theft and fraud do not necessarily alter data, which is also true for activities that result in either loss of confidentiality or loss of privacy.

Confidentiality refers to the need to maintain secrecy over data, usually only that which is critical to the organization, whereas privacy refers to the need to protect data about individuals. Breaches of security resulting in loss of confidentiality could, for instance, lead to loss of competitiveness, and loss of privacy could lead to legal action being taken against the organization.

Loss of data integrity results in invalid or corrupted data, which may seriously affect the operation of an organization. Many organizations are now seeking virtually continuous operation, the so-called 24×7 availability (that is, 24 hours a day, seven days a week). Loss of availability means that the data, or the system, or both, cannot be accessed, which can seriously impact on an organization's financial performance. In some cases, events that cause a system to be unavailable may also cause data corruption.

In recent times, computer-based criminal activities have significantly increased and are forecast to continue to rise over the next few years. Database security aims to minimize losses caused by anticipated events in a cost-effective manner without unduly constraining the users.

5.2.1 Threats

Threat

Any situation or event, whether intentional or unintentional, that may adversely affect a system and consequently the organization.

A threat may be caused by a situation or event involving a person, action, or circumstance that is likely to be detrimental to an organization. The loss to the organization may be tangible, such as loss of hardware, software, or data, or intangible, such as loss of credibility or client confidence. The problem facing any organization is to identify all possible threats. Therefore as a minimum, an organization should invest time and effort in identifying the most serious threats.

In the previous section, we identified outcomes that may result from intentional or unintentional activities. While some types of threat can be either intentional or unintentional, the impact remains the same. Intentional threats involve people, and may be carried out by both authorized users and unauthorized users, some of whom may be external to the organization.

Any threat must be viewed as a potential breach of security which, if successful, will have a certain impact. Table 5.4 presents examples of various types of threats and the possible outcomes for an organization. For example, 'Using another person's means of access' as a threat may result in theft and fraud, loss of confidentiality, and loss of privacy for an organization.

The extent that an organization suffers as a result of a threat succeeding depends upon a number of factors, such as the existence of countermeasures and contingency plans. For example, if a hardware failure occurs corrupting secondary storage, all processing activity must cease until the problem is resolved. The recovery will depend upon a number of factors, which include when the last backups were taken and the time needed to restore the system.

An organization needs to identify the types of threats it may be subjected to and initiate appropriate plans and countermeasures, bearing in mind the costs of implementing them. Obviously, it may not be cost-effective to spend considerable time, effort, and money on potential threats that may result only in

Table 5.4 Examples of threats and the possible outcomes.

Threat	Theft and fraud	Loss of confidentiality	Loss of privacy	Loss of integrity	Loss of availability
Using another person's means of access	√	√	√		
Unauthorized amendment or copying of data	√			√	
Program alteration	√			√	√
Inadequate policies and procedures that allow a mix of confidential and normal output	√	√	√		
Wire tapping	√	√	√		
Illegal entry by hacker	√	√	√		
Blackmail	√	√	√		
Creating 'trapdoor' into system	√	√	√		
Theft of data, programs, and equipment	√	√	√		√
Failure of security mechanisms, giving greater access than normal	√	√	√		
Staff shortage or strikes				√	√
Inadequate staff training		√	√	√	√
Viewing and disclosing unauthorized data	√	√	√		
Electronic interference and radiation				√	√
Data corruption due to power loss or surge				√	√
Fire (electrical fault, lightning strike, arson), flood, bomb				√	√
Physical damage to equipment				√	√
Breaking cables or disconnection of cables				√	√
Introduction of viruses				√	√

minor inconveniences. The organization's business may also influence the types of threat that should be considered, some of which may be rare. However, rare events should be taken into account, particularly if their impact would be significant. A summary of the potential threats to computer systems is represented in Figure 5.1.

5.2.2 Countermeasures – computer-based controls

The types of countermeasures to threats on database systems range from physical controls to administrative procedures. Despite the range of computer-based

Figure 5.1

Summary of potential threats to computer systems.

Hardware
Fire/flood/bombs
Data corruption due to power
loss or surge
Failure of security mechanisms
giving greater access
Theft of equipment
Physical damage to equipment
Electronic interference and radiation

DBMS and Application Software
Failure of security mechanism
giving greater access
Program alteration
Theft of programs

Communication networks
Wire tapping
Breaking or disconnection of cables
Electronic interference and radiation

Database
Unauthorized amendment or
copying of data
Theft of data
Data corruption due to power
loss or surge

Users
Using another person's means of
access
Viewing and disclosing
unauthorized data
Inadequate staff training
Illegal entry by hacker
Blackmail
Introduction of viruses

Programers/Operators
Creating trapdoors
Program alteration (such as creating
software that is insecure)
Inadequate staff training
Inadequate security policies and
procedures
Staff shortages or strikes

Data/Database Administrator
Inadequate security policies
and procedures

controls that are available, it is worth noting that, generally, the security of a DBMS is only as good as that of the operating system, owing to their close association. Representation of a typical multi-user computer environment is shown in Figure 5.2. In this section, we focus on the following computer-based security controls for a multi-user environment (some of which may not be available in the PC environment):

■ authorization;

■ views;

■ backup and recovery;

- integrity;
- encryption;
- Redundant Array of Independent Disks (RAID).

RAID discussed
in Chapter 16

Authorization

> **Authorization**
> _____
> The granting of a right or privilege that enables a subject to have legitimate access to a
> database system or a database system's object.

Authorization controls can be built into the software, and govern not only
what database system or object a specified user can access, but also what the
user may do with it. For this reason, authorization controls are sometimes
referred to as *access controls*. The process of authorization involves authentication of a subject requesting access to an object, where 'subject' represents a user
or program and 'object' represents a database table, view, procedure, trigger, or
any other object that can be created within the database system.

Access controls
discussed in Step 6
of Chapter 14

Figure 5.2

Representation of a
typical multi-user
computer
environment.

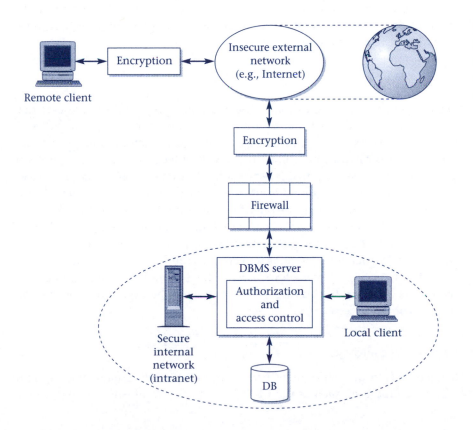

Authentication

A mechanism that determines whether a user is who he or she claims to be.

A system administrator is usually responsible for permitting users to have access to a computer system by creating individual user accounts. Each user is given a unique identifier, which is used by the operating system to determine who they are. Associated with each identifier is a password, chosen by the user and known to the operating system, which must be supplied to enable the operating system to authenticate (or verify) who the user claims to be.

This procedure allows authorized use of a computer system, but does not necessarily authorize access to the DBMS or any associated application programs. A separate, similar procedure may have to be undertaken to give a user the right to use the DBMS. The responsibility to authorize use of the DBMS usually rests with the DBA, who must also set up individual user accounts and passwords using the DBMS.

Some DBMSs maintain a list of valid user identifiers and associated passwords, which can be distinct from the operating system's list. However, other DBMSs maintain a list whose entries are validated against the operating system's list based on the current user's login identifier. This prevents a user from logging onto the DBMS with one name, having already logged onto the operating system using a different name.

Privileges

Privileges discussed in Step 6 of Chapter 14

Once a user is given permission to use a DBMS, various other privileges may also be automatically associated with it. For example, privileges may include the right to access or create certain database objects such as tables, views, and indexes, or to run various DBMS utilities. Privileges are granted to users to accomplish the tasks required for their jobs. As excessive granting of unnecessary privileges can compromise security, a privilege should only be granted to a user who absolutely requires the privilege to accomplish his or her work.

Some DBMSs operate as *closed systems* so that while users may be authorized to access the DBMS, they require authorization to access specific objects. Either the DBA or owners of particular objects provide this authorization. On the other hand, an *open system* allows users to have complete access to all objects within the database. In this case, privileges have to be explicitly removed from users to control access.

Ownership and privileges

Some objects in the DBMS are owned by the DBMS itself, usually in the form of a specific superuser, such as the DBA. Accordingly, ownership of objects gives the owner all appropriate privileges on the objects owned. The same situation applies to other authorized users if they own objects. The creator of an object owns the object and can assign appropriate privileges for the object. For example, although a user owns a view, he or she may only be authorized to query the view. This may happen when the user is only authorized to query the underlying base table. These privileges can be passed on to other authorized users. For example, an owner of several tables may authorize other users to query the tables, but not to carry out any updates.

Where a DBMS supports several different types of authorization identifier, there may be different priorities associated with each type. For example, a DBMS may permit both individual user identifiers and group identifiers to be created, with the user identifier having a higher priority than the group identifier. For such a DBMS, user and group identifiers may be defined as shown in Tables 5.5(a) and (b).

Table 5.5(a) User identifiers.

User Identifier	Type
S0099	User
S2345	User
S1500	User
Sales	Group

Table 5.5(b) Group identifiers.

Group	Member Identifier
Sales	S0099
Sales	S2345

In Table 5.5(a) the columns with headings *User Identifier* and *Type* list each user on the system together with the user type, which distinguishes individuals from groups. In Table 5.5(b) the columns with headings *Group* and *Member Identifier* list each group and the user members of that group. Certain privileges may be associated with specific identifiers, which indicate what kind of privilege (such as Select, Update, Insert, Delete, or All) is allowed with certain database objects.

On some DBMSs, a user has to tell the system under which identifier he or she is operating, especially if the user is a member of more than one group. It is essential to become familiar with the available authorization and other control mechanisms provided by the DBMS, particularly where priorities may be applied to different authorization identifiers and where privileges can be passed on. This will enable the correct types of privileges to be granted to users based on their requirements and those of the application programs that many of them will use.

Views

> **View**
> ___
> A *virtual table* that does not necessarily exist in the database but can be produced upon request by a particular user, at the time of request.

Views discussed in Section 1.2.4

The view mechanism provides a powerful and flexible security mechanism by hiding parts of the database from certain users. The user is not aware of the existence of any columns or rows that are missing from the view. A view can be defined over several tables with a user being granted the appropriate privilege to use it, but not to use the base tables. In this way, using a view is more restrictive than simply having certain privileges granted to a user on the base table(s).

Backup and recovery

> **Backup**
> ___
> The process of periodically taking a copy of the database and log file (and possibly programs) onto offline storage media.

A DBMS should provide backup facilities to assist with the recovery of a database following failure. To keep track of database transactions, the DBMS maintains a special file called a **log file** (or journal) that contains information about all updates to the database. It is always advisable to make backup copies of the database and log file at regular intervals and to ensure that the copies are in a secure location. In the event of a failure that renders the database unusable, the backup copy and the details captured in the log file are used to restore the database to the latest possible consistent state.

> **Journaling**
> ___
> The process of keeping and maintaining a log file (or journal) of all changes made to the database to enable recovery to be undertaken effectively in the event of a failure.

A DBMS should provide logging facilities, sometimes referred to as journaling, which keep track of the current state of transactions and database changes, to provide support for recovery procedures. The advantage of journaling is that, in the event of a failure, the database can be recovered to its last known consistent state using a backup copy of the database and the information contained in the log file. If no journaling is enabled on a failed system, the only means of recovery is to restore the database using the latest backup version of the database. However, without a log file, any changes made after the last backup to the database will be lost.

Integrity

Integrity constraints also contribute to maintaining a secure database system by preventing data from becoming invalid, and hence giving misleading or incorrect results. Integrity constraints were introduced in Section 1.3 and will be discussed in detail in Step 2.4 of Chapter 10.

Encryption

Encryption
The encoding of the data by a special algorithm that renders the data unreadable by any program without the decryption key.

If a database system holds particularly sensitive data, it may be deemed necessary to encode it as a precaution against possible external threats or attempts to access it. Some DBMSs provide an encryption facility for this purpose. The DBMS can access the data (after decoding it), although there is degradation in performance because of the time taken to decode it. Encryption also protects data transmitted over communication lines. There are a number of techniques for encoding data to conceal the information; some are termed irreversible and others reversible. *Irreversible techniques*, as the name implies, do not permit the original data to be known. However, the data can be used to obtain valid statistical information. *Reversible techniques* are more commonly used. To transmit data securely over insecure networks requires the use of a **cryptosystem**, which includes:

- an encryption key to encrypt the data (plaintext);
- an encryption algorithm that, with the encryption key, transforms the plaintext into ciphertext;
- a decryption key to decrypt the ciphertext;
- a decryption algorithm that, with the decryption key, transforms the ciphertext back into plaintext.

One technique, called *symmetric encryption*, uses the same key for both encryption and decryption and relies on safe communication lines for exchanging the key. However, most users do not have access to a secure communication line and, to be really secure, the keys need to be as long as the message. However, most working systems are based on using keys shorter than the message. One scheme used for encryption is the Data Encryption Standard (DES), which is a standard encryption algorithm developed by IBM. This scheme uses one key for both encryption and decryption, which must be kept secret, although the algorithm need not be. The algorithm transforms each 64-bit block of plaintext using a 56-bit key. The DES is not universally regarded as being very secure, and some authors maintain that a larger key is required. For example, a scheme called PGP (Pretty Good Privacy) uses a 128-bit symmetric algorithm for encryption of the data it sends.

Keys with 64 bits are now probably breakable with special hardware, albeit at substantial costs. However, this technology will be within the reach of organized criminals, major organizations, and smaller governments in a few years. While it is envisaged that keys with 80 bits will also become breakable in the future, it is probable that keys with 128 bits will remain unbreakable for the foreseeable future. The terms 'strong authentication' and 'weak authentication' are sometimes used to distinguish algorithms that, to all intents and purposes, cannot be broken with existing technologies and knowledge, from those that can be.

Another type of cryptosystem uses different keys for encryption and decryption, and is referred to as *asymmetric encryption*. One example is *public key cryptosystems*, which use two keys, one of which is public and the other private. The encryption algorithm may also be public, so that anyone wishing to send a user a message can use the user's publicly known key in conjunction with the algorithm to encrypt it. Only the owner of the private key can then decipher the message. Public key cryptosystems can also be used to send a 'digital signature' with a message and prove that the message came from the person who claimed to have sent it. The most well-known asymmetric encryption is RSA (the name is derived from the initials of the three designers of the algorithm).

Generally, symmetric algorithms are much faster to execute on a computer than those that are asymmetric. However, in practice, they are often used together, so that a public key algorithm is used to encrypt a randomly generated encryption key, and the random key is used to encrypt the actual message using a symmetric algorithm.

Redundant Array of Independent Disks (RAID)

The hardware that the DBMS is running on must be *fault-tolerant*, meaning that the DBMS should continue to operate even if one of the hardware components fails. This suggests having redundant components that can be seamlessly integrated into the working system whenever there is one or more component failures. The main hardware components that should be fault-tolerant include disk drives, disk controllers, CPU, power supplies, and cooling fans. Disk drives are the most vulnerable components, with the shortest times between failures of any of the hardware components.

One solution is the use of Redundant Array of Independent Disks (RAID) technology. RAID works by having a large disk array comprising an arrangement of several independent disks that are organized to improve reliability and at the same time increase performance.

RAID discussed in Chapter 16

Chapter summary

 Data administration is the management and control of the corporate data, including database planning, development and maintenance of standards, policies, and procedures, and logical database design.

 Database administration is the management and control of the physical realization of the corporate database system, including physical database design and implementation, setting security and integrity controls, monitoring system performance, and reorganizing the corporate database as necessary.

Database security is concerned with the mechanisms that protect the database against intentional or accidental threats.

A **threat** is any situation or event, whether intentional or unintentional, that may adversely affect a system and consequently an organization.

Computer-based security controls for the multi-user environment include: authorization, views, backup and recovery, integrity, encryption, and RAID.

Authorization is the granting of a right or privilege that enables a subject to have legitimate access to a system or a system's object.

Authentication is a mechanism that determines whether a user is who he or she claims to be.

A **view** is a *virtual table* that does not necessarily exist in the database but can be produced upon request by a particular user, at the time of request.

 Backup is the process of periodically taking a copy of the database and log file (and possibly programs) onto offline storage media.

 Journaling is the process of keeping and maintaining a log file (or journal) of all changes made to the database to enable recovery to be undertaken effectively in the event of a failure.

Integrity constraints also contribute to maintaining a secure database system by preventing data from becoming invalid, and hence giving misleading or incorrect results.

Encryption is the encoding of the data by a special algorithm that renders the data unreadable by any program without the decryption key.

✔ **Redundant Array of Independent Disks (RAID)** works by having a large disk array comprising an arrangement of several independent disks that are organized to improve reliability and at the same time increase performance.

Review questions

5.1 Define the purpose and tasks associated with data administration and database administration.

5.2 Compare and contrast the main tasks carried out by the DA and DBA.

5.3 Explain the purpose and scope of database security.

5.4 List the main types of threat that could affect a database system, and for each, describe the possible outcomes for an organization.

5.5 Explain the following in terms of providing security for a database:

(a) authorization;
(b) views;
(c) backup and recovery;
(d) integrity;
(e) encryption;
(f) RAID.

Part 2

Database analysis and design techniques

Chapter 6

Fact-finding

In this chapter you will learn:

When fact-finding techniques are used in the database system development lifecycle. ◀

The types of facts collected throughout the database system development lifecycle. ◀

The types of documentation produced throughout the database system development lifecycle. ◀

The most commonly used fact-finding techniques. ◀

How to use each fact-finding technique and the advantages and disadvantages of each. ◀

About a video rental company called *StayHome*. ◀

How to use fact-finding techniques in the early stages of the database system development lifecycle. ◀

In Chapter 4, we learned about the stages of the database system development lifecycle. There are many occasions during these stages when it's critical that the database developer captures the necessary facts to build the required database system. The necessary facts cover the business and the users of the database system, including the terminology, problems, opportunities, constraints, requirements, and priorities. These facts are captured using **fact-finding** techniques.

Fact-finding

The formal process of using techniques such as interviews and questionnaires to collect facts about systems, requirements, and preferences.

In this chapter, we discuss when a database developer might use fact-finding techniques and what types of facts should be captured. We present an overview of how these facts are used to generate the main types of documentation used throughout the database system development lifecycle. We briefly describe the most commonly used fact-finding techniques and identify the advantages and disadvantages of each. We finally demonstrate how some of these techniques may be used during the earlier stages of the database system development lifecycle using a video rental company called *StayHome*. In Chapters 9 and 10, and 12 to 16, we'll use the *StayHome* case study to demonstrate the methodology for database design.

Throughout this chapter we use the term 'database developer' to refer to a person or group of people responsible for the analysis, design, and implementation of a database system.

6.1   When are fact–finding techniques used?

There are many occasions for fact-finding during the database system development lifecycle. However, fact-finding is particularly crucial to the early stages of the lifecycle, including the database planning, system definition, and requirements collection and analysis stages. It's during these early stages that the database developer learns about the terminology, problems, opportunities, constraints, requirements, and priorities of the business and the users of the system. Fact-finding is also used during database design and the later stages of the lifecycle, but to a lesser extent. For example, during physical database design, fact-finding becomes technical as the developer attempts to learn more about the DBMS selected for the database system. Also, during the final stage, operational maintenance, fact-finding is used to determine whether a system requires tuning to improve performance or further development to include new requirements.

> **TIP**
>
> It's important to have a rough estimate of how much time and effort is to be spent on fact-finding for a database project. Too much study too soon leads to *paralysis by analysis*. However, too little thought can result in an unnecessary waste of both time and money due to working on the wrong solution to the wrong problem.

6.2   What facts are collected?

Throughout the database system development lifecycle, the database developer needs to capture facts about the current or future system. Table 6.1 provides examples of the sorts of data captured and the documentation produced for each stage of the lifecycle. As we mentioned in Chapter 4, the stages of the database system development lifecycle are not strictly sequential, but involve some amount of repetition of previous stages through feedback loops. This is also true for the data captured and the documentation produced at each stage. For example, problems encountered during database design may necessitate additional data capture on the requirements for the new system.

6.1 Examples of the data captured and the documentation produced for each stage of database system development lifecycle.

Stage of database system development lifecycle	Examples of data captured	Examples of documentation produced
Database planning	Aims and objectives of database project	Mission statement and objectives of database system
System definition	Description of major user views (includes job roles and/or business application areas)	Definition of scope and boundary of database system; definition of user views to be supported
Requirements collection and analysis	Requirements for user views; systems specifications, including performance and security requirements	Users' requirements specifications and system specifications
Database design	Users' responses to checking the logical database design; functionality provided by target DBMS	Logical database design (includes ER diagram(s), data dictionary, and tables); physical database design
Application design	Users' responses to checking interface design	Application design (includes description of programs and user interface)
DBMS selection	Functionality provided by target DBMS	DBMS evaluation and recommendations
Prototyping	Users' responses to prototype	Modified users' requirements specifications and systems specification
Implementation	Functionality provided by target DBMS	
Data conversion and loading	Format of current data; data import capabilities of target DBMS	
Testing	Test results	Testing strategies used; analysis of test results
Operational maintenance	Performance testing results; new or changing user and system requirements	User manual; analysis of performance results; modified users' requirements and systems specification

In Section 6.4, we'll return to examine the first three stages of the database system development lifecycle, namely database planning, system definition, and requirements collection and analysis. For each stage, we demonstrate the process of collecting data using fact-finding techniques and the production of documentation for the *StayHome* video rental company. However, before this section, we first present a review of the most commonly used fact-finding techniques.

6.3   Fact-finding techniques

A database developer normally uses several fact-finding techniques during a single database project. There are five common fact-finding techniques:

- Examining documentation
- Interviewing
- Observing the business in operation
- Research
- Questionnaires.

6.3.1   Examining documentation

Examining documentation can be useful when you're trying to gain some insight as to how the need for a database arose. You also may find that documentation can be helpful to provide information on the business (or part of the business) associated with the problem. If the problem relates to the current system there should be documentation associated with that system. Examining documents, forms, reports, and files associated with the current system is a good way to gain some understanding of the system quickly. Examples of the types of documentation that you should examine are listed in Table 6.2.

6.3.2   Interviewing

Interviewing is the most commonly used, and normally most useful, fact-finding technique. You can interview to collect information from individuals face-to-face. There can be several objectives to using interviewing such as finding out facts, checking facts, generating user interest and feelings of involvement, identifying requirements, and gathering ideas and opinions. However, using the interviewing technique requires good communication skills for dealing effectively with people who have different values, priorities, opinions, motivations, and personalities. As with other fact-finding techniques, interviewing isn't always the best method for all situations. The advantages and disadvantages of using interviewing as a fact-finding technique are listed in Table 6.3.

Table 6.2 Examples of types of documentation that should be examined.

Purpose of documentation	Examples of useful sources
Describes problem and need for database	Internal memos, e-mails, and minutes of meetings Employee/customer complaints, and documents that describe the problem Performance reviews/reports
Describes business (or part of business) affected by problem	Organizational chart, mission statement, and strategic plan of the business Objectives for the business being studied Task/job descriptions Samples of manual forms and reports Samples of computerized forms and reports Completed forms/reports
Describes current system	Various types of flowcharts and diagrams Data dictionary Database system design Program documentation User/training manuals

Table 6.3 Advantages and disadvantages of using interviewing as a fact-finding technique.

Advantages	Disadvantages
Allows interviewer to follow up on interesting comments made by interviewee	Very time-consuming and costly, and therefore may be impractical
Allows interviewer to adapt or re-word questions during interview	Success is dependent on communication skills of interviewer
Allows interviewer to observe interviewee's body language	
Allows interviewee to respond freely and openly to questions	
Allows interviewee to feel part of project	

There are two types of interviews, unstructured and structured. *Unstructured interviews* are conducted with only a general objective in mind and with few, if any, specific questions. The interviewer counts on the interviewee to provide a framework and direction to the interview. This type of interview frequently loses focus and, for this reason, you may find that it doesn't usually work well for database projects.

In *structured interviews*, the interviewer has a specific set of questions to ask the interviewee. Depending on the interviewee's responses, the interviewer will direct additional questions to obtain clarification or expansion. *Open-ended questions* allow the interviewee to respond in any way that seems appropriate. An example of an open-ended question is: 'Why are you dissatisfied with the report on member registration?' *Closed-ended questions* restrict answers to either specific choices or short, direct responses. An example of such a question might be: 'Are you receiving the report on member registration on time?' or 'Does the report on member registration contain accurate information?' Both questions require only a 'Yes' or 'No' response.

> **TIP**
>
> To ensure a successful interview you should select appropriate individuals to interview, prepare extensively for the interview, and conduct the interview in an efficient and effective manner.

6.3.3   Observing the business in operation

Observation is one of the most effective fact-finding techniques you can use to understand a system. With this technique, you can either participate in, or watch a person perform, activities to learn about the system. This technique is particularly useful when the validity of data collected through other methods is in question or when the complexity of certain aspects of the system prevents a clear explanation by the end-users.

As with the other fact-finding techniques, successful observation requires much preparation. To ensure that the observation is successful, you need to know as much about the individuals and the activity to be observed as possible. For example, when are the low, normal, and peak periods for the activity being observed and will the individuals be upset by having someone watch and record their actions? The advantages and disadvantages of using observation as a fact-finding technique are listed in Table 6.4.

6.3.4   Research

A useful fact-finding technique is to research the application and problem. Computer trade journals, reference books, and the Internet are good sources of information. They can provide you with information on how others have solved similar problems, plus you can learn whether or not software packages exist to solve your problem. The advantages and disadvantages of using research as a fact-finding technique are listed in Table 6.5.

Table 6.4 Advantages and disadvantages of using observation as a fact-finding technique.

Advantages	Disadvantages
Allows the validity of facts and data to be checked	People may knowingly or unknowingly perform differently when being observed
Observer can see exactly what is being done	May miss observing tasks involving different levels of difficulty or volume normally experienced during that time period
Observer can also obtain data describing the physical environment of the task	Some tasks may not always be performed in the manner in which they are observed
Relatively inexpensive	May be impractical
Observer can do work measurements	

Table 6.5 Advantages and disadvantages of using research as a fact-finding technique.

Advantages	Disadvantages
Can save time if solution already exists	Can be time-consuming
Researcher can see how others have solved similar problems or met similar requirements	Requires access to appropriate sources of information
Keeps researcher up to date with current developments	May ultimately not help in solving problem because problem is not documented elsewhere

6.3.5 Questionnaires

Another fact-finding technique is to conduct surveys through questionnaires. Questionnaires are special-purpose documents that allow you to gather facts from a large number of people while maintaining some control over their responses. When dealing with a large audience, no other fact-finding technique can tabulate the same facts as efficiently. The advantages and disadvantages of using questionnaires as a fact-finding technique are listed in Table 6.6.

Table 6.6 Advantages and disadvantages of using questionnaires as a fact-finding technique.

Advantages	Disadvantages
People can complete and return questionnaires at their convenience	Number of respondents can be low, possibly only 5–10 percent (particularly if the postal service or e-mail is used to deliver the questionnaires)
Relatively inexpensive way to gather data from a large number of people	Questionnaires may be returned incomplete
People more likely to provide the real facts as responses can be kept confidential	No opportunity to adapt or re-word questions that may have been misinterpreted
Responses can be tabulated and analyzed quickly	Can't observe and analyze the respondent's body language
Can be delivered using various modes, including person-to-person, postal service, and e-mail	Can be time-consuming to prepare questionnaire

There are two formats for questionnaires, free-format and fixed-format. *Free-format questionnaires* offer the respondent greater freedom in providing answers. A question is asked and the respondent records the answer in the space provided after the question. Examples of free-format questions are: 'What reports do you currently receive and how are they used?' and 'Are there any problems with these reports? If so, please explain.' The problems with free-format questions are that the respondent's answers may prove difficult to tabulate and, in some cases, may not match the questions asked.

Fixed-format questionnaires contain questions that require specific responses from individuals. Given any question, the respondent must choose from the available answers. This makes the results much easier to tabulate. On the other hand, the respondent cannot provide additional information that might prove valuable. An example of a fixed-format question is: 'The current format of the report on video rentals is ideal and should not be changed.' The respondent may be given the option to answer 'Yes' or 'No' to this question, or be given the option to answer from a range of responses, including 'Strongly Agree', 'Agree', 'No opinion', 'Disagree', and 'Strongly Disagree'.

6.4 The *StayHome* case study

In this section, we first describe the *StayHome* case study. We then use the *StayHome* case study to illustrate how you would establish a database project in the early stages of the database system development lifecycle by going through database planning, system definition, and requirements collection and analysis stages.

6.4.1 The *StayHome* case study – an overview

This case study describes a company called *StayHome*, which rents out videos to its members. The first branch of *StayHome* was established in 1982 in Seattle but the company has now grown and has many branches throughout the United States. The company's success is due to the first-class service it provides to its members and the wide and varied stock of videos available for rent.

StayHome currently has about 2000 staff working in 100 branches. When a member of staff joins the company, the *StayHome* staff registration form is used. The staff registration form for Mary Martinez is shown in Figure 6.1.

Each branch has a Manager and several Supervisors. The Manager is responsible for the day-to-day running of a given branch and each Supervisor is responsible for supervising a group of staff. An example of the first page of a report listing the members of staff working at the branch in Seattle is shown in Figure 6.2.

Figure 6.1

The *StayHome* staff registration form for Mary Martinez.

StayHome
Staff Registration Form

Staff Number S0010	**Branch Number** B002
Full Name	**Branch Address**
Mary Martinez	City Center Plaza,
Position	Seattle, WA 98122
Manager	
Salary	**Telephone Number(s)**
50000	205-555-6756/206-555-8836

Figure 6.2

Example of the first page of a report listing the members of staff working at a *StayHome* branch in Seattle.

Each branch of *StayHome* has a stock of videos for hire. Each video is uniquely identified using a catalog number. However, in most cases, there are several copies of each video at a branch, and the individual copies are identified using the video number. An example of the first page of a report listing the videos available at the branch in Seattle is shown in Figure 6.3.

Before renting a video, a customer must first join as a member of *StayHome*. When a customer joins, he or she is requested to complete the *StayHome* member registration form. The member registration form for Don Nelson is shown in Figure 6.4. *StayHome* currently has about 100 000 members. A customer may choose to register at more than one branch; however, a new member registration form must be filled out on each occasion. An example of the first page of a Manager's report listing the members registered at the branch in Seattle is shown in Figure 6.5.

Once registered, a member is free to rent videos, up to a maximum of 10 at any one time. When a member chooses to rent one or more videos, the *StayHome* video rental form is completed. An example of a completed form for Claire Sinclair renting *Harry Potter* and *Shrek* is shown in Figure 6.6.

StayHome
Videos for Rent Listing

Branch Number   B002

Telephone Number(s)

206-555-6756/206-555-8836

Branch Address

City Center Plaza, Seattle,

WA 98122

Catalog Number	Video Number	Video Title	Category	Daily Rental
207132	199004	Die Another Day	Action	5.00
207132	245456	Die Another Day	Action	5.00
634817	178643	Independence Day	Sci-Fi	4.50
634817	243431	Independence Day	Sci-Fi	4.50
989001	456778	Spider-man	Sci-Fi	5.00
989001	456880	Spider-man	Sci-Fi	5.00
989001	456887	Spider-man	Sci-Fi	5.00

Page 1

Figure 6.3

Example of the first page of a report listing the videos available at the *StayHome* branch in Seattle.

StayHome
Member Registration Form

Member Number   M284354
(Enter if known)

Full Name

Don Nelson

Member Address

123 Suffolk Lane,

Seattle, WA 98117

Date Registered   09-Oct-01

Branch Number   B002

Branch Address

City Center Plaza,

Seattle, WA 98122

Registered By

Robert Chin

Figure 6.4

The *StayHome* member registration form for Don Nelson.

Figure 6.5

Example of the first page of a report listing the members registered at the *StayHome* branch in Seattle.

		StayHome Members Listing	

Branch Number   B002   Branch Address

City Center Plaza,

Telephone Number(s)

206-555-6756/206-555-8836   Seattle, WA 98122

Member Number	Name	Address	Date Joined
M129906	Karen Homer	634–12th Avenue, Seattle, WA 98123	10-Jan-97
M189976	John Hood	4/4 Rosie Lane, Seattle	21-May-98
M220045	Jamie Peters	5A–22nd Street, Seattle, WA 98451	20-May-99
M228877	Claire Sinclair	44B–16th Street, Seattle, WA 98123	28-Aug-99
M265432	Janet McDonald	1 Lincoln Way, Seattle, WA 98234	19-Aug-00
M284354	Don Nelson	123 Suffolk Lane, Seattle, WA 98117	09-Oct-01
M284666	William Carring	1 Sparrowhill Way, Seattle, WA 98111	10-Oct-02

Page 1

As *StayHome* has grown, so have the difficulties in managing the increasing amount of data used and generated by the company. To ensure the continued success of the company, the Director of *StayHome* has urgently requested that a database system be built to help solve the increasing problems of data management.

6.4.2   The *StayHome* case study – database planning

The first step in developing a database system is to define clearly the **mission statement** for the database project. The mission statement defines the major aims of the database system. Those driving the database project within the business (such as the Director and/or owner) normally define the mission

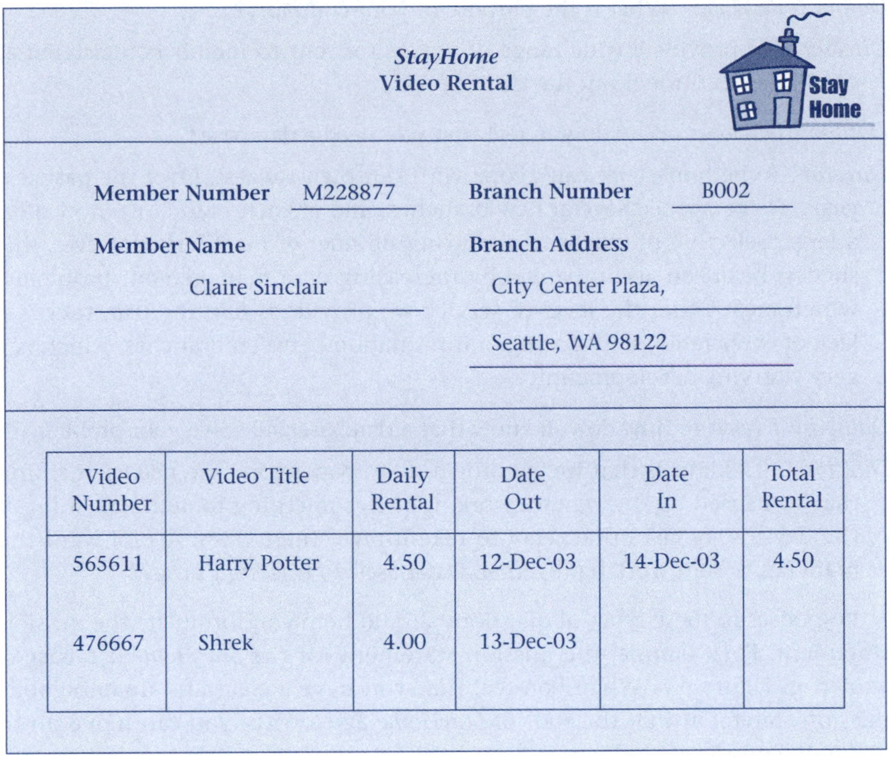

Figure 6.6

Example of a
StayHome video
rental form for
Claire Sinclair.

**StayHome
Video Rental**

Stay
Home

Member Number   M228877   Branch Number   B002

Member Name   Branch Address

        Claire Sinclair   City Center Plaza,

                                         Seattle, WA 98122

Video Number	Video Title	Daily Rental	Date Out	Date In	Total Rental
565611	Harry Potter	4.50	12-Dec-03	14-Dec-03	4.50
476667	Shrek	4.00	13-Dec-03		

statement. A mission statement helps to clarify the purpose of the database project and provides a clearer path towards the efficient and effective creation of the required database system.

Once the mission statement is defined, the next activity involves identifying the **mission objectives**. Each mission objective should identify a particular task that the database must support. The assumption is that if the database supports the mission objectives then the mission statement should be met. The mission statement and objectives may be accompanied by additional information that specifies, in general terms, the work to be done, the resources with which to do it, and the money to pay for it all.

Creating the mission statement for the StayHome database system

You should begin the process of creating a mission statement for the *StayHome* database system by conducting interviews with the Director of the company and any other appropriate staff, as indicated by the Director. Open-ended questions are normally the most useful at this stage of the process. For example, you (the database developer) may start the interview by asking the Director of *StayHome* the following questions:

Database developer 'What is the purpose of your company?'

Director 'We provide a wide range of videos for rent to members registered at our branches throughout the US.'

Database developer 'Why do you feel that you need a database?'

Director 'To be honest we can't cope with our own success. Over the past few years, we've opened several new branches, and at each branch we now offer a larger selection of videos to a growing number of members. However, this success has been accompanied by increasing data management problems, which means that the level of service we provide is falling. Also, there's a lack of cooperation and sharing of information between branches, which is a very worrying development.'

Database developer 'How do you know that a database will solve your problems?'

Director 'All I know is that we are drowning in paperwork. We need something that will speed up the way we work, that is, something to automate a lot of the day-to-day tasks that seem to take forever these days. Also, I want the branches to start working together. Databases do this, don't they?'

Responses to these types of questions should help you formulate the mission statement. For example, the mission statement for the *StayHome* database is shown in Figure 6.7. When you feel that you have a clear and unambiguous mission statement that the staff of *StayHome* agree with, you can move on to define the mission objectives.

Creating the mission objectives for the StayHome database system

The process of creating mission objectives involves conducting interviews with appropriate members of staff. Again, open-ended questions are normally the most useful at this stage of the process. To obtain the complete range of mission objectives, you should interview various members of staff with different roles in *StayHome*. Examples of typical questions you might ask are as follows:

'What is your job description?'
'What kinds of tasks do you perform in a typical day?'
'What kinds of data do you work with?'
'What types of reports do you use?'
'What types of things do you need to keep track of?'
'What service does your company provide to your members?'

These questions (or similar) are put to the Director and members of staff in the role of Manager, Supervisor, Assistant, and Buyer of *StayHome*. Of course, it may be necessary to adapt the questions as required depending on whom you are interviewing.

Figure 6.7

Mission statement
for the *StayHome*
database system.

'The purpose of the *StayHome* database system is to collect, store, manage, and control access to the data that supports the video rentals business for our members, and to facilitate the cooperation and sharing of information between branches.'

Director

Database developer 'What role do you play for the company?'

Director 'I oversee the running of the company to ensure that we continue to provide the best possible video rental service to our members.'

Database developer 'What kinds of tasks do you perform in a typical day?'

Director 'I monitor the running of each branch by our Managers. I try to ensure that the branches work well together and share important information about videos and members. I oversee the work carried out by the Buyer for our company; that's the person responsible for buying videos for all our branches. I normally try to keep a high profile with our branch Managers by calling into each branch once or twice a month.'

Database developer 'What kinds of data do you work with?'

Director 'I need to be able to get my hands on everything used or generated by our company. That includes data about staff, videos, rentals, members, video suppliers, and video orders. I mean everything!'

Database developer 'What types of reports do you use?'

Director 'I need to know what's going on at all the branches. I get my information from various reports on staff, videos in stock, video rentals, members, video suppliers, and orders.'

Database developer 'What types of things do you need to keep track of?'

Director 'As I said before, I need to track everything, I need to see the whole picture, OK?'

Database developer 'What service does your company provide to your members?'

Director 'We try to provide the best and most competitively priced video rental service in the US.'

Manager

Database developer 'What is your job description?'

Manager 'My job title is Manager. I oversee the day-to-day running of my branch to provide the best service to our members.'

Database developer 'What kinds of tasks do you perform in a typical day?'

Manager 'I ensure that the branch has the appropriate type and number of staff on duty at any time of the day. I monitor the hiring of videos to ensure that we have an appropriate selection of videos for our membership, although I don't actually do the buying of videos myself – that's done by the company Buyer. I monitor the registering of new members and the hiring activity of our current members.'

Database developer 'What kinds of data do you work with?'

Manager 'I need data about staff, videos, rentals, and members.'

Database developer 'What types of reports do you use?'

Manager 'Various reports on staff, videos in stock, video rentals, and members.'

Database developer 'What types of things do you need to keep track of?'

Manager 'Staff, videos in stock, video rentals, and members.'

Database developer 'What service does your company provide to your members?'

Manager 'We try to provide the best video rentals service in the area.'

Supervisor

Database developer 'What is your job description?'

Supervisor 'My job title is Supervisor. I supervise a small group of staff and deal directly with our members in providing a video rental service.'

Database developer 'What kinds of tasks do you perform in a typical day?'

Supervisor 'I allocate staff to particular duties, such as dealing with members, restocking shelves, and the filing of paperwork. I answer queries from members about videos for rent. I process the renting out and return of videos. I keep members' details up to date and register customers when they want to join the company as one of our members.'

Database developer 'What kinds of data do you work with?'

Supervisor 'I work with data about staff, videos, rentals, and members.'

Database developer 'What types of reports do you use?'

Supervisor 'Reports on staff and videos in stock.'

Database developer 'What types of things do you need to keep track of?'

Supervisor 'Whether certain videos are available for hire and whether the details on our members are up to date.'

Assistant

Database developer 'What is your job description?'

Assistant My job title is Assistant. I deal directly with our members in providing a video rental service.'

Database developer 'What kinds of tasks do you perform in a typical day?'

Assistant 'I answer queries from members about videos for rent. You know what I mean: "Do you have such and such a video?" I process the renting out and return of videos. I restock the shelves with returned videos and when we are not too busy I try to file paperwork.'

Database developer 'What kinds of data do you work with?'

Assistant 'Data about videos, rentals, and members.'

Database developer 'What types of reports do you use?'

Assistant 'None.'

Database developer 'What types of things do you need to keep track of?'

Assistant 'Whether certain videos are available for hire.'

Database developer 'What service does your company provide to your members?'

Assistant 'We try to answer questions about videos in stock such as: "Do you have videos starring Ewan MacGregor?" and "Who starred in or directed *2001 A Space Odyssey*?" You wouldn't believe what our members expect us to know, but luckily most of us work here because we're really into films, so if I don't know the answer, one of the others will.'

Buyer

Database developer 'What is your job description?'

Buyer 'My job title is Buyer. I'm responsible for buying videos for rent for all branches of the company.'

Database developer 'What kinds of tasks do you perform in a typical day?'

Buyer 'I work directly with branch Managers and video suppliers. I respond to requests from Managers to supply them with certain videos. It's my job to ensure that I get the best possible deal for the company when dealing with video suppliers. Of course, I depend on Managers doing their homework – I don't want to order videos that a branch doesn't need or find that a branch doesn't stock sufficient copies of a popular video. When I have time, I do my own checking by monitoring the renting of videos at each branch to check that they have an appropriate selection of videos.'

Database developer 'What kinds of data do you work with?'

Buyer 'I need access to data on branches, videos, video rentals, members, video orders, and suppliers.'

Database developer 'What types of reports do you use?'

Buyer 'I need reports on orders I have placed for videos. I need various reports that show me videos in stock, video rentals, and members at each branch and across all branches.'

Database developer 'What types of things do you need to keep track of?'

Buyer 'I need to have up-to-date information about my orders for videos; it's important to deal only with suppliers who won't let us down. I also need to know what's going on at each branch in terms of their stock of videos and video rentals. As I said before, I don't want to order videos that a branch doesn't need.'

Database developer 'What service does your company provide to your members?'

Buyer 'We try to provide the best selection of videos at the cheapest possible rental rate.'

Responses to these types of questions should help you formulate the mission objectives. For example, the mission objectives for the *StayHome* database are shown in Figure 6.8.

Figure 6.8

Mission objectives for the *StayHome* database system.

To maintain (enter, update, and delete) data on branches.
To maintain (enter, update, and delete) data on staff.
To maintain (enter, update, and delete) data on videos.
To maintain (enter, update, and delete) data on members.
To maintain (enter, update, and delete) data on video rentals.
To maintain (enter, update, and delete) data on video suppliers.
To maintain (enter, update, and delete) data on orders to suppliers for videos.
To perform searches on branches.
To perform searches on videos.
To perform searches on staff.
To perform searches on video rentals.
To perform searches on members.
To perform searches on video suppliers.
To perform searches on video orders.
To track the status of videos in stock.
To track the status of video rentals.
To track the status of video orders.
To report on branches.
To report on staff.
To report on videos.
To report on members.
To report on video rentals.
To report on video suppliers.
To report on video orders.

6.4.3   The *StayHome* case study – system definition

The purpose of the system definition stage is to define the scope and boundary of the database system and its major user views. A user view represents the requirements that should be supported by a database system as defined by a particular job role (such as Manager or Assistant) or business application area (such as video rentals or stock control).

Defining the systems boundary for the StayHome database system

During this stage of the database system development lifecycle, you should use interviews to clarify or expand on data captured in the previous stage. However, you may also use additional fact-finding techniques, including examining the sample documentation shown in Section 6.4.1. You should now analyze the data collected so far to define the boundary of the database system. The boundary for the *StayHome* database system is shown in Figure 6.9. Contained within the boundary is a representation of the main types of data mentioned in the interviews and a rough guide as to how this data is related.

Identifying the major user views for the StayHome database system

You should now analyze the data collected so far to define the user views of the database system. The majority of data about the user views was collected during interviews with the Director and members of staff in the role of Manager, Supervisor, Assistant, and Buyer. The user views for the *StayHome* database system are shown in Figure 6.10.

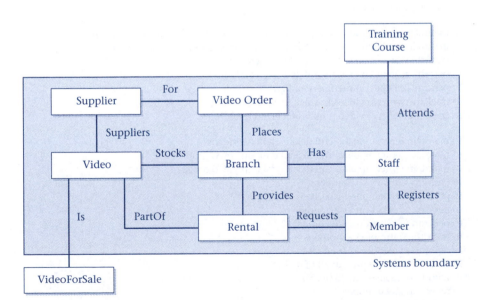

Figure 6.9

Boundary for the *StayHome* database system.

Figure 6.10

User views for the *StayHome* database system.

User view	Requirements
Director	To report on all branches. To report on staff at all branches. To report on videos at all branches. To report on members at all branches. To report on video rentals at all branches. To report on video suppliers. To report on video orders.
Manager	To maintain (enter, update, and delete) data on a given branch. To maintain (enter, update, and delete) data on staff at a given branch. To perform searches on branches. To perform searches on staff at all branches. To report on staff at a given branch. To report on videos at all branches. To report on members at all branches. To report on video rentals at all branches.
Supervisor	To maintain (enter, update, and delete) data on videos at a given branch. To maintain (enter, update, and delete) data on members at a given branch. To maintain (enter, update, and delete) data on video rentals at a given branch. To perform searches on videos at all branches. To perform searches on video rentals at a given branch. To perform searches on members at a given branch. To track the status of videos in stock at a given branch. To track the status of video rentals at a given branch. To report on staff at a given branch.
Assistant	To maintain (enter, update, and delete) data on video rentals at a given branch. To maintain (enter, update, and delete) data on members at a given branch. To perform searches on videos at all branches. To perform searches on video rentals at a given branch. To perform searches on members at a given branch. To track the status of videos in stock at a given branch. To track the status of video rentals at a given branch.
Buyer	To maintain (enter, update, and delete) data on videos. To maintain (enter, update, and delete) data on video suppliers. To maintain (enter, update, and delete) data on video orders. To perform searches on branches. To perform searches on videos at all branches. To perform searches on video suppliers. To perform searches on video orders. To track the status of video orders. To report on videos at all branches. To report on video rentals at all branches. To report on members at all branches. To report on video suppliers. To report on video orders.

6.4.4 The *StayHome* case study – requirements collection and analysis

During this stage, you should continue to gather more details on the user views identified in the previous stage, to create a *users' requirements specification* that describes in detail the data to be held in the database and how the data is to be used. While gathering more information on the user views, you should also try to collect any general requirements for the system. The purpose of gathering this information is to create a *systems specification*, which describes any features to be included in the new database system such as networking and shared access requirements, performance requirements, and the levels of security required.

While you are collecting the data on the requirements for the user views and the system in general, you will learn about how the current system works. Of course, you are building a new database system and should try to retain the good things about the old system while introducing the benefits that will be part of using the new system.

An important activity associated with this stage is deciding how you want to deal with the situation where you have more than one user view. As we discussed in Section 4.6, there are three approaches to dealing with multiple user views, namely the *centralized approach*, the *view integration approach*, and a combination of both approaches. We'll show how you can use these approaches shortly.

Gathering more information on the user views of the StayHome database system

To find out more about the requirements for each user view, you may again use a selection of fact-finding techniques, including interviews and observing the business in operation. Examples of the types of questions that you may ask about the data (represented as X) required by a user view includes:

'What type of data do you need to hold on X?'
'What sorts of things do you do with the data on X?'

For example, you may ask a branch Manager the following questions:

Database developer 'What type of data do you need to hold on staff?'

Manager 'The type of data held on a member of staff is his or her name, position, and salary. Each member of staff is given a staff number, which is unique throughout the company.'

Database developer 'What sorts of things do you do with the data on staff?'

Manager 'I need to be able to enter the details of new members of staff and delete their details when they leave. I need to keep the details of staff up to date and print reports that list the name, position, and salary of each member of staff at my branch. I need to be able to allocate Supervisors to look after staff. Sometimes when I need to communicate with other branches, I need to find out the names of Managers.'

You need to ask similar questions about all the important data to be stored in the database. Responses to these questions should help you identify the necessary details for the users' requirements specification.

Gathering information on the system requirements of the StayHome database system

While conducting interviews about user views, you should also collect more general information on the system requirements. Examples of the types of questions that you may ask about the system include:

'What transactions run frequently on the database?'
'What transactions are critical to the operation of the business?'
'When do the critical transactions run?'
'When are the low, normal, and high workload periods for the critical transactions?'
'What type of security do you want for the database system?'
'Is there any highly sensitive data that should only be accessed by certain members of staff?'
'What historical data do you want to hold?'
'What are the networking and shared access requirements for the database system?'
'What type of protection from failures or data loss do you want for your database system?'

For example, you may ask a Manager the following questions:

Database developer 'What transactions run frequently on the database?'

Manager 'We frequently get requests either by phone or by members who call into our branch to search for a particular video and see if it's available for rent. Of course, we also do a lot of renting out and returning of videos.'

Database developer 'What transactions are critical to the operation of the business?'

Manager 'Again, critical operations include being able to search for particular videos and the renting out and returning of videos. Members would go elsewhere if we couldn't provide these basic services.'

Database developer 'When do the critical transactions run?'

Manager 'Every day.'

Database developer 'When are the low, normal, and high workload periods for the critical transactions?'

Manager 'We tend to be quiet in the mornings and get busier as the day progresses. The busiest time each day for dealing with members is between 6 and 9pm. We even have to double the staff on duty during this period on Fridays and Saturdays.'

You may ask the Director the following questions:

Database developer 'What type of security do you want for the database system?'

Director 'I don't suppose a database holding information for a video rental company holds very sensitive data, but I wouldn't want any of our competitors to see our data on members and their video rentals. Staff should see only the data necessary to do their job in a form that suits what they're doing. For example, although it's necessary for Supervisors and Assistants to see member details, member records should only be displayed one at a time and not as a report.'

Database developer 'Is there any highly sensitive data that should only be accessed by certain members of staff?'

Director 'As I said before, staff should see only the data necessary to do their jobs. For example, although Supervisors need to see staff details, I should be the only one to see salary details.'

Database developer 'What historical data do you want to hold?'

Director 'I want to be able to keep members' details for a couple of years after their last video rental, so that we can mailshot them, tell them about our latest promotional offers, and generally try to attract them back. I also want to be able to keep rental information for a couple of years so that we can analyze it to find out which types of videos are the most popular, which age groups hire videos most frequently, and so on.'

Database developer 'What are the networking and shared access requirements for the database system?'

Director 'I want all the branches networked to our Headquarters here in Seattle, so that staff can access the system from wherever and whenever they need to. At most branches, I would expect about two or three staff to be accessing the system at any one time, but remember we have about 100 branches. Most of the time the staff should be just accessing local branch data. However, I don't really want there to be any restrictions about how or when the system can be accessed, unless it's got real financial implications.'

Database developer 'What type of protection from failures or data loss do you want for your database system?'

Director 'The best, of course. All our business is going to be conducted using the database, so if it goes down, we're sunk. To be serious for a minute, I think we probably have to back up our data every evening when the branch closes, what do you think?'

You need to ask similar questions about all the important aspects of the system. Responses to these questions should help you identify the necessary details for the systems specification.

Managing the user views of the StayHome database system

How do you decide whether to use the centralized or view integration approach to manage multiple user views? One way to help you make a decision is to examine the overlap in terms of the data used between the user views identified during the system definition stage. Table 6.7 cross-references the Director, Manager, Supervisor, Assistant, and Buyer user views with the main types of data used by the *StayHome* database system (namely, Supplier, Video Order, Video, Branch, Staff, Rental, and Member).

Table 6.7 Cross-reference of user views with the main types of data used by the *StayHome* database system.

	Supplier	Video Order	Video	Branch	Staff	Rental	Member
Director	X	X	X	X	X	X	X
Manager			X	X	X	X	X
Supervisor			X	X	X	X	X
Assistant			X	X		X	X
Buyer	X	X	X	X		X	X

You can see from this table that there is an overlap in the data used by all the user views. However, the Director and Buyer user views are distinct in requiring additional data (namely, Supplier and Video Order) to that used by the other user views. Based on this analysis, you could use the centralized approach first to merge the requirements for the Director and Buyer user views (given the collective name of *Business user views*) and the requirements for the Manager, Supervisor, and Assistant user views (given the collective name of *Branch user views*). You could then develop data models representing the Business and Branch user views and then use the view integration approach to merge the two data models. Of course, for a simple case study like *StayHome*, we could easily use the centralized approach for all user views. However, to allow us to demonstrate both the centralized and view integration approaches working in practice we'll stay with our decision to identify two collective user views for *StayHome*.

It's difficult to give precise rules as to when it's appropriate to use the centralized or view integration approaches. As the database developer, you should base your decision on an assessment of the complexity of the database system and the degree of overlap between the various user views. However, whether you use the centralized or view integration approach or a mixture of both to build the underlying database, ultimately you need to create the original user views for the working database system. We'll discuss the establishment of the user views for the database in Chapter 14. In the remainder of this chapter, we present the users' requirements specification for the Branch user views of *StayHome* and the systems specification for the database system.

Creating the users' requirements specification for the Branch user views of the StayHome database system

The users' requirements specification for the Branch user views is listed in two sections: the first describes the data used by the Branch user views and the second provides examples of how the data is used by the Branch user views (that is, the transactions performed on the data).

Data requirements

The data held on a branch of *StayHome* is the branch address made up of street, city, state, and zip code, and the telephone numbers (maximum of 3 lines). Each branch is given a branch number, which is unique throughout the company.

Each branch of *StayHome* has staff, which includes a Manager, one or more Supervisors, and a number of other staff. The Manager is responsible for the day-to-day running of a given branch. Each branch has several Supervisors and each Supervisor is responsible for supervising a group of staff. The data held on a member of staff is his or her name, position, and salary. Each member of staff is given a staff number, which is unique throughout the company.

Each branch of *StayHome* is allocated a stock of videos. The data held on a video is the catalog number, video number, title, category, daily rental rate, purchase price, status, and the names of the main actors (and the characters played), and the director. The catalog number uniquely identifies each video. In most cases, there are several copies of each video at a branch, and the individual copies are identified using the video number. A video is given a category such as Action, Adult, Children, Fantasy, Horror, Sci-Fi, or Thriller. The status indicates whether a specific copy of a video is available for rent.

Before renting a video from the company, a customer must first register as a member of a local branch of *StayHome*. The data held on a member is the first and last name, address, and the date that the member registered at the branch. Each member is given a member number, which is unique across all branches and is used even when a member chooses to register at more than one branch. The name of the member of staff responsible for processing the registration of a member at a branch is also noted.

Once registered, a member is free to rent videos, up to a maximum of 10 at any one time. The data held on each video rented is the rental number, the member's full name and member number, the video number, title, and daily rental cost, and the dates the video is rented out and returned. The rental number is unique throughout the company.

Transaction requirements

Data entry

(a) Enter the details of a new branch.

(b) Enter the details of a new member of staff at a branch (such as an employee Tom Daniels at branch B001).

(c) Enter the details for a newly released video (such as details of a video called *Return of the King*).

(d) Enter the details of copies of a new video at a given branch (such as three copies of *Return of the King* at branch B001).

(e) Enter the details of a new member registering at a given branch (such as a member Bob Adams registering at branch B002).

(f) Enter the details of a rental agreement for a member renting a video (such as member Don Nelson renting *Return of the King* on 4-May-2004).

Data update/deletion

(g) Update/delete the details of a branch.

(h) Update/delete the details of a member of staff at a branch.

(i) Update/delete the details of a given video.

(j) Update/delete the details of a copy of a video.

(k) Update/delete the details of a given member.

(l) Update/delete the details of a given rental agreement for a member renting a video.

Data queries

The database should be capable of supporting the following sample queries:

(m) List the details of branches in a given city.

(n) List the name, position, and salary of staff at a given branch, ordered by staff name.

(o) List the name of each Manager at each branch, ordered by branch number.

(p) List the title, category, and availability of all videos at a specified branch, ordered by category.

(q) List the title, category, and availability of all videos for a given actor at a specified branch, ordered by title.

(r) List the title, category, and availability of all videos for a given director at a specified branch, ordered by title.

(s) List the details of all videos a specified member currently has on rent.

(t) List the details of copies of a given video at a specified branch.

(u) List the titles of all videos in a specified category, ordered by title.

(v) List the total number of videos in each video category at each branch, ordered by branch number.

(w) List the total cost of the videos at all branches.

(x) List the total number of videos featuring each actor, ordered by actor name.

(y) List the total number of members at each branch who joined in 1999, ordered by branch number.

(z) List the total possible daily rental for videos at each branch, ordered by ·branch number.

Creating the systems specification for the StayHome database system

The systems specification should list all the important features for the *StayHome* database system. Examples of the types of features that should be described in the systems specification include:

- Initial database size
- Database rate of growth
- The types and average number of record searches
- Networking and shared access requirements
- Performance
- Security
- Backup and recovery
- User interface
- Legal issues.

Initial database size

(a) There are approximately 20 000 video titles and 400 000 videos for rent distributed over 100 branches. There are an average of 4000 and a maximum of 10 000 videos for rent at each branch.

(b) There are approximately 2000 staff working across all branches. There are an average of 15 and a maximum of 25 members of staff working at each branch.

(c) There are approximately 100 000 members registered across all branches. There are an average of 1000 and a maximum of 1500 members registered at each branch.

(d) There are approximately 400 000 video rentals across all branches. There are an average of 4000 and a maximum of 10 000 video rentals at each branch.

(e) There are approximately 1000 directors and 30 000 main actors in 60 000 starring roles.

(f) There are approximately 50 video suppliers and 1000 video orders.

Database rate of growth

(a) Approximately 100 new video titles and 20 copies of each video are added to the database each month.

(b) Once a copy of a video is no longer suitable for renting out (this includes those of poor visual quality, lost, or stolen), the corresponding record is deleted from the database. Approximately 100 records of videos for rent are deleted each month.

(c) Approximately 20 members of staff join and leave the company each month. The records of staff who have left the company are deleted after one year. Approximately 20 staff records are deleted each month.

(d) Approximately 1000 new members register at branches each month. If a member does not rent out a video at any time within a period of two years, his or her record is deleted. Approximately 100 member records are deleted each month.

(e) Approximately 5000 new video rentals are recorded across 100 branches each day. The details of video rentals are deleted two years after the creation of the record.

(f) Approximately 50 new video orders are placed each week. The details of video orders are destroyed two years after the creation of the record.

The types and average number of record searches

(a) Searching for the details of a branch – approximately 10 per day.

(b) Searching for the details of a member of staff at a branch – approximately 20 per day.

(c) Searching for the details of a given video – approximately 5000 per day (Sunday to Thursday), approximately 10 000 per day (Friday and Saturday). Peak workload 6–9pm daily.

(d) Searching for the details of a copy of a video – approximately 10 000 per day (Sunday to Thursday), approximately 20 000 per day (Friday and Saturday). Peak workload 6–9pm daily.

(e) Searching for the details of a specified member – approximately 100 per day.

(f) Searching for the details of a rental agreement for a member renting a video – approximately 10 000 per day (Sunday to Thursday), approximately 20 000 per day (Friday and Saturday). Peak workload 6–9pm daily.

Networking and shared access requirements

(a) All branches should be securely networked to a centralized database located at the company's HQ in Seattle.

(b) The system should allow for at least three people concurrently accessing the system from each branch. Consideration needs to be given to the licensing requirements for this number of concurrent accesses.

Performance

(a) During opening hours but not during peak periods expect less than 1 second response for all single record searches. During peak periods (6–9pm daily) expect less than 5 second response for all single record searches.

(b) During opening hours but not during peak periods expect less than 5 second response for all multiple record searches. During peak periods (6–9pm daily) expect less than 10 second response for all multiple record searches.

(c) During opening hours but not during peak periods expect less than 1 second response for all updates/saves. During peak periods (6–9pm daily) expect less than 5 second response for all updates/saves.

Security

(a) The database should be password protected.

(b) Each member of staff should be assigned database access privileges appropriate to a particular user view, namely Director, Manager, Supervisor, Assistant, or Buyer.

(c) Staff should see only the data necessary to do their job in a form that suits what they're doing.

Backup and recovery

The database should be backed up each day at 12 midnight.

User interface

The user interface should be menu-driven. Online help should be easy to locate and access.

Legal issues

Each country has laws that govern the way that the computerized storage of personal data is handled. As the *StayHome* database holds data on staff and members, any legal issues that must be complied with should be investigated and implemented.

6.4.5 The *StayHome* case study – database design

In this chapter, we demonstrated the creation of the users' requirements specification for the Branch user views and the systems specification for the *StayHome* database system. These documents are the source of information for the next stage of the lifecycle called database design. In Chapters 9, 10, and 12 to 16, we'll provide a step-by-step methodology for database design, and we'll use the documents created in this chapter to demonstrate the methodology in practice.

For those of you interested in developing more complex multi-user-view database systems, we'll demonstrate how the view integration approach works in practice in Appendix C using the branch and business user views of *StayHome*.

Chapter summary

✓ **Fact–finding** is the formal process of using techniques such as interviews and questionnaires to collect facts about systems, requirements, and preferences.

✓ Fact-finding is particularly crucial to the early stages of the database system development lifecycle, including the database planning, system definition, and requirements collection and analysis stages.

✓ The five most common fact-finding techniques are examining documentation, interviewing, observing the business in operation, research, and questionnaires.

✓ The first step in the **database planning stage** is to define clearly the mission statement and mission objectives for the database project. The **mission statement** defines the major aims of the database system. Each **mission objective** should identify a particular task that the database must support.

✓ The purpose of the **system definition stage** is to define the boundaries and user views of the database system.

✓ There are two main documents created during the **requirements collection and analysis stage**, namely the users' requirements specification and the systems specification.

✓ The **users' requirements specification** describes in detail the data to be held in the database and how the data is to be used.

✓ The **systems specification** describes any features to be included in the database system such as the required performance and the levels of security.

Review questions

6.1 Briefly describe what the process of fact-finding attempts to achieve for a database developer.

6.2 Describe how fact-finding is used throughout the stages of the database system development lifecycle.

6.3 For each stage of the database system development lifecycle identify examples of the facts captured and the documentation produced.

6.4 A database developer normally uses several fact-finding techniques during a single database project. The five most commonly used techniques are examining documentation, interviewing, observing the business in operation, conducting research, and using questionnaires. Describe each fact-finding technique and identify the advantages and disadvantages of each.

6.5 Describe the purpose of defining a mission statement and mission objectives for a database system.

6.6 What is the purpose of the systems definition stage?

6.7 How do the contents of a users' requirements specification differ from a systems specification?

6.8 Describe one approach to deciding whether to use centralized, view integration, or a combination of both when developing a database system for multiple user views.

Chapter 7

Entity–Relationship modeling

In this chapter you will learn:

➤ How to use ER modeling in database design.

➤ The basic concepts of an ER model called entities, relationships, and attributes.

➤ A diagrammatic technique for displaying an ER model.

➤ How to identify and solve connection traps in an ER model.

Database system development lifecycle discussed in Chapter 4

In Chapter 6, you learned about techniques for gathering and capturing information about what the users require of the database system. Once the requirements collection and analysis stage of the database system development lifecycle is complete and you have documented the requirements for the database system, you are now ready to begin database design.

One of the most difficult aspects of database design is the fact that designers, programmers, and end-users tend to view data and its use in different ways. Unfortunately, unless we can gain a common understanding that reflects how the organization operates, the design we produce will fail to meet the users' requirements. To ensure that we get a precise understanding of the nature of the data and how the organization uses it, we need to have a model for communication that is non-technical and free of ambiguities. The Entity–Relationship (ER) model is one such example. Since the introduction of ER modeling in 1976, the model has been extended to include additional enhanced modeling concepts. We cover the basic ER concepts in this chapter and introduce some of the more popular enhanced ER concepts in Chapter 11.

Entity–Relationship modeling is a top-down approach to database design. We begin ER modeling by identifying the important data (called entities) and relationships between the data that must be represented in the model. We then add more details such as the information we want to hold about the entities and relationships (called attributes) and any constraints on the entities, relationships, and attributes.

Throughout this chapter, you are introduced to the basic concepts that make up an ER model. Although there is general agreement about what each concept means, there are a number of different ways that you can represent each concept in a diagram. We have chosen a diagrammatic notation that uses an increasingly popular object-oriented modeling language called **UML (Unified Modeling Language)**. However, examples of alternative popular notations for ER models are shown in Appendix A.

> UML is the successor to a number of object-oriented analysis and design methods introduced in the 1980s and 1990s and is the standard modeling language.

As the ER model forms the basis of the methodology we'll present in Chapters 9, 10, and 12 to 16, this chapter may prove to be one of the most important in this book. If you don't understand the concepts immediately, don't worry. Try reading the chapter again, and then look at the examples we give in the methodology for additional help. We start by introducing the basic concepts of the ER model, namely entities, relationships, and attributes.

7.1   Entities

> **Entity**
>
> A set of objects with the same properties, which are identified by a user or organization as having an independent existence.

The basic concept of the ER model is an **entity**, which represents a set of objects in the 'real world' that share the same properties. Each object, which should be uniquely identifiable within the set, is called an **entity occurrence**. An entity has an independent existence and can represent objects with a physical (or 'real') existence or objects with a conceptual (or 'abstract') existence, as shown in Figure 7.1.

We identify each entity by a unique name and a list of properties, called **attributes**. Although an entity has a distinct set of attributes, each entity has its own values for each attribute. A database normally contains many different entities.

Figure 7.1

Examples of entities
with physical
and conceptual
existence.

Physical existence	Conceptual existence
Member	Role
Video	Rental
Branch	Registration

Attributes are
discussed in
Section 7.3

Diagrammatic representation of entities

Each entity is shown as a rectangle labeled with the name of the entity, which is normally a singular noun. In UML, the first letter of each word in the entity name is uppercase (for example, Video, Role, Actor, VideoForRent). Figure 7.2 demonstrates the diagrammatic representation of the Video, Role, and Actor entities.

7.2 Relationships

Relationship

A set of meaningful associations among entities.

A **relationship** is a set of associations between participating entities. As with entities, each association should be uniquely identifiable within the set. A uniquely identifiable association is called a **relationship occurrence**.

Each relationship is given a name that describes its function. For example, the Actor entity is associated with the Role entity through a relationship called *Plays*, and the Role entity is associated with the Video entity through a relationship called *Features*.

Diagrammatic representation of relationships

Each relationship is shown as a line connecting the associated entities, labeled with the name of the relationship. Normally, a relationship is named using a verb (for example, *Plays* or *Features*) or a short phrase including a verb (for exam-

Figure 7.2

Diagrammatic
representation of
the Video, Role, and
Actor entities.

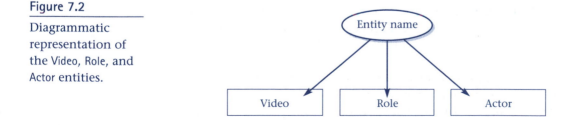

ple, *IsPartOf* or *WorksAt*). Again, the first letter of each word in the relationship name is shown in uppercase. Whenever possible, a relationship name should be unique for a given ER model.

A relationship is only labeled in one direction, which usually means that the name of the relationship only makes sense in one direction (for example, Actor *Plays* Role makes sense but not Role *Plays* Actor). So once the relationship name is chosen, an arrow symbol is placed beside the name indicating the correct direction for a reader to interpret the relationship name (for example, Actor *Plays* ▶ Role). Figure 7.3 demonstrates the diagrammatic representation of the relationships Video *Features* Role and Actor *Plays* Role.

7.2.1 Degree of a relationship

Degree of a relationship

The number of participating entities in the relationship.

The entities involved in a particular relationship are referred to as participants. The number of participants in a relationship is called the **degree** and indicates the number of entities involved in a relationship. A relationship of degree one is called **unary**, which is commonly referred to as a *recursive* relationship. We discuss this type of relationship in more detail in the following section. A relationship of degree two is called **binary**. The two relationships shown in Figure 7.3 are **binary relationships**. A relationship of a degree higher than binary is called a **complex relationship**.

A relationship of degree three is called **ternary**. An example of a ternary relationship is *Registers* with three participating entities, namely Branch, Staff, and Member, as shown in Figure 7.4. The purpose of this relationship is to represent the situation where a member of staff registers a member at a particular branch, allowing for members to register at more than one branch, and members of staff to move between branches.

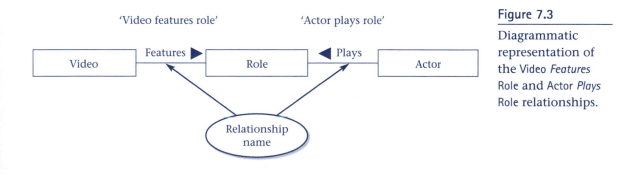

Figure 7.3

Diagrammatic representation of the Video *Features* Role and Actor *Plays* Role relationships.

Figure 7.4

Example of a
ternary relationship
called *Registers*.

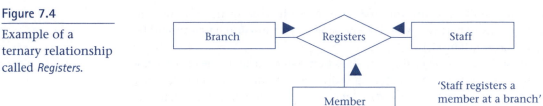

'Staff registers a
member at a branch'

A relationship of degree four is called **quaternary**, and a relationship of a higher degree is called ***n*-ary**. The most popular type of relationship you'll come across is binary, but occasionally you'll come across unary or ternary, and less frequently quaternary.

7.2.2 Recursive relationships

Recursive relationship

A relationship where the *same* entity participates more than once in *different* roles.

Let's consider a recursive relationship called *Supervises*, which represents an association of staff with a supervisor where the supervisor is also a member of staff. In other words, the Staff entity participates twice in the *Supervises* relationship: the first participation as a supervisor, and the second participation as a member of staff who is supervised (supervisee), as shown in Figure 7.5.

Relationships may be given role names to indicate the purpose that each participating entity plays in a relationship. Role names are important for recursive relationships to determine the function of each participating entity. Figure 7.5 shows the use of role names to describe the *Supervises* recursive relationship. The first participation of the Staff entity in the *Supervises* relationship is given the role name Supervisor and the second participation is given the role name Supervisee.

Figure 7.5

Example of a
recursive
relationship called
Supervises.

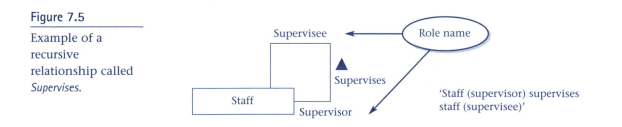

'Staff (supervisor) supervises
staff (supervisee)'

7.3   Attributes

Attribute

A property of an entity or a relationship.

The particular properties of entities are called attributes. Attributes represent what we want to know about entities. For example, a Video entity may be described by the catalogNo, title, category, dailyRental, and price attributes. These attributes hold values that describe each video occurrence, and represent the main source of data stored in the database.

A relationship between entities can also have attributes similar to those of an entity, but we'll defer the discussion of relationships that have attributes until Section 7.6.

As we now discuss, we can classify attributes as being: simple or composite; single-valued or multi-valued; or derived.

7.3.1 Simple and composite attributes

Simple attribute

An attribute composed of a single component.

Simple attributes cannot be further subdivided. Examples of simple attributes include the category and price attributes for a video. Simple attributes are sometimes called *atomic attributes*.

Composite attribute

An attribute composed of multiple components.

Composite attributes can be further divided to yield smaller components with an independent existence. For example, the name attribute of the Member entity with the value 'Don Nelson' can be subdivided into fName ('Don') and lName ('Nelson').

The decision to model the name attribute as a simple attribute or to subdivide the attribute into fName and lName is dependent on whether the users' transactions access the name attribute as a single component or as individual components.

7.3.2 Single-valued and multi-valued attributes

Single-valued attribute

An attribute that holds a single value for an entity occurrence.

The majority of attributes are **single-valued** for a particular entity. For example, each occurrence of the Video entity has a single value for the catalogNo attribute (for example, 207132), and therefore the catalogNo attribute is referred to as being single-valued.

Multi-valued attribute

An attribute that holds multiple values for an entity occurrence.

Some attributes have multiple values for a particular entity. For example, each occurrence of the Video entity may have multiple values for the category attribute (for example, 'Children' and 'Comedy'), and therefore the category attribute in this case would be **multi-valued**. A multi-valued attribute may have a set of values with specified lower and upper limits. For example, the category attribute may have between one and three values.

> The classification of simple and composite, and the classification of single-valued and multi-valued, are not mutually exclusive. In other words, you can have simple single-valued, composite single-valued, simple multi-valued, and composite multi-valued attributes.

7.3.3 Derived attributes

Derived attribute

An attribute that represents a value that is derivable from the value of a related attribute, or set of attributes, not necessarily in the same entity.

Some attributes may be related for a particular entity. For example, the age of a member of staff (age) is derivable from the date of birth (DOB) attribute, and therefore the age and DOB attributes are related. We refer to the age attribute as a derived attribute, the value of which is derived from the DOB attribute.

> **TIP**
>
> Age is not normally stored in a database because it would have to be updated regularly. On the other hand, as date of birth never changes and age can be derived from date of birth, date of birth is stored instead, and age is derived from the DOB attribute, when needed.

In some cases, the value of an attribute is derived from the values in a single entity, like age. But in other cases, the value of an attribute may be derived from the values in more than one entity.

7.3.4 Keys

In Section 2.2.3, we introduced the concept of keys associated with tables. These concepts also apply to entities.

Superkey

An attribute, or set of attributes, that uniquely identifies each entity occurrence.

Candidate key

A superkey that contains only the minimum number of attributes necessary for unique identification of each entity occurrence.

Primary key

The candidate key that is selected to identify each entity occurrence.

Alternate keys

The candidate keys that are not selected as the primary key of the entity.

For example, branchNo (the branch number) and zipCode (the branch's zip code) are candidate keys for the Branch entity, as each has a distinct value for every branch occurrence. If we choose branchNo as the primary key for the Branch entity, then zipCode becomes an alternate key.

Diagrammatic representation of attributes

If an entity is to be displayed with its attributes, we display the rectangle representing the entity in two parts. The upper part of the rectangle displays the name of the entity and the lower part lists the names of the attributes. For example, Figure 7.6 shows the ER model for the Video, Role, and Actor entities and their associated attributes.

The first attribute(s) to be listed is the primary key for the entity, if known. The name(s) of the primary key attribute(s) can be labeled with the tag {PK}. In UML, the name of an attribute is displayed with the first letter in lowercase and, if the name has more than one word, with the first letter of each subsequent word in uppercase (for example, character, actorNo, catalogNo). Additional tags that can be used include partial primary key {PPK}, when an attribute forms only part of a composite primary key, and alternate key {AK}.

For simple, single-valued attributes, there is no need to use tags and so we simply display the attribute names in a list below the entity name.

Figure 7.6

Diagrammatic representation of the attributes for the Video, Role, and Actor entities.

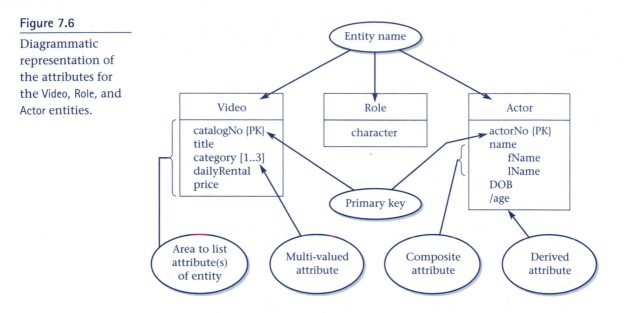

For composite attributes, we list the name of the composite attribute followed below and indented to the right by the names of its simple component parts. For example, in Figure 7.6 the composite attribute name is shown followed below by the names of its component attributes, fName and lName.

For multi-valued attributes, we label the attribute name with an indication of the range of values available for the attribute. For example, if we label the category attribute with the range [1..*], this means that there are one or more values for the category attribute. If we know the precise maximum number of values, we can label the attribute with an exact range. For example, if the category attribute can hold one to a maximum of three values, we would label the attribute with [1..3].

For derived attributes, we prefix the attribute name with a '/'. For example, the derived attribute age is shown in Figure 7.6 as /age.

No primary key has been identified for the Role entity. The presence or absence of a primary key allows us to identify whether an entity is strong or weak. We discuss the concept of strong and weak entities next.

For a simple database, it's possible to show all the attributes for each entity on the data model. However, for a more complex database, you normally display just the attribute, or attributes, that form the primary key of each entity. When only the primary key attributes are shown in the ER model, you can omit the {PK} tag.

7.4 Strong and weak entities

We can classify entities as being either strong or weak.

Strong entity

Entity that is *not* dependent on the existence of another entity for its primary key.

Weak entity

Entity that is partially or wholly dependent on the existence of another entity, or entities, for its primary key.

For example, as we can distinguish one actor from all other actors and one video from all other videos without the existence of any other entity, Actor and Video are referred to as being **strong entities**. In other words, the Actor and Video entities are strong because they have their own primary keys, as shown in Figure 7.6.

Figure 7.6 also has an example of a **weak entity** called Role, which represents characters played by actors in videos. If we are unable to uniquely identify one Role entity occurrence from another without the existence of the Actor and Video entities, then Role is referred to as being a weak entity. In other words, the Role entity is weak because it has no primary key of its own.

Strong entities are sometimes referred to as *parent, owner,* or *dominant entities* and weak entities as *child, dependent,* or *subordinate entities*.

7.5 Multiplicity constraints on relationships

We now examine the constraints that may be placed on entities that participate in a relationship. Examples of such constraints include the requirements that a branch must have members and each branch must have staff. The main type of constraint on relationships is called **multiplicity**.

Multiplicity

The number of occurrences of one entity that may relate to a single occurrence of an associated entity.

Multiplicity constrains the number of entity occurrences that relate to other entity occurrences through a particular relationship. Multiplicity is a representation of the policies established by the user or organization, and is referred to as a **business rule**. Ensuring that all appropriate business rules are identified and represented is an important part of modeling an organization.

As we mentioned earlier, the most common degree for relationships is binary. The multiplicity for a binary relationship is generally referred to as one-to-one (1:1), one-to-many (1:*), or many-to-many (*:*). We examine these three types of relationships using the following business rules:

- A member of staff manages a branch.
- A branch has members of staff.
- Actors play in videos.

For each business rule, we demonstrate how to work out the multiplicity if, as is sometimes the case, it's not clearly specified in the rule, and show how to represent it in an ER model. In Section 7.5.4, we'll examine multiplicity for relationships of degrees higher than binary.

> Not all business rules are easily and clearly represented in an ER model. For example, the requirement that a member of staff receives an additional day's holiday for every year of employment with the organization may be difficult to represent clearly in an ER model.

7.5.1   One-to-one (1:1) relationships

Let's consider the relationship called *Manages*, which relates the Staff and Branch entities. Figure 7.7(a) displays individual examples of the *Manages* relationship using values for the primary key attributes of the Staff and Branch entities.

Working out the multiplicity

Working out the multiplicity normally requires examining the precise relationships between the data given in a business rule using sample data. The sample data may be obtained by examining filled-in forms or reports or, if possible, from further discussions with the users. However, to reach the right conclusions about a business rule, it's essential that the sample data examined or discussed is a true representation of all the data.

In Figure 7.7(a), we see that staffNo S1500 manages branchNo B001 and staffNo S0010 manages branchNo B002, but staffNo S0003 does not manage any branch. In other words, a member of staff can manage zero or one branch and each branch is managed by a single member of staff. As there is a maximum of *one* branch for each member of staff and a maximum of *one* member of staff for each branch involved in the relationship, we refer to this relationship as *one-to-one*, which we usually abbreviate as (1:1).

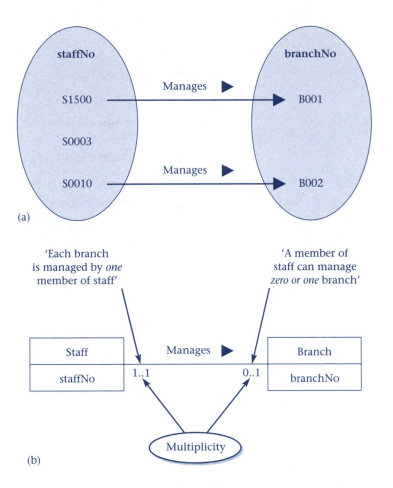

Figure 7.7
Staff *Manages* Branch
(1:1) relationship:
(a) individual
examples;
(b) multiplicity.

Diagrammatic representation of 1:1 relationships

An ER model of the Staff *Manages* Branch relationship is shown in Figure 7.7(b). To represent that a member of staff can manage zero or one branch, we place a '0..1' beside the Branch entity. To represent that a branch always has one manager, we place a '1..1' beside the Staff entity. (Note that for a 1:1 relationship, we may choose a relationship name that makes sense in either direction.)

7.5.2 One-to-many (1:*) relationships

Let's consider the relationship called *Has*, which also relates the Branch and Staff entities. Figure 7.8(a) displays individual examples of the Branch *Has* Staff relationship using values for the primary key attributes of the Branch and Staff entities.

Figure 7.8

Branch *Has* Staff (1:*)
relationship:
(a) individual
examples;
(b) multiplicity.

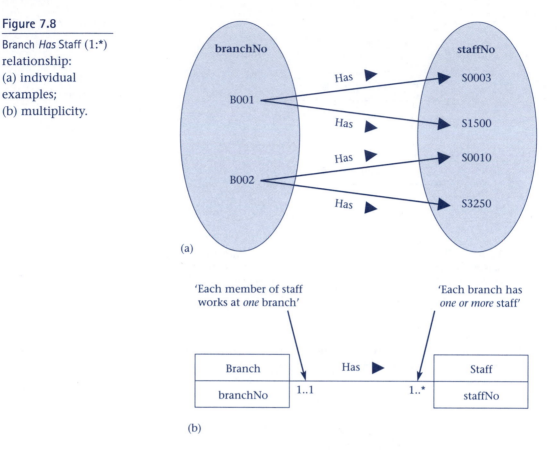

(a)

(b)

Working out the multiplicity

In Figure 7.8(a), we see that branchNo B001 has staffNo S0003 and S1500, and branchNo B002 has staffNo S0010 and S3250. Therefore, each branch has one or more members of staff and each member of staff works at a single branch. As *one* branch can have *many* staff, we refer to this type of relationship as *one-to-many*, which we usually abbreviate as (1:*).

Diagrammatic representation of 1:* relationships

An ER model of the Branch *Has* Staff relationship is shown in Figure 7.8(b). To represent that each branch can have one or more staff, we place a '1..*' beside the Staff entity. To represent that each member of staff works at a single branch, we place a '1..1' beside the Branch entity. (Note that with 1:* relationships, we choose a relationship name that makes sense in the 1:* direction.)

> **TIP**
>
> If you know the actual minimum and maximum values for the multi-plicity, you can display these instead. For example, if a branch has between two and ten staff, we can replace the '1..*' with '2..10'.

7.5.3 Many-to-many (*:*) relationships

Let's consider the relationship called *PlaysIn*, which relates the Actor and Video enti-ties. Figure 7.9(a) displays individual examples of the Actor *PlaysIn* Video relationship using values for the primary key attributes of the Actor and Video entities.

Working out the multiplicity

In Figure 7.9(a), we see that actorNo A2019 plays in video catalogNo 634817 and 445624, and actorNo A7525 plays in video catalogNo 445624. In other words, a single actor can play in one or more videos. We also see that video catalogNo 445624 has two starring actors but catalogNo 781132 does not have any actors in it, and so we conclude that a single video can star zero or more actors.

In summary, the *PlaysIn* relationship is 1:* from the viewpoint of both the Actor and Video entities. We represent this relationship as two 1:* relationships in both directions, which are collectively referred to as a *many-to-many* relation-ship, which we usually abbreviate as (*:*).

*Diagrammatic representation of *:* relationships*

An ER model of the Actor *PlaysIn* Video relationship is shown in Figure 7.9(b). To represent that each actor can star in one or more videos, we place a '1..*' beside the Video entity. To represent that each video can star zero or more actors, we place a '0..*' beside the Actor entity. (Note that for a *:* relationship, we may choose a relationship name that makes sense in either direction.)

7.5.4 Multiplicity for complex relationships

Multiplicity for relationships beyond degree two is slightly more complex. For example, the multiplicity for a ternary relationship represents the potential number of entity occurrences in the relationship when the other two values are fixed. Let's consider the ternary *Registers* relationship between Branch, Staff, and Member shown in Figure 7.4. Figure 7.10(a) displays individual examples of the *Registers* relationship when the values for the Staff and Member entities are fixed.

Figure 7.9

Actor *PlaysIn* Video
relationship (*:*):
(a) individual
examples;
(b) multiplicity.

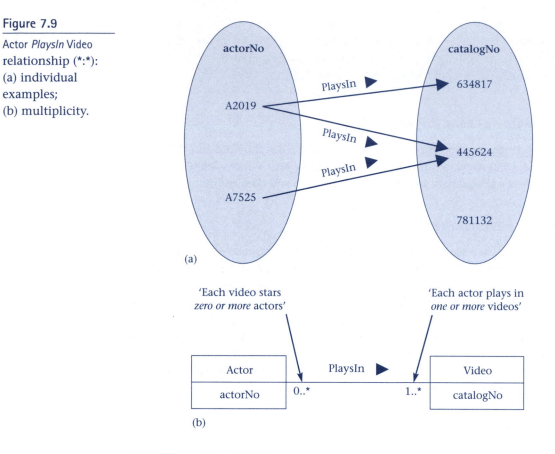

Working out the multiplicity

In Figure 7.10(a), we see that for every combination of staffNo/memberNo values
there is always at least one corresponding branchNo value. In particular, staffNo
S0003 registers memberNo M166884 at branchNo B001 and B002. This represents
the situation where member M166884 has been registered at branch B001 by
staff S0003, and has subsequently been registered at B002 by the same member
of staff, who has transferred to branch B002 in the intervening period. In other
words, from the Branch perspective the multiplicity is 1..*.

If we repeat this test from the Staff perspective, we find that the multiplicity
for this relationship is 1..1, and if we examine it from the Member perspective,
we find it is 0..*. An ER model of the ternary *Registers* relationship showing multiplicity is shown in Figure 7.10(b).

In general, the multiplicity for *n*-ary relationships represents the potential
number of entity occurrences in the relationship when the other $(n-1)$ values
are fixed.

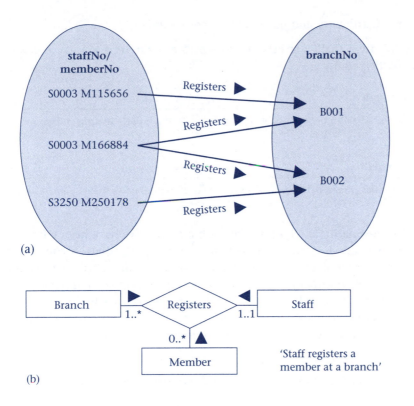

Figure 7.10

The ternary *Registers* relationship from the Branch perspective with the values for Staff and Member fixed: (a) individual examples; (b) multiplicity of relationship.

A summary of the possible ways that you may represent multiplicity constraints along with a description of the meaning for each is shown in Table 7.1.

Table 7.1 A summary of ways to represent multiplicity constraints.

Alternative ways to represent multiplicity constraints	Meaning
0..1	Zero or one entity occurrence
1..1 (or just 1)	Exactly one entity occurrence
0..* (or just *)	Zero or many entity occurrences
1..*	One or many entity occurrences
5..10	Minimum of 5 up to a maximum of 10 entity occurrences
0, 3, 6–8	Zero or three or six, seven, or eight entity occurrences

7.5.5 Cardinality and participation constraints

Multiplicity actually consists of two separate constraints known as cardinality and participation.

Cardinality

Describes the number of possible relationships for each participating entity.

Participation

Determines whether all or only some entity occurrences participate in a relationship.

The **cardinality** of a binary relationship is what we have been referring to as one-to-one, one-to-many, and many-to-many. A **participation constraint** represents whether all entity occurrences are involved in a particular relationship (*mandatory participation*) or only some (*optional participation*). In Figure 7.11, we illustrate the cardinality and participation constraints for the Staff *Manages* Branch relationship shown in Figure 7.7(b). We'll use the participation constraint during the logical database design methodology to determine:

(a) how to create tables for one-to-one relationships (covered in Step 2.1);

(b) whether a foreign key can have nulls (covered in Step 2.4).

Foreign key defined in Section 2.2.3

7.6 Attributes on relationships

As we briefly mentioned in Section 7.3, attributes can also be assigned to relationships. For example, let's consider the relationship *PlaysIn*, which associates

Figure 7.11

Multiplicity shown as cardinality and participation constraints for the Staff *Manages* Branch (1:1) relationship shown in Figure 7.7(b).

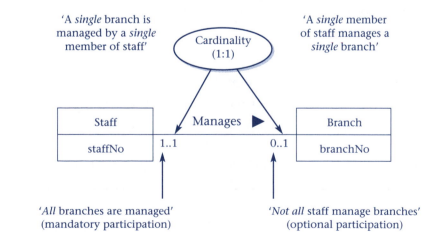

'A *single* branch is managed by a *single* member of staff'

Cardinality (1:1)

'A *single* member of staff manages a *single* branch'

Staff — staffNo

Manages ▶

Branch — branchNo

1..1   0..1

'*All* branches are managed' (mandatory participation)

'*Not all* staff manage branches' (optional participation)

the Actor and Video entities. We may wish to record the character played by an actor in a given video. This information is associated with the *PlaysIn* relationship rather than the Actor or Video entities. We create an attribute called character to store this information and assign it to the *PlaysIn* relationship, as illustrated in Figure 7.12. Note that in this figure the character attribute is shown using the symbol for an entity; however, to distinguish between a relationship with an attribute and an entity, the rectangle representing the attribute is associated with the relationship using a dashed line.

The presence of one or more attributes assigned to a relationship may indicate that the relationship conceals an unidentified entity. For example, the character attribute associated with an entity called Role was shown earlier in Figure 7.6.

7.7 Design problems with ER models

In this section, we examine two types of problems that may arise when designing an ER model. These problems are collectively referred to as *connection traps*, and normally occur due to a misinterpretation of the meaning of certain relationships. We examine the two main types of connection traps, called fan traps and chasm traps, and illustrate how to identify and resolve such problems in ER models.

In general, to identify connection traps we must ensure that the meaning of a relationship (and the business rule that it represents) is fully understood and clearly defined. If we don't understand the relationships we may create a model that is not a true representation of the 'real world'.

7.7.1 Fan traps

> **Fan trap**
>
> Two entities have a 1:* relationship that fan out from a third entity, but the two entities should have a direct relationship between them to provide the necessary information.

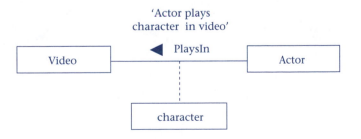

'Actor plays character in video'

Figure 7.12

A relationship called *PlaysIn* with an attribute called character.

A **fan trap** may exist where two or more one-to-many (1:*) relationships fan out from the same entity. A potential fan trap is illustrated in Figure 7.13(a), which shows two 1:* relationships (*Has* and *IsAssigned*) emanating from the same entity called Branch. This model tells us that a single branch has many staff and is assigned many cars. However, a problem arises if we want to know which member of staff uses a particular car. To appreciate the problem, let's examine some examples of the *Has* and *IsAssigned* relationships, using values for the primary key attributes of the Staff, Branch, and Car entities, as shown in Figure 7.13(b).

If we attempt to answer the question: 'Which member of staff uses car SH34?', it's impossible to give a specific answer with the current structure. We can determine that car SH34 is assigned to branch B001 but we cannot tell whether staff S0003 or S1500 uses this car. The inability to answer this question specifically is the result of a fan trap.

We resolve this fan trap by adding a new relationship called Staff *Uses* Car to the original ER model, as shown in Figure. 7.13(c). If we now examine the examples of the *Has*, *IsAssigned*, and *Uses* relationships shown in Figure 7.13(d), we can see that staff S1500 uses car SH34.

Figure 7.13(a)

Example of a fan trap.

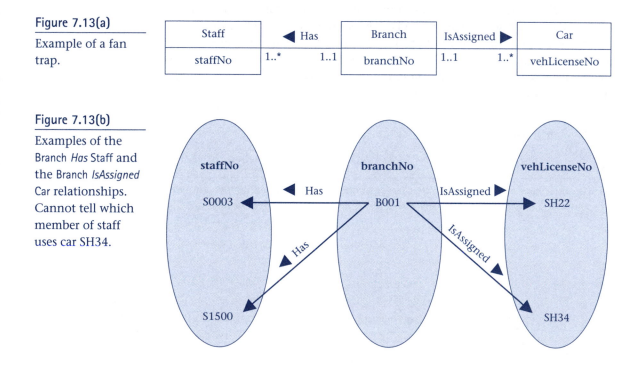

Figure 7.13(b)

Examples of the Branch *Has* Staff and the Branch *IsAssigned* Car relationships. Cannot tell which member of staff uses car SH34.

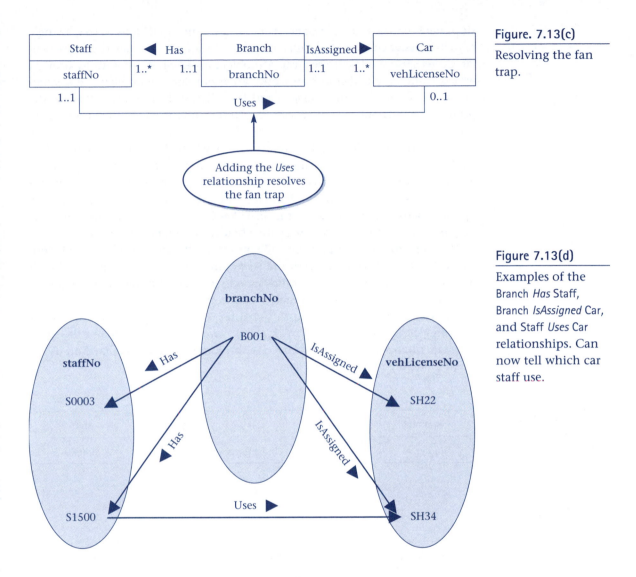

Figure. 7.13(c)

Resolving the fan trap.

Figure 7.13(d)

Examples of the Branch *Has* Staff, Branch *IsAssigned* Car, and Staff *Uses* Car relationships. Can now tell which car staff use.

7.7.2 Chasm traps

Chasm trap

A model suggests the existence of a relationship between entities, but the pathway does not exist between certain entity occurrences.

A **chasm trap** may occur where there is a relationship with optional participation that forms part of the pathway between entities that are related. A potential chasm trap is illustrated in Figure 7.14(a), which shows the relationships between the Branch, Car, and Staff entities. This model tells us that a single branch is assigned many cars and a member of staff may use one car. In particular, note that not all staff use a car. A problem arises when we want to know at which branch a member of staff works. To appreciate the problem, let's examine some examples of the *IsAssigned* and *Uses* relationships, using values for the primary key attributes of the Branch, Car, and Staff entities, as shown in Figure 7.14(b).

If we attempt to answer the question: 'At which branch does staff S0003 work?', we can't tell with the current structure as not all staff use cars. The inability to answer this question is considered to be a loss of information (as we know a member of staff must work at a branch), and is the result of a chasm trap. The optional participation of Staff in the Staff *Uses* Car relationship means that some members of staff are not associated with a branch through the use of cars.

Therefore, to solve this problem and remove the chasm trap, we add a relationship called *Has* between the Branch and Staff entities, as shown in Figure 7.14(c). If we now examine the examples of the *Has*, *IsAssigned*, and *Uses* relationships shown in Figure 7.14(d), we can see that staff S0003 works at branch B001.

The ER concepts described in this chapter sometimes prove inadequate for modeling complex databases. In Chapter 11, we'll introduce some of the more popular enhanced concepts associated with ER models that you may find useful when modeling more complex data.

Figure 7.14(a)

Example of a chasm trap.

Branch	IsAssigned ▶	Car	◀ Uses	Staff
branchNo	1..1 1..*	vehLicenseNo	0..1 1..1	staffNo

Figure 7.14(b)

Examples of the Branch *IsAssigned* Car and Staff *Uses* Car relationships. Cannot tell which branch staff S0003 works at.

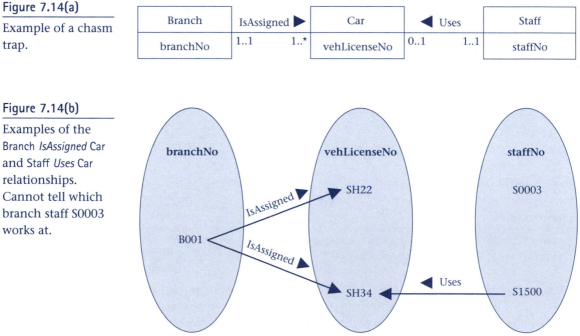

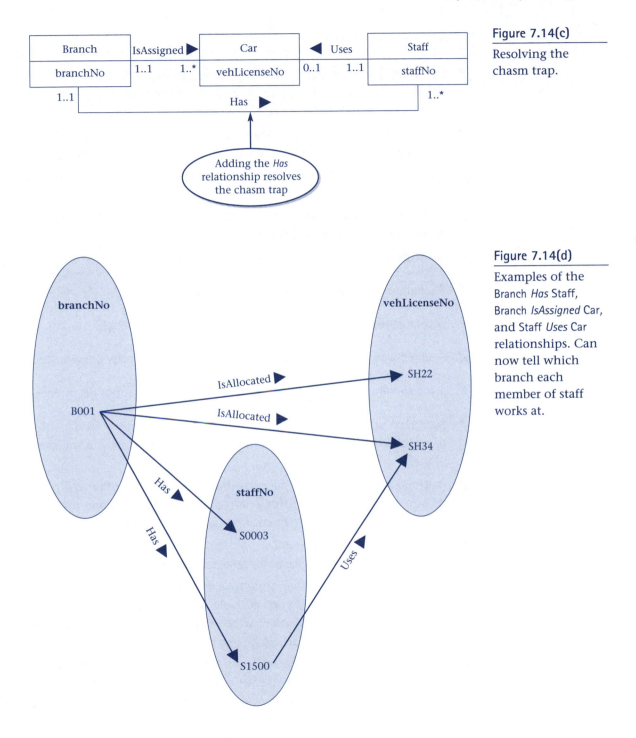

Figure 7.14(c)

Resolving the chasm trap.

Figure 7.14(d)

Examples of the Branch *Has* Staff, Branch *IsAssigned* Car, and Staff *Uses* Car relationships. Can now tell which branch each member of staff works at.

Chapter summary

✔ An **entity** is a set of objects with the same properties that are identified by a user or organization as having an independent existence. A uniquely identifiable object is called an **entity occurrence**.

✔ A **relationship** is a set of meaningful associations among entities. A uniquely identifiable association is called a **relationship occurrence**.

✔ The **degree** of a relationship is the number of participating entities in a relationship.

✔ A **recursive relationship** is a relationship where the *same* entity participates more than once in *different* roles.

✔ An **attribute** is a property of an entity or a relationship.

✔ A **simple attribute** is composed of a single component.

✔ A **composite attribute** is composed of multiple components.

✔ A **single-valued attribute** holds a single value for an entity occurrence.

✔ A **multi-valued attribute** holds multiple values for an entity occurrence.

✔ A **derived attribute** represents a value that is derivable from the value of a related attribute, or a set of attributes, not necessarily in the same entity.

✔ A **strong entity** is *not* dependent on the existence of another entity for its primary key. A **weak entity** is partially or wholly dependent on the existence of another entity, or entities, for its primary key.

✔ **Multiplicity** defines the number of occurrences of one entity that may relate to a single occurrence of an associated entity.

✔ Multiplicity consists of two separate constraints; namely **cardinality**, which describes the number of possible relationships for each participating entity, and **participation**, which determines whether all or only some entity occurrences participate in a relationship.

✔ A **fan trap** occurs when two entities have 1:* relationships that fan out from a third entity, but the two entities should have a direct relationship between them to provide the necessary information.

✔ A **chasm trap** suggests the existence of a relationship between entities, but the pathway does not exist between certain entity occurrences.

Review questions

7.1 Describe what entities represent in an ER model and provide examples of entities with a physical or conceptual existence.

7.2 Describe what relationships represent in an ER model and provide examples of unary, binary, and ternary relationships.

7.3 Describe what attributes represent in an ER model and provide examples of simple, composite, single-value, multi-value, and derived attributes.

7.4 Describe what multiplicity represents for a relationship.

7.5 What are business rules and how does multiplicity model these constraints?

7.6 How does multiplicity represent both the cardinality and the participation constraints on a relationship?

7.7 Provide an example of a relationship with attributes.

7.8 Describe how strong and weak entities differ and provide an example of each.

7.9 Describe how fan and chasm traps can occur in an ER model and how they can be resolved.

Exercises

7.10 Create an ER diagram for each of the following descriptions:

(a) Each company operates four departments, and each department belongs to one company.

(b) Each department in part (a) employs one or more employees, and each employee works for one department.

(c) Each of the employees in part (b) may or may not have one or more dependants, and each dependant belongs to one employee.

(d) Each employee in part (c) may or may not have an employment history.

(e) Represent all the ER diagrams described in (a), (b), (c), and (d) as a single ER diagram.

7.11 Create an ER diagram to represent the data requirements for a company that specializes in IT training. The company has 30 instructors and can handle up to 100 trainees per training session. The company offers five advanced technology courses, each of which is taught by a teaching team of two or more instructors. Each instructor is assigned to a maximum of two teaching teams or may be assigned to do research. Each trainee undertakes one advanced technology course per training session.

(a) Identify the main entities for the company.

(b) Identify the main relationships and specify the multiplicity for each relationship. State any assumptions you make about the data.

(c) Using your answers for (a) and (b), draw a single ER diagram to represent the data requirements for the company.

7.12 Read the following case study which describes the data requirements for the *EasyDrive School of Motoring*.

The *EasyDrive School of Motoring* was established in Glasgow in 1992. Since then, the School has grown steadily and now has several offices in most of the main cities of Scotland. Each office has a Manager (who tends also to be a Senior Instructor), several Senior Instructors, Instructors, and administrative staff. The Manager is responsible for the day-to-day running of the office. Clients must first register at an office and this requires that they complete an application form, which records their personal details. A client may request individual lessons or book a block of lessons. An individual lesson is for one hour, which begins and ends at the office. A lesson is with a particular Instructor in a particular car at a given time. Lessons can start as early as 8am and as late as 8pm. After each lesson, the Instructor records the progress made by the client and notes the mileage used during the lesson. The School has a pool of cars, which are adapted for the purposes of teaching. Each Instructor is allocated to a particular car. Once ready, a client applies for a driving test date. To obtain a full driving license the client must pass both the practical and theoretical parts of the test. If a client fails to pass, the Instructor must record the reasons for the failure.

(a) Identify the main entities of the *EasyDrive School of Motoring*.
(b) Identify the main relationships between the entities described in (a) and represent each relationship as an ER diagram.
(c) Determine the multiplicity constraints for each relationship described in (b). Represent the multiplicity for each relationship in the ER diagrams created in (b).
(d) Identify attributes and associate them with an entity or relationship. Represent each attribute in the ER diagrams created in (c).
(e) Determine candidate and primary key attributes for each (strong) entity.
(f) Using your answers (a) to (e), attempt to represent the data requirements of the *EasyDrive School of Motoring* as a single ER diagram. State any assumptions necessary to support your design.

Chapter 8

Normalization

In this chapter you will learn:

How tables that contain redundant data can suffer from update anomalies, which can introduce inconsistencies into a database. ◀

The rules associated with the most commonly used normal forms, namely first (1NF), second (2NF), and third (3NF) normal forms. ◀

How tables that break the rules of 1NF, 2NF, or 3NF are likely to contain redundant data and suffer from update anomalies. ◀

How to restructure tables that break the rules of 1NF, 2NF, or 3NF. ◀

In the previous chapter, we learned about Entity–Relationship (ER) modeling, a commonly used top-down approach to database design. In this chapter, we consider another commonly used approach to database design called normalization. Normalization can be used in database design in two ways: the first is to use normalization as a bottom-up approach to database design; the second is to use normalization in conjunction with ER modeling.

Using normalization as a **bottom-up approach** involves analyzing the associations between attributes and, based on this analysis, grouping the attributes together to form tables that represent entities and relationships. However, this approach becomes difficult with a large number of attributes, where it's difficult to establish all the important associations between the attributes. For this reason, in this book we present a methodology that recommends that you should first attempt to understand the data using a **top-down approach** to database design. In this approach, we use ER modeling to create a data model that represents the main entities and relationships. We then translate the ER model into a set of tables that represents the data. It's at this point that we use normalization to check whether the tables are well designed.

Normalization used in Step 2.2

The purpose of this chapter is to examine why normalization is a useful technique in database design and, in particular, how normalization can be used to check the structure of tables created from an ER model.

8.1 Introduction

> **Normalization**
>
> A technique for producing a set of tables with desirable properties that support the requirements of a user or company.

Relational model discussed in Chapter 2

In 1972, Dr E.F. Codd developed the technique of **normalization** to support the design of databases based on the *relational model*. Normalization is often performed as a series of tests on a table to determine whether it satisfies or violates the rules for a given **normal form**. There are several normal forms, although the most commonly used ones are called first normal form (1NF), second normal form (2NF), and third normal form (3NF). All these normal forms are based on rules about relationships among the columns of a table.

In the following sections, we first demonstrate how badly structured tables that contain redundant data can potentially suffer from problems called *update anomalies*. Badly structured tables may occur due to errors in the original ER model or in the process of translating the ER model into tables. We then present a definition for first normal form (1NF), second normal form (2NF), and third normal form (3NF), and demonstrate how each normal form can be used to identify and correct different types of problems in our tables.

8.2 Data redundancy and update anomalies

Base tables defined in Section 2.3.2

A major aim of relational database design is to group columns into tables to minimize data redundancy and reduce the file storage space required by the implemented base tables. To illustrate the problems associated with data redundancy, let's compare the Staff and Branch tables shown in Figure 8.1 with the StaffBranch table shown in Figure 8.2.

DBDL discussed in Chapter 10

The StaffBranch table is an alternative form of the Staff and Branch tables. The structure of these tables is described using a Database Definition Language (DBDL):

Staff (staffNo, name, position, salary, branchNo)
Primary Key staffNo
Foreign Key branchNo references Branch(branchNo)

Branch (branchNo, branchAddress, telNo)
Primary Key branchNo

Primary and foreign keys defined in Section 2.2.3

StaffBranch (staffNo, name, position, salary, branchNo, branchAddress, telNo)
Primary Key staffNo

Staff

staffNo	name	position	salary	branchNo
S1500	Tom Daniels	Manager	46000	B001
S0003	Sally Adams	Assistant	30000	B001
S0010	Mary Martinez	Manager	50000	B002
S3250	Robert Chin	Supervisor	32000	B002
S2250	Sally Stern	Manager	48000	B004
S0415	Art Peters	Manager	41000	B003

Branch

branchNo	branchAddress	telNo
B001	8 Jefferson Way, Portland, OR 97201	503-555-3618
B002	City Center Plaza, Seattle, WA 98122	206-555-6756
B003	14 – 8th Avenue, New York, NY 10012	212-371-3000
B004	16 – 14th Avenue, Seattle, WA 98128	206-555-3131

Figure 8.1

The Staff and Branch tables.

Figure 8.2

The StaffBranch table.

staffNo	name	position	salary	branchNo	branchAddress	telNo
S1500	Tom Daniels	Manager	46000	B001	8 Jefferson Way, Portland, OR 97201	503-555-3618
S0003	Sally Adams	Assistant	30000	B001	8 Jefferson Way, Portland, OR 97201	503-555-3618
S0010	Mary Martinez	Manager	50000	B002	City Center Plaza, Seattle, WA 98122	206-555-6756
S3250	Robert Chin	Supervisor	32000	B002	City Center Plaza, Seattle, WA 98122	206-555-6756
S2250	Sally Stern	Manager	48000	B004	16 – 14th Avenue, Seattle, WA 98128	206-555-3131
S0415	Art Peters	Manager	41000	B003	14 – 8th Avenue, New York, NY 10012	212-371-3000

In the StaffBranch table there is **redundant data**: the details of a branch are repeated for every member of staff located at that branch. In contrast, the details of each branch appear only once in the Branch table and only the branch number (branchNo) is repeated in the Staff table, to represent where each member of staff is located. Tables that have redundant data may have problems called **update anomalies**, which are classified as insertion, deletion, or modification anomalies.

8.2.1   Insertion anomalies

There are two main types of insertion anomalies, which we illustrate using the StaffBranch table shown in Figure 8.2.

(1) To insert the details of a new member of staff located at a given branch into the StaffBranch table, we must also enter the correct details for that branch. For example, to insert the details of a new member of staff at branch B002, we must enter the correct details of branch B002 so that the branch details are consistent with values for branch B002 in other records of the StaffBranch table. The tables shown in Figure 8.1 do not suffer from this potential inconsistency, because for each staff member we only enter the appropriate branch number into the Staff table. In addition, the details of branch B002 are recorded only once in the database as a single record in the Branch table.

(2) To insert details of a new branch that currently has no members of staff into the StaffBranch table, it's necessary to enter nulls into the staff-related columns, such as staffNo. However, as staffNo is the primary key for the StaffBranch table, attempting to enter nulls for staffNo violates entity integrity, and is not allowed. The design of the tables shown in Figure 8.1 avoids this problem because new branch details are entered into the Branch table separately from the staff details. The details of staff ultimately located at a new branch can be entered into the Staff table at a later date.

Entity integrity defined in Section 2.3.2

8.2.2   Deletion anomalies

If we delete a record from the StaffBranch table that represents the last member of staff located at a branch, the details about that branch are also lost from the database. For example, if we delete the record for staff Art Peters (S0415) from the StaffBranch table, the details relating to branch B003 are lost from the database. The design of the tables in Figure 8.1 avoids this problem because branch records are stored separately from staff records and only the column branchNo relates the two tables. If we delete the record for staff Art Peters (S0415) from the Staff table, the details on branch B003 in the Branch table remain unaffected.

8.2.3   Modification anomalies

If we want to change the value of one of the columns of a particular branch in the StaffBranch table, for example the telephone number for branch B001, we must update the records of all staff located at that branch. If this modification is not carried out on all the appropriate records of the StaffBranch table, the database will become inconsistent. In this example, branch B001 would have different telephone numbers in different staff records.

   The above examples illustrate that the Staff and Branch tables of Figure 8.1 have more desirable properties than the StaffBranch table of Figure 8.2. In the following sections, we examine how normal forms can be used to formalize the identification of tables that have desirable properties from those that may potentially suffer from update anomalies.

8.3 First normal form (1NF)

Only first normal form (1NF) is critical in creating appropriate tables for relational databases. All the subsequent normal forms are optional. However, to avoid the update anomalies discussed in Section 8.2, it's normally recommended that you proceed to third normal form (3NF).

First normal form (1NF)

A table in which the intersection of every column and record contains only *one* value.

Let's examine the Branch table shown in Figure 8.3, with primary key branchNo. We can see that all the columns of this version of the Branch table comply with our definition of 1NF with the exception of the column telNos. There are multiple values at the intersection of the telNos column with every record. For example, branchNo B001 has three telephone numbers, 503-555-3618, 503-555-2727, and 503-555-6534. As a result, the Branch table is not in 1NF.

Note that although the branchAddress column may appear to hold multiple values, this representation of address does not break 1NF. In this example, we have simply chosen the option to hold all the details of an address as a single value.

Figure 8.3

This version of the Branch table is not in 1NF.

branchNo	branchAddress	telNos
B001	8 Jefferson Way, Portland, OR 97201	503-555-3618, 503-555-2727, 503-555-6534
B002	City Center Plaza, Seattle, WA 98122	206-555-6756, 206-555-8836
B003	14 – 8th Avenue, New York, NY 10012	212-371-3000
B004	16 – 14th Ayenue, Seattle, WA 98128	206-555-3131, 206-555-4112

Primary key

More than one value, so *not* in 1NF

Converting to 1NF

To convert this version of the Branch table to 1NF, we create a separate table called BranchTelephone to hold the telephone numbers of branches, by removing the telNos column from the Branch table along with a copy of the primary key of the Branch table (branchNo). The primary key for the new BranchTelephone table is the new telNo column. The structures for the altered Branch table and the new BranchTelephone table are shown in Figure 8.4. The Branch and BranchTelephone tables are in 1NF as there is a single value at the intersection of every column with every record for each table.

Figure 8.4

Altered Branch table is in 1NF due to the removal of the telNos column and the creation of a new table called BranchTelephone.

Branch (Not 1NF)

branchNo	branchAddress	telNos
B001	8 Jefferson Way, Portland, OR 97201	503-555-3618, 503-555-2727, 503-555-6534
B002	City Center Plaza, Seattle, WA 98122	206-555-6756, 206-555-8836
B003	14 – 8th Avenue, New York, NY 10012	212-371-3000
B004	16 – 14th Avenue, Seattle, WA 98128	206-555-3131, 206-555-4112

Take copy of branchNo column to new table to become foreign key

Remove telNos column and create new column called telNo in the new table

Branch (1NF)

branchNo	branchAddress
B001	8 Jefferson Way, Portland, OR 97201
B002	City Center Plaza, Seattle, WA 98122
B003	14 – 8th Avenue, New York, NY 10012
B004	16 – 14th Avenue, Seattle, WA 98128

Primary key

BranchTelephone (1NF)

branchNo	telNo
B001	503-555-3618
B001	503-555-2727
B001	503-555-6534
B002	206-555-6756
B002	206-555-8836
B003	212-371-3000
B004	206-555-3131
B004	206-555-4112

Becomes foreign key

Becomes primary key

8.4   Second normal form (2NF)

Second normal form applies only to tables with composite primary keys, that is tables with a primary key composed of two or more columns. A 1NF table with a single column primary key is automatically in at least 2NF. A table that is not in 2NF may suffer from the update anomalies discussed in Section 8.2.

Second normal form (2NF)

A table that is already in 1NF and in which the values in each non-primary-key column can be worked out from the values in *all* the columns that make up the primary key.

Let's examine the TempStaffAllocation table shown in Figure 8.5. This table represents the hours worked per week for temporary staff at each branch. The primary key for the TempStaffAllocation table is made up of both the staffNo and branchNo columns. Note that we use the term 'non-primary-key' columns to refer to those columns that are not part of the primary key. For example, the non-primary-key columns for the TempStaffAllocation table are branchAddress, name, position, and hoursPerWeek. The arrows shown below the TempStaffAllocation table indicate particular relationships between the primary key columns and the non-primary-key columns.

The particular relationships that we show between the columns of the TempStaffAllocation table in Figure 8.5 are more formally referred to as **functional dependencies**. Functional dependency is a property of the meaning of the columns in a table and indicates how columns relate to one another.

For example, consider a table with columns A and B, where column B is functionally dependent on column A (denoted A → B). If we know the value of A, we find only *one* value of B in all the records that has this value for A, at any moment in time. So, when two records have the same value of A, they also have the same value of B. However, for a given value of B there may be several different values of A.

We can see that the TempStaffAllocation table contains redundant data and may suffer from the update anomalies described in Section 8.2. For example, to change the name of 'Ellen Layman', we have to update two records in the TempStaffAllocation table. If only one record is updated, the database will be inconsistent. The reason that the TempStaffAllocation table contains redundant data is that this table does not comply with our definition for 2NF.

Figure 8.5

TempStaffAllocation table is not in 2NF.

staffNo	branchNo	branchAddress	name	position	hoursPerWeek
S4555	B002	City Center Plaza, Seattle, WA 98122	Ellen Layman	Assistant	16
S4555	B004	16 – 14th Avenue, Seattle, WA 98128	Ellen Layman	Assistant	9
S4612	B002	City Center Plaza, Seattle, WA 98122	Dave Sinclair	Assistant	14
S4612	B004	16 – 14th Avenue, Seattle, WA 98128	Dave Sinclair	Assistant	10

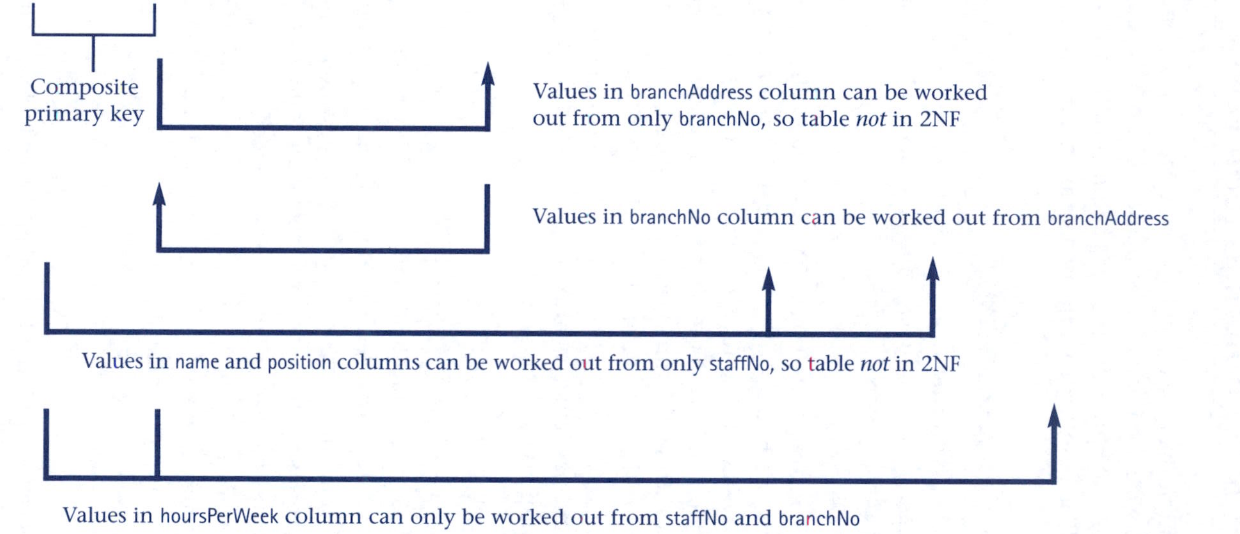

Composite primary key

Values in branchAddress column can be worked out from only branchNo, so table *not* in 2NF

Values in branchNo column can be worked out from branchAddress

Values in name and position columns can be worked out from only staffNo, so table *not* in 2NF

Values in hoursPerWeek column can only be worked out from staffNo and branchNo

Consider the non-primary-key column branchAddress of the TempStaffAllocation table. The values in the branchAddress column can be worked out from the values in the branchNo column (part of the primary key). In other words, every unique value in the branchNo column is associated with the same value in the branchAddress column. For example, every time the value B002 appears in the branchNo column, the same address 'City Center Plaza, Seattle, WA 98122' appears in the branchAddress column. In this example, the reverse is also true. Every time the value 'City Center Plaza, Seattle, WA 98122' appears in the branchAddress column, the same branch number B002 appears in the branchNo column.

Now consider the non-primary-key columns name and position. The values in the name and position columns can be worked out from the values in the staffNo column (part of the primary key). For example, every time S4555 appears in the staffNo column, the name 'Ellen Layman' and position 'Assistant' appear in the name and position columns.

Finally, consider the non-primary-key column hoursPerWeek. The values in the hoursPerWeek column can only be worked out from the values in both the staffNo and branchNo columns (the whole primary key). For example, when S4555 appears in the staffNo column at the same time that B002 appears in the branchNo column, then the value '16' appears in the hoursPerWeek column.

> The formal definition of **second normal form (2NF)** is a table that is in first normal form and every non-primary-key column is **fully functionally dependent** on the primary key. Full functional dependency indicates that if A and B are columns of a table, B is fully functionally dependent on A, if B is not dependent on any subset of A. If B is dependent on a subset of A, this is referred to as a **partial dependency**. If a partial dependency exists on the primary key, the table is not in 2NF. The partial dependency must be removed for a table to achieve 2NF.

Converting to 2NF

To convert the TempStaffAllocation table shown in Figure 8.5 to 2NF, we need to remove the non-primary-key columns that can be worked out using only part of the primary key. In other words, we need to remove the columns that can be worked out from either the staffNo or the branchNo column but do not require both. For the TempStaffAllocation table, this means that we must remove the branchAddress, name, and position columns and place them in new tables.

To do this we create two new tables called Branch and TempStaff. The Branch table will hold the columns describing the details of branches and the TempStaff table will hold the columns describing the details of temporary staff.

(1) The Branch table is created by removing the branchAddress column from the TempStaffAllocation table along with a copy of the part of the primary key that the column is related to, which in this case is the branchNo column.

(2) In a similar way, the TempStaff table is created by removing the name and position columns from the TempStaffAllocation table along with a copy of the part of the primary key that the columns are related to, which in this case is the staffNo column.

It's not necessary to remove the hoursPerWeek column as the presence of this column in the TempStaffAllocation table does not break the rules of 2NF.

To ensure that we maintain the relationship between a temporary member of staff and the branches at which he or she works for a set number of hours, we leave a copy of the staffNo and branchNo columns to act as foreign keys in the TempStaffAllocation table.

The structure for the altered TempStaffAllocation table and the new Branch and TempStaff tables are shown in Figure 8.6. The primary key for the new Branch table is branchNo and the primary key for the new TempStaff table is staffNo.

The TempStaff and Branch tables must be in 2NF because the primary key for each table is a single column. The altered TempStaffAllocation table is also in 2NF because the non-primary-key column hoursPerWeek is related to both the staffNo and branchNo columns.

8.5 Third normal form (3NF)

Although 2NF tables have less redundancy than tables in 1NF, they may still suffer from update anomalies.

> **Third normal form (3NF)**
>
> A table that is already in 1NF and 2NF, and in which the values in all non-primary-key columns can be worked out from *only* the primary key column(s) and no other columns.

Let's examine the StaffBranch table shown in Figure 8.2, with primary key staffNo. In Figure 8.7, we indicate the particular relationships between the columns in this table. We can see that the StaffBranch table contains redundant data and may suffer from the update anomalies described in Section 8.2. For example, to change the telephone number of branch B001, we have to update two records in the StaffBranch table. If only one record is updated, the database will be inconsistent. The reason that the StaffBranch table contains redundant data is that this table does not comply with our definition for 3NF.

Figure 8.6

Altered TempStaffAllocation table is in 2NF due to the removal of the branchAddress, name, and position columns and the creation of the new Branch and TempStaff tables.

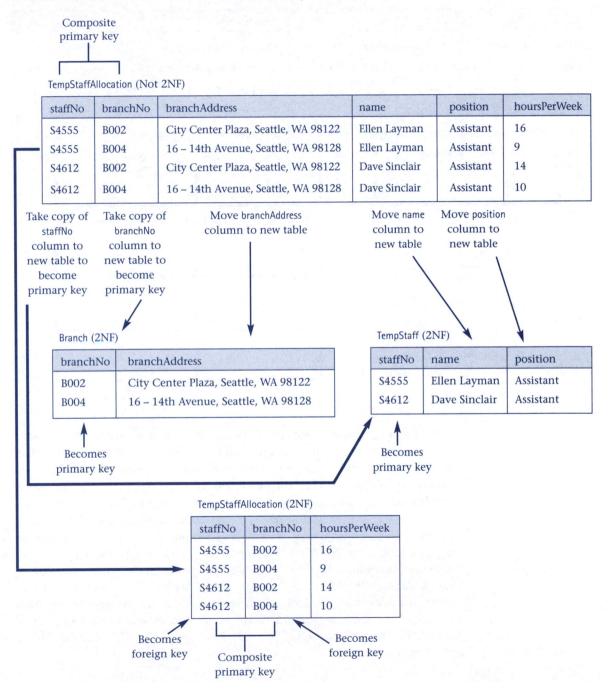

Figure 8.7

The StaffBranch table is not in 3NF.

StaffBranch (Not 3NF)

staffNo	name	position	salary	branchNo	branchAddress	telNo
S1500	Tom Daniels	Manager	46000	B001	8 Jefferson Way, Portland, OR 97201	503-555-3618
S0003	Sally Adams	Assistant	30000	B001	8 Jefferson Way, Portland, OR 97201	503-555-3618
S0010	Mary Martinez	Manager	50000	B002	City Center Plaza, Seattle, WA 98122	206-555-6756
S3250	Robert Chin	Supervisor	32000	B002	City Center Plaza, Seattle, WA 98122	206-555-6756
S2250	Sally Stern	Manager	48000	B004	16 – 14th Avenue, Seattle, WA 98128	206-555-3131
S0415	Art Peters	Manager	41000	B003	14 – 8th Avenue, New York, NY 10012	212-371-3000

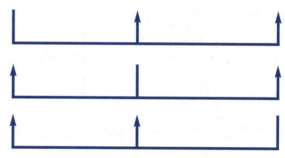

Primary key

Values in all non-primary-key columns can be worked out from the primary key, staffNo

Values in branchAddress and telNo columns can be worked out from branchNo, so table *not* in 3NF

Values in branchNo and telNo columns can be worked out from branchAddress, so table *not* in 3NF

Values in branchNo and branchAddress columns can be worked out from telNo, so table *not* in 3NF

The StaffBranch table is not in 3NF because of the presence of the branchNo, branchAddress, and telNo columns. Although we can work out the branch number, branch address, and telephone number of a member of staff from the primary key, staffNo, we can also work out the details for a given branch, if we know the branch number, branch address, or branch telephone number. In other words, we can work out information using values from non-primary-key columns, namely branchNo, branchAddress, or telNo. For example, when S1500 appears in the staffNo column, '8 Jefferson Way, Portland, OR 97201' appears in the branchAddress column. However, when B001 appears in branchNo, '8 Jefferson Way, Portland, OR 97201' also appears in the branchAddress column. In other words, the address that a member of staff works at can be worked out from knowing the value in branchNo. This is not allowed in 3NF as the values in all non-primary-key columns must be worked out from only the values in the primary key column(s).

The formal definition for **third normal form (3NF)** is a table that is in first and second normal forms and in which no non-primary-key column is **transitively dependent** on the primary key. Transitive dependency is a type of functional dependency that occurs when a particular type of relationship holds between columns of a table.

For example, consider a table with columns A, B, and C. If B is functionally dependent on A (A → B) and C is functionally dependent on B (B → C), then C is transitively dependent on A via B (provided that A is not functionally dependent on B or C). If a transitive dependency exists on the primary key, the table is not in 3NF. The transitive dependency must be removed for a table to achieve 3NF.

Converting to 3NF

To convert the StaffBranch table shown in Figure 8.7 to 3NF, we need to remove the non-primary-key columns that can be worked out using another non-primary-key column. In other words, we need to remove the columns that describe the branch at which the member of staff works. We remove the branchAddress and telNo columns and take a copy of the branchNo column. We create a new table called Branch to hold these columns and nominate branchNo as the primary key for this table. The branchAddress and telNo columns are candidate keys in the Branch table as these columns can be used to uniquely identify a given branch. The relationship between a member of staff and the branch at which he or she works is maintained as the copy of the branchNo column in the StaffBranch table acts as a foreign key.

The structure for the altered StaffBranch table and the new Branch tables are shown in Figure 8.8. The altered StaffBranch table is in 3NF because each non-primary-key column can only be worked out from the primary key, staffNo.

The new Branch table is also in 3NF as all of the non-primary-key columns can be worked out from the primary key, branchNo. Although the other two non-primary-key columns in this table, branchAddress and telNo, can also be used to work out the details of a given branch, this does not violate 3NF because these columns are candidate keys for the Branch table. This example illustrates that the definition for 3NF can be generalized to include all candidate keys of a table, if any exist.

Therefore, for tables with more than one candidate key you can use the generalized definition for 3NF, which is a table that is in 1NF and 2NF, and in which the values in all the non-primary-key columns can be worked out from only *candidate key* column(s) and no other columns. Furthermore, this generalization is also true for the definition of 2NF, which is a table that is in 1NF and in which the values in each non-primary-key column can be worked out from

Figure 8.8

The StaffBranch table is in 3NF due to the removal of the branchAddress and telNo columns and the creation of a new table called Branch.

StaffBranch (Not 3NF)

staffNo	name	position	salary	branchNo	branchAddress	telNo
S1500	Tom Daniels	Manager	46000	B001	8 Jefferson Way, Portland, OR 97201	503-555-3618
S0003	Sally Adams	Assistant	30000	B001	8 Jefferson Way, Portland, OR 97201	503-555-3618
S0010	Mary Martinez	Manager	50000	B002	City Center Plaza, Seattle, WA 98122	206-555-6756
S3250	Robert Chin	Supervisor	32000	B002	City Center Plaza, Seattle, WA 98122	206-555-6756
S2250	Sally Stern	Manager	48000	B004	16 – 14th Avenue, Seattle, WA 98128	206-555-3131
S0415	Art Peters	Manager	41000	B003	14 – 8th Avenue, New York, NY 10012	212-371-3000

Take copy of branchNo column to new table to become primary key

Move branchAddress column to new table

Move telNo column to new table

Branch (3NF)

branchNo	branchAddress	telNo
B001	8 Jefferson Way, Portland, OR 97201	503-555-3618
B002	City Center Plaza, Seattle, WA 98122	206-555-6756
B003	14 – 8th Avenue, New York, NY 10012	212-371-3000
B004	16 – 14th Avenue, Seattle, WA 98128	206-555-3131

Becomes primary key

Becomes candidate key

Becomes candidate key

Staff (3NF)

staffNo	name	position	salary	branchNo
S1500	Tom Daniels	Manager	46000	B001
S0003	Sally Adams	Assistant	30000	B001
S0010	Mary Martinez	Manager	50000	B002
S3250	Robert Chin	Supervisor	32000	B002
S2250	Sally Stern	Manager	48000	B004
S0415	Art Peters	Manager	41000	B003

Primary key

Becomes foreign key

all the columns that make up a *candidate key* and no other columns. Note that this generalization does not alter the definition for 1NF as this normal form is independent of keys and particular relationships between columns of a table.

The trade-off is whether it is better to keep the process of normalization simpler by examining the relationships between the non-primary-key columns and those that make up the primary keys, which allows the identification of the most problematic and obvious redundancy in tables, or to use the general definitions and increase the opportunity to identify missed redundancy. In fact, it is often the case that whether you use the definitions based on primary keys or the general definitions of 2NF and 3NF, the decomposition of tables is the same.

There are normal forms that go beyond 3NF such as Boyce–Codd normal form (BCNF), fourth normal form (4NF), and fifth normal form (5NF). However, these later normal forms are not commonly used as they attempt to identify and solve problems in tables that occur relatively infrequently. However, if you would like to find out more about BCNF, 4NF, and 5NF you should consult the book *Database Systems* by Connolly and Begg (2002).

Chapter summary

✓ **Normalization** is a technique for producing a set of tables with desirable properties that supports the requirements of a user or company.

✓ Tables that have redundant data may have problems called **update anomalies**, which are classified as insertion, deletion, or modification anomalies.

✓ The definition for **first normal form (1NF)** is a table in which the intersection of every column and record contains only *one* value.

✓ The definition for **second normal form (2NF)** is a table that is already in 1NF and in which the values in each non-primary-key column can be worked out from the values in *all* the column(s) that make up the primary key.

✓ The definition for **third normal form (3NF)** is a table that is already in 1NF and 2NF, and in which the values in all non-primary-key columns can be worked out from *only* the primary key column(s) and no other columns.

Review questions

8.1 Discuss how normalization may be used in database design.

8.2 Describe the types of update anomalies that may occur on a table that has redundant data.

8.3 Describe the characteristics of a table that violates first normal form (1NF) and then describe how such a table is converted to 1NF.

8.4 What is the minimal normal form that a table must satisfy? Provide a definition for this normal form.

8.5 Describe an approach to converting a first normal form (1NF) table to second normal form (2NF) table(s).

8.6 Describe the characteristics of a table in second normal form (2NF).

8.7 Describe what is meant by full functional dependency and describe how this type of dependency relates to 2NF. Provide an example to illustrate your answer.

8.8 Describe the characteristics of a table in third normal form (3NF).

8.9 Describe what is meant by transitive dependency and describe how this type of dependency relates to 3NF. Provide an example to illustrate your answer.

Exercises

8.10 The table shown in Figure 8.9 lists dentist/patient appointment data. A patient is given an appointment at a specific time and date with a dentist located at a particular surgery.

(a) The table shown in Figure 8.9 is susceptible to update anomalies. Provide examples of insertion, deletion, and modification anomalies.

(b) Describe and illustrate the process of normalizing the table shown in Figure 8.9 to 3NF. State any assumptions you make about the data shown in this table.

Figure 8.9

Details of patient dental appointments.

staffNo	dentistName	patientNo	patientName	appointment date	time	surgeryNo
S1011	Tony Smith	P100	Gillian White	12-Aug-03	10.00	S10
S1011	Tony Smith	P105	Jill Bell	13-Aug-03	12.00	S15
S1024	Helen Pearson	P108	Ian MacKay	12-Sept-03	10.00	S10
S1024	Helen Pearson	P108	Ian MacKay	14-Sept-03	10.00	S10
S1032	Robin Plevin	P105	Jill Bell	14-Oct-03	16.30	S15
S1032	Robin Plevin	P110	John Walker	15-Oct-03	18.00	S13

8.11 An agency called *InstantCover* supplies part-time/temporary staff to hotels throughout Scotland. The table shown in Figure 8.10 lists the time spent by agency staff working at two hotels. The National Insurance Number (NIN) is unique for every employee.

(a) The table shown in Figure 8.10 is susceptible to update anomalies. Provide examples of insertion, deletion, and modification anomalies.

(b) Describe and illustrate the process of normalizing the table shown in Figure 8.10 to 3NF. State any assumptions you make about the data shown in this table.

NIN	contractNo	hoursPerWeek	eName	hotelNo	hotelLocation
113567WD	C1024	16	John Smith	H25	Edinburgh
234111XA	C1024	24	Diane Hocine	H25	Edinburgh
712670YD	C1025	28	Sarah White	H4	Glasgow
113567WD	C1025	16	John Smith	H4	Glasgow

Figure 8.10

Employees of *InstantCover* and their contracts to work at hotels.

Part 3

Logical database design

Logical database design
Step 1 Create ER model
Step 2 Map ER model to tables

Physical database design
Step 3 Translate logical design
Step 4 Choose file organizations
Step 5 Design user views
Step 6 Design security
Step 7 Controlled redundancy
Step 8 Monitor and tune

Chapter 9

Logical database design – Step 1

In this chapter you will learn:

What a design methodology is. ◄

Database design has two main phases: logical and physical design. ◄

Critical success factors in database design. ◄

About a methodology for logical and physical database design. ◄

The tasks in Step 1 of the database design methodology, which build an ER model. ◄

The documentation produced during Step 1 of database design, including Entity–Relationship (ER) diagrams and a data dictionary. ◄

In Chapter 4, we described the stages of the database system development life-cycle, one of which is database design. This stage starts only after a complete analysis of the organization's requirements has been undertaken, as discussed in Chapter 6. Database design is made up of two main phases: *logical database design* and *physical database design*. In this chapter and Chapter 10 we'll present a methodology for logical database design and in Chapters 12 to 16 we'll present a methodology for physical database design. We begin by presenting an overview of the database design methodology and then describe in detail the tasks associated with Step 1 of logical database design.

9.1 Introduction to the database design methodology

If the database you require is reasonably complex, you'll need a systematic approach to design and build your database to ensure that it satisfies users' requirements and achieves stated performance requirements (such as response times). This systematic approach is called a *database design methodology*. Before presenting an overview of the methodology, we first discuss what a database design methodology is and then identify the critical success factors in database design.

9.1.1 What is a design methodology?

> **Design methodology**
>
> A structured approach that uses procedures, techniques, tools, and documentation aids to support and facilitate the process of design.

Logical design described in this chapter and Chapter 10

A design methodology consists of phases made up of steps, which guide the designer in the techniques appropriate at each stage of the project. The phases also help the designer to plan, manage, control, and evaluate development projects. In addition, it is a structured approach for analyzing and modeling a set of requirements in a standardized and organized manner.

9.1.2 Phases of database design

In this book we present a methodology, which separates database design into two main phases: logical and physical database design.

> **Logical database design**
>
> The process of constructing a model of the data used in an organization based on a specific data model, but independent of a particular DBMS and other physical considerations.

In the logical database design phase we build the logical representation of the database, which includes identification of the important entities and relationships, and then translate this representation to a set of tables. The logical database design is a source of information for the physical design phase, providing the physical database designer with a vehicle for making trade-offs that are very important to the design of an efficient database.

Physical database design

The process of producing a description of the implementation of the database on secondary storage; it describes the base tables, file organizations, and indexes used to achieve efficient access to the data, and any associated integrity constraints and security restrictions.

In the physical database design phase we decide how the logical design is to be physically implemented in the target relational DBMS. This phase allows the designer to make decisions on how the database is to be implemented. Therefore, physical design is tailored to a specific DBMS.

Physical design discussed in Chapters 12–16

Strictly speaking, there is a phase before logical database design known as *conceptual database design*. This phase begins with the creation of a conceptual data model of the data used by the organization, which is entirely independent of *all* implementation details such as the underlying data model (for example, the relational data model) or any other physical considerations. However, as we're designing databases specifically for relational DBMSs, we've combined the conceptual and logical phases together and used the more general term 'logical database design'.

Relational model discussed in Chapter 2

9.1.3 Critical success factors in database design

The following guidelines are important to the success of database design:

■ Work interactively with the users as much as possible.
■ Follow a structured methodology throughout the data modeling process.
■ Employ a data-driven approach.
■ Incorporate structural and integrity considerations into the data models.
■ Use normalization and transaction validation techniques in the methodology.
■ Use diagrams to represent as much of the data models as possible.
■ Use a Database Design Language (DBDL).
■ Build a data dictionary to supplement the data model diagrams.
■ Be willing to repeat steps.

All these guidelines are built into the methodology we're about to introduce in the next section.

9.2   Overview of the database design methodology

In this section, we present an overview of the database design methodology. The steps in the methodology are shown in Figure 9.1 and the chapter in which the step is discussed in detail is displayed in the adjacent column.

The logical database design phase of the methodology is divided into two main steps.

■ In *Step 1* we create an ER model and check that the model has minimal redundancy and is capable of supporting user transactions. The output of this step is the creation of an ER model, which is a complete and accurate representation of the data requirements of the organization (or part of the organization) that is to be supported by the database.

Step 1 described
in this chapter

Figure 9.1

Steps in the
methodology for
logical and physical
database design.

Logical database design		Chapter
Step 1	Create and check ER model	9
	Step 1.1 Identify entities	
	Step 1.2 Identify relationships	
	Step 1.3 Identify and associate attributes with entities or relationships	
	Step 1.4 Determine attribute domains	
	Step 1.5 Determine candidate, primary, and alternate key attributes	
	Step 1.6 Specialize/Generalize entities (optional step)	
	Step 1.7 Check model for redundancy	
	Step 1.8 Check model supports user transactions	
	Step 1.9 Review model with users	
Step 2	Map ER model to tables	10
	Step 2.1 Create tables	
	Step 2.2 Check table structures using normalization	
	Step 2.3 Check tables support user transactions	
	Step 2.4 Check business rules	
	Step 2.5 Review logical database design with users	
Physical database design		
Step 3	Translate logical database design for target DBMS	12
	Step 3.1 Design base tables	
	Step 3.2 Design representation of derived data	
	Step 3.3 Design remaining business rules	
Step 4	Choose file organizations and indexes	13
	Step 4.1 Analyze transactions	
	Step 4.2 Choose file organizations	
	Step 4.3 Choose indexes	
Step 5	Design user views	14
Step 6	Design security mechanisms	14
Step 7	Consider the introduction of controlled redundancy	15
Step 8	Monitor and tune the operational system	16

■ In *Step 2* we map the ER model to a set of tables. The structure of each table is checked using normalization. Normalization is an effective means of ensuring that the tables are structurally consistent, logical, with minimal redundancy. The tables are also checked to ensure that they are capable of supporting the required transactions. The required integrity constraints on the database are also defined.

Step 2 described in Chapter 10

For database systems that have numerous and varied user views, it may be necessary to create one or more logical data model designs that are merged at a later stage of the database design process. We'll describe the typical tasks associated with the merging of the data models in Appendix C.

Physical database design is divided into six main steps:

Step 3 described in Chapter 12

■ *Step 3* involves the design of the base tables and integrity constraints using the available functionality of the target DBMS.

■ *Step 4* involves choosing the file organizations and indexes for the base tables. Typically, DBMSs provide a number of alternative file organizations for data, with the exception of PC DBMSs, which tend to have a fixed storage structure.

Step 4 described in Chapter 13

■ *Step 5* involves the design of the user views originally identified in the requirements analysis and collection stage of the database system development lifecycle.

Step 5 described in Chapter 14

■ *Step 6* involves designing the security measures to protect the data from unauthorized access.

■ *Step 7* considers relaxing the normalization constraints imposed on the tables to improve the overall performance of the system. This is a step that you should undertake only if necessary, because of the inherent problems involved in introducing redundancy while still maintaining consistency.

Step 6 described in Chapter 14

■ *Step 8* is an ongoing process of monitoring and tuning the operational system to identify and resolve any performance problems resulting from the design and to implement new or changing requirements.

Step 7 described in Chapter 15

Appendix B presents a summary of the methodology for those of you who are already familiar with database design and simply require an overview of the main steps.

Throughout this methodology, users play a critical role in continually reviewing and checking the data model and the supporting documentation. Some steps may not be necessary depending on the complexity of the organization you're analyzing and your need for performance and security.

Step 8 described in Chapter 16

> Database design is an iterative process that has a starting point and an **TIP** almost endless procession of refinements. Although we present our database design methodology as a procedural process, it must be emphasized that this does not imply that it should be performed in this manner. It is likely that the knowledge you gain in one step may alter decisions you made in a previous step. Similarly, you may find it useful to briefly look at a later step to help with an earlier step. The methodology should act as a framework to help guide you through the database design activity effectively.

9.3 Introduction to Step 1 of the logical database design methodology

This section covers the first step of our logical database design methodology. In this step, you build an ER model for one of the user views identified during the earlier analysis stage.

Centralized approach discussed in Section 4.6

> During analysis, you will have identified a number of user views, and depending on the amount of overlap between these views and the complexity of your database system, you may have combined some user views together. In the requirements collection and analysis stage discussed in Section 6.4.4, we used the centralized approach to create two collections of user views for *StayHome* that represent the merged requirements for the following user views:
>
> ■ *Branch user views* representing the Manager, Supervisor, and Assistant user views;
> ■ *Business user views* representing the Director and Buyer user views.

In this section and in the following chapter, you're going to build a logical data model for the Branch user views of *StayHome*. In Chapter 4, we introduced the term 'local logical data model' to describe a model that describes one or more, but not all, user views of a database. However, throughout the chapters that describe the database design methodology, we simply use the more general term 'logical data model'.

For those of you interested in building more complex databases that first require the creation of separate local logical data models to represent different user views of a database, we describe and demonstrate the merging of the data models using the Branch and Business user views of *StayHome* in Appendix C.

Step 1 Create and check ER model

Objective
To build an ER model of the data requirements of the organization (or part of the organization) to be supported by the database.

Each ER model comprises:

■ entities,

■ relationships,

■ attributes and attribute domains,

■ primary keys and alternate keys,

■ integrity constraints.

The ER model is supported by documentation, including a data dictionary and ER diagrams, which you'll produce throughout the development of the model. We'll detail the types of supporting documentation that you may want to produce as we go through the various steps. The tasks involved in Step 1 are:

■ Step 1.1   Identify entities

■ Step 1.2   Identify relationships

■ Step 1.3   Identify and associate attributes with entities or relationships

■ Step 1.4   Determine attribute domains

■ Step 1.5   Determine candidate, primary, and alternate key attributes

■ Step 1.6   Specialize/Generalize entities (optional step)

■ Step 1.7   Check model for redundancy

■ Step 1.8   Check model supports user transactions

■ Step 1.9   Check model with users

So, let's start to build the ER model for the Branch user views of *StayHome*.

Step 1.1 Identify entities

Objective
To identify the required entities.

The first step in building an ER model is to define the main objects that the users are interested in. These objects are the entities for the model. One method of identifying entities is to examine the users' requirements specification. From this

Entities defined
in Section 7.1

Users' requirements for Branch user views given in Section 6.4.4

specification, you can identify nouns or noun phrases that are mentioned (for example, staff number, staff name, catalog number, title, daily rental rate, purchase price). You should also look for major objects such as people, places, or concepts of interest, excluding those nouns that are merely qualities of other objects.

For example, you could group staff number and staff name with an entity called Staff and group catalog number, title, daily rental rate, and purchase price with an entity called Video.

An alternative way of identifying entities is to look for objects that have an existence in their own right. For example, Staff is an entity because staff exist whether or not you know their names, addresses, and salaries. If possible, you should get the user to assist with this activity.

It's sometimes difficult to identify entities because of the way they are presented in the users' requirements specification. Users often talk in terms of examples or analogies. Instead of talking about staff in general, users may mention people's names. In some cases, users talk in terms of job roles, particularly where people or companies are involved. These roles may be job titles or responsibilities, such as Manager, Supervisor, or Assistant. To further confuse matters, users frequently use synonyms and homonyms.

> Two words are *synonyms* when they have the same meaning, for example 'branch' and 'outlet'. *Homonyms* occur when the same word can have different meanings depending on the context. For example, the word 'program' has several alternative meanings such as a series of events, a plan of work, a piece of software, and a course of study.

It's not always obvious whether a particular object is an entity, a relationship, or an attribute. For example, how would you model marriage? In fact, depending on the actual requirements you could model marriage as any or all of these. You'll find that analysis is subjective, and different designers may produce different, but equally valid, interpretations. The activity therefore relies, to a certain extent, on judgment and experience. Database designers must take a very selective view of the world and categorize the things that they observe within the context of the organization. Thus, there may be no unique set of entities deducible from a given users' requirements specification. However, successive iterations of the analysis process should lead you to the choice of entities that are at least adequate for the system required.

> **TIP**
>
> The fact that database design is subjective can initially be quite off-putting. However, by following the methodology we present in this book, you'll find that the task is achievable and that it gets easier with some practice and experience. To help, in Chapters 17 and 18 we'll go through a second case study, and in Appendix E we provide a number of common business data models you're likely to encounter in one form or another.

StayHome entities

For the Branch user views of *StayHome*, you may identify the following entities:

Branch	Staff
Video	VideoForRent
Member	RentalAgreement
Actor	Director

Document entities

As you identify entities, assign them names that are meaningful and obvious to the users. Record the names and descriptions of entities in a data dictionary. If possible, document the expected number of occurrences of each entity. If an entity is known by different names, the names are referred to as synonyms or aliases, which you should also record in the data dictionary. Figure 9.2 shows an extract from the data dictionary that documents the entities for the Branch user views of *StayHome*.

Step 1.2 Identify relationships

Objective
To identify the important relationships that exist between the entities.

Having identified the entities, the next step is to identify all the relationships that exist between these entities. When you identify entities, one method is to look for nouns in the users' requirements specification. Again, you can use the

Relationships defined in Section 7.2

Figure 9.2

Extract from the data dictionary for the Branch user views of *StayHome* showing a description of entities.

Entity name	Description	Aliases	Occurrence
Branch	Place of work	Outlet and Branch Outlet	One or more *StayHome* branches are located in main cities throughout the US.
Staff	General term describing all staff employed by *StayHome*	Employee	Each member of staff works at a particular branch.

grammar of the requirements specification to identify relationships. Typically, relationships are indicated by verbs or verbal expressions. For example:

- Branch *Has* Staff
- Branch *IsAllocated* VideoForRent
- VideoForRent *IsPartOf* RentalAgreement

The fact that the users' requirements specification records these relationships suggests that they are important to the users, and should be included in the model.

> **TIP**
>
> We're interested only in required relationships between entities. In the previous example, you identified the Branch *IsAllocated* VideoForRent and VideoForRent *IsPartOf* RentalAgreement relationships. You may also be inclined to include a relationship between Branch and RentalAgreement (for example, Branch *Handles* RentalAgreement). However, although this is a possible relationship, from the requirements it's not a relationship that we're interested in modeling. We discuss this further in Step 1.7.

Transaction check described in Steps 1.8 and 2.3

Take great care to ensure that all the relationships that are either explicit or implicit in the users' requirements specification are noted. In principle, it should be possible to check each pair of entities for a potential relationship between them, but this would be a daunting task for a large system comprising hundreds of entities. On the other hand, it's unwise not to perform some such check. However, missing relationships should become apparent when you check that the model supports the transactions that the users require. On the other hand, it is possible that an entity can have no relationship with other entities in the database but still play an important part in meeting the users' requirements.

In most instances, the relationships you find will be binary; in other words, the relationships exist between exactly two entities. However, you should be careful to look out for complex relationships that may involve more than two entities and recursive relationships that involve only one entity. For the Branch user views of *StayHome*, you should identify the following non-binary relationships:

Complex and recursive relationships defined in Sections 7.2.1 and 7.2.2

Registers a ternary relationship between *Branch*, *Member*, and *Staff*
Supervises a recursive relationship between *Staff*.

StayHome relationships

For the Branch user views of *StayHome*, you may identify the relationships shown in Figure 9.3.

Entity	Relationship	Entity
Branch	Has	Staff
	IsAllocated	VideoForRent
Branch, Staff[†]	Registers	Member
Staff	Manages	Branch
	Supervises	Staff
Video	Is	VideoForRent
VideoForRent	IsPartOf	RentalAgreement
Member	Requests	RentalAgreement
Actor	PlaysIn	Video
Director	Directs	Video

[†] represents a ternary relationship

Figure 9.3

First draft of the relationships for the Branch user views of *StayHome*.

Use Entity–Relationship (ER) modeling

It's often easier to visualize a complex system rather than decipher long textual descriptions of such a system. The use of Entity–Relationship (ER) diagrams helps you more easily to represent entities and how they relate to one another. You can represent the above entities and relationships in the first draft ER diagram shown in Figure 9.4.

> **TIP**
>
> Throughout the database design phase, we recommend that ER diagrams are used whenever necessary, to help build up a picture of what you're attempting to model. Different people use different notations for ER diagrams. In this book, we've used the latest object-oriented notation called **UML (Unified Modeling Language)**, but other notations perform a similar function.

Other notations shown in Appendix A

Determine the multiplicity constraints of relationships

Having identified the relationships you wish to model, you now want to determine the multiplicity of each relationship. If specific values for the multiplicity are known, or even upper or lower limits, document these values as well.

Multiplicity defined in Section 7.5

A model that includes multiplicity constraints more explicitly represents the meaning of the relationship and consequently results in a better representation of what you're trying to model. Multiplicity constraints are used to check and maintain the quality of the data. These constraints can be applied when the database is updated to determine whether or not the updates violate the stated business rules.

Figure 9.4

First draft ER diagram of the Branch user views for *StayHome* showing entities and relationships.

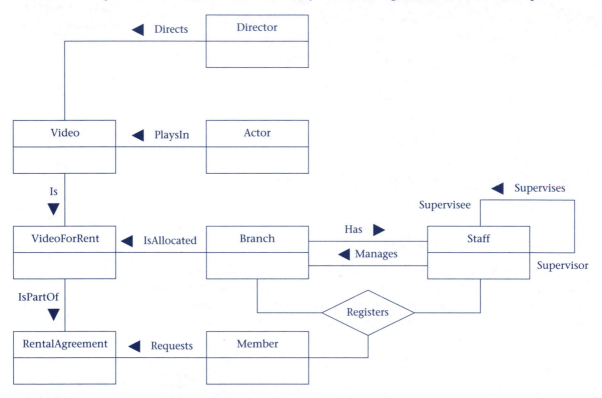

StayHome multiplicity constraints

For the *StayHome* case study, you should identify the multiplicity constraints shown in Figure 9.5. Figure 9.6 shows the updated ER diagram with this information added.

Check for fan and chasm traps

Fan and chasm traps discussed in Section 7.7

Having identified the relationships, you should check that each one correctly represents what you want it to represent, and that you've not inadvertently created any fan traps or chasm traps.

Document relationships

As you identify relationships, assign them names that are meaningful and obvious to the user, and also record relationship descriptions and the multiplicity constraints in the data dictionary. Figure 9.7 shows an extract from the data dictionary that documents the relationships for the Business user views of *StayHome*.

Entity	Multiplicity	Relationship	Multiplicity	Entity
Branch	1..1	Has	1..*	Staff
	1..1	IsAllocated	1..*	VideoForRent
Branch, Staff[†]	1..*, 1..1	Registers	0..*	Member
Staff	1..1	Manages	0..1	Branch
	0..1	Supervises	0..*	Staff
Video	1..1	Is	1..*	VideoForRent
VideoForRent	1..1	IsPartOf	0..*	RentalAgreement
Member	1..1	Requests	0..*	RentalAgreement
Actor	0..*	PlaysIn	1..*	Video
Director	1..1	Directs	1..*	Video

[†] represents a ternary relationship

Figure 9.5

Multiplicity constraints for the relationships identified for the Branch user views of *StayHome*.

Figure 9.6

Adding multiplicity constraints to the ER diagram for the Branch user views of *StayHome*.

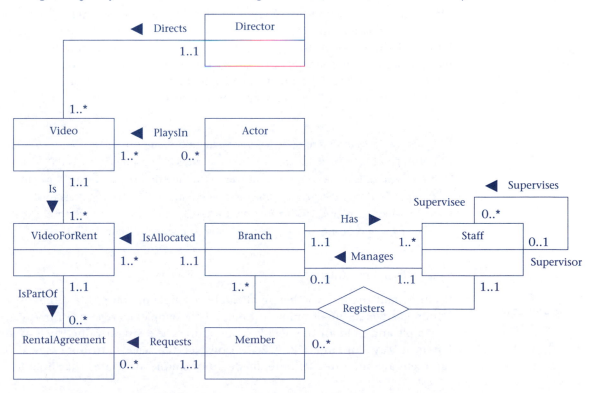

Figure 9.7

Extract from the
data dictionary for
the Branch user
views of *StayHome*
showing
descriptions of
relationships.

Entity	Multiplicity	Relationship	Multiplicity	Entity
Branch	1..*	Has	1..1	Staff
Branch	1..*	IsAllocated	1..1	VideoForRent
Staff	0..1	Manages	1..1	Branch
Staff	0..*	Supervises	0..1	Staff

Step 1.3 Identify and associate attributes with entities or relationships

Objective
To associate attributes with the appropriate entities or relationships.

Attributes
defined in
Section 7.3

The next step in the methodology is to identify the types of facts about the
entities and relationships that you've chosen to be represented in the database.
In a similar way to identifying entities, look for nouns or noun phrases in the
users' requirements specification. The attributes can be identified where the
noun or noun phrase is a property, quality, identifier, or characteristic of one of
the entities or relationships that you've previously found.

> **TIP**
>
> By far the easiest thing to do when you've identified an entity or a rela-
> tionship in the users' requirements specification is to consider '*What information
> are we required to hold on . . .?*' The answer to this question should be described in
> the specification. However, in some cases, you may need to ask the users to clar-
> ify the requirements. Unfortunately, they may give you answers that also
> contain other concepts, so users' responses must be carefully considered.

Simple/Composite attributes

Simple/Composite
attributes defined
in Section 7.3.1

It's important to note whether an attribute is simple or composite. Composite
attributes are made up of simple attributes. For example, an address attribute can
be simple and hold all the details of an address as a single value, such as '8
Jefferson Way, Portland, OR, 97201'. However, the address attribute may also
represent a composite attribute, made up of simple attributes that hold the

address details as separate values in the attributes street ('8 Jefferson Way'), city ('Portland'), state ('OR'), and zipCode ('97201').

> The option to represent address details as a simple or composite attribute is determined by the users' requirements. If users do not need to access the separate components of an address, you should represent the address attribute as a simple attribute. On the other hand, if users do need to access the individual components of an address, you should represent the address attribute as being composite, made up of the required simple attributes.

Single/Multi-valued attributes

In addition to being simple or composite, an attribute can also be single-valued or multi-valued. Most attributes you encounter will be single-valued, but occasionally you may encounter a multi-valued attribute; that is, an attribute that holds multiple values for a single entity occurrence. For example, you may identify the Branch attribute telNo (telephone number) as a multi-valued attribute.

Single/ Multi-valued attributes defined in Section 7.3.2

> You may have identified branch telephone numbers as a separate entity. This is an alternative, and equally valid, way to model this. As you'll see shortly in Step 2.1, multi-valued attributes are mapped to tables anyway, so both approaches produce the same end result.

Derived attributes

Attributes whose values can be found by examining the values of other attributes are known as derived attributes. All derived attributes must be shown in the data model to avoid a potential loss of information, which may occur if the attribute or attributes on which the derived attribute is based are deleted or modified.

Derived attributes defined in Section 7.3.3

We'll consider the representation of derived attributes during physical database design. Depending on how the attribute is used, new values for a derived attribute may be calculated each time it's accessed or when the value(s) it's derived from changes. However, this issue is not the concern of logical database design, and we'll discuss how best to physically represent derived attributes in Step 3.2 in Chapter 12.

Potential problems

When identifying attributes, it's not uncommon for it to become apparent that one or more entities have been omitted from the original selection. In this case, return to the previous steps, document the new entities, and re-examine the associated relationships.

> **TIP**
>
> It may be useful to produce a list of all attributes given in the users' requirements specification. As you associate an attribute with a particular entity or relationship, you can remove the item from the list. In this way, you can ensure that an attribute is associated with only one entity or relationship and, when the list is empty, that all attributes are associated with some entity or relationship.

You must also be aware of cases where attributes appear to be associated with more than one entity as this can indicate the following:

(1) You've identified several entities that can be represented as a single entity. For example, you may have identified entities Manager and Supervisor both with the attributes staffNo (staff number), name, and salary, which can be represented as a single entity called Staff with the attributes staffNo, name, position, and salary.

> On the other hand, it may be that these entities share many attributes but there are also attributes that are unique to each entity. In Chapter 11, we'll look at some enhanced ER modeling concepts known as specialization and generalization, and provide guidelines for their use. These enhanced concepts allow you to represent this type of situation more accurately. We omit these concepts here and consider them as a separate optional step (Step 1.6) to keep the basic methodology as simple as possible.

(2) You've identified a relationship between entities. In this case, you must associate the attribute with only *one* entity, namely the parent entity, and ensure that the relationship was previously identified in Step 1.2. If this is not the case, the documentation should be updated with details of the newly identified relationship. For example, you may have identified the entities Branch and Staff with the following attributes:

Branch   branchNo, street, city, state, zipCode, managerName
Staff   staffNo, name, position, salary

The presence of the managerName attribute in Branch is intended to represent the relationship Staff *Manages* Branch. In this case, however, the managerName attribute should be omitted from Branch and the relationship *Manages* should be added to the model.

StayHome attributes for entities

For the Branch user views of the *StayHome* case study, you should identify and associate attributes with entities as follows:

Branch	branchNo, address (composite: street, city, state, zipCode), telNo (multi-valued)
Staff	staffNo, name, position, salary
Video	catalogNo, title, category, dailyRental, price
Director	directorName
Actor	actorName
Member	memberNo, name (composite: fName, lName), address
RentalAgreement	rentalNo, dateOut, dateReturn
VideoForRent	videoNo, available

Note that the address attribute in Branch and the name attribute in Member have been identified as composite, whereas the address attribute in Member and the name attributes in Staff, Director, and Actor have been identified as simple. This reflects the users' access requirements for these attributes.

StayHome attributes for relationships

You may have difficulty associating the attribute representing the date a member registered at a branch, dateJoined, with a particular entity. There are potentially three entities associated with this attribute, namely Member, Branch, and Staff. However, this attribute cannot be associated with any of these entities because a member can register at many branches, a member of staff can register many members at many branches, and a branch has many members. The solution is to associate the dateJoined attribute with the *Registers* ternary relationship, which relates the Member, Branch, and Staff entities. Similarly, the attribute representing the name of the character an actor plays in a video, character, has to be associated with the *PlaysIn* binary relationship between Actor and Video.

Document attributes

As you identify attributes, assign them names that are meaningful and obvious to the user. Where appropriate, record the following information for each attribute:

■ attribute name and description;
■ data type and length;
■ any aliases that the attribute is known by;

Nulls defined in
Section 2.3.1

- whether the attribute must always be specified (in other words, whether the attribute allows or disallows nulls);
- whether the attribute is multi-valued;
- whether the attribute is composite, and if so, which simple attributes make up the composite attribute;
- whether the attribute is derived and, if so, how it is to be computed;
- default values for the attribute (if specified).

Figure 9.8 shows an extract from the data dictionary that documents the attributes for the Branch user views of *StayHome*.

Step 1.4 Determine attribute domains

Objective
To determine domains for the attributes in the ER model.

Figure 9.8

Extract from the data dictionary for the Branch user views of *StayHome* showing descriptions of attributes.

Entity	Attributes	Description	Data type and length	Nulls	Multi-valued	...
Branch	branchNo	Uniquely identifies a branch	4 fixed characters	No	No	
	address: street	Street of branch address	30 variable characters	No	No	
	city	City of branch address	20 variable characters	No	No	
	state	State of branch address	2 fixed characters	No	No	
	zipCode	Zip code of branch address	5 variable characters	No	No	
	telNo	Telephone numbers of branch	10 variable characters	No	Yes	
Staff	staffNo	Uniquely identifies a member of staff	5 fixed characters	No	No	
	name	Name of staff member	30 variable characters	No	No	

The objective of this step is to determine domains for the attributes in the ER model. A **domain** is a pool of values from which one or more attributes draw their values. Examples of the attribute domains for *StayHome* include:

■ The attribute domain of valid branch numbers as being a four-character fixed-length string, with the first character as a letter and the next three characters as digits in the range 000–999.

■ The attribute domain for valid telephone numbers as being a 10-digit string.

■ The possible values for the available attribute of the VideoForRent entity as being either 'Y' or 'N'. The domain of this attribute is a single character string consisting of the values 'Y' or 'N'.

A fully developed data model specifies the domains for each of the model's attributes and includes:

■ allowable set of values for the attribute;

■ size and format of the attribute.

Document attribute domains

As you identify attribute domains, record their names and characteristics in the data dictionary. Update the data dictionary entries for attributes to record their domain in place of the data type and length information.

Step 1.5 Determine candidate, primary, and alternate key attributes

> **Objective**
> To identify the candidate key(s) for each entity and, if there is more than one candidate key, to choose one to be the primary key, and to identify the others as alternate keys.

This step is concerned with identifying the candidate key(s) for an entity and then selecting one to be the primary key. Be careful to ensure that you choose a candidate key that can never be null (if the candidate key consists of more than one attribute, then this applies to each attribute). If you identify more than one candidate key, you must choose one to be the primary key; the remaining candidate keys are called alternate keys.

Keys defined in Section 2.2.3 and Section 7.3.4

When choosing a primary key from among the candidate keys, you should use the following guidelines to help make the selection:

■ the candidate key with the minimal set of attributes;

■ the candidate key that is less likely to have its values changed;

Weak entities
defined in
Section 7.4

> **TIP**
>
> People's names generally do not make good candidate keys, as we pointed out in Section 2.2.3. For example, you may think that a suitable candidate key for the Staff entity would be *name*, the member of staff's name. However, it's possible for two people with the same name to join *StayHome*, which would clearly invalidate the choice of *name* as a candidate key. We could make a similar argument for the names of *StayHome's* members. In such cases, rather than coming up with combinations of attributes that may provide uniqueness, it may be better to define a new attribute that would always ensure uniqueness, such as a *staffNo* attribute for the Staff entity and a *memberNo* attribute for the Member entity.

■ the candidate key that is less likely to lose uniqueness in the future;

■ the candidate key with fewest characters (for those with textual attribute(s));

■ the candidate key with the smallest maximum value (for numerical attributes);

■ the candidate key that is easiest to use from the users' point of view.

In the process of identifying primary keys, note whether an entity is strong or weak. If you can assign a primary key to an entity, the entity is referred to as being **strong**. On the other hand, if you can't identify a primary key for an entity, the entity is referred to as being **weak**. However, it's possible that one or more of the attributes associated with a weak entity may form part of the final primary key, but they don't provide uniqueness by themselves.

> The primary key of a weak entity can only be identified when you map the weak entity to a table, which we'll describe in Step 2.1 of Chapter 10.

StayHome primary keys

For the Branch user views of the *StayHome* case study, you should identify the primary keys shown in Figure 9.9.

> In the users' requirements for *StayHome* there are no obvious keys for the Director and Actor entities. In fact, the only attributes that have been identified for the entities are the director's name for the Director entity and the actor's name for the Actor entity. As we've just said, these are not suitable as primary keys, so we've made up a primary key for each of these entities, which we've called directorNo and actorNo, respectively.

Figure 9.9

ER diagram for the Branch user views of *StayHome* showing primary keys.

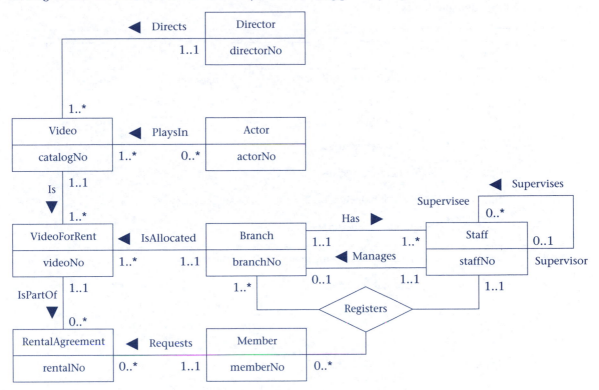

Document candidate, primary, and alternate keys

Record the identification of candidate, primary, and alternate keys (when available) in the data dictionary. Figure 9.10 shows an extract from the data dictionary that documents the attributes for *StayHome* with the keys identified.

Step 1.6 Specialize/Generalize entities (optional step)

Objective
To identify superclass and subclass entities, where appropriate.

In this step, you have the option to continue the development of the ER model using the process of specialization or generalization. The modeling of superclasses and subclasses adds more information to the data model, but also adds

Figure 9.10

Extract from the data dictionary for the Branch user views of *StayHome* showing attributes with primary and alternate keys identified.

Entity	Attributes	Description	Key	Nulls	...
Branch	branchNo	Uniquely identifies a branch	Primary key	No	
	address: street	Street of branch address		No	
	city	City of branch address		No	
	state	State of branch address		No	
	zipCode	Zip code of branch address	Alternate key	No	
	telNo	Telephone numbers of branch		No	
Staff	staffNo	Uniquely identifies a member of staff	Primary key	No	
	name	Name of staff member		No	

more complexity as well. Consequently, as this is an optional step, we'll omit the details of specialization and generalization just now and consider it separately in Chapter 11 for those readers who may be interested.

Step 1.7 Check model for redundancy

Objective
To check for the presence of redundancy in the ER model.

In this step, you examine the ER model with the specific objectives of identifying whether there is any redundancy present and removing any that does exist. The three activities in this step are:

(1) re-examine one-to-one (1:1) relationships;

(2) remove redundant relationships;

(3) consider the time dimension when assessing redundancy.

Re-examine one-to-one (1:1) relationships

In the identification of entities, you may have identified two entities that represent the same object in the organization. For example, you may have identified two entities named Branch and Outlet that are actually the same; in other words, Branch is a synonym for Outlet. In this case, the two entities should be merged together. If the primary keys are different, choose one of them to be the primary key and leave the other as an alternate key.

1:1 relationships defined in Section 7.5.1

Remove redundant relationships

A relationship is redundant if the same information can be obtained via other relationships. You're trying to develop a minimal data model and, as redundant relationships are unnecessary, they should be removed. It's relatively easy to identify whether there is more than one path between two entities. However, this does not necessarily imply that one of the relationships is redundant, as they may represent different associations in the organization.

For example, consider the relationships between the VideoForRent, RentalAgreement, and Member entities shown in Figure 9.11. There are two ways to find out which members rent out which videos. There is the direct route using the *Rents* relationship between the Member and VideoForRent entities and there's the indirect route using the *Requests* and *IsPartOf* relationships via the RentalAgreement entity. Before we can assess whether both routes are required, we need to establish the purpose of each relationship. The *Rents* relationship indicates which members rent out which videos. On the other hand, the *Requests* relationship indicates which members hold which rental agreements, and the *IsPartOf* relationship indicates which videos are associated with which rental agreements. Although it's true that there is a relationship between members and the videos they rent, this is not a direct relationship and the association is more accurately represented through a rental agreement. The *Rents* relationship is therefore redundant and does not convey any additional information about

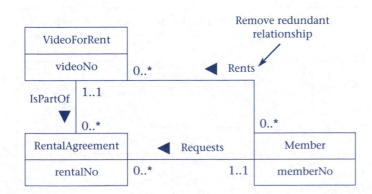

Figure 9.11

Remove redundant relationships.

the relationship between VideoForRent and Member that cannot more easily be found out through the RentalAgreement entity. To ensure that we create a minimal model, the redundant *Rents* relationship must be removed.

Consider the time dimension when assessing redundancy

The time dimension of relationships is also important when assessing redundancy. For example, consider the situation where you wish to model the relationships between the entities Man, Woman, and Child, as illustrated in Figure 9.12. Clearly, there are two paths between Man and Child: one via the direct relationship *FatherOf* and the other via the relationships *MarriedTo* and *MotherOf*. Consequently, you may think that the relationship *FatherOf* is unnecessary. However, this would be incorrect for two reasons:

(1) The father may have children from a previous marriage, and you're modeling only the father's current marriage through a 1:1 relationship.

(2) The father and mother may not be married, or the father may be married to someone other than the mother (or the mother may be married to someone who is not the father).

In either case, the required relationship could not be modeled without the *FatherOf* relationship.

> **TIP**
>
> The message here is that it's important you examine the meaning of each relationship between entities when assessing redundancy.

Figure 9.12

Non-redundant relationships.

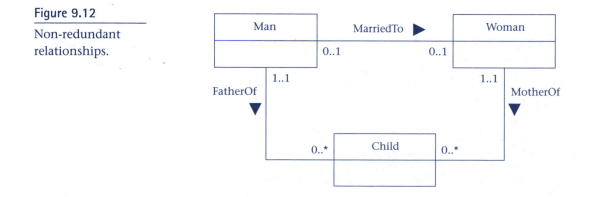

Step 1.8 Check model supports user transactions

> **Objective**
> To ensure that the ER model supports the required transactions.

You now have an ER model that represents the data requirements of the organization (or part of the organization). The objective of this step is to check the ER
model to ensure that the model supports the required transactions. In our case,
the transaction requirements for the Branch user views of *StayHome* are listed in
Section 6.4.4.

Using the ER model and the data dictionary, you attempt to perform the
operations manually. If you can resolve all transactions in this way, you have
checked the ER model supports the required transactions. However, if you're
unable to perform a transaction manually, there must be a problem with the
data model, which must be resolved. In this case, it's likely that you've omitted
an entity, a relationship, or an attribute from the data model.

We examine two possible approaches to ensuring that the ER model supports
the required transactions.

Describing the transaction

Using the first approach, you check that all the information (entities, relationships, and their attributes) required by each transaction is provided by the
model, by documenting a description of each transaction's requirements. Let's
examine the requirements for an example transaction for *StayHome*:

Transaction (o) List the name of each manager at each branch, ordered by
branch number

The name of each manager is held in the Staff entity and branch details are
held in the Branch entity. In this case, you can use the Staff *Manages* Branch relationship to find the name of each manager for each branch.

Using transaction pathways

The second approach to validating the data model against the required transactions involves representing the pathway taken by each transaction directly on
the ER diagram. An example of this approach using the data queries listed in
Section 6.4.4 is shown in Figure 9.13. Clearly, the more transactions that exist,
the more complex this diagram would become, so for readability you may need
several such diagrams to cover all the transactions.

Figure 9.13

Using pathways to check that the ER model supports the user transactions.

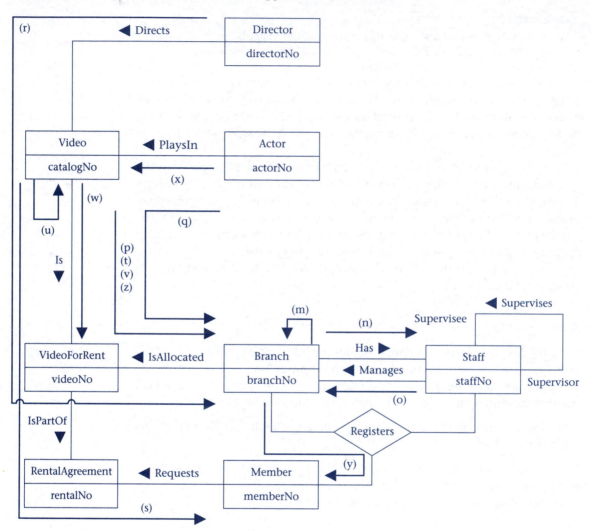

Step 1.9 Review model with user

Objective

To review the ER model with the user to ensure that the model is a 'true' representation of the organization (or the part of the organization) to be supported by the database.

Before completing Step 1, you should review the ER model with the users. The ER model includes the data dictionary, ER diagrams, and any additional documentation that describes the data model. If any anomalies are present in the data model, you must make the appropriate changes, which may require repeating the previous step(s). You should repeat this process until the user is prepared to 'sign off' the model as being a 'true' representation of the organization (or part of the organization) that you're attempting to model.

In the following chapter we proceed to the next major step, which maps the data model to a set of tables and checks that the tables will satisfy user requirements.

Chapter summary

✓ A **design methodology** is a structured approach that uses procedures, techniques, tools, and documentation aids to support and facilitate the process of design.

✓ The **database design methodology** used in this book has two main phases: logical and physical database design.

✓ **Logical database design** is the process of constructing a model of the data used in an organization based on a specific data model, but independent of a particular DBMS and other physical considerations. In our case, logical design is tailored to the relational model.

✓ **Physical database design** is the process of producing a description of the implementation of the database on secondary storage; it describes the file organizations and indexes used to achieve efficient access of the data, and any associated integrity constraints and security restrictions. Physical design is tailored to a specific DBMS.

✓ There are **critical factors** for the success of the database design stage, including, for example, working interactively with users and being willing to repeat steps.

✓ The main objective of **Step 1** of the methodology is to build an ER model to represent the data requirements of the organization (or part of the organization) to be supported by the database.

✓ An ER model includes entities, relationships, attributes, attribute domains, candidate keys, primary keys, and alternate keys.

✓ An ER model is described by documentation, which includes ER diagrams and a data dictionary.

✓ An ER model should be checked to ensure that it does not have any redundancy and supports the transactions required by the users.

Review questions

9.1   Describe the purpose of a design methodology.

9.2   Describe the main phases involved in database design.

9.3   Identify important factors in the success of database design.

9.4   Discuss the important role played by users in the process of database design.

9.5   Discuss the main activities associated with each step of the logical database design methodology.

9.6   Discuss the main activities associated with each step of the physical database design methodology.

9.7   Discuss the purpose of Step 1 of logical database design.

9.8   Identify the main tasks associated with Step 1 of logical database design.

9.9   Discuss an approach to identifying entities and relationships from a users' requirements specification.

9.10 Discuss an approach to identifying attributes from a users' requirements specification and the association of attributes with entities or relationships.

9.11 Discuss an approach to checking an ER model for redundancy. Give an example to illustrate your answer.

9.12 Describe two approaches to checking that an ER model supports the transactions required by the user.

9.13 Identify and describe the purpose of the documentation generated during Step 1 of logical database design.

Exercise

9.14 Identify entities, relationships, and the associated attributes in each case study given in Appendix E and then create an ER diagram without first looking at the answer ER diagram that accompanies each case study. Compare your ER diagram with the answer ER diagram and justify any differences found.

Logical database design
Step 1 Create ER model
Step 2 Map ER model to tables

Physical database design
Step 3 Translate logical design
Step 4 Choose file organizations
Step 5 Design user views
Step 6 Design security
Step 7 Controlled redundancy
Step 8 Monitor and tune

Chapter 10

Logical database design – Step 2

In this chapter you will learn:

How to map a set of tables from an ER model. ◄

How to check that the tables are well structured using normalization. ◄

How to check that the tables are capable of supporting the transactions required by the user. ◄

How to define and document integrity constraints on the tables. ◄

This chapter covers the second step of our logical database design methodology. In this step, you create a set of tables for the ER model created in Step 1. You then check that the tables are well structured using normalization, and that they support the user transactions. Finally, you check that all business rules are represented in the final logical data model.

Methodology summarized in Appendix B

Step 2 Map ER model to tables

Objective
To create tables for the ER model and to check the structure of the tables.

The main purpose of this step is to produce a description of the tables for the ER model created in Step 1 of the methodology. The set of tables produced should represent the entities, relationships, attributes, and constraints described by the ER model. The structure of each table is checked to ensure that no errors have been introduced in creating the tables. If errors exist in the tables this may indicate that errors were introduced during the process of creating the tables or that the ER model still has errors that have not yet been identified. The tasks involved in Step 2 are:

- Step 2.1 Create tables
- Step 2.2 Check table structures using normalization
- Step 2.3 Check tables support user transactions
- Step 2.4 Check business rules
- Step 2.5 Review logical database design with users

We demonstrate Step 2 of the methodology using the ER model created in Step 1 of the last chapter for the Branch user views of *StayHome*, which represent the merged requirements for the Manager, Supervisor, and Assistant user views.

Step 2.1 Create tables

> **Objective**
> To map a set of tables from the ER model.

In this step, you create tables for the ER model to represent the entities, relationships, attributes, and constraints. The structure of each table is created from the information that describes the ER model, including the ER diagrams, data dictionary, and any other supporting documentation. To describe the composition of each table you use a Database Design Language (DBDL) for relational databases. Using the DBDL, you first specify the name of the table, followed by a list of the names of the table's simple attributes enclosed in parentheses. You then identify the primary key and any alternate and/or foreign key(s) of the table. For each foreign key, the table containing the referenced primary key is also given.

We illustrate this process using the ER diagram for the Branch user views of *StayHome* shown in Figure 9.9. However, in some cases it's necessary to add examples not shown in this model to illustrate particular points.

Relational keys defined in Section 2.2.3

How to represent entities

For each entity in the ER model, create a table that includes all the entity's simple attributes. For composite attributes, include only the simple attributes that make up the composite attribute in the table. For example, for the composite address attribute, you would include its simple attributes street, city, state, and zipCode. Where possible, identify the column(s) that make up the primary key in

Simple and composite attributes defined in Section 7.3.1

each table. For the entities shown in Figure 9.9, you should document the initial table structures shown in Figure 10.1.

In some cases, you have not yet identified the full set of columns that make up the tables, as you have still to represent the relationships between entities. In particular, this means that you cannot identify the columns that make up the primary key for weak entities. As we have no weak entities in Figure 9.9, we use an example of a weak entity called VideoOrderLine in Figure C.1. We discuss the identification of primary key columns for this weak entity at the end of this step.

Weak entities defined in Section 7.4

How to represent relationships

The relationship that an entity has with another entity is represented by the primary key/foreign key mechanism. In deciding where to *post* (or place) the foreign key attribute(s), you must first identify the 'parent' and 'child' entities involved in the relationship. The parent entity refers to the entity that posts a copy of its primary key into the table that represents the child entity, to act as the foreign key.

Relationships discussed in Section 7.2

We consider the identification of parent/child entities for different types of relationships and for multi-valued attributes.

(a) one-to-many (1:*) binary relationships;

(b) one-to-many (1:*) recursive relationships;

(c) one-to-one (1:1) binary relationships;

Figure 10.1

Initial table structures for the entities in the Branch user views of *StayHome* as shown in Figure 9.9.

Actor (actorNo, actorName) **Primary Key** actorNo	**Branch** (branchNo, street, city, state, zipCode) **Primary Key** branchNo **Alternate Key** zipCode
Director (directorNo, directorName) **Primary Key** directorNo	**Member** (memberNo, fName, lName, address) **Primary Key** memberNo
RentalAgreement (rentalNo, dateOut, dateReturn) **Primary Key** rentalNo	**Staff** (staffNo, name, position, salary) **Primary Key** staffNo
Video (catalogNo, title, category, dailyRental, price) **Primary Key** catalogNo	**VideoForRent** (videoNo, available) **Primary Key** videoNo

(d) one-to-one (1:1) recursive relationships;

(e) many-to-many (*:*) binary relationships;

(f) complex relationships;

(g) multi-valued attributes.

One-to-many (1:*) binary relationships

1:* relationships
defined in
Section 7.5.2

For each 1:* binary relationship, the entity on the 'one side' of the relationship is designated as the parent entity and the entity on the 'many side' is designated as the child entity. To represent this relationship, a copy of the primary key of the parent entity is placed into the table representing the child entity, to act as a foreign key.

Let's consider the Branch *Has* Staff relationship shown in Figure 9.9 to illustrate how to represent a 1:* relationship as tables. In this example, Branch is on the 'one side' and represents the parent entity, and Staff is on the 'many side' and represents the child entity. The relationship between these entities is established by placing a copy of the primary key of the Branch (parent) entity, namely branchNo, into the Staff (child) table. Figure 10.2(a) shows the Branch *Has* Staff ER diagram and Figure 10.2(b) shows the corresponding tables.

Figure 10.2

The 1:* Branch *Has* Staff relationship: (a) ER diagram; (b) representation as tables.

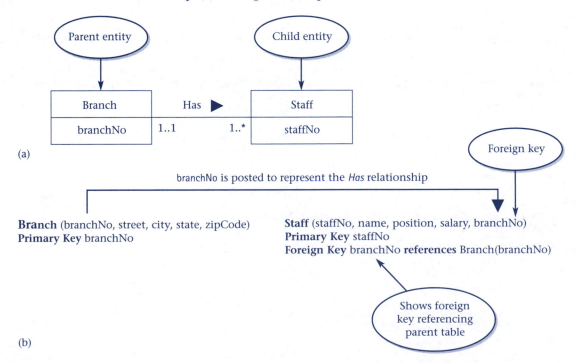

(a)

branchNo is posted to represent the *Has* relationship

Branch (branchNo, street, city, state, zipCode)
Primary Key branchNo

Staff (staffNo, name, position, salary, branchNo)
Primary Key staffNo
Foreign Key branchNo **references** Branch(branchNo)

(b)

There are several other examples of 1:* relationships in Figure 9.9 such as Director *Directs* Video and Member *Requests* RentalAgreement. You should repeat the rule given above for every 1:* relationship in the ER model.

> In the case where a 1:* relationship has one or more attributes, these attributes should follow the posting of the primary key to the child table. For example, if the Branch *Has* Staff relationship had an attribute called dateStart representing when a member of staff started at the branch, this attribute should also be posted to the Staff table along with the copy of the primary key of the Branch table, namely branchNo.

One-to-many (1:*) recursive relationships

The representation of a 1:* recursive relationship is similar to that described above. In Figure 9.9, there is a 1:* recursive relationship Staff *Supervises* Staff. In this case, both the parent and the child entity is Staff. Following the rule given above, you represent the *Supervises* relationship by posting a copy of the primary key of the Staff (parent) entity, staffNo, to the Staff (child) table, creating a second copy of this column to act as the foreign key. This copy of the column is renamed supervisorStaffNo to indicate its purpose. Figure 10.3(a) shows the Staff *Supervises* Staff ER diagram and Figure 10.3(b) shows the corresponding table (with BranchNo included to represent the Branch *Has* Staff relationship).

Recursive relationships defined in Section 7.2.2

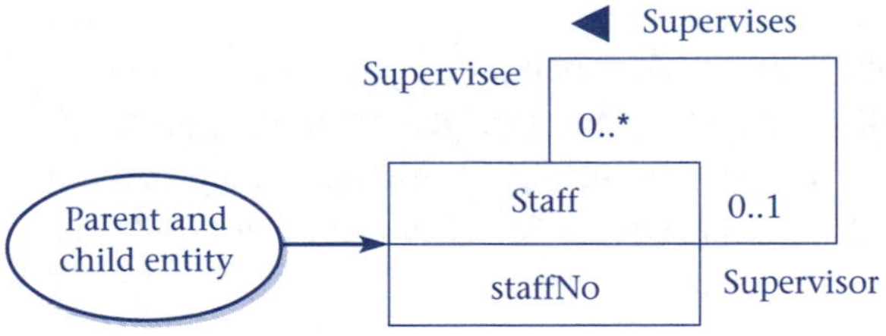

(a)

staffNo is posted to represent the *Supervises* relationship
and renamed supervisorStaffNo

Staff (staffNo, name, position, salary, branchNo, supervisorStaffNo)
Primary Key staffNo
Foreign Key branchNo **references** Branch(branchNo)
Foreign Key supervisorStaffNo **references** Staff(staffNo)

branchNo is posted
to represent Branch *Has* Staff
relationship

(b)

Figure 10.3

The 1:* Staff *Supervises* Staff recursive relationship:
(a) ER diagram;
(b) representation as a table.

One-to-one (1:1) binary relationships

1:1 relationships
defined in
Section 7.5.1

Participation
defined in
Section 7.5.5

Creating tables to represent 1:1 relationships is slightly more complex as you cannot use the cardinality to help identify the parent and child entities in a relationship. Instead, you need to use participation to help decide whether it's best to represent the relationship by combining the entities involved into one table or by creating two tables and posting a copy of the primary key from one table to the other. We consider how to create tables to represent the following participation constraints:

(1) *Mandatory* participation on *both* sides of 1:1 relationship

(2) *Mandatory* participation on *one* side of 1:1 relationship

(3) *Optional* participation on *both* sides of 1:1 relationship.

Mandatory participation on both sides of 1:1 relationship
In this case, you should combine the entities involved into one table and choose one of the primary keys of the original entities to be the primary key of the new table, while the other is used as an alternate key.

We don't have an example of such a relationship in Figure 9.9. However, let's consider how to represent a 1:1 relationship called Staff *Uses* Car with mandatory participation for both entities, as shown in Figure 10.4(a). The primary key for the Car entity is the vehicle license number (vehLicenseNo), and the other attributes include make and model. In this example, you place all the attributes for the Staff and Car entities into one table. You choose one of the primary keys to be the primary key of the new table, say staffNo, and the other becomes an alternate key, as shown in Figure 10.4(b).

In the case where a 1:1 relationship with mandatory participation on both sides has one or more attributes, these attributes should also be included in the table that represents the entities and relationship. For example, if the Staff *Uses* Car relationship had an attribute called dateAssigned, this attribute would also appear as a column in the StaffCar table.

Note that it is only possible to merge two entities into one table when there are no other relationships between these entities that would prevent this, such as a 1:* relationship. If this were the case, you would need to represent the Staff *Uses* Car relationship using the primary key/foreign key mechanism. We discuss how to designate the parent and child entities in this type of situation shortly.

Mandatory participation on one side of a 1:1 relationship
In this case, you are able to identify the parent and child entities for the 1:1 relationship using the participation constraints. The entity that has optional

Figure 10.4

The 1:1 Staff *Uses* Car relationship with mandatory participation for both entities: (a) ER diagram; (b) representation as a table.

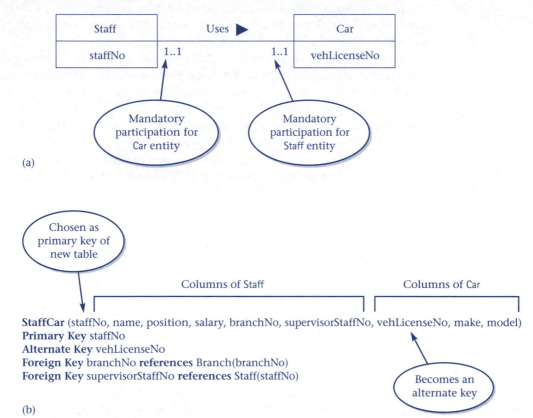

(a)

(b)

participation in the relationship is designated as the parent entity, and the entity that has mandatory participation in the relationship is designated as the child entity. As described above, a copy of the primary key of the parent entity is placed in the table representing the child entity.

The reason for posting a copy of the primary key of the entity that has optional participation (parent entity) to the entity that has mandatory participation (child entity) is that this copy of the primary key (foreign key) will always hold a value and hence avoid the presence of nulls in this column of the resulting table. If we did not follow this rule and chose to represent this relationship by positioning the foreign key column in the table representing the entity with optional participation, this column would contain nulls.

Let's now consider how you would represent the 1:1 Staff *Uses* Car relationship with mandatory participation only for the Car entity, as shown in Figure

10.5(a). The entity that has optional participation in the relationship (Staff) is designated as the parent entity, and the entity that has mandatory participation in the relationship (Car) is designated as the child entity. Therefore, a copy of the primary key of the Staff (parent) entity, staffNo, is placed in the Car (child) table, as shown in Figure 10.5(b). In this case, staffNo also becomes an alternate key for the Car table.

Figure 9.9 has a second example of a 1:1 relationship with mandatory participation on only one side, namely Staff *Manages* Branch with mandatory participation only for the Branch entity. Following the rule given above, the Staff entity is designated as the parent entity and the Branch entity is designated as the child entity. Therefore, a copy of the primary key of the Staff (parent) entity, staffNo, is placed in the Branch (child) table and renamed as mgrStaffNo, to indicate the purpose of the foreign key in the Branch table. Figure 10.6(a) shows the Staff *Manages* Branch ER diagram and Figure 10.6(b) shows the corresponding tables.

Figure 10.5

The 1:1 Staff *Uses* Car relationship with mandatory participation for the Car entity and optional participation for the Staff entity:
(a) ER diagram;
(b) representation as tables.

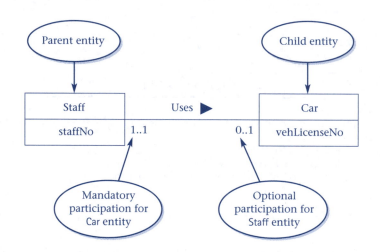

Figure 10.6

The 1:1 Staff *Manages* Branch relationship with mandatory participation for the Branch entity and optional participation for the Staff entity: (a) ER diagram; (b) representation as tables.

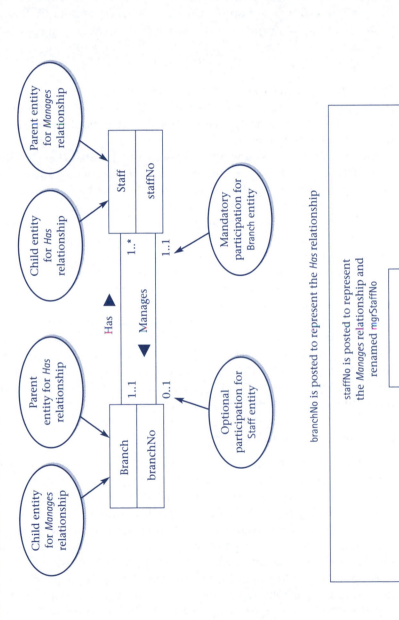

(a)

Branch (branchNo, street, city, state, zipCode, mgrStaffNo)
Primary Key branchNo
Foreign Key mgrStaffNo **references** Staff(staffNo)

Staff (staffNo, name, position, salary, branchNo, supervisorStaffNo)
Primary Key staffNo
Foreign Key branchNo **references** Branch(branchNo)
Foreign Key supervisorStaffNo **references** Staff(staffNo)

(b)

In the case where a 1:1 relationship with only mandatory participation for one entity in a relationship has one or more attributes, these attributes should follow the posting of the primary key to the child table. For example, if the Staff *Manages* Branch relationship had an attribute called dateStart, this attribute would appear as a column in the Branch table along with a copy of staffNo (renamed mgrStaffNo).

Optional participation on both sides of a 1:1 relationship

In this case, the designation of the parent and child entities is arbitrary unless you can find out more about the relationship that can help you reach a decision one way or the other.

Let's consider how you would represent the 1:1 Staff *Uses* Car relationship, with optional participation on both sides of the relationship, as shown in Figure 10.7(a). (Note that the discussion that follows is also relevant for 1:1 relationships with mandatory participation for both entities where you cannot select the option to put everything into a single table.) If you don't have any additional information to help you select the parent and child entities, your choice is arbitrary. In other words, you have the choice to post a copy of the primary key of the Staff entity to the Car entity, or vice versa.

However, let's assume you find that the majority of cars, but not all, are used by staff and only a minority of staff use cars. Now you can say that the Car entity, although optional, is closer to being mandatory than the Staff entity. You can therefore designate Staff as the parent entity and Car as the child entity, and post a copy of the primary key of the Staff entity (staffNo) into the Car table, as shown in Figure 10.7(b). (Note that the composition of the Staff and Car tables is the same as the example used in the discussion above on 1:1 relationships with mandatory participation on only one side.)

One-to-one (1:1) recursive relationships

For a 1:1 recursive relationship, you should follow the rules for participation as described above for a 1:1 relationship. However, in this special case of a 1:1 relationship, the entity on both sides of the relationship is the same. For a 1:1 recursive relationship with mandatory participation on both sides, you should represent the recursive relationship as a single table with two copies of the primary key. As before, one copy of the primary key represents a foreign key and should be renamed to indicate the relationship it represents.

For a 1:1 recursive relationship with mandatory participation on only one side, you have the option to create a single table with two copies of the primary key as described above, or to create a new table to represent the relationship. The new table would only have two columns, both copies of the primary key. As before, the copies of the primary keys act as foreign keys and have to be renamed to indicate the purpose of each in the table.

Figure 10.7

The 1:1 Staff *Uses* Car relationship with optional participation for both entities: (a) ER diagram; (b) representation as tables.

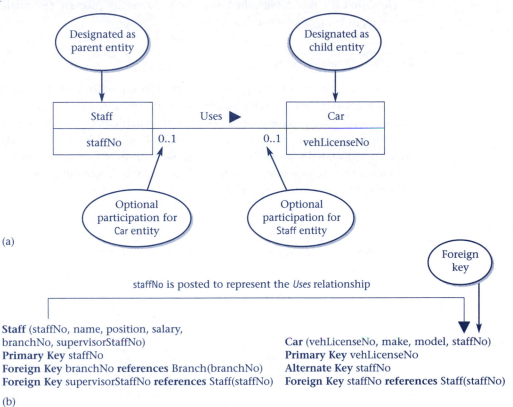

(a)

staffNo is posted to represent the *Uses* relationship

Staff (staffNo, name, position, salary, branchNo, supervisorStaffNo)
Primary Key staffNo
Foreign Key branchNo **references** Branch(branchNo)
Foreign Key supervisorStaffNo **references** Staff(staffNo)

Car (vehLicenseNo, make, model, staffNo)
Primary Key vehLicenseNo
Alternate Key staffNo
Foreign Key staffNo **references** Staff(staffNo)

(b)

For a 1:1 recursive relationship with optional participation on both sides, you should create a new table.

Many-to-many (*:*) binary relationships

For each *:* binary relationship, create a table to represent the relationship and include any attributes that are part of the relationship. We post a copy of the primary key attribute(s) of the entities that participate in the relationship into the new table, to act as foreign keys. One or both of the foreign keys will also form the primary key of the new table, possibly in combination with some of the attributes of the relationship.

: relationship discussed in Section 7.5.3

For example, consider the *:* relationship Actor *PlaysIn* Video shown in Figure 9.9. The two entities enclosing the *:* relationship, namely Actor and Video, act as parent entities and post copies of their primary keys (actorNo and catalogNo) to a new table called Role that represents the relationship. Note that the *PlaysIn* relationship has an attribute called character, which is also included in the Role table. Figure 10.8(a) shows the Actor *PlaysIn* Video ER diagram and Figure 10.8(b) shows the corresponding tables.

Note that the new table called Role has a composite primary key made up of two foreign keys, catalogNo and actorNo.

Complex relationship types

Complex relationship discussed in Section 7.5.4

For each complex relationship, that is a relationship with more than two participating entities, create a table to represent the relationship. We post a copy of the primary key attribute(s) of the entities that participate in the complex relationship into the new table, to act as foreign keys, and include any attributes that are associated with the relationship. One or more of the foreign keys will also form the primary key of the new table, possibly in combination with some of the attributes of the relationship.

Figure 10.8

The *:* Actor *PlaysIn* Video relationship: (a) ER diagram; (b) representation as tables.

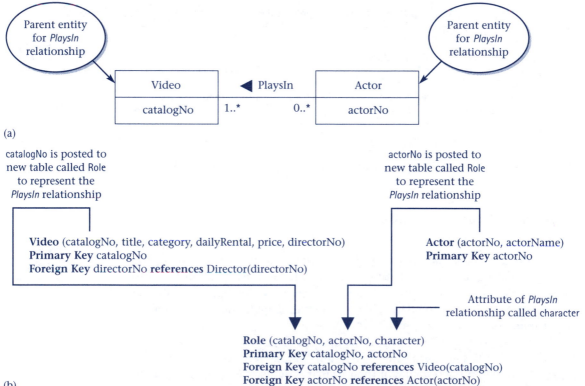

For example, the complex (ternary) *Registers* relationship represents the association between a member of staff who registers a new member at a branch as shown in Figure 9.9. The entities enclosing the complex relationship, namely Staff, Member, and Branch, act as parent entities and we post copies of their primary keys (staffNo, memberNo, and branchNo) to a new table called Registration that represents the relationship. Note that the *Registers* relationship has an attribute called dateJoined, which is also included in the Registration table. Figure 10.9(a) shows the *Registers* complex (ternary) relationship ER diagram and Figure 10.9(b) shows the corresponding tables.

Note that the new table called Registration has a composite primary key made up of two foreign keys, branchNo and memberNo.

Multi-valued attributes

For each multi-valued attribute associated with an entity, you should follow the rule described above for 1:* relationships. The entity is on the one side and is designated the parent entity while the multi-valued attribute is on the many side and is designated the child entity. A new table is created to hold the multi-valued attribute and the parent entity posts a copy of its primary key, to act as a foreign key. Unless the multi-valued attribute is itself an alternate key of the parent entity, the primary key of the new table is composed of the multi-valued attribute and the original primary key of the parent entity.

Figure 10.9

The complex *Registers* relationship: (a) ER diagram

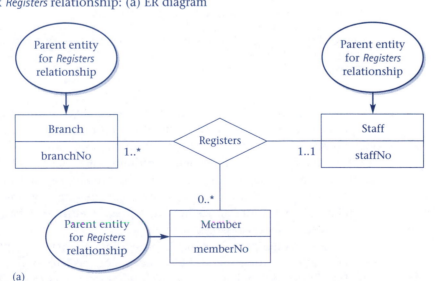

(a)

Figure 10.9 *Continued*

The complex *Registers* relationship: (b) representation as tables.

branchNo is posted to a
new table called Registration
to represent the
Registers relationship

Branch (branchNo, street, city, state, zipCode, mgrStaffNo)
Primary Key branchNo
Foreign Key mgrStaffNo **references** Staff(staffNo)

staffNo is posted to a new table called Registration
to represent the *Registers* relationship

Staff (staffNo, name, position, salary, branchNo, supervisorStaffNo)
Primary Key staffNo
Foreign Key branchNo **references** branch(branchNo)
Foreign Key supervisorStaffNo **references**

memberNo is posted to a new table
called Registration to represent the
Registers relationship

Member (memberNo, fName, IName, address)
Primary Key memberNo

Registration (branchNo, memberNo, staffNo, dataJoined)
Primary Key branchNo, memberNo
Foreign Key branchNo **references** Branch(branchNo)
Foreign Key memberNo **references** Member(memberNo)
Foreign Key staffNo **references** Staff(staffNo)

Attribute of *Registers*
relationship called
dataJoined

(b)

For example, to represent the situation where a single branch has up to three telephone numbers, the telNo attribute of the Branch entity has been defined as being a multi-valued attribute. To represent this, we create a new table called Telephone to represent the multi-valued attribute telNo. Figure 10.10(a) shows the ER diagram of the Branch entity with only the primary key and the telNo multi-valued attribute and Figure 10.10(b) shows the corresponding tables.

In Table 10.1 we summarize how to represent entities, relationships, and multi-valued attributes as tables.

In Step 1.6 of the database design methodology we have the option to represent entities using the enhanced ER concepts of specialization/generalization, which we'll describe in Chapter 11. We therefore also leave the discussion on how to map those enhanced concepts to tables until this chapter.

Figure 10.10

The multi-valued telNo attribute of the Branch entity: (a) ER diagram; (b) representation as tables.

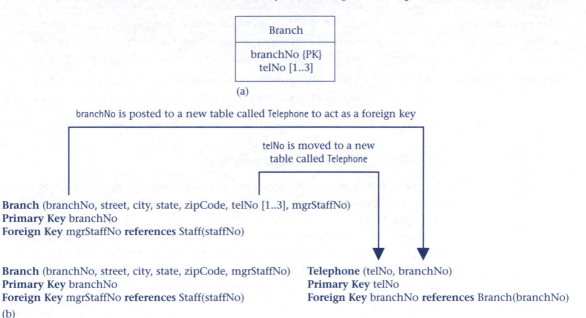

(a)

branchNo is posted to a new table called Telephone to act as a foreign key

telNo is moved to a new table called Telephone

Branch (branchNo, street, city, state, zipCode, telNo [1..3], mgrStaffNo)
Primary Key branchNo
Foreign Key mgrStaffNo **references** Staff(staffNo)

Branch (branchNo, street, city, state, zipCode, mgrStaffNo)   **Telephone** (telNo, branchNo)
Primary Key branchNo   **Primary Key** telNo
Foreign Key mgrStaffNo **references** Staff(staffNo)   **Foreign Key** branchNo **references** Branch(branchNo)

(b)

Table 10.1 Summary of how to represent entities, relationships, and multi-valued attributes as tables.

Entity/Relationship/Attribute	Representation as table(s)
Strong or weak entity	Create table that includes all simple attributes.
1:* binary relationship	Post copy of primary key of entity on 'one' side to table representing entity on 'many' side. Any attributes of relationship are also posted to 'many' side.
1:* recursive relationship	As entity on 'one' and 'many' side is the same, the table representing the entity receives a second copy of the primary key, which is renamed, and also any attributes of the relationship.
1:1 binary relationship:	
Mandatory participation on *both* sides	Combine entities into one table.
Mandatory participation on *one* side	Post copy of primary key of entity with optional participation to table representing entity with mandatory participation. Any attributes of relationship are also posted to table representing entity with mandatory participation.
Optional participation on *both* sides	Without further information, post copy of primary key of one entity to the other. However, if information is available, treat entity that is closer to having mandatory participation as being the child entity.

▶

Table 10.1 *Continued*

Entity/Relationship/Attribute	Representation as table(s)
: binary relationship/ complex relationship	Create a table to represent the relationship and include any attributes associated with the relationship. Post a copy of the primary key from each parent entity into the new table to act as foreign keys.
Multi-valued attribute	Create a table to represent the multi-valued attribute and post a copy of the primary key of the parent entity into the new table to act as a foreign key.

Document tables and foreign key attributes

At the end of Step 2.1, you document the full composition of the tables created from the ER model. The tables for the Branch user views of *StayHome* are shown in Figure 10.11.

Now that each table has its full set of columns, you're in a position to identify any new primary and/or alternate keys. This is particularly important for weak entities that rely on the posting of the primary key from the parent entity (or entities) to form all or part of a primary key of their own. For example, the weak entity VideoOrderLine shown in Figure C.1 of Appendix C has a composite primary key made up of a copy of the primary key of the Video entity (catalogNo) and a copy of the primary key of the VideoOrder entity (orderNo) as described in Figure C.2.

The DBDL syntax that describes each table can be extended to show integrity constraints on the foreign keys, as you'll see in Step 2.4. The data dictionary should also be updated to indicate the presence of foreign keys, and any new primary and alternate keys identified in this step. For example, following the posting of primary keys, the RentalAgreement table has gained a new alternate key, which is a combination of memberNo, videoNo, and dateOut.

Step 2.2 Check table structures using normalization

> **Objective**
> To check that each table has an appropriate structure, using normalization.

Normalization discussed in Chapter 8

The purpose of this step is to examine the groupings of columns in each table created in Step 2.1. You check the composition of each table using the rules of normalization, to avoid unnecessary duplication of data.

You should ensure that each table created in Step 2.1 is in at least third normal form (3NF). If you identify tables that are not in 3NF, this may indicate

Figure 10.11

Tables for the Branch user views of *StayHome*.

Actor (actorNo, actorName) **Primary Key** actorNo	**Branch** (branchNo, street, city, state, zipCode, mgrStaffNo) **Primary Key** branchNo **Alternate Key** zipCode **Foreign Key** mgrStaffNo **references** Staff(staffNo)
Director (directorNo, directorName) **Primary Key** directorNo	**Member** (memberNo, fName, lName, address) **Primary Key** memberNo
Registration (branchNo, memberNo, staffNo, dateJoined) **Primary Key** branchNo, memberNo **Foreign Key** branchNo **references** Branch(branchNo) **Foreign Key** memberNo **references** Member(memberNo) **Foreign Key** staffNo **references** Staff(staffNo)	**RentalAgreement** (rentalNo, dateOut, dateReturn, memberNo, videoNo) **Primary Key** rentalNo **Alternate Key** memberNo, videoNo, dateOut **Foreign Key** memberNo **references** Member(memberNo) **Foreign Key** videoNo **references** VideoForRent(videoNo)
Role (catalogNo, actorNo, character) **Primary Key** catalogNo, actorNo **Foreign Key** catalogNo **references** Video(catalogNo) **Foreign Key** actorNo **references** Actor(actorNo)	**Staff** (staffNo, name, position, salary, branchNo, supervisorStaffNo) **Primary Key** staffNo **Foreign Key** branchNo **references** Branch(branchNo) **Foreign Key** supervisorStaffNo **references** Staff(staffNo)
Telephone (telNo, branchNo) **Primary Key** telNo **Foreign Key** branchNo **references** Branch(branchNo)	**Video** (catalogNo, title, category, dailyRental, price, directorNo) **Primary Key** catalogNo **Foreign Key** directorNo **references** Director(directorNo)
VideoForRent (videoNo, available, catalogNo, branchNo) **Primary Key** VideoNo **Foreign Key** catalogNo **references** Video(catalogNo) **Foreign Key** branchNo **references** Branch(branchNo)	

that part of the ER model is incorrect, or that you have introduced an error while creating the tables from the model. If necessary, you may need to restructure the data model and/or tables.

Step 2.3 Check tables support user transactions

Objective
To ensure that the tables support the required transactions.

The objective of this step is to check that the tables created in Step 2.1 support the required transactions, as documented in the users' requirements specification. This type of check was carried out in Step 1.8 to ensure that the ER model supported the required transactions. In this step, you check that the tables created in the previous steps also support these transactions, and thereby ensure that no error has been introduced while creating tables.

One approach to checking that the tables support a transaction is to examine the transaction's data requirements to ensure that the data is present in one or more tables. Also, if a transaction requires data in more than one table you should check that these tables are linked through the primary key/foreign key mechanism. We demonstrate this approach by examining the transactions given in Section 6.4.4. Table 10.2(a) presents the data entry and update/deletion transactions and Table 10.2(b) presents the query transactions for the Branch user views of *StayHome*, together with the tables required by each. In each case, you highlight the columns required by the transaction, including, where necessary, those involved in joining tables.

Table 10.2(a) The tables required by the data entry and update/delete transactions of the Branch user views of *StayHome*.

Transaction	Table(s) required
(a) Enter the details of a new branch. (g) Update/delete the details of a branch.	**Branch (branchNo, street, city, state, zipCode, mgrStaffNo)** **Telephone (telNo, branchNo)** Foreign Key branchNo references Branch(branchNo)
(b) Enter the details of a new member of staff at a branch. (h) Update/delete the details of a member of staff at a branch.	**Staff (staffNo, name, position, salary, branchNo, supervisorStaffNo)**
(c) Enter the details for a newly released video. (i) Update/delete the details of a given video.	**Video (catalogNo, title, category, dailyRental, price, directorNo)** Foreign Key directorNo references Director (directorNo) **Director (directorNo, directorName)** **Role (catalogNo, actorNo, character)** Foreign Key catalogNo references Video(catalogNo) Foreign Key actorNo references Actor(actorNo) **Actor (actorNo, actorName)**
(d) Enter the details of copies of a new video at a given branch. (j) Update/delete the details of a copy of a video.	**VideoForRent (videoNo, available, catalogNo, branchNo)**
(e) Enter the details of a new member registering at a given branch. (k) Update/delete the details of a given member.	**Member (memberNo, fName, lName, address)** **Registration (branchNo, memberNo, staffNo, dateJoined)** Foreign Key memberNo references Member(memberNo)
(f) Enter the details of a rental agreement for a member renting a video. (l) Update/delete the details of a given rental agreement for a member renting a video.	**RentalAgreement (rentalNo, dateOut, dateReturn, memberNo, videoNo)**

From this analysis, you conclude that the tables shown in Figure 10.11 support all the transactions for the Branch user views of *StayHome*.

Table 10.2(b) The tables required by the query transactions of the Branch user views of *StayHome*.

Transaction	Table(s) required
(m) List the details of branches in a given city.	**Branch (branchNo**, **street**, **city**, **state**, **zipCode**, **mgrStaffNo)** **Telephone (telNo**, **branchNo)** Foreign Key branchNo references Branch(branchNo)
(n) List the name, position, and salary of staff at a given branch, ordered by staff name.	**Staff (**staffNo, **name**, **position**, **salary**, **branchNo**, supervisorStaffNo)
(o) List the name of each Manager at each branch, ordered by branch number.	**Branch (branchNo**, street, city, state, zipCode, **mgrStaffNo)** Foreign Key mgrStaffNo references Staff (staffNo) **Staff (**staffNo, **name**, position, salary, branchNo, supervisorStaffNo)
(p) List the title, category, and availability of all videos at a specified branch, ordered by category.	**Video (catalogNo**, **title**, **category**, dailyRental, price, directorNo) **VideoForRent (**videoNo, **available**, **catalogNo**, **branchNo)** Foreign Key catalogNo references Video (catalogNo)
(q) List the title, category, and availability of all videos for a given actor's name at a specified branch, ordered by title.	**Actor (actorNo**, **actorName)** **Role (catalogNo**, **actorNo**, character) Foreign Key catalogNo references Video(catalogNo) Foreign Key actorNo references Actor(actorNo) **Video (catalogNo**, **title**, **category**, dailyRental, price, directorNo) **VideoForRent (**videoNo, **available**, **catalogNo**, **branchNo)** Foreign Key catalogNo references Video (catalogNo)
(r) List the title, category, and availability of all videos for a given director's name at a specified branch, ordered by title.	**Director (directorNo**, **directorName)** **Video (catalogNo**, **title**, **category**, dailyRental, price, **directorNo)** Foreign Key directorNo references Director (directorNo) **VideoForRent (**videoNo, **available**, **catalogNo**, **branchNo)** Foreign Key catalogNo references Video (catalogNo)
(s) List the details of all videos a specified member currently has on rent.	**Video (catalogNo**, **title**, **category**, **dailyRental**, **price**, **directorNo)** **VideoForRent (**videoNo, **available**, **catalogNo**, branchNo) Foreign Key catalogNo references Video (catalogNo) **RentalAgreement (**rentalNo, **dateOut**, **dateReturn**, **memberNo**, **videoNo)** Foreign Key videoNo references VideoForRent (videoNo) Foreign Key memberNo references Member (memberNo) **Member (memberNo**, **fName**, **lName**, address)

Table 10.2(b) *Continued*

Transaction	Table(s) required
(t) List the details of copies of a given video at a specified branch.	**Video (catalogNo, title, category, dailyRental, price, directorNo)** **VideoForRent (videoNo, available, catalogNo, branchNo)** Foreign Key videoNo references VideoForRent (videoNo)
(u) List the titles of all videos in a specified category, ordered by title.	**Video (catalogNo, title, category,** dailyRental, price, directorNo)**
(v) List the total number of videos in each video category at each branch, ordered by branch number.	**Video (catalogNo, title, category,** dailyRental, price, directorNo)** **VideoForRent (videoNo, available, catalogNo, branchNo)** Foreign Key catalogNo references Video (catalogNo)
(w) List the total cost of the videos at all branches.	**Video (catalogNo,** title, category, dailyRental, **price,** directorNo)** **VideoForRent (videoNo, available, catalogNo, branchNo)** Foreign Key catalogNo references Video (catalogNo)
(x) List the total number of videos featuring each actor, ordered by actor name.	**Video (catalogNo,** title, category, dailyRental, price, directorNo)** **Role (catalogNo, actorNo, character)** Foreign Key catalogNo references Video(catalogNo) Foreign Key actorNo references Actor(actorNo) **Actor (actorNo, actorName)**
(y) List the total number of members at each branch who joined in 2002, ordered by branch number.	**Registration (branchNo, memberNo, staffNo, dateJoined)**
(z) List the total possible daily rental for videos at each branch, ordered by branch number.	**Video (catalogNo,** title, category, **dailyRental,** price, directorNo)** **VideoForRent (videoNo, available, catalogNo, branchNo)** Foreign Key catalogNo references Video(catalogNo)

> **TIP**
>
> As with Step 1.8 covered in the last chapter, this may look like a lot of hard work and it certainly can be. As a result, you may be tempted to omit this step. However, it's very important that you do these checks now rather than later when you'll find it much more difficult and costly to resolve any errors in your data model.

Step 2.4 Check business rules

Objective
To check business rules are represented in the logical database design.

Business rules are the constraints that you wish to impose in order to protect the database from becoming incomplete, inaccurate, or inconsistent. Although you may not be able to implement some business rules within the DBMS, this is not the question here. At this stage, you are concerned only with high-level design: that is, specifying *what* business rules are required irrespective of *how* this might be achieved. Having identified the business rules, you will have a logical data model that is a complete and accurate representation of the data requirements of the organization (or part of the organization) to be supported by the database. If necessary, you could produce a physical database design from the logical data model, for example to prototype the system for the user.

Prototyping discussed in Section 4.10

We consider the following types of business rules:

- required data,
- column domain constraints,
- entity integrity,
- multiplicity,
- referential integrity,
- other business rules.

Required data

Some columns must always contain a value; in other words, they are not allowed to hold nulls. For example, every member of staff must have a job position (such as Manager or Supervisor). These constraints should have been identified when you documented the columns (attributes) in the data dictionary in Step 1.3.

Nulls defined in Section 2.3.1

Column domain constraints

Every column has a domain (a set of values that are legal for it). For example, the position of a member of staff is Director, Manager, Supervisor, Assistant, or Buyer so the domain of the position column consists of only these values. These constraints should have been identified when you chose the column (attribute) domains for the data in Step 1.4.

Domains defined in Section 2.2.1

Entity integrity

Entity integrity
defined in
Section 2.3.2

The primary key of an entity cannot hold nulls. For example, each record of the Staff table must have a value for the primary key column, staffNo. These constraints should have been considered when you identified the primary keys for each entity in Step 1.5.

Multiplicity

Multiplicity
discussed in
Section 7.5

Multiplicity represents the constraints that are placed on relationships between data in the database. Examples of such constraints include the requirements that a branch must have members and each branch must have staff. Ensuring that all appropriate business rules are identified and represented is an important part of modeling the organization's data requirements. In Step 1.2 we defined the relationships between entities and all business rules that can be represented in this way were defined and documented in this step.

Referential integrity

Referential
integrity defined
in Section 2.3.3

A foreign key links each record in the child table to the record in the parent table containing the matching primary key value. Referential integrity means that, if the foreign key contains a value, that value must refer to an existing record in the parent table. For example, the branchNo column in the Staff table links the member of staff to the record in the Branch table where he or she works. If branchNo is not null, it must contain a value that exists in the branchNo column of the Branch table, or the member of staff will be assigned to a non-existent branch.

There are two issues regarding foreign keys that must be addressed.

(1) Are nulls allowed for the foreign key?

Participation
defined in
Section 7.5.5

For example, can you store the details of a member of staff without having a branch number for the employee? The issue is not whether the branch number exists, but whether a branch number must be specified. In general, if the participation of the child table in the relationship is mandatory, then nulls are not allowed. On the other hand, if the participation of the child table is optional, then nulls should be allowed.

(2) How do you ensure referential integrity?

To do this, you specify **existence constraints**, which define conditions under which a primary key or foreign key may be inserted, updated, or deleted. Consider the 1:* relationship Branch *Has* Staff. The primary key of the Branch table (branchNo) is a foreign key in the Staff table. Let's consider the following six cases.

*Case 1: Insert record into child table (*Staff*)*
To ensure referential integrity, check that the foreign key column (branchNo) of the new Staff record is set to null or to a value of an existing Branch record.

*Case 2: Delete record from child table (*Staff*)*
If a record in the child table is deleted, referential integrity is unaffected.

*Case 3: Update foreign key of child record (*Staff*)*
This is similar to Case 1. To ensure referential integrity, check that the foreign key column (branchNo) of the updated Staff record is set to null or to a value of an existing Branch record.

*Case 4: Insert record into parent table (*Branch*)*
Inserting a record into the parent table (Branch) does not affect referential integrity; it simply becomes a parent without any children – in other words, a branch without members of staff.

*Case 5: Delete record from parent table (*Branch*)*
If a record of the parent table is deleted, referential integrity is lost if there is a child record referencing the deleted parent record. In other words, referential integrity is lost if the deleted branch currently has one or more members of staff working at it. There are several strategies you can consider in this case:

■ NO ACTION Prevent a deletion from the parent table if there are any refer-encing child records. In our example, 'You cannot delete a branch if there are currently members of staff working there'.

■ CASCADE When the parent record is deleted, automatically delete any refer-encing child records. If any deleted child record also acts as a parent record in another relationship then the delete operation should be applied to the records in this child table, and so on in a cascading manner. In other words, deletions from the parent table cascade to the child table. In our example, 'Deleting a branch automatically deletes all members of staff working there'. Clearly, in this situation, this strategy would not be wise.

■ SET NULL When a parent record is deleted, the foreign key values in all related child records are automatically set to null. In our example, 'If a branch is deleted, indicate that the current branch for those members of staff previously working there is unknown'. You can only consider this strategy if the columns comprising the foreign key can accept nulls, as defined in Step 1.3.

■ SET DEFAULT When a parent record is deleted, the foreign key values in all related child records are automatically set to their default values. In our example, 'If a branch is deleted, indicate that the current assignment of members of staff previously working there is being assigned to another (default) branch'. You can only consider this strategy if the columns comprising the foreign key have default values, as defined in Step 1.3.

■ NO CHECK When a parent record is deleted, do nothing to ensure that referential integrity is maintained. This strategy should only be considered in extreme circumstances.

Case 6: Update primary key of parent record (Branch)

If the primary key value of a parent table record is updated, referential integrity is lost if there exists a child record referencing the old primary key value; that is, if the updated branch currently has staff working there. To ensure referential integrity, the strategies described above can be used. In the case of CASCADE, the updates to the primary key of the parent record are reflected in any referencing child records, and so on in a cascading manner.

The referential integrity constraints for the tables that have been created for the Branch user views of *StayHome* are shown in Figure 10.12.

Other business rules

Finally, you consider constraints for any remaining business rules that have not been defined so far. Business rules should be represented as constraints on the database to ensure that only permitted updates to tables governed by 'real world' transactions are allowed. For example, *StayHome* has a business rule that prevents a member from renting more than 10 videos at any one time.

Document all business rules

Document all business rules for consideration during physical database design.

Step 2.5 Review logical database design with users

> **Objective**
> To ensure that the logical database design is a true representation of the data requirements of the organization (or part of the organization) to be supported by the database.

The logical database design should now be complete and fully documented. However, to finish this step you should review the design with the users.

If you're designing a database that has only a single user view or you are using the centralized approach and have merged the user requirements for two or more user views, then you are ready to proceed to physical database design, which we'll describe in Chapters 12 to 16. If, however, you're designing a more

Centralized and view integration approaches discussed in Sections 4.5 and 6.4.4

Figure 10.12

The referential integrity constraints for the tables in the Branch user views of *StayHome*.

Branch
Foreign Key mgrStaffNo **references** Staff(staffNo) ON UPDATE CASCADE ON DELETE NO ACTION

Registration
Foreign Key branchNo **references** Branch(branchNo) ON UPDATE CASCADE ON DELETE NO ACTION
Foreign Key memberNo **references** Member(memberNo) ON UPDATE CASCADE ON DELETE NO ACTION
Foreign Key staffNo **references** Staff(staffNo) ON UPDATE CASCADE ON DELETE NO ACTION

RentalAgreement
Foreign Key memberNo **references** Member(memberNo) ON UPDATE CASCADE ON DELETE NO ACTION
Foreign Key videoNo **references** VideoForRent(videoNo) ON UPDATE CASCADE ON DELETE NO ACTION

Role
Foreign Key catalogNo **references** Video(catalogNo) ON UPDATE CASCADE ON DELETE CASCADE
Foreign Key actorNo **references** Actor(actorNo) ON UPDATE CASCADE ON DELETE NO ACTION

Staff
Foreign Key branchNo **references** Branch(branchNo) ON UPDATE CASCADE ON DELETE NO ACTION
Foreign Key supervisorStaffNo **references** Staff(staffNo) ON UPDATE CASCADE ON DELETE SET NULL

Telephone
Foreign Key branchNo **references** Branch(branchNo) ON UPDATE CASCADE ON DELETE CASCADE

Video
Foreign Key directorNo **references** Director(directorNo) ON UPDATE CASCADE ON DELETE NO ACTION

VideoForRent
Foreign Key catalogNo **references** Video(catalogNo) ON UPDATE CASCADE ON DELETE NO ACTION
Foreign Key branchNo **references** Branch(branchNo) ON UPDATE CASCADE ON DELETE NO ACTION

complex database that has numerous and varied user views and you're using the view integration approach to manage those user views then you should read Appendix C before you proceed to physical database design.

Chapter summary

✓ The main purpose of Step 2 of logical database design is to create tables for the ER model and to check the structure of the tables.

✓ The structures of the tables are checked using normalization.

✓ The tables are checked to ensure that they support the transactions defined in the users' requirements.

✓ Business rules can protect the database from becoming incomplete, inaccurate, or inconsistent. These rules include: integrity constraints, required data, column domain constraints, entity integrity, multiplicity, referential integrity, and any additional business rules.

✓ Existence constraints ensure referential integrity by defining conditions under which a primary key or foreign key may be inserted, updated, or deleted.

✓ There are several strategies to consider when a child record references the parent record that you're attempting to delete/update: NO ACTION, CASCADE, SET NULL, SET DEFAULT, and NO CHECK.

Review questions

10.1 Describe the main purpose and tasks of Step 2 of the logical database design methodology.

10.2 Describe the rules for creating tables that represent:

(a) strong and weak entities;

(b) one-to-many (1:*) binary relationships;

(c) one-to-many (1:*) recursive relationships;

(d) one-to-one (1:1) binary relationships;

(e) one-to-one (1:1) recursive relationships;

(f) many-to-many (*:*) binary relationships;

(g) complex relationships;

(h) multi-valued attributes.

Give examples to illustrate your answers.

10.3 Discuss how the technique of normalization can be used to check the structure of the tables created from the ER model and supporting documentation.

10.4 Discuss one approach that can be used to check that the tables support the transactions required by the users.

10.5 Discuss what business rules represent. Give examples to illustrate your answers.

10.6 Describe the alternative strategies that can be applied if there is a child record referencing a parent record that we wish to delete.

Exercise

10.7 Create a description of the tables for each answer ER diagram given in Appendix E without first looking at the answer table descriptions that accompany each case study. Compare your tables with the answer tables and justify any differences found.

Chapter 11

Enhanced ER modeling techniques

In this chapter you will learn:

▶ The limitations of the basic ER modeling concepts and the requirements to model more complex applications using enhanced data modeling concepts.

▶ The main concepts associated with the Enhanced Entity–Relationship (EER) model called specialization/generalization.

▶ A notation for displaying specialization/generalization in an EER diagram.

▶ How to create tables that represent specialization/generalization in an EER model.

Methodology
summarized in
Appendix B

We covered the basic concepts associated with Entity–Relationship (ER) modeling in Chapter 7, and used these concepts in the construction of ER models in the logical database design methodology presented in Chapters 9 and 10. These basic concepts are often perfectly adequate for the representation of the data requirements for many different database applications. However, the basic ER concepts can be limiting when modeling more complex database applications with a large amount of data and/or data with complex interrelationships. This stimulated the need to develop additional 'semantic' modeling concepts. The original ER model with additional semantic concepts is referred to as the **Enhanced Entity–Relationship (EER)** model. In this chapter, we describe one of the most useful concepts associated with the EER model called specialization/generalization and show how it can be used.

The database design methodology presented in this book provides an option to use the enhanced concepts of the EER model in Step 1.6. The choice of whether to include this step is largely dependent on whether the designer considers that using these enhanced modeling concepts facilitates or hinders the process of database design.

11.1 Specialization/Generalization

The concept of specialization/generalization is associated with special types of entities known as **superclasses** and **subclasses**, and the process of **attribute inheritance**. We begin this section by defining what superclasses and subclasses are and by examining superclass/subclass relationships. We describe the process of attribute inheritance and contrast the process of specialization with generalization. We also show how to represent specialization/generalization in a diagram using the UML (Unified Modeling Language) notation.

11.1.1 Superclasses and subclasses

Superclass

An entity that includes one or more distinct groupings of its occurrences, which require to be represented in a data model.

Subclass

A distinct grouping of occurrences of an entity, which require to be represented in a data model.

A general entity called a superclass includes groupings of more specific kinds of entities called subclasses. For example, an entity that may have many distinct subclasses is Staff. The entities that are members of the Staff entity may be classified as Manager, Secretary, and SalesPersonnel. In other words, the Staff entity is the superclass of the Manager, Secretary, and SalesPersonnel subclasses.

11.1.2 Superclass/Subclass relationships

The relationship between a superclass and any one of its subclasses is one-to-one (1:1) and is called a superclass/subclass relationship. For example, Staff/Manager forms a superclass/subclass relationship. Each member of a subclass is also a member of the superclass but has a distinct role.

We can use superclasses and subclasses to avoid describing different types of entities with possibly different attributes within a single entity. For example, SalesPersonnel may have special attributes such as salesArea and carAllowance, and

1:1 relationships defined in Section 7.5.1

so on. If all staff attributes and those specific to particular jobs are represented by a single Staff entity, this may result in a lot of nulls for the job-specific attributes. Clearly, Sales Personnel have common attributes with other staff, such as staffNo, name, position, and salary, but it's the unshared attributes that cause problems when we try to represent all members of staff within a single entity. Defining superclasses/subclasses can also allow us to show relationships that are associated only with particular subclasses of staff and not with staff in general. For example, Sales Personnel may have distinct relationships that are not appropriate for all staff, such as SalesPersonnel *Requires* Car.

To illustrate the points being made above, let's consider the table called AllStaff in Figure 11.1. This table holds the details of all members of staff no matter what position they hold. A consequence of holding the details of all members of staff in one table is that while the columns appropriate to all staff are filled (namely, staffNo, name, position, salary, and branchNo), those that are only applicable to particular job roles will only be partially filled. For example, the columns associated with the SalesPersonnel subclass (namely salesArea, vehLicenseNo, and carAllowance) have no values for those members of staff not in this subclass.

Figure 11.1

The AllStaff table holding details of all members of staff.

Columns appropriate for all staff | Columns appropriate for Sales Personnel

AllStaff

staffNo	name	position	salary	branchNo	salesArea	vehLicenseNo	carAllowance
S1500	Tom Daniels	Manager	46000	B001			
S0003	Sally Adams	Assistant	30000	B001			
S0010	Mary Martinez	Manager	50000	B002			
S0099	Joe Hope	Sales Personnel	35000	B002	WA 1A	SH22	5000
S3250	Robert Chin	Supervisor	32000	B002			
S2250	Sally Stern	Manager	48000	B004			
S2345	Linda Haven	Sales Personnel	37500	B002	WA 2B	SH34	5000
S0415	Art Peters	Manager	41000	B003			

There are two important reasons for introducing the concepts of superclasses and subclasses into an ER model. The first reason is that it avoids describing similar concepts more than once, thereby saving you time and making the ER model more readable. The second reason is that it adds more semantic information to the design in a form that is familiar to many people. For example, the assertions that 'Manager IS-A member of staff' and 'van IS-A type of vehicle' communicate significant semantic content in an easy-to-follow form.

11.1.3 Attribute inheritance

As mentioned above, an entity occurrence in a subclass represents the same 'real world' object as in the superclass. Hence, a member of a subclass inherits those attributes associated with the superclass, but may also have subclass-specific attributes. For example, a member of the SalesPersonnel subclass has subclass-specific attributes, salesArea, vehLicenseNo, and carAllowance, and all the attributes of the Staff superclass, namely staffNo, name, position, salary, and branchNo.

A subclass is an entity in its own right and so it may also have one or more subclasses. A subclass with more than one superclass is called a *shared subclass*. In other words, a member of a shared subclass must be a member of the associated superclasses. As a consequence, the attributes of the superclasses are inherited by the shared subclass, which may also have its own additional attributes. This process is referred to as *multiple inheritance*.

An entity and its subclasses and their subclasses, and so on, is called a **type hierarchy**. Type hierarchies are known by a variety of names including: **specialization hierarchy** (for example, Manager is a specialization of Staff), **generalization hierarchy** (for example, Staff is a generalization of Manager), and **IS-A hierarchy** (for example, Manager IS-A (member of) Staff). We describe the process of specialization and generalization in the following sections.

11.1.4 Specialization process

Specialization

The process of maximizing the differences between members of an entity by identifying their distinguishing characteristics.

Specialization is a top-down approach to defining a set of superclasses and their related subclasses. The set of subclasses is defined on the basis of some distinguishing characteristics of the entities in the superclass. When we identify a subclass of an entity, we then associate attributes specific to the subclass (where necessary), and also identify any relationships between the subclass and other entities or subclasses (where necessary).

11.1.5 Generalization process

> **Generalization**
>
> The process of minimizing the differences between entities by identifying their common features.

The process of generalization is a bottom-up approach, which results in the identification of a generalized superclass from the original subclasses. The process of generalization can be viewed as the reverse of the specialization process. For example, consider a model where Manager, Secretary, and SalesPersonnel are represented as distinct entities. If we apply the process of generalization on these entities, we attempt to identify any similarities between them such as common attributes and relationships. As stated earlier, these entities share attributes common to all staff, and therefore we would identify Manager, Secretary, and SalesPersonnel as subclasses of a generalized Staff superclass.

Diagrammatic representation

UML has a special notation for representing subclasses and superclasses. For example, consider the specialization/generalization of the Staff entity into subclasses that represent job roles. The Staff superclass and the Manager, Secretary, and SalesPersonnel subclasses can be represented in an EER diagram as illustrated in Figure 11.2. Note that the Staff superclass and the subclasses, being entities, are represented as rectangles. Specialization/generalization subclasses are attached by lines to a triangle that points towards the superclass. The label below the triangle, shown as {Optional, And}, describes the constraints on the specialization/generalization relationship. These constraints are discussed in more detail in the following section.

Attributes that are specific to a given subclass are listed in the lower section of the rectangle representing that subclass. For example, the salesArea, vehLicenseNo, and carAllowance attributes are associated only with the SalesPersonnel subclass, and are not applicable to the Manager or Secretary subclasses. Similarly, we show attributes that are specific to the Manager (bonus) and Secretary (typingSpeed) subclasses.

Figure 11.2 also shows relationships that are applicable to specific subclasses or just to the superclass. For example, the Manager subclass is related to the Branch entity through the *Manages* relationship, whereas the Staff entity is related to the Branch entity through the *Has* relationship.

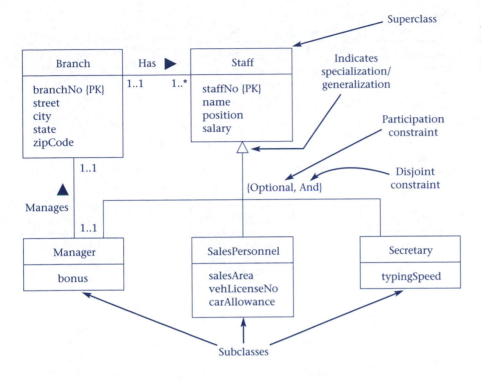

Figure 11.2

Specialization/
generalization of the
Staff entity into
subclasses
representing job
roles.

Note that the multiplicity of Manager in the *Manages* relationship is 1..1, whereas previously the multiplicity of Staff in the *Manages* relationship was 0..1 (in other words, Manager has mandatory participation whereas Staff had optional participation).

In Figure 11.3, the Staff specialization/generalization has been expanded to show a shared subclass called SalesManager and a subclass called Secretary with its own subclass called AssistantSecretary. In other words, a member of the SalesManager shared subclass must be a member of the SalesPersonnel and Manager subclasses and Staff superclass. As a consequence, the attributes of the Staff superclass (staffNo, name, position, salary), and the attributes of the subclasses SalesPersonnel (salesArea, vehLicenseNo, carAllowance) and Manager (bonus), are inherited by the SalesManager subclass, which also has its own additional attribute called salesTarget.

AssistantSecretary is a subclass of Secretary, which is a subclass of Staff. This means that a member of the AssistantSecretary subclass must be a member of the Secretary subclass and the Staff superclass. As a consequence, the attributes of the Staff superclass (staffNo, name, position, salary) and the attribute of the Secretary subclass (typingSpeed) are inherited by the AssistantSecretary subclass, which also has its own additional attribute called startDate.

Figure 11.3

Specialization/
generalization of
the Staff entity
including a shared
subclass called
SalesManager and a
subclass called
Secretary with its
own subclass called
AssistantSecretary.

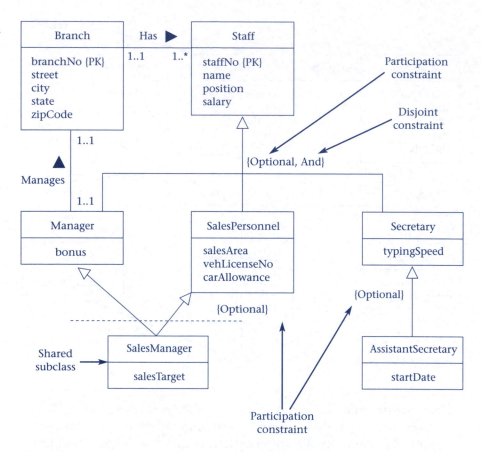

11.1.6 Constraints on superclass/subclass relationships

There are two constraints that may apply to a superclass/subclass relationship,
called participation constraints and disjoint constraints.

Participation constraints

> **Participation constraint**
>
> Determines whether every occurrence in the superclass must participate as a member
> of a subclass.

A **participation constraint** may be mandatory or optional. A superclass/sub-
class relationship with a *mandatory participation* specifies that every entity
occurrence in the superclass must also be a member of a subclass. To represent
mandatory participation, a 'Mandatory' is placed in curly brackets below the

triangle that points towards the superclass. For example, in Figure 11.4 the Vehicle specialization/generalization (Van, Bus, and Car) has mandatory participation, which means that every vehicle must be a van, bus, or car.

A superclass/subclass relationship with *optional participation* specifies that a member of a superclass need not belong to any of its subclasses. To represent optional participation, an 'Optional' is placed in curly brackets below the triangle that points towards the superclass. For example, in Figure 11.2 the job role specialization/generalization has optional participation, which means that a member of staff need not have an additional job role such as a Manager, Secretary, or Sales Personnel.

Disjoint constraints

> **Disjoint constraint**
>
> Describes the relationship between members of the subclasses and indicates whether it's possible for a member of a superclass to be a member of one, or more than one, subclass.

The **disjoint constraint** only applies when a superclass has more than one subclass. If the subclasses are *disjoint*, then an entity occurrence can be a member of only one of the subclasses. To represent a disjoint superclass/subclass relationship, an 'Or' is placed next to the participation constraint within the curly brackets. For example, in Figure 11.4 the subclasses of the Vehicle specialization/generalization (Van, Bus, and Car) are disjoint, which means that a vehicle is a van, bus, or car.

If subclasses of a specialization/generalization are not disjoint (called nondisjoint), then an entity occurrence may be a member of more than one subclass.

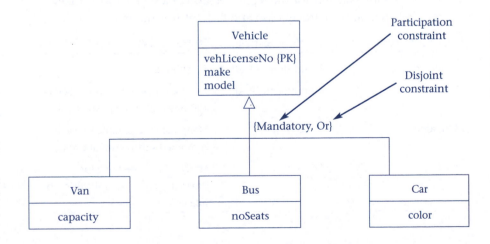

Figure 11.4

Specialization/ generalization of the Vehicle entity into vehicle types.

To represent a *nondisjoint* superclass/subclass relationship, an 'And' is placed next to the participation constraint within the curly brackets. For example, in Figure 11.2 (and Figure 11.3) the subclasses of the job role specialization/generalization (Manager, Secretary, SalesPersonnel) are nondisjoint, which means that an entity occurrence can be a member of both the Manager and SalesPersonnel subclasses. This is also confirmed by the presence of the shared subclass called SalesManager.

The participation and disjoint constraints of specialization/generalization are distinct giving the following four categories: mandatory and nondisjoint, optional and nondisjoint, mandatory and disjoint, and optional and disjoint.

11.2 Creating tables to represent specialization/generalization

In Chapter 10, we described how to create tables from a data model built using the basic concepts of the ER model. In this section, we show how to create tables for a specialization/generalization hierarchy. We illustrate this process for the EER models shown in Figures 11.2 and 11.4. As before, we describe each table using the Database Definition Language (DBDL) for relational databases.

DBDL defined in Step 2.1 of Chapter 10

For each superclass/subclass relationship in the EER model, you identify the superclass as the parent entity and the subclass as the child entity. There are various options on how you may best represent such a relationship as one or more tables. The selection of the most appropriate option is dependent on the participation and disjoint constraints on the superclass/subclass relationship, as shown in Table 11.1.

Parent/child entities covered in Step 2.1 of Chapter 10

Table 11.1 Options available for the representation of a superclass/subclass relationship based on the participation and disjoint constraints.

Participation constraint	Disjoint constraint	Tables required
Mandatory	Nondisjoint {And}	Single table
Optional	Nondisjoint {And}	Two tables: one table for superclass and one table for all subclasses
Mandatory	Disjoint {Or}	Many tables: one table for each combined superclass/subclass
Optional	Disjoint {Or}	Many tables: one table for superclass and one table for each subclass

We use the Staff specialization/generalization in Figure 11.2 as our first example. The relationship that the Staff superclass has with its subclasses (Manager, SalesPersonnel, or Secretary) is *optional*, as a member of staff may not belong to any of the subclasses, and *nondisjoint*, as a member of staff may belong to more than one subclass. Based on the options given in Table 11.1, you should represent the Staff superclass/subclass relationship by creating a table for the superclass and a table for all of the subclasses, as shown in Figure 11.5. For clarification, we also include a table to represent the Branch entity and its relationship with Staff.

We use the Vehicle specialization/generalization in Figure 11.4 as our second example. The relationship that the Vehicle superclass has with its subclasses (Van, Bus, or Car) is *mandatory*, as all members of the Vehicle superclass must belong to one of the subclasses, and *disjoint*, as a member of the Vehicle superclass can belong to only one subclass. Based on the options given in Table 11.1, you should represent the Vehicle superclass/subclass relationship by creating a table for each combined superclass/subclass, as shown in Figure 11.6.

Although the options described in Table 11.1 provide some guidelines for how best to represent a superclass/subclass relationship, there are other factors that may influence the final selection such as:

■ whether the subclasses are involved in distinct relationships;

■ the number of attributes that are distinct to each subclass;

■ the relative number of entity occurrences represented by the superclass and by each subclass.

Figure 11.5

Tables to represent the Staff specialization/generalization and the Branch entity shown in Figure 11.2.

Staff superclass
staff (staffNo, name, position, salary, branchNo)
Primary Key staffNo
Foreign Key branchNo **references** Branch(branchNo)

Staff subclasses
AllStaffSubclasses (subclassStaffNo, bonus, salesArea, vehLicenseNo, carAllowance, typingSpeed)
Primary Key subclassStaffNo
Foreign Key subclassStaffNo **references** Staff(staffNo)

Branch
Branch (branchNo, street, city, state, zipCode, mgrStaffNo)
Primary Key branchNo
Foreign Key mgrStaffNo **references** AllStaffSubclasses(subclassStaffNo)

Figure 11.6

Tables to represent the Vehicle specialization/generalization shown in Figure 11.4.

Van subclass
Van (vehLicenseNo, make, model, capacity)
Primary Key vehLicenseNo

Bus subclass
Bus (vehLicenseNo, make, model, noSeats)
Primary Key vehLicenseNo

Car subclass
Car (vehLicenseNo, make, model, color)
Primary Key vehLicenseNo

Chapter summary

✓ A **superclass** is an entity that includes one or more distinct groupings of its occurrences, which require to be represented in a model.

✓ A **subclass** is a distinct grouping of occurrences of an entity, which require to be represented in a data model.

✓ **Attribute inheritance** is the process by which a member of a subclass may possess subclass-specific attributes, and inherit those attributes associated with the superclass.

✓ **Specialization** is the process of maximizing the differences between members of an entity by identifying their distinguishing characteristics.

✓ **Generalization** is the process of minimizing the differences between entities by identifying their common features.

✓ The constraints that may apply on a superclass/subclass relationship are called participation and disjoint constraints.

✓ A **participation constraint** determines whether every occurrence in the superclass must participate as a member of a subclass.

✓ A **disjoint constraint** describes the relationship between members of the subclasses and indicates whether it's possible for a member of a super-class to be a member of one, or more than one, subclass.

Review questions

11.1 Describe what a superclass and a subclass represent.

11.2 Describe the relationship between a superclass and its subclass.

11.3 Describe, and illustrate using an example, the process of attribute inheritance.

11.4 What are the main reasons for introducing the concepts of superclasses and subclasses into an EER model?

11.5 Describe what a shared subclass represents.

11.6 Describe and contrast the process of specialization with the process of generalization.

11.7 Describe the two main constraints that apply to a specialization/generalization relationship.

Exercises

11.8 Examine how specialization/generalization has been applied to some of the case studies described in Appendix E.

11.9 Consider whether it is appropriate to introduce the enhanced concepts of specialization/generalization into the ER model for the case study described in Exercise 7.12. If appropriate, redraw the ER diagram as an EER diagram with the additional enhanced concepts.

Part 4

Physical database design

Chapter 12

Logical database design
Step 1 Create ER model
Step 2 Map ER model to tables

Physical database design
Step 3 Translate logical design
Step 4 Choose file organizations
Step 5 Design user views
Step 6 Design security
Step 7 Controlled redundancy
Step 8 Monitor and tune

Physical database design – Step 3

In this chapter you will learn:

The purpose of physical database design. ◄

How to map the logical database design to a physical database design. ◄

How to design base tables for the target DBMS. ◄

How to design the representation of derived data. ◄

How to design business rules for the target DBMS. ◄

In these next few chapters, we describe and illustrate by example a physical database design methodology for relational databases. The starting point for this chapter is the logical data model and the documentation that describes the model created in Steps 1 and 2 of the methodology. The methodology started by producing a logical data model in Step 1 and then used the logical model to derive a set of tables in Step 2. The logical model and derived tables were checked to ensure they were correctly structured using the technique of normalization, and to ensure they supported the transactions the users require.

Steps 1 and 2 covered in Chapters 9 and 10

In the second phase of the database design methodology, namely **physical database design**, you must decide how to translate the logical database structure (that is, the entities, attributes, relationships, and constraints) into a physical database design that can be implemented using the target DBMS. As many parts of physical database design are highly dependent on the target DBMS, you may find that there may be more than one way of implementing any given part of the database. Therefore, to carry out physical database design properly, you need to be fully aware of the functionality of the target DBMS, and you need to understand the advantages and disadvantages of each alternative for a particular implementation. For some systems, you may also need to select a suitable storage strategy that takes account of intended database usage. PC RDBMSs, such as Microsoft Access, generally have a fixed storage structure and so, for such a system, you probably won't have to worry about this step.

In this chapter, we convert the tables derived from the logical data model into a specific database implementation. In Chapter 13, we'll discuss how to choose file organizations for the base tables and decide when to create indexes. In Chapter 14, we'll look at ways to ensure the security of the database through the creation of user views and appropriate database security mechanisms. In Chapter 15, we'll give guidelines for deciding when to denormalize the physical data model and introduce redundancy to improve performance and in Chapter 16 we'll discuss the ongoing process of monitoring and tuning the operational system.

Throughout the following chapters we sometimes show physical implementation details to clarify the discussion. To illustrate the differences between DBMSs, we use Microsoft Access to illustrate implementation issues for the *StayHome* case study. In contrast, we'll use the Oracle DBMS for the second case study we'll work through in Chapters 17 and 18.

Before we present the methodology for physical database design, we briefly review the design process.

12.1 Comparison of logical and physical database design

Logical database design is independent of implementation details, such as the specific functionality of the target DBMS, application programs, programming languages, or any other physical considerations. The output of this process is a logical data model that includes a set of relational tables together with supporting documentation, such as a data dictionary. These represent the sources of information for the physical design process, and they provide you with a vehicle for making trade-offs that are so important to an efficient database design.

Whereas logical database design is concerned with the *what*, physical database design is concerned with the *how*. In particular, the physical database designer must know how the computer system hosting the DBMS operates, and must also be fully aware of the functionality of the target DBMS. As the functionality provided by current systems varies widely, physical design must be tailored to a specific DBMS. However, physical database design is not an isolated activity – there is often feedback between physical, logical, and application design. For example, decisions taken during physical design to improve performance, such as merging tables together, might affect the logical data model.

Application
design discussed
in Section 4.9

12.2 Overview of the physical database design methodology

Physical database design

The process of producing a description of the implementation of the database on secondary storage; it describes the base tables, file organizations, and indexes used to achieve efficient access to the data, and any associated integrity constraints and security restrictions.

The steps for physical database design are shown in Figure 12.1. We've divided the physical database design methodology into six main steps, numbered consecutively from 3 to follow the two steps of the logical database design methodology. The chapter in which each step is discussed is noted in the adjacent column.

Step 3 of physical database design involves the design of the base tables and integrity constraints using the available functionality of the target DBMS. This step also considers how we should represent any derived data present in the model and any associated business rules.

Step 4 involves analyzing the transactions that have to be supported and, based on this analysis, choosing appropriate file organizations and indexes for the base tables. Typically, PC DBMSs have a fixed storage structure but other DBMSs tend to provide a number of alternative file organizations for data. From the user's viewpoint, the internal storage representation for tables should be invisible – the user should be able to access tables and records without having to specify where or how the records are stored. The physical database designer must provide the physical design details to both the DBMS and the operating system. For the DBMS, this includes specifying the file organizations that are to be used to represent each table; for the operating system, this includes specify-

		Chapter
Step 3	Translate logical database design for target DBMS	12
	Step 3.1 Design base tables	
	Step 3.2 Design representation of derived data	
	Step 3.3 Design remaining business rules	
Step 4	Choose file organizations and indexes	13
	Step 4.1 Analyze transactions	
	Step 4.2 Choose file organizations	
	Step 4.3 Choose indexes	
Step 5	Design user views	14
Step 6	Design security mechanisms	14
Step 7	Consider the introduction of controlled redundancy	15
Step 8	Monitor and tune the operational system	16

Figure 12.1

Steps in the physical database design methodology.

ing details such as the location and protection for each file. We recommend that you review Appendix D on file organizations and indexes before reading Step 4 of the methodology.

Step 5 involves deciding how each user view should be implemented. **Step 6** involves designing the security measures to protect data from unauthorized access, including the access controls that are required on the base tables.

Step 7 considers relaxing the normalization constraints imposed on the logical data model to improve the overall performance of the system. This is a step that you should undertake only if necessary because of the inherent problems involved in introducing redundancy while still maintaining data consistency. **Step 8** is an ongoing process of monitoring and tuning the operational system to identify and resolve any performance problems resulting from the design, and to design and then implement new or changing requirements.

Appendix B presents a summary of the methodology for those of you who are already familiar with database design and simply require an overview of the main steps. In the remainder of this chapter, we examine Step 3 of the database design methodology. In these next few chapters, we demonstrate the close association between physical database design and implementation by describing how alternative designs can be implemented.

Step 3 Translate logical database design for target DBMS

Objective
To produce a basic working relational database from the logical data model.

The first step of physical database design involves the translation of the tables in the logical data model into a form that can be implemented in the target relational DBMS. The first part of this process entails collating the information gathered during logical database design and documented in the data dictionary along with the information gathered during the requirements collection and analysis stage and documented in the systems specification. The second part of the process uses this information to produce the design of the base tables. This process requires intimate knowledge of the functionality offered by the target DBMS. For example, you will need to know:

Base tables:
Section 2.3.2

Keys: Section 2.2.3

■ how to create base tables;

■ whether the system supports the definition of primary keys, foreign keys, and alternate keys;

- whether the system supports the definition of required data (that is, whether the system allows columns to be defined as NOT NULL);

Nulls: Section 2.3.1

- whether the system supports the definition of domains;
- whether the system supports relational integrity rules;
- whether the system supports the definition of business rules.

Domains:
Section 2.2.1

The three tasks in Step 3 are:

- Step 3.1 Design base tables
- Step 3.2 Design representation of derived data

Rules: Section 2.3

- Step 3.3 Design remaining business rules

Step 3.1 Design base tables

Objective
To decide how to represent the base tables identified in the logical data model in the target DBMS.

To start the physical design process, you first need to collate and assimilate the information about the tables that was produced during logical database design. The necessary information is obtained from the data dictionary and the definition of the tables that were defined using the Database Design Language (DBDL). For each table identified in the logical data model, you should have a definition consisting of:

DBDL defined in
Step 2.1 in
Chapter 10

- the name of the table;
- a list of simple columns in brackets;
- the primary key and, where appropriate, alternate keys (AK) and foreign keys (FK);
- referential integrity constraints for any foreign keys identified.

You should also have for each column:

- its domain, consisting of a data type, length, and any constraints on the domain;
- an optional default value for the column;
- whether the column can hold nulls;
- whether the column is derived and, if so, how it should be computed.

To represent the design of the base tables, we use an extended form of the DBDL to define domains, default values, and null indicators. For example, for the Branch table of the *StayHome* database application defined in Figure 10.8, you may produce the design shown in Figure 12.2.

Figure 12.2

The physical design of the Branch table using an extended DBDL.

domain Branch_Numbers	fixed length character string length 4
domain Street_Names	variable length character string maximum length 30
domain City_Names	variable length character string maximum length 20
domain State_Codes	fixed length character string length 2
domain Zip_Codes	fixed length character string length 5
domain Staff_Numbers	fixed length character string length 5

```
Branch(  branchNo        Branch_Numbers       NOT NULL,
         street          Street_Names         NOT NULL,
         city            City_Names           NOT NULL,
         state           State_Names          NOT NULL,
         zipCode         Zip_Codes            NOT NULL,
         mgrStaffNo      Staff_Numbers        NOT NULL)
         Primary Key branchNo
         Alternate Key zipCode
         Foreign Key mgrStaffNo References Staff(staffNo) ON UPDATE CASCADE ON DELETE NO ACTION
```

Implementing base tables in Microsoft Access 2002

The next step is to decide how to implement the base tables. As we've already said, this decision is dependent on the target DBMS; some systems provide more facilities than others for defining base tables and integrity constraints. To illustrate this process, we show how to create base tables and integrity constraints in Microsoft Access 2002. In Chapter 18, we'll look at how to create tables and integrity constraints in Oracle 9i.

> When discussing Microsoft Access we use the vendor's terminology, which uses the term 'field' in place of 'column'.

Microsoft Access provides five ways to create a blank (empty) table:

■ Use the Database Wizard to create in one operation all the tables, forms, and reports that are required for the entire database. The Database Wizard creates a new database, although this particular wizard cannot be used to add new tables, forms, or reports to an existing database.

■ Use the Table Wizard to choose the fields for the table from a variety of predefined tables such as business contacts, household inventory, or medical records.

■ Enter data directly into a blank table (called a **datasheet**). When the new datasheet is saved, Access will analyze the data and automatically assign the appropriate data type and format for each field.

■ Use the CREATE TABLE statement in SQL View.

■ Use Design View to specify all table details from scratch.

We now demonstrate the last two methods of creating a new table.

Creating a blank table in Microsoft Access using SQL

In Section 3.3.1, we examined the SQL CREATE TABLE statement, which allows you to create a base table. Microsoft Access 2002 does not fully comply with the SQL3 standard (for example, the Access CREATE TABLE statement has no support for the DEFAULT clause). However, default values and certain business rules can still be specified outside SQL, as we'll see shortly. In addition, the data types are slightly different from the SQL standard, as shown in Table 12.1. Figure 12.3 shows the SQL View with the SQL statement to create the Branch table (compare this with the equivalent SQL statement in Section 3.3.1).

Table 12.1 Microsoft Access data types.

Data type	Use	Size
Text	Text or text/numbers. Also numbers that do not require calculations, such as phone numbers.	Up to 255 characters
Memo	Lengthy text and numbers, such as notes or descriptions.	Up to 64 000 characters
Number	Numeric data to be used for mathematical calculations, except calculations involving money (use Currency type).	1, 2, 4, or 8 bytes
Date/Time	Dates and times.	8 bytes
Currency	Currency values. Use the Currency data type to prevent rounding off during calculations.	8 bytes
Autonumber	Unique sequential (incrementing by 1) or random numbers automatically inserted when a record is added.	4 bytes
Yes/No	Fields that will contain only one of two values, such as Yes/No, True/False, On/Off.	1 bit

Table 12.1 *Continued*

Data type	Use	Size
OLE Object	Objects (such as Microsoft Word documents, Microsoft Excel spreadsheets, pictures, sounds, or other binary data), created in other programs using the OLE protocol, that can be linked to, or embedded in, a Microsoft Access table.	Up to 1 gigabyte
Hyperlink	Field that will store hyperlinks.	Up to 64 000 characters
Lookup Wizard	Creates a field that allows you to choose a value from another table or from a list of values using a combo box. Choosing this option in the data type list starts a wizard to define this for you.	Typically 4 bytes

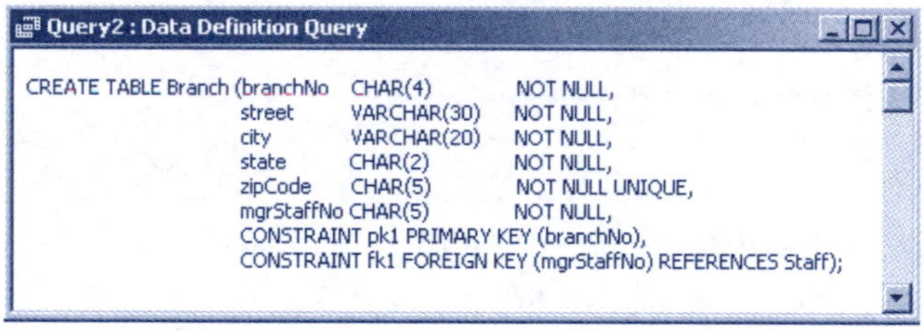


```
CREATE TABLE Branch (branchNo   CHAR(4)        NOT NULL,
                     street     VARCHAR(30)    NOT NULL,
                     city       VARCHAR(20)    NOT NULL,
                     state      CHAR(2)        NOT NULL,
                     zipCode    CHAR(5)        NOT NULL UNIQUE,
                     mgrStaffNo CHAR(5)        NOT NULL,
                     CONSTRAINT pk1 PRIMARY KEY (branchNo),
                     CONSTRAINT fk1 FOREIGN KEY (mgrStaffNo) REFERENCES Staff);
```

Figure 12.3
SQL View showing creation of the Branch table.

Creating a blank table in Microsoft Access using Design View

Figure 12.4 shows the Design View for the creation of the Branch table. Regardless of which method you use to create a table, you can use table Design View at any time to customize your table further, such as adding new fields, setting default values, or creating input masks.

Creating a relationship between two tables in Access

Relationships are created in the Relationships window. To create a relationship, you display the tables you want to create the relationships between, and then drag the primary key field of the parent table to the foreign key field of the child table. At this point, Access will display a window allowing you to specify the referential integrity constraints.

1:1 relationships defined in Section 7.5.1

Figure 12.5(a) shows the Edit Relationships dialog box that is displayed when creating the one-to-one (1:1) relationship Staff *Manages* Branch, and Figure 12.5(b) shows the Relationships window after the relationship has been created.

Figure 12.4

Design View showing creation of the Branch table.

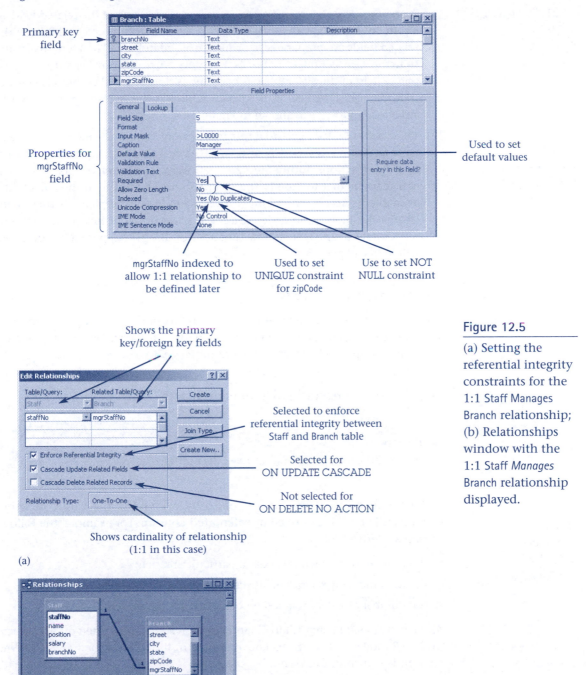

Primary key field

Properties for mgrStaffNo field

Used to set default values

Require data entry in this field?

mgrStaffNo indexed to allow 1:1 relationship to be defined later

Used to set UNIQUE constraint for zipCode

Use to set NOT NULL constraint

Shows the primary key/foreign key fields

Selected to enforce referential integrity between Staff and Branch table

Selected for ON UPDATE CASCADE

Not selected for ON DELETE NO ACTION

Shows cardinality of relationship (1:1 in this case)

(a)

(b)

Figure 12.5

(a) Setting the referential integrity constraints for the 1:1 Staff Manages Branch relationship;
(b) Relationships window with the 1:1 Staff *Manages* Branch relationship displayed.

There are a couple of things to note about setting referential integrity constraints in Microsoft Access:

1:* relationships
defined in
Section 7.5.2

(1) A one-to-many (1:*) relationship is created if only one of the related fields is a primary key or has a unique index; a 1:1 relationship is created if both the related fields are primary keys or have unique indexes. Therefore, to ensure that the *Manages* relationship is 1:1, you must not only ensure that the staffNo field in the Staff table has been set as the primary key, but also ensure that the mgrStaffNo field in the Branch table has the Indexed property set to Yes (No Duplicates), as shown in Figure 12.4.

Step 2.4 covered
in Chapter 10

(2) There are only two referential integrity actions for update and delete, which correspond to NO ACTION and CASCADE. Therefore, if you have identified other actions during Step 2.4 Define integrity constraints, you must consider whether to modify these constraints to fit in with the constraints available in Access, or you must investigate how to implement these constraints in application code. You'll see an example of how to implement referential integrity constraints that are not directly supported by the target DBMS in Chapter 18.

Document design of base tables

The design of the base tables should be fully documented along with the reasons for selecting the proposed design. In particular, document the reasons for selecting one approach where many alternatives exist.

Step 3.2 Design representation of derived data

Objective
To design the representation of derived data in the database.

Derived
attributes
defined in
Section 7.3.3

A column whose value can be found by examining the values of other columns is known as a **derived** or **calculated column**. For example, the following are all derived columns:

■ the number of staff who work at a particular branch;

■ the total monthly salaries of all staff at a particular branch;

■ the number of videos that a member currently has on rental.

As we mentioned in Step 1.3 in Chapter 9, derived columns often do not appear in the ER model, but are instead documented in the data dictionary. If a derived column is shown in the ER model, the name is preceded by a '/' to indicate it's derived. The first step, then, is to examine the logical data model and produce a list of all derived columns.

From a physical database design perspective, whether a derived column is stored in the database or calculated every time it's needed is a trade-off. To decide, you should calculate:

■ the additional cost to store the derived data and keep it consistent with the data from which it is derived, and

■ the cost to calculate it each time it's required,

and choose the less expensive option subject to performance constraints. For the last example given above, you could store an additional column in the Member table representing the number of rentals that each member currently has. The RentalAgreement table and the Member table with the new derived column are shown in Figure 12.6.

The additional storage overhead for this new derived column would not be particularly significant. However, the noOfRentals column would need to be updated every time a member rented or returned a video. You would need to ensure that this change was made consistently to maintain the correct count, and thereby ensure the integrity of the database. By storing the data in this way, when a query requires this information, the value is immediately available and does not have to be calculated.

Figure 12.6

The RentalAgreement table and the Member table with the additional derived column noOfRentals.

RentalAgreement

rentalNo	dateOut	dateReturn	memberNo	videoNo
R753461	4-Feb-03	6-Feb-03	M284354	245456
R753462	4-Feb-03	6-Feb-03	M284354	243431
R668256	5-Feb-03	7-Feb-03	M115656	199004
R668189	2-Feb-03		M115656	178643

Member

memberNo	fName	lName	address	noOfRentals
M250178	Bob	Adams	57 – 11th Avenue, Seattle, WA 98105	0
M166884	Art	Peters	89 Redmond Rd, Portland, OR 97117	0
M115656	Serena	Parker	22 W. Capital Way, Portland, OR 97201	2
M284354	Don	Nelson	123 Suffolk Lane, Seattle, WA 98117	2

On the other hand, if the noOfRentals column is not stored directly in the Member table, it must be calculated each time it's needed. This involves a join of the Member and RentalAgreement tables. For example, to calculate the number of videos that member 'Don Nelson' currently has on rental, you could use the following SQL query:

SELECT COUNT(*) **AS** noOfRentals
FROM Member m, RentalAgreement ra
WHERE m.memberNo= ra.memberNo **AND** m.fName = 'Don' **AND**
        m.lName = 'Nelson';

If this type of query is frequent or is considered to be critical for performance purposes, it may be more appropriate to store the derived column rather than calculate it each time. In our example, *StayHome* runs this type of query every time a member attempts to rent a new video. Through discussion with *StayHome* staff, it's estimated that the size of the RentalAgreement table is 400 000 records. Therefore, as the RentalAgreement table is likely to be large and the query frequent, you may decide that it is more efficient to add the derived column to the Member table. The same query could now be written as follows:

SELECT noOfRentals
FROM Member
WHERE fName = 'Don' **AND** lName = 'Nelson';

> **TIP**
>
> It may also be more appropriate to store derived columns whenever the system's query language cannot easily cope with the algorithm to calculate the derived column. For example, SQL has a limited set of aggregate functions and also cannot easily handle recursive queries.

Document design of derived data

The design of how to represent derived data should be fully documented along with the reasons for selecting the proposed design. In particular, document the reasons for selecting one approach where many alternatives exist.

Step 3.3 Design remaining business rules

> **Objective**
> To design the remaining business rules for the target DBMS.

Updates to tables may be constrained by business rules governing the 'real world' transactions that are represented by the updates. At this point, you have already designed domain constraints and relational integrity constraints. The objective of this step is to design any other business rules that have to be imposed on the data. The design of such rules is again dependent on the choice of DBMS; some systems provide more facilities than others for defining business rules. As in the previous step, if the system is compliant with the SQL standard, some rules may be easy to implement. For example, *StayHome* has a rule that prevents a member from renting more than 10 videos at any one time. You could design this rule into the SQL CREATE TABLE statement for the RentalAgreement table, using the following clause:

CONSTRAINT member_not_renting_too_many
CHECK (NOT EXISTS (SELECT memberNo
                             FROM RentalAgreement
                             GROUP BY memberNo
                             HAVING COUNT(*) >= 10))

Alternatively, in some systems a **trigger** could be used to enforce some constraints. For the previous example, in some systems we could create the **trigger** shown in Figure 12.7 to enforce this integrity constraint. This trigger is invoked before a record is inserted into the RentalAgreement table or an existing record is updated. If the member is currently renting 10 videos, the system displays a message and aborts the transaction.

> Don't worry too much about the details of this trigger. We'll discuss triggers in more detail in Step 3.3 in Chapter 18.

```
CREATE TRIGGER member_not_renting_too_many
BEFORE INSERT OR UPDATE ON RentalAgreement
FOR EACH ROW
DECLARE
        x  NUMBER;
BEGIN
        SELECT COUNT(*) INTO x
                FROM RentalAgreement r
                WHERE r.memberNo = :new.memberNo;
        IF x  >= 10 THEN
            raise_application_error(-20000,('Member' | | :new.memberNo | |
                                'already renting 10 videos');
        END IF;
END;
```

Figure 12.7

Trigger to enforce constraint that member cannot rent more than 10 videos at any one time.

Creating business rules in Microsoft Access 2002

There are several ways to create business rules in Microsoft Access using, for example:

(a) validation rules for fields;

(b) validation rules for records;

(c) validation for forms using VBA (Visual Basic for Applications).

We illustrate each of these below with some simple examples.

Validation rules for fields

You can ensure that data is entered correctly into a field by defining a field validation rule. A field validation rule is used to check the value entered into a field as the user leaves the field. A message you define is displayed if the value breaks the validation rule.

For example, *StayHome* has a simple constraint that all return dates for video rentals cannot be earlier than the current date, although the date may initially be left unspecified. You can implement this constraint at the field level in the RentalAgreement table using the function Date(), which returns the current date, as shown in Figure 12.8.

Validation rules for records

A record validation rule controls when an entire record can be saved. Unlike field validation rules, record validation rules can refer to other fields. This

Figure 12.8

Example of field validation in Microsoft Access.

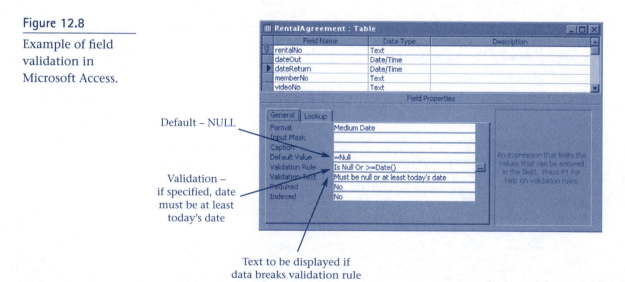

Default – NULL

Validation – if specified, date must be at least today's date

Text to be displayed if data breaks validation rule

makes them useful when you want to compare values from different fields in a table. For example, *StayHome* may have a constraint that the maximum rental period for videos is five days, although the date may initially be left unspecified. You can implement this constraint at the record level in the RentalAgreement table using the validation rule:

[dateReturn] Is Null OR [dateReturn] <= [dateOut] + 5

Figure 12.9 shows the ValidationRule property box for the table with this rule set.

Validation for forms using VBA (Visual Basic for Applications)

As we've just mentioned, *StayHome* has a constraint that members are not allowed to rent more than 10 videos at any one time. This is a more complex constraint, which requires you to check how many rentals the member currently has. One way to implement this constraint in Access is to use an event procedure (BeforeUpdate), as shown in Figure 12.10. The BeforeUpdate event is triggered before a record is updated and you can associate code with this event on a form.

In some systems, there will be no support for some or all of the business rules and it will be necessary to design the rules into the application, as we've shown with the last example which has built the constraint into the application's VBA code. Implementing a business rule in application code is, of course, potentially dangerous and can lead to duplication of effort and, worse still, to inconsistencies if the rule is not implemented everywhere it should be.

Document design of business rules

The design of business rules should be fully documented. In particular, document the reasons for selecting one approach where many alternatives exist.

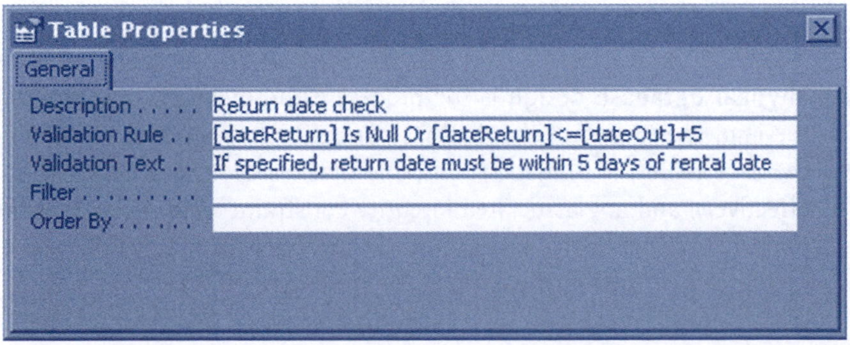

Figure 12.9

Example of record validation in Microsoft Access.

Figure 12.10

VBA code to check member does not have more than 10 videos currently rented.

```
Private Sub Form_BeforeUpdate(Cancel As Integer)
Dim MyDB As Database
Dim MySet As Recordset
Dim MyQuery As String


'Set up query to select all records for specified member'
MyQuery = "SELECT rentalNo FROM RentalAgreement WHERE memberNo ="'+ memberNoField +""'


'Open the database and run the query'
Set MyDB = DBEngine.Workspaces(0).Databases(0)
Set MySet = MyDB.OpenRecordset(MyQuery)


'Check if any records have been returned, then move to the end of the file to allow RecordCount'
'property to be correctly set'
If (NOT MySet.EOF) Then
        MySet.MoveLast
        If (MySet.RecordCount >= 10) Then 'If currently 10 - cannot rent any more'
                MsgBox "Member currently has 10 videos out"
                Me.Undo
        End If
End If


MySet.Close
MyDB.Close
End Sub
```

Name of field on form

Chapter summary

✓ **Physical database design** is the process of producing a description of the implementation of the database on secondary storage. It describes the base tables, file organizations, and indexes used to access this data effectively, and any associated integrity constraints and security restrictions. The design of the base tables can be undertaken only once you are fully aware of the facilities offered by the target DBMS.

In the initial step (Step 3) of physical database design, you translate the logical data model into a form that can be implemented in the target relational DBMS. This involves designing the base tables, the representation of derived data, and the business rules.

 In the next step (Step 4), you analyze the transactions and, based on this analysis, design the file organizations and indexes that will be used to store the base tables.

✓ A database represents an essential corporate resource, and so security of this resource is extremely important. The objective of Steps 5 and 6 is to design how the security measures identified during logical database design will be realized. This may include the creation of user views and the use of access control mechanisms.

✓ In Step 7, you consider the introduction of controlled redundancy to improve performance. Step 8 involves the ongoing process of monitoring and tuning the operational system to achieve maximum performance.

Review questions

12.1 Explain the difference between logical and physical database design. Why might these tasks be carried out by different people?

12.2 Describe the inputs and outputs of physical database design.

12.3 Describe the purpose of the main steps in the physical design methodology presented in this chapter.

12.4 Describe the types of information required to design the base tables.

12.5 Describe how you would you handle the representation of derived data in the database. Give an example to illustrate your answer.

Exercise

12.6 Work your way through some of the case studies presented in Appendix E and perform the steps of the physical design methodology discussed in this chapter for a target DBMS to which you have access.

Chapter 13

Physical database design – Step 4

In this chapter you will learn:

➤ How to analyze the users' transactions to determine characteristics that may impact performance.

➤ How to select appropriate file organizations based on an analysis of the transactions.

➤ When to select indexes to improve performance.

Methodology summarized in Appendix B

This chapter covers Step 4 of our database design methodology. In the previous step, we showed how to translate the logical database design into a set of tables and, if required, a set of business rules. However, even for the simplest database, there are additional considerations required to achieve acceptable performance. In this chapter, we consider the next step of physical database design which considers those aspects of performance that you can influence by the appropriate choice of file organizations and indexes.

> **TIP**
> If you are unfamiliar with file organization and indexing concepts, we strongly recommend reading Appendix D before reading this chapter.

As with logical database design, physical database design must be guided by the nature of the data and its intended use. In particular, you must understand the typical *workload* that the database must support. During the analysis phase, you may also have found that some users have requirements about how fast certain transactions must run or how many transactions must be processed per second. This information forms the basis for a number of decisions that you'll need to make during this step.

As we mentioned in the previous chapter, to undertake physical database design you must understand the workings of the target DBMS, particularly the file organizations, indexing, and query processing techniques that it supports. For example, there may be circumstances where the DBMS would not use a secondary index, even if one were available. Thus, adding a secondary index would not improve the performance of the query, and the resultant overhead would be unjustified.

Secondary indexes defined in Appendix D 5.2

> You may recall from Chapter 3 that SQL and QBE are *non-procedural* Data Manipulation Languages (DMLs). Such languages hide the low-level details of how to access the data on secondary storage. This is the responsibility of the DBMS, or to be more precise, the DBMS's *query optimizer*. Typically, the query optimizer will analyze a number of different strategies for carrying out the user's request and select the one it believes will give optimal performance. This analysis is based on the estimated cost of database operations using database statistics, such as the number of records in a table, the size of each record, and the availability of indexes.
>
> This might suggest that you have no influence over the final strategy that the DBMS will choose. In fact, you'll see that you can define some of the storage structures that will be available to the query optimizer to select the optimal strategy.

Step 4 Choose file organizations and indexes

> **Objective**
> To determine the optimal file organizations to store the base tables, and the indexes that are required to achieve acceptable performance.

We provide an introduction to file organizations and indexes in Appendix D for those readers who are unfamiliar with these terms. To recap, a **file organization** is a way of arranging the records in a file when the file is stored on disk; an **index** is a data structure that allows the DBMS to locate particular records in a file more quickly, and thereby increase the response to user queries.

The types of file organization available are dependent on the target DBMS; some systems provide more choice of file organizations than others. It's important that you fully understand the structures that are available, and how the target system uses these structures.

You also can't make meaningful physical design decisions until you understand in detail the transactions that have to be supported. In analyzing the transactions, you're attempting to identify performance criteria, such as:

■ the transactions that run frequently and will have a significant impact on performance;

■ the transactions that are critical to the operation of the business;

■ the times of the day/week when there will be a high demand made on the database (called the *peak load*).

You'll use this information to identify the parts of the database that may cause performance problems. At the same time, you need to identify the high-level functionality of the transactions, such as the columns that are updated in an update transaction or the columns that are retrieved in a query. You'll use this information to select appropriate file organizations and indexes.

As a result, we've broken the tasks in Step 4 into:

■ Step 4.1 Analyze transactions
■ Step 4.2 Choose file organizations
■ Step 4.3 Choose indexes

Step 4.1 Analyze transactions

Objective
To understand the functionality of the transactions that will run on the database and to analyze the important transactions.

To carry out physical database design effectively, you need to have a good understanding of the transactions that will run on the database.

TIP

In many situations it would be far too time-consuming to analyze all the expected transactions, so you should at least investigate the 'most important' ones. It has been suggested that the most active 20 percent of user queries account for 80 percent of the total data access. You may find this 80/20 rule is a useful guideline when carrying out the analysis.

To help identify which transactions to investigate, you could use a *transaction usage map*, which diagrammatically indicates which tables are potentially heavily used, and/or a *transaction/table cross-reference matrix*, which shows the tables each transaction accesses. To focus on areas that may be problematic, one way to proceed is to:

(1) Map all transaction paths to tables.

(2) Determine which tables are most frequently accessed by transactions.

(3) Analyze selected transactions that involve these tables.

Map all transaction paths to tables

In Steps 1.8 and 2.3 of the logical database design methodology, you checked that the model supported the transactions that the users require by mapping the transaction paths to entities/tables. If you used a transaction pathway diagram similar to the one shown in Figure 9.17, you'll be able to use this diagram to determine the tables that are most frequently accessed. On the other hand, if you checked the transactions in some other way, you may find it useful to create a transaction/table cross-reference matrix. The matrix shows the transactions that are required and the tables they access. For example, Table 13.1 shows a transaction/table cross-reference matrix for the following selection of entry, update/delete, and retrieval (also known as a *query*) transactions for *StayHome*:

StayHome transactions listed in Section 6.4.4

(e) Enter the details of a new member registering at a given branch.

(k) Update/delete the details of a given member.

(p) List the title, category, and availability of all videos at a specified branch, ordered by category.

Table 13.1 Cross-referencing transactions and tables.

Transaction/ Table	(e)				(k)				(p)				(q)				(r)				(s)			
	I	R	U	D	I	R	U	D	I	R	U	D	I	R	U	D	I	R	U	D	I	R	U	D
Branch																								
Staff		X																						
Video										X				X				X				X		
VideoForRent										X				X				X				X		
RentalAgreement																						X		
Member	X				X	X	X															X		
Registration	X																							
Actor														X										
Role														X										
Director																		X						

I = Insert; R = Read; U = Update; D = Delete

(q) List the title, category, and availability of all videos for a given actor at a specified branch, ordered by title.

(r) List the title, category, and availability of all videos for a given director at a specified branch, ordered by title.

(s) List the details of all videos a specified member currently has on rent.

The matrix summarizes, in a visual way, the access patterns of the transactions that will run on the database. For example, the matrix indicates that transaction (e) reads the Staff table and also inserts records into the Member and Registration tables. To be more useful, you should indicate the number of accesses over some time interval (for example, hourly, daily, weekly) in each cell. However, to keep the matrix simple, we do not show this information. This matrix shows that the Video and VideoForRent tables are accessed by the four query transactions (p, q, r, and s).

Determine frequency information

In discussion with the *StayHome* branch managers it's estimated that there are about 20 000 video titles and 400 000 videos for rent distributed over 100 branch offices, with an average of 4000 and a maximum of 10 000 videos for rent at each branch. In addition, *StayHome* holds data for about 10 000 directors and 30 000 main actors in 60 000 roles. Figure 13.1 shows a reduced logical data model with these numbers added.

Figure 13.2 shows the *transaction usage map* for transactions (p), (q), and (r). This figure shows that the VideoForRent and Video tables are accessed by all three transactions. Further, due to the size of the VideoForRent table, it is important that access to this table is as efficient as possible. You may now decide that a closer analysis of transactions involving these tables is useful.

In considering each transaction, it's important that you know not only the average and maximum number of times it runs per hour, but also the day and time that the transaction is run, including when the peak load is likely. For example, some transactions may run at the average rate for most of the time, but have a peak loading between 14.00 and 16.00 on a Thursday prior to a meeting on Friday morning. Other transactions may run only at specific times, for example 18.00–21.00 on Friday/Saturday, which is also their peak loading.

Where transactions require frequent access to particular tables, then their pattern of operation is very important. If these transactions operate in a mutually exclusive manner, the risk of likely performance problems is reduced. However, if their operating patterns conflict, potential problems may be alleviated by examining the transactions more closely to determine whether changes can be made to the structure of the tables to improve performance, as we'll discuss in Step 7 in Chapter 15.

Figure 13.1

Simplified logical data model showing expected occurrences.

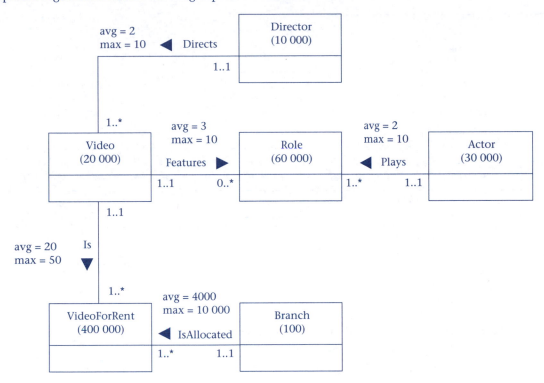

Data usage analysis

Having identified the important transactions, you now need to analyze each one in more detail. For each transaction, determine:

(a) The tables and columns accessed by the transaction and the type of access; that is, whether it's an insert, update, delete, or retrieval transaction.

 – For an update transaction, note the columns that are updated as these columns may be candidates for avoiding an *access structure* (such as a secondary index).

(b) The columns used in any *search conditions* (in SQL, these are the conditions specified in the WHERE clause). Check whether the conditions involve:

 (i) pattern matching; for example: (name LIKE '%Smith%');
 (ii) range searches; for example: (salary BETWEEN 30000 AND 40000);
 (iii) exact-match key retrieval; for example: (salary = 30000).

This applies not only to queries but also to update and delete transactions, which can restrict the records to be updated/deleted in a table.

 – These columns may be candidates for access structures.

Figure 13.2

Transaction usage map for sample transactions.

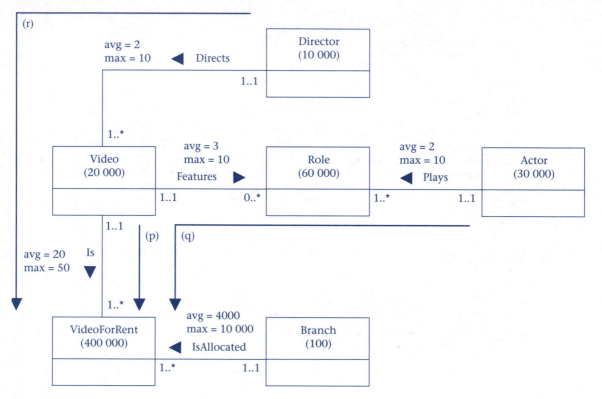

(c) For a query, the columns that are involved in the join of two or more tables.

   – Again, these columns may be candidates for access structures.

(d) The expected frequency at which the transaction will run; for example, the transaction will run approximately 50 times per day.

(e) The performance goals for the transaction; for example, the transaction must complete within 1 second.

   – The columns used in any search conditions for very frequent or critical transactions should have a higher priority for access structures.

Figure 13.3 shows an example of a *transaction analysis form* for transaction (p). This form shows that the average frequency of this transaction is 50 times per hour, with a peak loading of 100 times per hour between 18.00 and 21.00. In other words, typically half the branches will run this transaction per hour and at peak time all branches will run this transaction once per hour.

Figure 13.3

Example transaction analysis form.

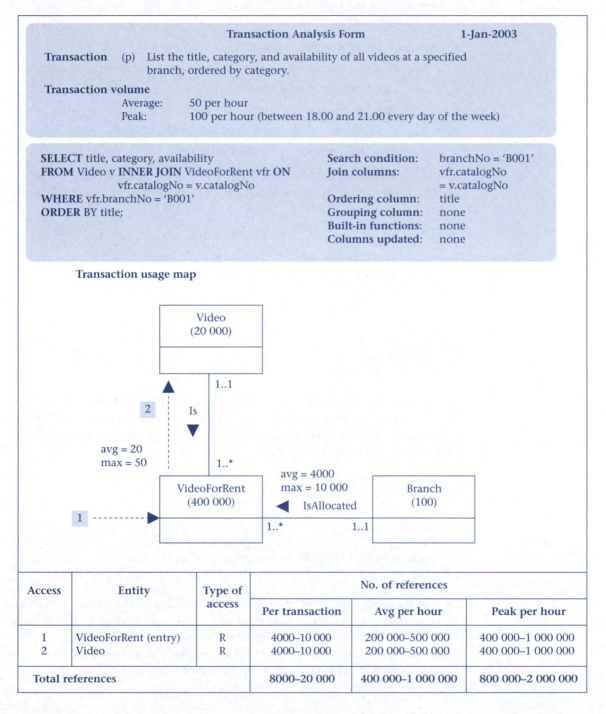

Transaction Analysis Form   1-Jan-2003

Transaction (p) List the title, category, and availability of all videos at a specified branch, ordered by category.

Transaction volume
     Average: 50 per hour
     Peak: 100 per hour (between 18.00 and 21.00 every day of the week)

SELECT title, category, availability   Search condition: branchNo = 'B001'
FROM Video v **INNER JOIN** VideoForRent vfr **ON**   Join columns: vfr.catalogNo
          vfr.catalogNo = v.catalogNo   = v.catalogNo
WHERE vfr.branchNo = 'B001'   Ordering column: title
ORDER BY title;   Grouping column: none
                                                  Built-in functions: none
                                                  Columns updated: none

Transaction usage map

Access	Entity	Type of access	No. of references		
			Per transaction	Avg per hour	Peak per hour
1	VideoForRent (entry)	R	4000–10 000	200 000–500 000	400 000–1 000 000
2	Video	R	4000–10 000	200 000–500 000	400 000–1 000 000
Total references			**8000–20 000**	**400 000–1 000 000**	**800 000–2 000 000**

The form also shows the required SQL statement and the transaction usage map. At this stage, the full SQL statement may be too detailed but you should at least identify the types of details that are shown adjacent to the SQL statement, namely:

■ any search conditions that are used;

■ any columns that are required to join tables together (for query transactions);

■ columns used to order results (for query transactions);

■ columns used to group data together (for query transactions);

■ any built-in functions that are used (such as AVG, SUM);

■ any columns that are updated by the transaction.

You use this information to determine the indexes that are required, which we discuss shortly. Below the transaction usage map, there is a detailed breakdown documenting:

■ how each table is accessed (reads in this case),

■ how many records are accessed each time the transaction is run,

■ how many records are accessed per hour on average and at peak loading times.

> Note, for an update transaction there are two accesses made on a table: one to read the data and one to update the data.

The frequency information identifies the tables that will need careful consideration to ensure that appropriate access structures are used. As mentioned above, the search conditions used by transactions that have time constraints become higher priority for access structures.

Step 4.2 Choose file organizations

> **Objective**
> To determine an efficient file organization for each base table.

One of the main objectives of physical database design is to store data in an efficient way. For example, if you want to retrieve staff records in alphabetical order of name, sorting the file by staff name is a good file organization. However, if you want to retrieve all staff whose salary is in a certain range, a file ordered by staff name would not be a good file organization.

To complicate matters, some file organizations are efficient for bulk loading data into the database but inefficient after that. In other words, you may use an efficient storage structure to set up the database and then change it for normal operational use.

The objective of this step therefore is to choose an optimal file organization for each table, if the target DBMS allows this. In many cases, you may find that a relational DBMS gives you little or no choice for choosing file organizations, although some may be established as you specify indexes.

We provide guidelines for selecting file organizations in Appendix D. If your target DBMS does not allow you to choose the file organization, you can omit this step and move on to the next step, Step 4.3.

Document choice of file organizations

The choice of file organizations should be fully documented, along with the reasons for the choice. In particular, document the reasons for selecting one file organization where many alternatives exist.

Step 4.3 Choose indexes

Objective
To determine whether adding indexes will improve the performance of the system.

Indexes discussed in Appendix D.5

One approach to selecting an appropriate file organization for a table is to keep the records unordered and create as many **secondary indexes** as you need. Another approach is to order the records in the table by specifying a **primary** or **clustering index**. In this case, you should choose the column for ordering or clustering the records as:

■ the column that is used most often for join operations, as this makes the join operation more efficient, or

■ the column that is used most often to access the records in a table in order of that column.

If the ordering column chosen is a key of the table, the index will be a primary index; if the ordering column is not a key, the index will be a clustering index. Remember that you can only have either a primary index or a clustering index for each file.

Specifying indexes

> The initial version of the SQL standard had statements for creating and drop-ping indexes. However, these statements were removed from the second major release of the standard in 1992 because they were considered to be a physical concept rather than a logical concept. Having said that, most of the major relational DBMSs support these statements in one form or another. The SQL statements we use below are typical of what current products support.

To create an index in SQL, typically the **CREATE INDEX** statement is used. For example, to create a primary index on the Video table based on the catalogNo column, you might use the following SQL statement:

CREATE UNIQUE INDEX catalogNoPrimaryIndex
  ON Video (catalogNo);

To create a clustering index on the VideoForRent table based on the catalogNo column, you might use the following SQL statement:

CREATE INDEX catalogNoClusteringIndex
  ON VideoForRent (catalogNo) **CLUSTER**;

Oracle discussed
in Chapter 18

As we've already mentioned, in some systems the file organization is fixed. For example, until recently Oracle only supported B$^+$-Trees, but has now added support for hash clusters. On the other hand, the RDBMS INGRES offers a wide set of different index structures that you can choose using the optional clause in the CREATE INDEX statement:

[STRUCTURE = BTREE | ISAM | HASH | HEAP];

To drop an index in SQL, typically the **DROP INDEX** statement is used. For example, to drop the primary index catalogNoPrimaryIndex, you might use the following SQL statement:

DROP INDEX catalogNoPrimaryIndex;

> Note that Microsoft Access doesn't support the CREATE INDEX statement. Instead, you create indexes through the field properties dialog box. We saw an example of this in Figure 12.4 and we discuss this in more detail shortly.

Choosing secondary indexes

Secondary indexes provide a mechanism for specifying an additional key for a base table that can be used to retrieve data more efficiently. For example, the

Member table may be hashed on the member number, memberNo, the *primary index*. On the other hand, there may be frequent access to this table based on the lName (last name) column. In this case, you may decide to add lName as a *secondary index*.

However, there is an overhead involved in the maintenance and use of secondary indexes that you have to balance against the performance improvement gained when retrieving data. This overhead includes:

■ adding an index record to every secondary index whenever a record is inserted in the table;

■ updating a secondary index when the corresponding record in the table is updated;

■ the increase in disk space needed to store the secondary index;

■ possible performance degradation during query optimization, as the query optimizer may consider all secondary indexes before selecting an optimal execution strategy.

Guidelines for choosing a 'wish-list' of indexes

One approach to determining which secondary indexes are needed is to produce a **wish-list** of columns you think are candidates for indexing, and then to consider the impact of maintaining each of these indexes. We provide the following guidelines to help produce such a 'wish-list':

(1) Do not index small tables. It may be more efficient to search the table in memory than to store an additional index structure.

(2) In general, index the primary key of a table if it's not a key of the file organization. Although the SQL standard provides a clause for the specification of primary keys as discussed in Step 3.1 covered in the last chapter, note that this does not guarantee that the primary key will be indexed in some RDBMSs.

(3) Add a secondary index to any column that is heavily used for data retrieval. For example, add a secondary index to the Member table based on the column lName, as discussed above.

(4) Add a secondary index to a foreign key if there is frequent access based on it. For example, you may frequently join the VideoForRent and Branch tables on the column branchNo (the branch number). Therefore, it may be more efficient to add a secondary index to the VideoForRent table based on branchNo.

(5) Add a secondary index on columns that are frequently involved in:
  (a) selection or join criteria;
  (b) ORDER BY;
  (c) GROUP BY;
  (d) other operations involving sorting (such as UNION or DISTINCT).

(6) Add a secondary index on columns involved in built-in functions, along with any columns used to aggregate the built-in functions. For example, to find the average staff salary at each branch, you could use the following SQL query:

SELECT branchNo, **AVG**(salary)
FROM Staff
GROUP BY branchNo;

From the previous guideline, you could consider adding an index to the branchNo column by virtue of the GROUP BY clause. However, it may be more efficient to consider an index on both the branchNo column and the salary column. This may allow the DBMS to perform the entire query from data in the index alone, without having to access the data file. This is sometimes called an *index-only plan*, as the required response can be produced using only data in the index.

(7) As a more general case of the previous guideline, add a secondary index on columns that could result in an index-only plan.

(8) Avoid indexing a column or table that is frequently updated.

(9) Avoid indexing a column if the query will retrieve a significant proportion (for example, 25 percent) of the records in the table, even if the table is large. In this case, it may be more efficient to search the entire table than to search using an index.

(10) Avoid indexing columns that consist of long character strings.

TIP

If the search criteria involve more than one condition, and one of the terms contains an OR clause, and the term has no index/sort order, then adding indexes for the other columns is not going to help improve the speed of the query, because a linear search of the table is still required. For example, assume that only the category and dailyRental columns of the Video table are indexed, and you use the following query:

SELECT *
FROM Video
WHERE (category = 'Action' **OR** dailyRental > 3 **OR** price > 15);

Although the two indexes could be used to find the records where (category = 'Action' **OR** dailyRental > 3), the fact that the price column is not indexed will mean that these indexes cannot be used for the full WHERE clause. Thus, unless there are other queries that would benefit from having the category and dailyRental columns indexed, there is no benefit gained in indexing them for this query.

On the other hand, if the search conditions in the WHERE clause were AND'ed together, the two indexes on the category and dailyRental columns could be used to optimize the query.

Removing indexes from the 'wish-list'

Having drawn up your 'wish-list' of potential indexes, consider the impact of each of these on update transactions. If the maintenance of the index is likely to slow down important update transactions, then consider dropping the index from the list. Note, however, that a particular index may also make update operations more efficient. For example, if you want to update a member of staff's salary given the member's staff number, staffNo, and there is an index on staffNo, then the record to be updated can be found more quickly.

> **TIP**
>
> It's a good idea to experiment when possible to determine whether an index is improving performance, providing very little improvement, or adversely impacting performance. In the last case, clearly you should remove this index from the 'wish-list'. If there is little observed improvement with the addition of the index, further examination may be necessary to determine under what circumstances the index will be useful, and whether these circumstances are sufficiently important to warrant the implementation of the index.

Some systems allow you to inspect the optimizer's strategy for executing a particular query or update, sometimes called the Query Execution Plan (QEP). For example, Oracle has an EXPLAIN PLAN diagnostic utility, Microsoft Access has a Performance Analyzer, DB2 has an EXPLAIN utility, and INGRES has an online QEP-viewing facility. When a query runs slower than expected, it's worth using such a facility to determine the reason for the slowness, and to find an alternative strategy that may improve the performance of the query.

> **TIP**
>
> If a large number of records are being inserted into a table with one or more indexes, it may be more efficient to drop the indexes first, perform the inserts, and then re-create the indexes afterwards. As a rule of thumb, if the insert will increase the size of the table by at least 10 percent, drop the indexes temporarily.

Updating the database statistics

Earlier we mentioned that the query optimizer relies on database statistics held in the system catalog to select the optimal strategy. Whenever you create an index, the DBMS automatically adds the presence of the index to the system catalog. However, you may find that the DBMS requires a utility to be run to update the statistics in the system catalog relating to the table and the index.

System catalog defined in Section 1.2.1

Document choice of secondary indexes

The choice of indexes should be fully documented, along with the reasons for the choice. In particular, if there are performance reasons why some columns should not be indexed, these should also be documented.

13.1 File organizations and indexes for *StayHome* with Microsoft Access 2002

Like most, if not all, PC DBMSs, Microsoft Access uses a fixed file organization, so if you're using Access, Step 4.2 can be omitted.

13.1.1 Guidelines for indexes

Microsoft Access does, however, support indexes, as we now briefly discuss. In Access, the primary key of a table is automatically indexed, but a field whose data type is Memo, Hyperlink, or OLE Object can't be indexed. For other fields, Microsoft advise you to consider indexing a field if all the following apply:

■ the field's data type is Text, Number, Currency, or Date/Time;

■ you anticipate searching for values stored in the field;

■ you anticipate sorting values in the field;

■ you anticipate storing many different values in the field. (If many of the values in the field are the same, the index may not significantly speed up queries.)

In addition, Microsoft advise that:

■ you should consider indexing fields on both sides of a join or create a relationship between these fields, in which case Access will automatically create an index on the foreign key field, if one does not exist already;

■ when grouping records by the values in a joined field, you should specify GROUP BY for the field that's in the same table as the field you're calculating the aggregate on.

Microsoft Access can optimize simple and complex search conditions (called *expressions* in Access). For certain types of complex expressions, Microsoft Access uses a data access technology called Rushmore, to achieve a greater level of optimization. A complex expression is formed by combining two simple expressions with the AND or OR operator, such as:

branchNo = 'B001' **AND** available = Yes
category = 'Action' **OR** dailyRental > 3

In Access, a complex expression is fully or partially optimizable depending on whether one or both simple expressions are optimizable, and which operator was used to combine them. A complex expression is *Rushmore-optimizable* if all three of the following conditions are true:

■ the expression uses AND or OR to join two conditions;

■ both conditions are made up of simple optimizable expressions;

■ both expressions contain indexed fields. The fields can be indexed individually or they can be part of a multiple-field index.

Creating indexes in Access

You create an index in Access by setting the Indexed property of a table in the Field Properties section in table Design View. The Indexed property has the following values:

No	No index (the default).
Yes (Duplicates OK)	The index allows duplicates.
Yes (No Duplicates)	The index doesn't allow duplicates.

We saw an example of setting an index for the mgrStaffNo field in Figure 12.4 in the previous chapter.

13.1.2 Indexes for *StayHome*

Based on the guidelines provided above, you should ensure that you create the primary key for each table, which will cause Access to automatically index this column. Secondly, you should ensure that all relationships are created in the Relationships window, which will cause Access to automatically index the foreign key columns.

From the *Stayhome* transactions listed in Section 6.4.4, you may decide to create the additional indexes shown in Table 13.2. This figure shows the columns in each table that should be indexed, the transaction(s) that use the column, and the reason for adding the index (either because the column is used in a *search condition*, as an *ordering* column, or as a *grouping* column). As an exercise, document the indexes for the transactions in the Business view of *StayHome* documented in Appendix C.

> Note that the available column in the VideoForRent table is used as a search condition by transaction (s). However, this column can only take on two values (Y or N) and so from guideline (9) above, it is not worthwhile indexing this column.

Table 13.2 Additional indexes for the Branch view of *StayHome*.

Table	Column	Transaction	Reason
Branch	city	(m)	search condition
Staff	name	(n)	ordering
Video	category	(p)	ordering
		(u)	search condition
		(v)	grouping
	title	(q), (r), (u)	ordering
		(t)	search condition
Actor	actorName	(q)	search condition
		(x)	grouping, ordering
Director	directorName	(r)	search condition
Member	fName/lName	(s)	search condition
RentalAgreement	dateReturn	(s)	search condition
Registration	dateJoined	(y)	search condition

Chapter summary

✓ In Step 4, you select the optimal file organizations to store the base tables, and the indexes that are required to achieve acceptable performance. This involves analyzing the transactions that will run on the database to help choose suitable file organizations and useful indexes.

✓ It's not possible to make meaningful physical design decisions until you understand in detail the transactions that have to be supported. This involves analyzing the most important transactions; that is, the transactions that run most frequently or are critical to the operation of the business.

✓ **Secondary indexes** provide a mechanism for specifying an additional key for a base table that can be used to retrieve data more efficiently. However, there is an overhead involved in the maintenance and use of secondary indexes that has to be balanced against the performance improvement gained when retrieving data.

✓ One approach to selecting an appropriate file organization for a table is to keep the records unordered and create as many secondary indexes as you need. Another approach is to order the records in the table by specifying a primary or clustering index.

 One approach to determining which secondary indexes you need is to produce a 'wish-list' of columns you think are candidates for indexing, and then to consider the impact of maintaining each of these indexes.

Review questions

13.1 Describe the purpose of Step 4 in the database design methodology.

13.2 Discuss the purpose of analyzing the transactions that have to be supported and describe the type of information you would collect and analyze.

13.3 When would you not add any indexes to a table?

13.4 Discuss some of the main reasons for selecting a column as a potential candidate for indexing. Give examples to illustrate your answer.

13.5 Having identified a column as a potential candidate, under what circumstances would you decide against indexing it?

Exercise

13.6 Work your way through some of the case studies presented in Appendix E and perform the steps of the physical design methodology discussed in this chapter for a target DBMS to which you have access.

Chapter 14

Physical database design – Steps 5 and 6

In this chapter you will learn:

➤ A database represents an essential corporate resource that must be made secure.

➤ How to design user views.

➤ How to design security mechanisms to satisfy user requirements.

Methodology
summarized in
Appendix B

This chapter covers Steps 5 and 6 of our database design methodology. In the previous two chapters, we translated the logical design into a set of tables and business rules and then selected appropriate file organizations and indexes based on an analysis of the most important transactions. In this chapter, we examine how to design the user views and security measures identified during the requirements analysis and collection stage of the database application lifecycle. As with the other steps of physical database design, the implementation of the user views and security mechanisms will be dependent on the target DBMS.

Step 5 Design user views

Objective
To design the user views that were identified during the requirements collection and analysis stage of the database application lifecycle.

The first step of the database design methodology involved the production of a logical data model for either the single user view or a number of combined user views identified during the requirements collection and analysis stage. In Section 6.4.4, we identified five user views for *StayHome* named Manager, Supervisor, Assistant, Director, and Buyer. Following an analysis of the data requirements for these user views, we used the centralized approach to merge the requirements for the user views as follows:

User views defined in Section 4.5

■ **Branch**, consisting of the Manager, Supervisor, and Assistant user views;

■ **Business**, consisting of the Director and Buyer user views.

The objective of this step is to design all the user views identified previously. In a standalone DBMS on a personal computer, views are usually a convenience, defined to simplify queries. However, in a multi-user DBMS views play a central role in defining the structure of the database and enforcing security. As with the design of base tables discussed in Chapter 12, to illustrate this process we show two particular ways to create views using:

(1) the 1999 ISO SQL standard (SQL3),

(2) Microsoft Access 2002.

The 1999 ISO SQL Standard (SQL3)

Normally, views are created using SQL or a QBE-like facility. For example, for Supervisors and Assistants at branch B001 you may create a view of the base table Staff that excludes salary information. The SQL statement to create this view would be:

CREATE TABLE covered in Section 3.3.1

```
CREATE VIEW Staff1_View
AS   SELECT staffNo, name, position
     FROM Staff
     WHERE branchNo = 'B001';
```

This creates a view called Staff1_View with the same columns as the Staff table, but excluding the salary and branchNo columns. If you query this view you get the data shown in Figure 14.1.

Staff1_View

staffNo	name	position
S1500	Tom Daniels	Manager
S0003	Sally Adams	Assistant

Figure 14.1

List of the Staff1_View view.

To ensure that only the branch manager can see the salary column, Supervisors and Assistants are not given access to the base table Staff. Instead, they are given *access privilege* to the view Staff1_View, thereby denying them access to sensitive salary data. We discuss access privileges further in Step 7.

Creating views in Microsoft Access 2002

Microsoft Access does not support the SQL CREATE VIEW statement. Instead, you can create a (stored) query using QBE or SQL. For example, you could create the view Staff1_View using the QBE query shown in Figure 14.2(a) or using the SQL statement shown in Figure 14.2(b). This query can now be used to create other queries, update/delete records in the base table Staff, and can be used as the basis for creating forms and reports.

Step 6 Design security mechanisms

Objective

To design the security measures for the database as specified by the users during the requirements collection and analysis stage of the database application lifecycle.

A database represents an essential corporate resource, and so security of this resource is extremely important. There may have been specific security requirements documented during the requirements collection and analysis stage of the database application lifecycle. The objective of this step is to decide how these security requirements are to be realized. Different DBMSs offer slightly different

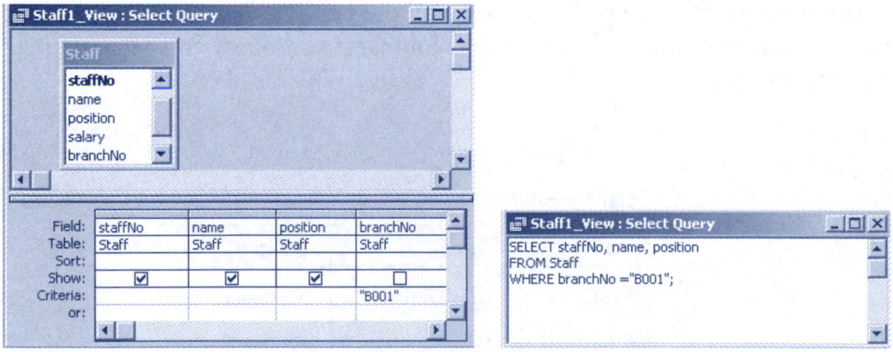

Figure 14.2

Creating a (stored) query in Microsoft Access: (a) using QBE; (b) using SQL.

(a)

(b)

security facilities and therefore you must be aware of the facilities offered by the target DBMS. As we discussed in Chapter 5, relational DBMSs generally provide two types of database security:

■ system security;
■ data security.

System security covers access and use of the database at the system level, such as a username and password. **Data security** covers access and use of database objects (such as tables and views) and the actions that users can have on the objects.

To illustrate the process of designing access rules we show two particular ways to design security mechanisms using:

(1) the 1999 ISO SQL standard (SQL3),

(2) Microsoft Access 2002.

> In Chapter 18, we'll show how to design security mechanisms in Oracle 9i using a different worked example.

The 1999 ISO SQL Standard (SQL3)

One way to provide data security is to use the access control facilities of SQL. As we've just mentioned, typically users should not be given direct access to the base tables. Instead, they should be given access to the base tables through the user views designed in Step 5. This provides a large degree of data independence and insulates users from changes in the database structure. We briefly review the access control mechanisms of SQL. For additional information, the interested reader is referred to Connolly and Begg (2002).

Data independence defined in Section 1.2.1

Each database user is assigned an **authorization identifier** by the Database Administrator (DBA); usually, the identifier has an associated password, for obvious security reasons. Every SQL statement that is executed by the DBMS is performed on behalf of a specific user. The authorization identifier is used to determine which database objects that user may reference, and what operations may be performed on those objects. Each object that is created in SQL has an owner, who is identified by the authorization identifier. By default, the owner is the only person who may know of the existence of the object and perform any operations on the object.

Privileges are the actions that a user is permitted to carry out on a given base table or view. For example, SELECT is the privilege to retrieve data from a table and UPDATE is the privilege to modify records of a table. When a user creates a table using the SQL CREATE TABLE statement, he or she automatically becomes the owner of the table and receives full privileges for the table. Other users initially have no privileges on the newly created table. To give them access to the table, the owner must explicitly grant them the necessary privileges using the SQL GRANT statement. A WITH GRANT OPTION clause can be specified with the GRANT statement to allow the receiving user(s) to pass the privilege(s) on to other users. Privileges can be revoked using the SQL REVOKE statement.

When a user creates a view with the CREATE VIEW statement, he or she automatically becomes the owner of the view, but does not necessarily receive full privileges on the view. To create the view, a user must have SELECT privilege to all the tables that make up the view. However, the owner will only get other privileges if he or she holds those privileges for every table in the view.

For example, to allow the user MANAGER to retrieve records from the Staff table and to insert, update, and delete data from the Staff table, you could use the following SQL statement:

GRANT ALL PRIVILEGES
ON Staff
TO Manager **WITH GRANT OPTION**;

In this case, MANAGER will also be able to reference the table and all the columns in any table he or she creates subsequently. The clause WITH GRANT OPTION is specified so that MANAGER can pass these privileges on to other users whom he or she sees fit. As another example, you could give the user with authorization identifier ADMIN the privilege SELECT on the Staff table using the following SQL statement:

GRANT SELECT
ON Staff
TO Admin;

The clause WITH GRANT OPTION is omitted this time so that ADMIN will not be able to pass this privilege on to other users.

Security in Microsoft Access 2002

Microsoft Access 2002 does not support the SQL GRANT and REVOKE statements. Instead, Access provides a number of security features, including the following two methods:

(a) setting a password for opening a database (system security);

(b) user-level security, which can be used to limit the parts of the database that a user can read or update (data security).

Setting a password

The simpler method is to set a password for opening the database. Once a password has been set (from the **Tools, Security** menu), a dialog box requesting the password will be displayed whenever the database is opened. The dialog box to set the password and the dialog box requesting the password whenever the database is opened are shown in Figure 14.3.

Only users who type the correct password will be allowed to open the database. This method is secure as Microsoft Access encrypts the password so that it cannot be accessed by reading the database file directly. However, once a database is open, all the objects contained within the database are available to the user.

User-level security

User-level security in Microsoft Access is similar to methods used in most network systems. Users are required to identify themselves and type a password when they start Microsoft Access. Within the workgroup information file, users are identified as members of a **group**. Access provides two default groups: administrators (*Admins* group) and users (*Users* group), but additional groups can be defined. Figure 14.4 displays the dialog box used to define the security level for user and group accounts. It shows a non-default group called Assistants, and a user called Assistant who is a member of the Users and Assistants groups.

Permissions are granted to groups and users to regulate how they are allowed to work with each object in the database using the User and Group Permissions dialog box. Table 14.1 shows the permissions that can be set in Microsoft Access. For example, Figure 14.5 shows the dialog box for a user called Assistant in

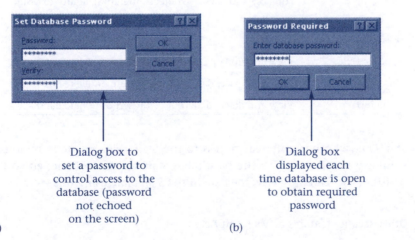

(a) Dialog box to set a password to control access to the database (password not echoed on the screen)

(b) Dialog box displayed each time database is open to obtain required password

Figure 14.3

Securing the *StayHome* database using a password: (a) the Set Database Password dialog box; (b) the Password Required dialog box shown at startup.

Figure 14.4

The User and Group Accounts dialog box for the *StayHome* database.

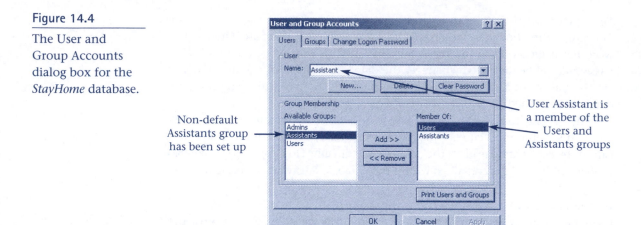

Non-default Assistants group has been set up

User Assistant is a member of the Users and Assistants groups

Table 14.1 Microsoft Access Permissions

Permission	Description
Open/Run	Open a database, form, report, or run a macro.
Open Exclusive	Open a database with exclusive access.
Read Design	View objects in Design view.
Modify Design	View and change database objects, and delete them.
Administer	For databases, set database password, replicate database, and change startup properties.
	Full access to database objects, including ability to assign permissions.
Read Data	View data.
Update Data	View and update data (but not insert or delete data).
Insert Data	View and insert data (but not update or delete data).
Delete Data	View and delete data (but not insert or update data).

StayHome who has only read access to the Staff1_View created previously. In a similar way, all access to the base table Staff would be removed so that the Assistant user can only view the data in the Staff table using this view.

Other security features of Microsoft Access

In addition to the above two methods of securing a Microsoft Access database, other security features include:

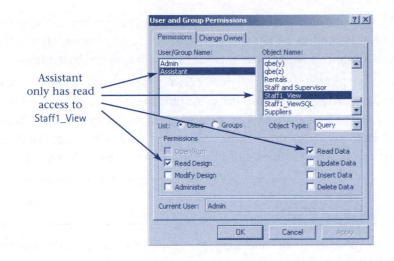

Assistant only has read access to Staff1_View

Figure 14.5

User and Group Permissions dialog box showing the Assistant user only has read access to the Staff1_View query.

■ *Encryption/decryption*: encrypting a database compacts a database file and makes it indecipherable by a utility program or word processor. This is useful if you wish to transmit a database electronically or when you store it on a floppy disk or compact disc. Decrypting a database reverses the encryption.

■ *Preventing users from replicating a database, setting passwords, or setting startup options.*

■ *Securing VBA code*: this can be achieved by setting a password that you enter once per session or by saving the database as an MDE file, which compiles the VBA source code before removing it from the database. Saving the database as an MDE file also prevents users from modifying forms and reports without requiring them to specify a log-on password or without you having to set up user-level security.

Document design of user views and security measures

The design of the individual user views and associated security mechanisms should be fully documented. If the physical design affects the logical data model, this model should also be updated.

Chapter summary

✓ A database represents an essential corporate resource, and so security of this resource is extremely important.

✓ In **Step 5**, you decide how each user view is to be implemented in the target DBMS.

✓ In **Step 6**, you decide how the security measures identified during the requirements collection and analysis stage are to be implemented in the target DBMS. This will include the access controls on the base tables.

✓ Relational DBMSs generally provide two types of database security: system security and data security. **System security** covers access and use of the database at the system level, such as a username and password. **Data security** covers access and use of database objects (such as tables and views) and the actions that users can have on the objects.

Review questions

14.1 Describe the purpose of the main steps in the physical design methodology presented in this chapter.

14.2 Discuss the difference between system security and data security.

14.3 Describe the access control facilities of SQL.

14.4 Describe the security features of Microsoft Access 2002.

Exercise

14.5 Work your way through some of the case studies presented in Appendix E and perform the steps of the physical design methodology discussed in this chapter for a target DBMS to which you have access. Create user views and security mechanisms that you think are appropriate. Justify your selection of these user views and security mechanisms.

Logical database design
Step 1 Create ER model
Step 2 Map ER model to tables

Physical database design
Step 3 Translate logical design
Step 4 Choose file organizations
Step 5 Design user views
Step 6 Design security
Step 7 Controlled redundancy
Step 8 Monitor and tune

Chapter 15

Physical database design – Step 7

In this chapter you will learn:

The meaning of denormalization. ◄

When to denormalize to improve performance. ◄

This chapter covers Step 7 of our database design methodology. In the previous three chapters, we translated the logical design into a set of tables and business rules and selected suitable file organizations and indexes based on an analysis of the transactions the database has to support. We then decided how to implement the user views and how to make the database secure. In some instances, additional performance improvements can be achieved by relaxing the normalization rules, which is what we consider in this chapter.

Methodology summarized in Appendix B

Normalization covered in Chapter 8

Step 7 Consider the introduction of controlled redundancy

Objective
To determine whether introducing redundancy in a controlled manner by relaxing the normalization rules will improve the performance of the system.

Normalization is a technique for deciding which columns belong together in a table. One of the basic aims of relational database design is to group columns

Functional
dependency defined
in Section 8.4

together in a table because there is a direct relationship (called a **functional dependency**) between them. The result of performing normalization on data is a logical database design that is structurally consistent and has minimal redundancy.

However, a normalized database design may not provide maximum processing efficiency. In these circumstances, you may wish to accept the loss of some of the benefits of a fully normalized design to achieve better performance. You should only consider this when you have estimated that the system will not be able to meet its performance requirements.

We are not advocating that normalization should be omitted from logical database design: normalization forces you to completely understand each column in each table in the database. Undertaking this process may be the most important factor that contributes to the overall success of the system. The following factors have to be considered if you're considering denormalization:

■ Denormalization makes implementation more complex.
■ Denormalization often sacrifices flexibility.
■ Denormalization may speed up retrievals but it slows down updates.

Formally, the term **denormalization** refers to a change to the structure of a base table, such that the new table is in a lower normal form than the original table. However, we also use the term more loosely to refer to situations where we combine two tables into one new table, where the new table is in the same normal form but contains more nulls than the original tables.

TIP

As a general rule of thumb, if performance is unsatisfactory and a table has a low update rate and a very high query rate, denormalization may be a viable option.

The transaction/table cross-reference matrix that was described in Step 4.1 provides useful information for this step. This matrix summarizes, in a visual way, the access patterns of the transactions that will run on the database. You can use it to highlight possible candidates for denormalization and to assess the effects this may have on the rest of the model. Indirectly, you've encountered an implicit example of denormalization when dealing with addresses. For example, consider the definition of the Branch table:

Branch   (<u>branchNo</u>, street, city, state, zipCode, mgrStaffNo)

Strictly speaking, this table is not in third normal form (3NF): city and state are functionally dependent on zipCode; in other words, if you know the zip code, you also know the city and state. Therefore, to normalize the table it is necessary to split the table into two, as follows:

Branch   (branchNo, street, zipCode, mgrStaffNo)
ZipCode   (zipCode, city, state)

3NF defined in Section 8.5

However, you rarely wish to access the branch address without the city and state columns. This means that you would have to perform a join whenever you wanted a complete address for a branch. As a result, we normally implement the original Branch table and settle for second normal form (2NF).

Unfortunately, there are no fixed rules for determining when to denormalize tables. Let's, however, discuss some of the more common situations for considering denormalization to speed up frequent or critical transactions:

- Step 7.1   Combining one-to-one (1:1) relationships
- Step 7.2   Duplicating nonkey columns in one-to-many (1:*) relationships to reduce joins
- Step 7.3   Duplicating foreign key columns in one-to-many (1:*) relationships to reduce joins
- Step 7.4   Duplicating columns in many-to-many (*:*) relationships to reduce joins
- Step 7.5   Introducing repeating groups
- Step 7.6   Creating extract tables
- Step 7.7   Partitioning tables

Step 7.1 Combining one–to–one (1:1) relationships

Re-examine one-to-one (1:1) relationships to determine the effects of combining the tables into a single table. You should only consider this for tables that are frequently referenced together and infrequently referenced separately. Let's consider a potential 1:1 relationship between Staff and NOK, as shown in Figure 15.1(a). The Staff entity contains information on staff and the NOK entity contains information about a member of staff's next of kin.

1:1 relationships defined in Section 7.5.1

We can combine the two tables together as shown in Figure 15.1(b). The relationship between Staff and NOK is 1:1 and the participation is optional. Since the participation is optional, when the two tables are combined together a number of the columns may have nulls appearing within them for some records, as shown in Figure 15.1(c). If the Staff table is large and the proportion of records involved in the participation is small, there will be a significant amount of wasted space. The amount of wastage has to be balanced against any performance improvements gained by combining the tables.

Participation defined in Section 7.5.5

Figure 15.1

Staff and NOK: (a) original table diagram; (b) revised table diagram; (c) resulting table.

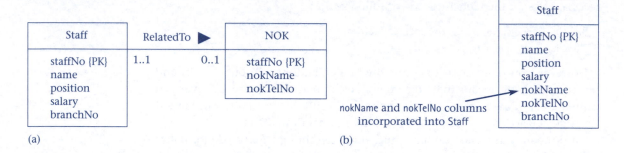

(a)

(b)

nokName and nokTelNo columns
incorporated into Staff

Staff

staffNo	name	position	salary	nokName	nokTelNo	branchNo
S1500	Tom Daniels	Manager	46000	Jane Daniels	207-878-2751	B001
S0003	Sally Adams	Assistant	30000	John Adams	518-474-5355	B001
S0010	Mary Martinez	Manager	50000			B002
S3250	Robert Chin	Supervisor	32000	Michelle Chin	206-655-9867	B002
S2250	Sally Stern	Manager	48000			B004
S0415	Art Peters	Manager	41000	Amy Peters	718-507-7923	B003

from original NOK

from original Staff

(c)

Step 7.2 Duplicating nonkey columns in one-to-many (1:*) relationships to reduce joins

With the specific aim of reducing or removing joins from frequent or critical queries, consider the benefits that may result from duplicating one or more nonkey columns of the parent table from the child table in a one-to-many (1:*) relationship. For example, whenever the VideoForRent table is accessed, it's very common for the video's daily rental rate to be accessed at the same time. A typical SQL query would be:

1:* relationships defined in Section 7.5.2

```
SELECT vfr.*, v.dailyRental
FROM VideoForRent vfr, Video v
WHERE vfr.catalogNo = v.catalogNo AND branchNo = 'B001';
```

based on the original table diagram shown in Figure 15.2(a).

Figure 15.2

Video and VideoForRent: (a) original table diagram; (b) revised table diagram.

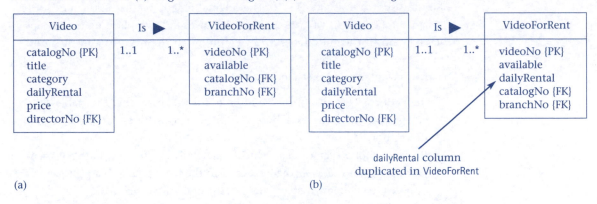

(a)   (b)

If you duplicate the dailyRental column in the VideoForRent table, you can remove the Video table from the query, which in SQL is now:

SELECT vfr.*
FROM VideoForRent vfr
WHERE branchNo = 'B001';

based on the revised table diagram shown in Figure 15.2(b).

The benefits that result from this change have to be balanced against the problems that may arise. For example, if you change the duplicated data in the parent table, you must also update it in the child table. Further, for a 1:* relationship there may be multiple occurrences of each data item in the child table. Thus, you also have to maintain consistency of the multiple copies. If the update of the dailyRental column in the Video and VideoForRent table cannot be automated, the potential for loss of integrity is considerable. Even if this process is automated, additional time is required to maintain consistency every time a record is inserted, updated, or deleted. In our case, it's likely that the daily rental rate will be reduced as the video becomes older, so the duplication may be unwarranted.

Another problem to consider is the increase in storage space resulting from the duplication. Again, with the relatively low cost of secondary storage nowadays, this may be less of a problem. However, this is not a justification for arbitrary duplication.

TIP

A special case of a one-to-many (1:*) relationship is a **lookup table**, sometimes called a **reference table** or **pick list**. Typically, a lookup table contains a code and a description. For example, you may define a lookup table for video category and modify the table diagram as shown in Figure 15.3(a). If the lookup table is used in frequent or critical queries, and the description is

▶

unlikely to change, consider duplicating the description column in the child table, as shown in Figure 15.3(b). The original lookup table is not redundant – it can still be used to validate user input. However, by duplicating the description column in the child table, you've eliminated the need to join the child table to the lookup table.

The advantages of using a lookup table are:

■ Reduction in the size of the child table (in this case, the Video table); the category code occupies 1 byte as opposed to 8 bytes for the category description.
■ If the description can change (which is generally not the case in this particular example), it's easier changing it once in the lookup table (VideoCategory) as opposed to changing it many times in the child table (Video).
■ The lookup table can be used to validate user input.

Figure 15.3

Lookup table for video category:
(a) original table diagram; (b) revised table diagram.

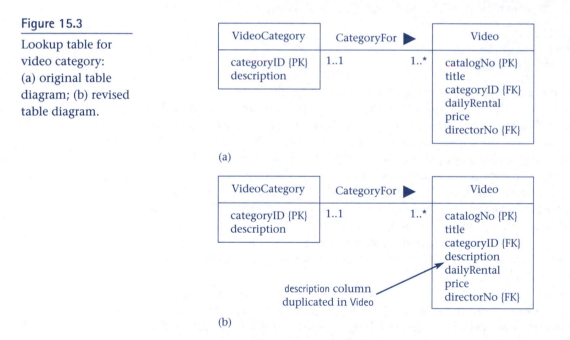

(a)

(b)

description column duplicated in Video

Step 7.3 Duplicating foreign key columns in one-to-many (1:*) relationships to reduce joins

Again, with the specific aim of reducing or removing joins from frequent or critical queries, consider the benefits that may result from duplicating one or more of the foreign key columns in a relationship. For example, a frequent query for *StayHome* is to list all rental agreements at a branch, using the following SQL query:

SELECT ra.*
FROM RentalAgreement ra, VideoForRent vfr
WHERE ra.videoNo = vfr.videoNo **AND** vfr.branchNo = 'B001';

based on the original table diagram shown in Figure 15.4(a).

As can be seen from this query, to get the list of rental agreements you have to use the VideoForRent table to gain access to the required branch number, branchNo. You can remove the need for this join by duplicating the foreign key branchNo in the RentalAgreement table; that is, you introduce a direct relationship between the Branch and RentalAgreement tables. In this case, you can simplify the SQL query to:

SELECT *
FROM RentalAgreement
WHERE branchNo = 'B001';

based on the revised table diagram shown in Figure 15.4(b). If this change is made, it will be necessary to introduce additional foreign key constraints, as discussed in Step 2.3.

Note that this only works because the new relationship between Branch and RentalAgreement is 1:*. In other words, for any one rental agreement there is one and only one associated branch. If the relationship was many-to-many (*:*), the above change would not work. For example, another frequent query might be to list the video titles in stock at a branch using the following SQL query:

: relationships defined in Section 7.5.3

SELECT v.title
FROM Video v, VideoForRent vfr
WHERE v.catalogNo = vfr.catalogNo **AND** vfr.branchNo = 'B001';

This query cannot be simplified by adding the branchNo column to the Video table, as the relationship between Branch and Video is *:*; that is, a video title is stocked by many branches, and a branch can have many video titles. However, in this case you could consider duplicating the title column of the Video table in the VideoForRent table, although the increased storage may be more significant in this case.

Figure 15.4

RentalAgreement and
VideoForRent:
(a) original table
diagram; (b) revised
table diagram.

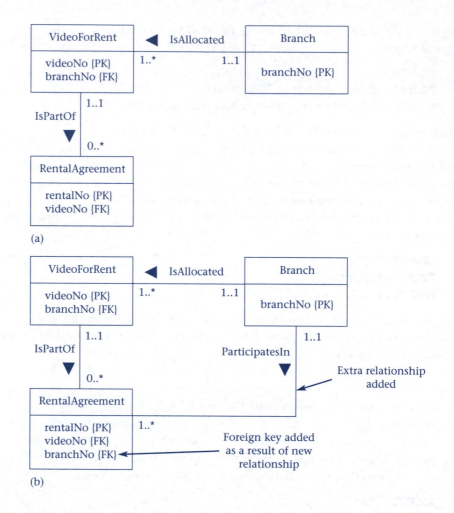

(a)

(b)

Step 7.4 Duplicating columns in many-to-many (*:*) relationships to reduce joins

In Step 2.1, you mapped each *:* relationship into three tables: the two tables derived from the original entities and a new table representing the relationship between the two entities. Now, if you wish to retrieve information from the *:* relationship, you have to join these three tables. In some circumstances, you may be able to reduce the number of tables to be joined by duplicating columns from one of the original entities in the intermediate table.

For example, a *:* relationship exists between Video and Actor, with Role acting as an intermediate entity. Consider the query that lists the video titles and roles that each actor has starred in:

SELECT v.title, a.*, r.*
FROM Video v, Role r, Actor a
WHERE v.catalogNo = r.catalogNo **AND** r.actorNo = a.actorNo;

based on the table diagram shown in Figure 15.5(a).

If you duplicate the title column in the Role table, you can remove the Video table from the query, giving the following revised SQL query:

SELECT a.*, r.*
FROM Role r, Actor a
WHERE r.actorNo = a.actorNo;

based on the revised table diagram shown in Figure 15.5(b).

Step 7.5 Introducing repeating groups

Repeating groups were eliminated from the logical data model as a result of the requirement that all entities be in first normal form (1NF). Repeating groups were separated out into a new table, forming a 1:* relationship with the original (parent) table. Occasionally, reintroducing repeating groups is an effective way to improve system performance.

For example, each *StayHome* branch office has a minimum of one and a maximum of three telephone numbers. In the logical data model, you created a Telephone table with a three-to-one (3:1) relationship with Branch, as shown in Figure 15.6(a).

Telephone entity created in Step 2.1 in Chapter 10

If access to this information is important or frequent, it may be more efficient to combine the tables and store the telephone details in the original Branch table, with one column for each telephone number, as shown in Figure 15.6(b).

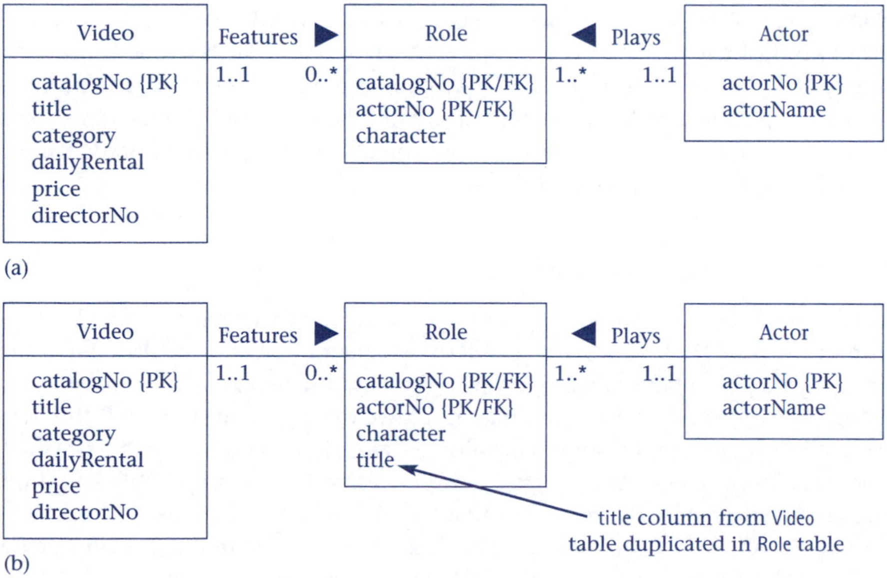

(a)

(b)

Figure 15.5

Video, Actor, and Role: (a) original table diagram; (b) revised table diagram.

Figure 15.6

Branch and Telephone: (a) original table diagram; (b) revised table diagram.

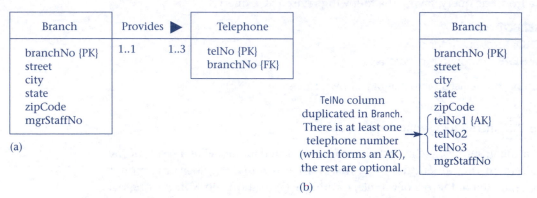

(a)

TelNo column
duplicated in Branch.
There is at least one
telephone number
(which forms an AK),
the rest are optional.

(b)

In general, you should only consider this type of denormalization in the following circumstances:

■ The absolute number of items in the repeating group is known (in this example, there is a maximum of three telephone numbers).

■ The number is static and will not change over time (the maximum number of telephone lines in a branch is fixed by *StayHome* and is not anticipated to change).

■ The number is not very large, typically not greater than 10, although this is not as important as the first two conditions.

Sometimes, it may be only the most recent or current value in a repeating group, or just the fact that there is a repeating group, that is needed most frequently. In the above example, you may choose to store one telephone number in the Branch table and leave the remaining numbers for the Telephone table. This would remove the presence of nulls from the Branch table, as each branch must have at least one telephone number.

Step 7.6 Creating extract tables

There may be situations where you have to run certain reports at peak times during the day. These reports access derived data and perform multi-table joins on the same set of base tables. However, the data the report is based on may be relatively static or, in some cases, may not have to be current (that is, if the data were a few hours old, the report would be perfectly acceptable). In this case, it may be possible to create a single, highly denormalized extract table based on the tables required by the reports, and allow the users to access the extract table directly instead of the base tables. The most common technique for producing extract tables is to create and populate the tables in an overnight batch run when the system is lightly loaded.

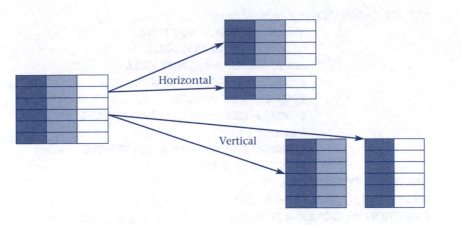

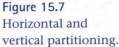Figure 15.7
Horizontal and
vertical partitioning.

Step 7.7 Partitioning tables

Rather than combining tables together, an alternative approach that addresses the key problem with supporting very large tables (and indexes) is to decompose them into a number of smaller and more manageable pieces called **partitions**. As illustrated in Figure 15.7, there are two main types of partitioning:

Horizontal partitioning
Distributing the **records** of a table across a number of (smaller) tables.

Vertical partitioning
Distributing the **columns** of a table across a number of (smaller) tables (the primary key is duplicated to allow the original table to be reconstructed).

Partitions are particularly useful in applications that store and analyze large amounts of data. For example, let's suppose there are hundreds of thousands of records in the VideoForRent table that are held indefinitely for analysis purposes. Searching for a particular record at a branch could be quite time-consuming; however, we could reduce this time by horizontally partitioning the table, with one partition for each branch. We can create a (*hash*) partition for this scenario in Oracle using the SQL statement shown in Figure 15.8.

As well as hash partitioning, other common types of partitioning are **range** (each partition is defined by a range of values for one or more columns) and **list** (each partition is defined by a list of values for a column). There are also composite partitions such as range-hash and list-hash (each partition is defined by a range or a list of values and then each partition is further subdivided based on a hash function).

There may also be circumstances where we frequently examine particular columns of a very large table and it may be appropriate to partition the table vertically into those columns that are frequently accessed together and another vertical partition for the remaining columns (with the primary key replicated in each partition to allow the original table to be reconstructed).

Figure 15.8

Oracle SQL
statement to create
a (hash) partition.

```
CREATE TABLE VideoForRent_Partition(
                videoNo CHAR(6) NOT NULL,
                available CHAR NOT NULL,
                catalogNo CHAR(6) NOT NULL,
                branchNo CHAR(4) NOT NULL,
                PRIMARY KEY videoNo,
                FOREIGN KEY catalogNo REFERENCES
                Video(videoNo),
                FOREIGN KEY branchNo REFERENCES
                Branch(branchNo))
PARTITION BY HASH (branchNo)
(PARTITION b1 TABLESPACE TB01,
PARTITION b2 TABLESPACE TB02,
PARTITION b3 TABLESPACE TB03,
PARTITION b4 TABLESPACE TB04);
```

Partitioning has a number of advantages:

■ *Improved load balancing*: Partitions can be allocated to different areas of secondary storage thereby permitting parallel access while at the same time minimizing the contention for access to the same storage area if the table was not partitioned.

■ *Improved performance*: By limiting the amount of data to be examined or processed, and by enabling parallel execution, performance can be enhanced.

■ *Increased availability*: If partitions are allocated to different storage areas and one storage area becomes unavailable, the other partitions will still be available.

■ *Improved recovery*: Smaller partitions can be recovered more efficiently (equally well, the DBA may find backing up smaller partitions easier than very large tables).

■ *Security*: Data in a partition can be restricted to only those users who require access to it, with different partitions having different access restrictions.

Partitioning can also have a number of disadvantages:

■ *Complexity*: Partitioning is not usually transparent to end-users and queries that utilize more than one partition become more complex to write.

■ *Reduced performance*: Queries that combine data from more than one partition may be slower than a non-partitioned approach.

■ *Duplication*: Vertical partitioning involves duplication of the primary key. This leads to increased storage requirements but also leads to potential inconsistencies arising.

Consider implications of denormalization

You should consider the implications of denormalization on the previous steps in the methodology. For example, you may have to reconsider the choice of indexes on the tables you have denormalized to check whether existing indexes should be removed or additional indexes added. In addition, you need to consider how data integrity will be maintained. Common solutions are:

■ *Triggers*: Triggers can be used to automate the updating of derived or duplicated data.

■ *Transactions*: Build transactions into each application that make the updates to denormalized data as a single (*atomic*) action.

■ *Batch reconciliation*: Run batch programs at appropriate times to make the denormalized data consistent.

In terms of maintaining integrity, triggers provide the best solution, although they can cause performance problems. The advantages and disadvantages of denormalization are summarized in Table 15.1.

Table 15.1 Advantages and disadvantages of denormalization.

Advantages	Disadvantages
Can improve performance by: – precomputing derived data; – minimizing the need for joins; – reducing the number of of foreign keys in tables; – reducing the number of indexes (thereby saving storage space); – reducing the number of tables.	May speed up retrievals but can slow down updates.
	Always application-specific and needs to be re-evaluated if the application changes.
	Can increase the size of tables.
	May simplify implementation in some cases but may make it more complex in others.
	Sacrifices flexibility.

Document introduction of redundancy

The introduction of redundancy should be fully documented, along with the reasons for introducing it. In particular, document the reasons for selecting one approach where many alternatives exist. Update the logical data model to reflect any changes made as a result of denormalization.

Chapter summary

✓ Step 7 considers the introduction of controlled redundancy to improve performance.

✓ There may be circumstances where it may be necessary to accept the loss of some of the benefits of a fully normalized design in favor of performance. This should be considered only when it's estimated that the system will not be able to meet its performance requirements.

✓ As a rule of thumb, if performance is unsatisfactory and a table has a low update rate and a very high query rate, **denormalization** may be a viable option.

✓ Consider denormalization in the following situations, specifically to speed up frequent or critical transactions: combining 1:1 relationships; duplicating nonkey columns in 1:* relationships to reduce joins; duplicating foreign key columns in 1:* relationships to reduce joins; duplicating columns in *:* relationships to reduce joins; introducing repeating groups; creating extract tables; partitioning tables that are very large.

Review questions

15.1 Describe the purpose of Step 7 in the database design methodology.

15.2 Explain the meaning of denormalization.

15.3 Discuss when it may be appropriate to denormalize a table. Give examples to illustrate your answer.

15.4 Describe the two main approaches to partitioning and discuss when each may be an appropriate way to improve performance. Give examples to illustrate your answer.

Exercise

15.5 For each of the case studies presented in Appendix E, discuss when denormalization may be appropriate.

Logical database design
Step 1 Create ER model
Step 2 Map ER model to tables

Physical database design
Step 3 Translate logical design
Step 4 Choose file organizations
Step 5 Design user views
Step 6 Design security
Step 7 Controlled redundancy
Step 8 Monitor and tune

Chapter 16

Physical database design – Step 8

In this chapter you will learn:

The importance of monitoring and tuning the operational system. ◄

How to measure efficiency. ◄

How system resources affect performance. ◄

This chapter covers the final step of our physical database design methodology. In the previous four chapters, we translated the logical database design into a set of tables and business rules, selected appropriate file organizations and indexes based on an analysis of the most important transactions, examined how to make the database secure, and considered the introduction of controlled redundancy to achieve additional performance improvements.

As user requirements evolve, it's usually necessary to *tune*, or adjust, the database to continue to achieve acceptable performance. In addition, you'll probably find that the requirements change, either as a result of the success of the system and users wanting more functionality, or as a result of the business evolving. In this chapter, we consider the remaining step of physical database design which takes these aspects into consideration.

Methodology summarized in Appendix B

Step 8 Monitor and tune the operational system

Objective
To monitor the operational system and improve the performance of the system to correct inappropriate design decisions or reflect changing requirements.

One of the main objectives of physical database design is to store data in an efficient way. There are a number of factors that we may use to measure efficiency:

■ *Transaction throughput*: this is the number of transactions processed in a given time interval. In some systems, such as airline reservations, high transaction throughput is critical to the overall success of the system.

■ *Response time*: this is the elapsed time for the completion of a single transaction.

From a user's point of view, you want to minimize response time as much as possible. However, there are some factors that influence response time over which you may have no control, such as system loading or communication times. You can shorten response time by:

– reducing contention and wait times, particularly disk I/O wait times;
– reducing the amount of time resources are required;
– using faster components.

■ *Disk storage*: this is the amount of disk space required to store the database files. You may wish to minimize the amount of disk storage used.

However, there is no one factor that is always correct. Typically, you have to trade one factor off against another to achieve a reasonable balance. For example, increasing the amount of data stored may decrease the response time or transaction throughput. You should not regard the initial physical database design as static, but as an estimate of how the operational system might perform. Once the initial design has been implemented, you should monitor the system and tune it as a result of observed performance and changing requirements. Many DBMSs provide the Database Administrator (DBA) with utilities to monitor the operation of the system and tune it.

There are many benefits to be gained from tuning the database:

■ It may avoid the procurement of additional hardware.

■ It may be possible to downsize the hardware configuration. This results in less, and cheaper, hardware and potentially less expensive maintenance.

■ A well-tuned system produces faster response times and better throughput, which in turn makes the users, and hence the organization, more productive.

■ Improved response times can improve staff morale.

■ Improved response times can increase customer satisfaction.

These last two benefits are more intangible than the others. However, we can certainly state that slow response times demoralize staff and potentially lose customers. To tune a database system, you need to understand how the various system components interact and affect database performance.

Understanding system resources

To improve performance, you must be aware of how the four basic hardware components interact and affect system performance:

- main memory
- CPU
- disk I/O
- network.

Each of these resources may affect other system resources. Equally well, an improvement in one resource may effect an improvement in other system resources. For example:

- Adding more main memory should result in less paging. This should help avoid CPU bottlenecks.
- More effective use of main memory may result in less disk I/O.

Main memory

Main memory accesses are significantly faster than secondary storage accesses, sometimes tens or even hundreds of thousands of times faster. In general, the more main memory available to the DBMS and the database applications, the faster the application programs will run. However, it's sensible always to have a minimum of 5 percent of main memory available. Equally well, it's advisable not to have any more than 10 percent available, otherwise main memory is not being used optimally. When there is insufficient memory to accommodate all processes, the operating system transfers pages of processes to disk to free up memory. When one of these pages is next required, the operating system has to transfer it back from disk. Sometimes, it's necessary to swap entire processes from main memory to disk and back again to free up memory. Problems occur with main memory when paging (also called swapping) becomes excessive.

To ensure efficient usage of main memory, you need to understand how the target DBMS uses main memory, what buffers it keeps in main memory, what parameters exist to allow you to adjust the size of these buffers, and so on. For example, Oracle keeps a data dictionary cache in main memory that ideally should be large enough to handle 90 percent of data dictionary accesses without having to retrieve the information from disk. You also need to understand the access patterns of users: an increase in the number of concurrent users accessing the database will result in an increase in the amount of memory being utilized.

CPU

The CPU controls the tasks of the other system resources and executes user processes, and is the most costly resource in the system so needs to be correctly utilized. The main objective for this component is to prevent **CPU contention** in which processes are waiting for the CPU. CPU bottlenecks occur when either the operating system or application programs make too many demands on the CPU. This is often a result of excessive paging.

You need to understand the typical workload through a 24-hour period and ensure that sufficient resources are available for not only the normal workload but also the peak workload (if you find that you have, for example, 90 percent CPU utilization and 10 percent idle during the normal workload then there may not be sufficient scope to handle the peak workload). One option is to ensure that during peak load no unnecessary jobs are being run and that such jobs are instead run in off-hours. Another option may be to consider multiple CPUs, which allow the processing to be distributed and operations to be processed in parallel.

CPU MIPS (Millions of Instructions Per Second) can be used as a guide in comparing platforms and determining their ability to meet the organization's throughput requirements.

Disk I/O

With any large DBMS, there's a significant amount of disk I/O involved in storing and retrieving data. While CPU clock speeds have increased dramatically in recent years, I/O speeds have not increased proportionately. The way in which data is organized on disk can have a major impact on the overall disk performance. One problem that can arise is **disk contention**. This occurs when multiple processes try to access the same disk simultaneously. Most disks have limits on both the number of accesses and the amount of data they can transfer per second and when these limits are reached, processes may have to wait to access the disk. To avoid this, it's recommended that storage should be evenly distributed across available drives to reduce the likelihood of performance problems occurring. Figure 16.1 illustrates the basic principles of distributing the data across disks:

■ The operating system files should be separated from the database files.

■ The main database files should be separated from the index files.

■ The recovery log file, if available and if used, should be separated from the rest of the database.

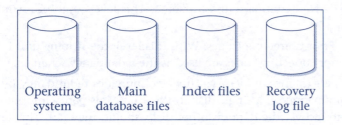

Figure 16.1

Typical disk configuration.

If a disk still appears to be overloaded, you can move one or more of its heavily accessed files to a less active disk (this is known as *distributing I/O*). You can achieve **load balancing** by applying this principle to each of your disks until they all have roughly the same amount of I/O. Once again, you have to understand how the DBMS operates, the characteristics of your hardware, and the access patterns of the users.

RAID

Disk I/O has been revolutionized with the introduction of RAID technology. RAID originally stood for *Redundant Array of Inexpensive Disks*, but more recently the 'I' in RAID has come to stand for *Independent*. RAID works on having a large disk array comprising an arrangement of several independent disks that are organized to increase performance and at the same time improve reliability.

Performance is increased through *data striping*: the data is segmented into equal-size partitions (the *striping unit*), which are transparently distributed across multiple disks. This gives the appearance of a single large, very fast disk where in fact the data is distributed across several smaller disks. Striping improves overall I/O performance by allowing multiple I/Os to be serviced in parallel. At the same time, data striping also balances the load among disks. Reliability is improved through storing redundant information across the disks using a *parity* scheme or an *error-correcting* scheme. In the event of a disk failure, the redundant information can be used to reconstruct the contents of the failed disk.

There are a number of disk configurations, referred to as **RAID levels**, each providing a slightly different trade-off between performance and reliability. The RAID levels are:

■ RAID 0 – Nonredundant: This level maintains no redundant data and so has the best write performance since updates do not have to be replicated. Data striping is performed at the level of blocks.

■ RAID 1 – Mirrored: This level maintains (*mirrors*) two identical copies of the data across different disks. To maintain consistency in the presence of disk failure, writes may not be performed simultaneously. This is the most expensive storage solution.

- RAID 0+1 – Nonredundant and Mirrored: This level combines striping and mirroring.
- RAID 2 – Error-Correcting Codes: With this level, the striping unit is a single bit and error-correcting codes are used as the redundancy scheme.
- RAID 3 —Bit-Interleaved Parity: This level provides redundancy by storing parity information on a single disk in the array. This parity information can be used to recover the data on other disks should they fail. This level uses less storage space than RAID 1 but the parity disk can become a bottleneck.
- RAID 4 – Block-Interleaved Parity: With this level, the striping unit is a disk block – a parity block is maintained on a separate disk for corresponding blocks from a number of other disks. If one of the disks fails, the parity block can be used with the corresponding blocks from the other disks to restore the blocks of the failed disk.
- RAID 5 – Block-Interleaved Distributed Parity: This level uses parity data for redundancy in a similar way to RAID 3 but stripes the parity data across all the disks, similar to the way in which the source data is striped. This alleviates the bottleneck on the parity disk.
- RAID 6 – P + Q Redundancy: This level is similar to RAID 5 but additional redundant data is maintained to protect against multiple disk failures. Error-correcting codes are used instead of using parity.

For most database applications, you will tend to choose between RAID 1, RAID 0+1, and RAID 5. Oracle, for example, recommends use of RAID 1 for the redo log files. For the database files, Oracle recommends RAID 5, provided the write overhead is acceptable, otherwise Oracle recommends either RAID 1 or RAID 0+1. Again, you should be aware of the RAID options available for your particular hardware configuration and know how the various DBMS components use disk I/O to allow you to select an appropriate solution.

Network

When the amount of data being transferred across the network is too great, network bottlenecks occur.

Summary

Tuning is an activity that is never complete. Throughout the life of the system, you'll need to monitor performance, particularly to account for changes in the environment and user requirements. However, making a change to one area of an operational system to improve performance may have an adverse effect on another area. For example, adding an index to a table may improve the performance of one application, but it may adversely affect another, perhaps more important, application. Therefore, care must be taken when making changes to an operational system. If possible, test the changes either on a test database, or alternatively, when the system is not being fully used (for example, out of working hours).

> **TIP**
>
> Most of the gains in performance come from good database design, through transaction analysis and use of appropriate indexes, as we discussed in Step 4 of the methodology. Although it's tempting to skip or rush through some of the steps, we strongly advocate against this and believe that spending sufficient time on database design will pay dividends subsequently.

Document tuning activity

The mechanisms you have used to tune the system should be fully documented, along with the reasons for tuning it the way you have. In particular, document the reasons for selecting one approach where many alternatives exist.

New requirement from *StayHome*

As well as tuning the system to maintain optimal performance, you may also have to cope with changing requirements. For example, *StayHome* have decided that the Video table should hold a picture of the video cover together with a brief story line, in preparation for making the video catalog available over the Web. You can accommodate the storing of images in Microsoft Access using the OLE (Object Linking and Embedding) data type, which is used to store data such as Microsoft Word or Excel documents, pictures, sound, and other types of binary data created in other programs. OLE objects can be linked to, or embedded in, a field in a Microsoft Access table and then displayed in a form or report.

To satisfy this new requirement, we restructure the Video table to add:

(1) a column called videoCover specified as an OLE Object data type; this column field holds graphical images of video covers, created by scanning photographs of the covers and saving the images as BMP (Bit Mapped) graphic files;

(2) a column called storyLine specified as a Memo data type, capable of storing lengthy text.

A form using these new columns is shown in Figure 16.2. The main problem with the addition of these two extra columns is the potentially large amount of disk space required to store the graphics files and the large amounts of text for the story line. You will therefore need to continue to monitor the performance of the *StayHome* database to ensure that satisfying this new requirement does not compromise the system's performance.

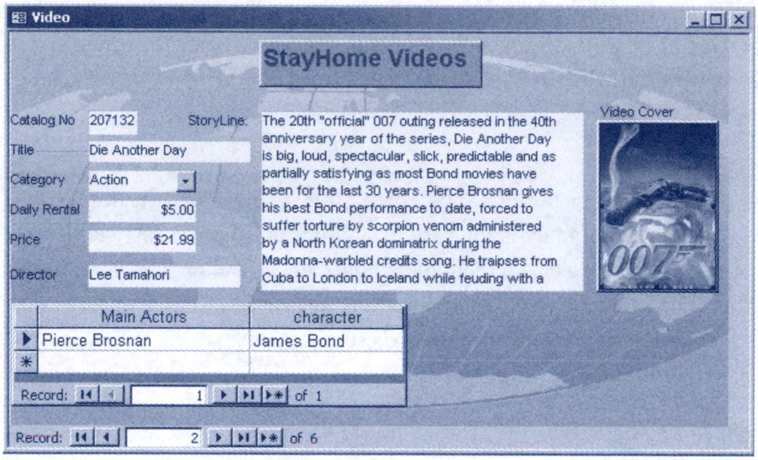

Figure 16.2

Form based on a revised Video table with the new videoCover and storyLine columns added.

Now that you have gone through all the steps in the methodology, you might like to look back at Section 9.1.3 to revisit the factors that we said were critical for successful database design. Possibly when you first read this section, it may have been difficult to see the relevance of some of these factors, but hopefully now you will see the importance of them all.

Chapter summary

✓ Step 8, the final step of physical database design, involves the ongoing process of monitoring and tuning the operational system to achieve maximum performance or to reflect changing requirements.

✓ One of the main objectives of physical database design is to store data in an efficient way. There are a number of factors that we may use to measure efficiency, including throughput, response time, and disk storage.

✓ To improve performance, you must be aware of how the following four basic hardware components interact and affect system performance: main memory, CPU, disk I/O, and network.

✓ Disk I/O has been revolutionized through the introduction of **RAID** (Redundant Array of Independent Disks) technology. RAID works on having a large disk array comprising an arrangement of independent disks that are organized to increase performance and at the same time improve reliability.

Review questions

16.1 Describe the purpose of the main steps in the physical design methodology presented in this chapter.

16.2 What factors can be used to measure efficiency?

16.3 Discuss how the four basic hardware components interact and affect system performance.

16.4 How should you distribute data across disks?

16.5 What is RAID technology and how does it improve performance and reliability?

Part 5

Second worked example

Chapter 17

PerfectPets – Logical database design

In this chapter, we provide a second case study to help reinforce the methodology we've covered in Chapters 9 to 16. We go through the steps of the logical database design methodology in this chapter and then the steps of physical database design in the next chapter. To demonstrate some of the physical implementation aspects we also use a different relational DBMS, namely Oracle 9i. We recommend that you read the case study in the following section and then attempt the steps in the methodology yourself. You can then check your solution against our sample solution. You may find the summary of the methodology given in Appendix B helpful.

17.1 *PerfectPets*

A practice called *PerfectPets* provides private health care for domestic pets throughout the US. This service is provided through various clinics located in the main cities of the US. The Director of *PerfectPets* is concerned that there is a lack of communication within the practice and particularly in the sharing of information and resources across the various clinics. To resolve this problem the Director has requested the creation of a centralized database system to assist in the more effective and efficient running of the practice. The Director has provided the following description of the current system.

17.1.1 Data requirements

Veterinary clinics

PerfectPets has many veterinary clinics located in the main cities of the US. The details of each clinic include the clinic number, clinic address (consisting of the street, city, state, and zip code), and the telephone and fax numbers. Each clinic has a Manager and a number of staff (for example, vets, nurses, secretaries, cleaners). The clinic number is unique throughout the practice.

Staff

The details stored on each member of staff include the staff number, name (first and last), address (street, city, state, and zip code), telephone number, date of birth, sex, social security number (SSN), position, and current annual salary. The staff number is unique throughout the practice.

Pet owners

When a pet owner first contacts a clinic of *PerfectPets* the details of the pet owner are recorded, which include an owner number, owner name (first name and last name), address (street, city, state, and zip code), and home telephone number. The owner number is unique to a particular clinic.

Pets

The details of the pet requiring treatment are noted, which include a pet number, pet name, type of pet, description, date of birth (if unknown, an approximate date is recorded), date registered at clinic, current status (alive/deceased), and the details of the pet owner. The pet number is unique to a particular clinic.

Examinations

When a sick pet is brought to a clinic, the vet on duty examines the pet. The details of each examination are recorded and include an examination number, the date and time of the examination, the name of the vet, the pet number, pet name, and type of pet, and a full description of the examination results. The examination number is unique to a particular clinic. As a result of the examination, the vet may propose treatment(s) for the pet.

Treatments

PerfectPets provides various treatments for all types of pets. These treatments are provided at a standard rate across all clinics. The details of each treatment include a treatment number, a full description of the treatment, and the cost to the pet owner. For example, treatments include:

T123	Penicillin antibiotic course	$50.00
T155	Feline hysterectomy	$200.00
T112	Vaccination course against feline flu	$70.00
T56	Small dog – stay in pen per day (includes feeding)	$20.00

A standard rate of $20.00 is charged for each examination, which is recorded as a type of treatment. The treatment number uniquely identifies each type of treatment and is used by all *PerfectPets* clinics.

Pet treatments

Based on the results of the examination of a sick pet, the vet may propose one or more types of treatment. For each type of treatment, the information recorded includes the examination number and date, the pet number, name and type, treatment number, description, quantity of each type of treatment, and date the treatment is to begin and end. Any additional comments on the provision of each type of treatment are also recorded.

Pens

In some cases, it's necessary for a sick pet to be admitted to the clinic. Each clinic has 20–30 animal pens, each capable of holding between one and four pets. Each pen has a unique pen number, capacity, and status (an indication of availability). The sick pet is allocated to a pen and the details of the pet, any treatment(s) required by the pet, and any additional comments about the care of the pet are recorded. The details of the pet's stay in the pen are also noted, which include a pen number, and the date the pet was put into and taken out of the pen. Depending on the pet's illness, there may be more than one pet in a pen at the same time. The pen number is unique to a particular clinic.

Invoices

The pet owner is responsible for the cost of the treatment given to a pet. The owner is invoiced for the treatment arising from each examination, and the details recorded on the invoice include the invoice number, invoice date, owner number, owner name and full address, pet number, pet name, and the details of the treatment given. The invoice provides the cost for each type of treatment and the total cost of all treatments given to the pet.

Additional data is also recorded on the payment of the invoice, including the date the invoice was paid and the method of payment (for example, check, cash, credit card). The invoice number is unique throughout the practice.

Surgical, non-surgical, and pharmaceutical supplies

Each clinic maintains a stock of surgical supplies (for example, syringes, sterile dressings, bandages) and non-surgical supplies (for example, plastic bags, aprons, litter trays, pet name tags, pet food). The details of surgical and non-surgical supplies include the item number and name, item description, quantity in stock (this is ascertained on the last day of each month), reorder level, reorder quantity, and cost. The item number uniquely identifies each type of surgical or non-surgical supply. The item number is unique for each surgical or non-surgical item and used throughout the practice.

Each clinic also maintains a stock of pharmaceutical supplies (for example, antibiotics, pain killers). The details of pharmaceutical supplies include a drug number and name, description, dosage, method of administration, quantity in stock (this is ascertained on the last day of each month), reorder level, reorder quantity, and cost. The drug number uniquely identifies each type of pharmaceutical supply. The drug number is unique for each pharmaceutical supply and used throughout the practice.

Appointments

If the pet requires to be seen by the vet at a later date, the owner and pet are given an appointment. The details of an appointment are recorded and include an appointment number, owner number, owner name (first name and last name), home telephone number, the pet number, pet name, type of pet, and the appointment date and time. The appointment number is unique to a particular clinic.

17.1.2 Transaction requirements

Listed below are the transactions that should be supported by the *PerfectPets* database application.

(1) The database should be capable of supporting the following maintenance transactions:

    (a) Create and maintain records recording the details of *PerfectPets* clinics and the members of staff at each clinic.

    (b) Create and maintain records recording the details of pet owners.

    (c) Create and maintain the details of pets.

    (d) Create and maintain records recording the details of the types of treatments available for pets.

    (e) Create and maintain records recording the details of examinations and treatments given to pets.

    (f) Create and maintain records recording the details of invoices to pet owners for treatment to their pets.

    (g) Create and maintain records recording the details of surgical, non-surgical, and pharmaceutical supplies at each clinic.

    (h) Create and maintain records recording the details of pens available at each clinic and the allocation of pets to pens.

    (i) Create and maintain pet owner/pet appointments at each clinic.

(2) The database should be capable of supporting the following example query transactions:

    (a) Present a report listing the Manager's name, clinic address, and telephone number for each clinic, ordered by clinic number.

(b) Present a report listing the names and owner numbers of pet owners with the details of their pets.

(c) List the historic details of examinations for a given pet.

(d) List the details of the treatments provided to a pet based on the results of a given examination.

(e) List the details of an unpaid invoice for a given pet owner.

(f) Present a report on invoices that have not been paid by a given date, ordered by invoice number.

(g) List the details of pens available on a given date for clinics in New York, ordered by clinic number.

(h) Present a report that provides the total monthly salary for staff at each clinic, ordered by clinic number.

(i) List the maximum, minimum, and average cost for treatments.

(j) List the total number of pets in each pet type, ordered by pet type.

(k) Present a report of the names and staff numbers for all vets and nurses over 50 years old, ordered by staff name.

(l) List the appointments for a given date and for a particular clinic.

(m) List the total number of pens in each clinic, ordered by clinic number.

(n) Present a report of the details of invoices for pet owners between 2000 and 2002, ordered by invoice number.

(o) List the pet number, name, and description of pets owned by a particular owner.

(p) Present a report listing the pharmaceutical supplies that need to be reordered at each clinic, ordered by clinic number.

(q) List the total cost of the non-surgical and surgical supplies currently in stock at each clinic, ordered by clinic number.

17.2 Using the logical database design methodology

Methodology summarized in Appendix B

In this section, we're going to work through the steps in the logical database design methodology to produce a logical data model that satisfies the above requirements for *PerfectPets*. We assume that the requirements collection and analysis stage has identified only one user view.

Step 1.1 Identify entities

Entities defined in Section 7.1

The first step in logical database design is to identify the main entities that you have to represent in the database. From the description of the practice given above, you may identify the following entities:

Clinic   Staff
PetOwner   Pet
Examination   Treatment
Pen   PetTreatment
Invoice   Appointment
Stock (with specializations Surgical, NonSurgical, and Pharmaceuticals)

Document entities

As you identify entities, assign them names that are meaningful and obvious to the user, and record this information in a data dictionary. Figure 17.1 shows an extract from the data dictionary that documents the entities for *PerfectPets*.

Step 1.2 Identify relationships

Relationships defined in Section 7.2

Having identified the entities, your next step is to identify all the relationships that exist between these entities. For *PerfectPets*, you may identify the relationships shown in Figure 17.2.

Determine the multiplicity constraints of relationships

Multiplicity defined in Section 7.5

Having identified the relationships you wish to model, you now want to determine the multiplicity of each relationship. For *PerfectPets*, you should identify the multiplicity constraints shown in Figure 17.3.

Figure 17.1

Extract from the data dictionary for *PerfectPets* showing description of entities.

Entity name	Description	Aliases	Occurrence
Clinic	Veterinary clinics.	Surgery	One or more *PerfectPets* clinics located in main cities throughout the US.
Staff	General term describing all staff employed by *PerfectPets*.	Vet, Nurse, Secretary	Each member of staff works at a particular clinic.
PetOwner	Owners of pets taken to *PerfectPets*.		Owner takes his/her pet to a particular clinic.

Entity	Relationship	Entity
Clinic	Has	Staff
	Holds	Stock
	Registers	Pet
	Provides	Pen
	Schedules	Appointment
	IsContactedBy	PetOwner
Staff	Manages	Clinic
	Performs	Examination
PetOwner	Owns	Pet
	Pays	Invoice
	Attends	Appointment
Pet	Undergoes	Examination
	IsAllocatedTo	Pen
	Attends	Appointment
Examination	ResultsIn	PetTreatment
Treatment	UsedIn	PetTreatment
Invoice	ResultsFrom	Examination

Figure 17.2

First draft of relationships for *PerfectPets*.

Entity	Multiplicity	Relationship	Multiplicity	Entity
Clinic	1..1	Has	1..*	Staff
	1..*	Holds	1..*	Stock
	1..1	Registers	1..*	Pet
	1..1	Provides	20..30	Pen
	1..1	Schedules..*	1..*	Appointment
	1..1	IsContactedBy	1..*	PetOwner
Staff	1..1	Manages	0..1	Clinic
	1..1	Performs	0..*	Examination
PetOwner	1..1	Owns	1..*	Pet
	1..1	Pays	1..*	Invoice
	1..1	Attends	1..*	Appointment
Pet	1..1	Undergoes	1..*	Examination
	1..*	IsAllocatedTo	0..*	Pen
	1..1	Attends	1..*	Appointment
Examination	1..1	ResultsIn	1..*	PetTreatment
Treatment	1..1	UsedIn	1..*	PetTreatment
Invoice	1..1	ResultsFrom	1..1	Examination

Figure 17.3

Multiplicity constraints for relationships identified above.

Use Entity–Relationship (ER) modeling

Throughout the database design phase, you'll create several versions of the ER diagram representing *PerfectPets*. Figure 17.4 shows the first draft ER diagram for *PerfectPets*.

Step 1.3 Identify and associate attributes with entities or relationships

Attributes defined in Section 7.3

The next step is to identify the attributes that are associated with the entities and relationships that you've identified. For *PerfectPets*, you should identify the attributes with the associated entities, as shown in Figure 17.5(a).

However, when examining the information on pens, you may have difficulty associating the attributes dateIn and dateOut, representing the date a pet was put in and taken out of a pen, and the attribute comments with either the Pen or Pet entity. Similarly, you may have difficulty associating the attribute inStock, representing the amount of quantity in stock for the different categories of supplies, and the attributes reorderLevel and reorderQty with either the Clinic or Stock entities. In both these cases, you should ensure that you have not missed one or more entities for these attributes in Step 1.1 or associate the attributes with the corresponding relationships, as shown in Figure 17.5(b).

You should also be careful not to include the same attribute in two entities, when the occurrence of the attribute actually represents a relationship between the entities. For example, in the requirements specification given in Section 17.1.1 under Examinations, it states that the details of each examination includes 'the name of the vet'. You might be misled here to include the name of the vet in both the Staff and Examination entities. However, this would be incorrect: the appearance of the vet's name in this situation represents a relationship and you should not include it as an attribute of the Examination entity. If you were to do this, it would subsequently result in the Examination table not conforming to third normal form (3NF).

3NF discussed in Section 8.5

TIP

This is quite a common mistake for inexperienced designers to make, so you should look out for it.

Document attributes

As you identify attributes, assign them names that are meaningful and obvious to the user, and record their details in a data dictionary, as discussed in Step 1.3 in Chapter 9.

Figure 17.4

First draft ER diagram for *PerfectPets*.

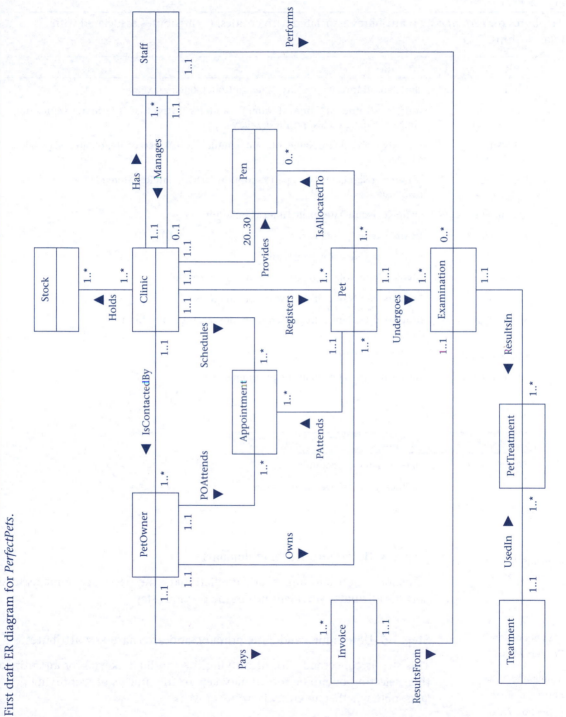

Figure 17.5

Attributes for *PerfectPets*: (a) attributes associated with entities; (b) attributes associated with relationships.

Entity	Attributes
Clinic	clinicNo, address (street, city, state, zipCode), telNo, faxNo
Staff	staffNo, sName (sFName, sLName), sAddress (sStreet, sCity, sState, sZipCode), sTelNo, DOB, sex, SSN, position, salary
PetOwner	ownerNo, oName (oFName, oLName), oAddress (oStreet, oCity, oState, oZipCode), oTelNo
Pet	petNo, petName, petType, petDescription, pDOB, dateRegistered, petStatus
Examination	examNo, examDate, examTime, examResults
Treatment	treatNo, description, cost
Pen	penNo, penCapacity, penStatus
Invoice	invoiceNo, invoiceDate, datePaid, paymentMethod
Stock: Item	itemNo, itemName, itemDescription, itemCost
Stock: Pharmacy	drugNo, drugName, drugDescription, dosage, methodAdmin, drugCost
Appointment	appNo, aDate, aTime
PetTreatment	startDate, endDate, quantity, ptComments

(a)

Relationship	Attributes
IsAllocatedTo	dateIn, dateOut, comments
Holds	inStock, reorderLevel, reorderQty

(b)

Domains defined in Section 2.2.1

Step 1.4 Determine attribute domains

You should now add into your data dictionary the necessary domains to support the attributes you identified in the previous step.

Keys defined in Section 2.2.3

Strong and weak entities defined in Section 7.4

Step 1.5 Determine candidate, primary, and alternate key attributes

This step is concerned with identifying the candidate key(s) for an entity and then selecting one to be the primary key. In the process of identifying primary keys, note whether an entity is strong or weak.

In trying to identify candidate keys, you should observe that the clinic number for the Clinic entity, the staff number for the Staff entity, the treatment number for the Treatment entity, the invoice number for the Invoice entity, and the item/drug number for the Stock entity are unique for the entire practice. On the other hand, the owner number for the PetOwner entity, the pet number for the Pet entity, and the pen number for the Pen entity are only unique for a particular clinic. It's not uncommon for a company to give different offices a degree of local autonomy. However, in a centralized database system it's sometimes more appropriate to have uniqueness throughout the company. In discussion with the *PerfectPets* management, it's agreed that all numbers should be allocated across the entire practice, as opposed to each clinic. If this had not been the decision, it would have been necessary to add the clinic number to those numbers only unique within each clinic to gain uniqueness across the practice.

With this in mind, you should now identify the primary keys shown in Figure 17.6 (other alternate keys are shown in Figure 17.9). In particular, you should identify PetTreatment as a weak entity.

Step 1.6 Specialize/Generalize entities (optional step)

The identification of the Stock entity in its current form is perfectly acceptable to continue with the logical database design methodology. However, there is additional information given that you may wish to add, to model the practice more accurately. The requirements specification states that there are surgical and non-surgical supplies that have a unique item number to distinguish them. There are also pharmaceutical supplies that have a unique drug number to distinguish them. In addition, these two types of supplies have slightly different attributes associated with them. Therefore, we could consider Surgical/Non-Surgical Stock and Pharmaceuticals to be particular types of the Stock entity. This specialization/generalization is shown in Figure 17.6. For simplicity, we have renamed Surgical/Non-Surgical Stock as Item and Pharmaceuticals as Pharmacy.

Specialization/ Generalization covered in Chapter 11

You may also identify Vet, Nurse, Secretary, and Cleaner as particular types of Staff. Although these job titles all have the same attributes, only the Vet entity participates in the *Performs* relationship with Examination. This is a perfectly valid way of modeling staff. However, to keep the model simple, we omit this specialization/generalization.

Step 1.7 Check model for redundancy

At this point, you now have a logical data model for *PerfectPets*. However, the data model may contain some redundancy which should be removed. More specifically, you have to:

(1) Re-examine one-to-one (1:1) relationships.

(2) Remove redundant relationships.

Figure 17.6

ER diagram for *PerfectPets* with primary keys shown and specialization/generalization of Stock.

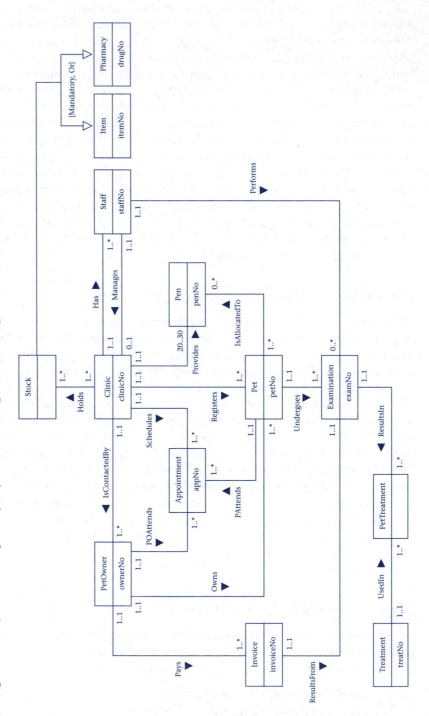

One-to-one (1:1) relationships

From Figure 17.6, there are two 1:1 relationships: Staff *Manages* Clinic and Invoice *ResultsFrom* Examination. However, in both cases the two entities are clearly distinct and should not be merged together.

1:1 relationships defined in Section 7.5.1

Redundant relationships

From Figure 17.6, there are a number of relationships between PetOwner, Pet, Clinic, and Appointment, and a closer examination is useful to identify any redundant relationships. First of all, note that the PetOwner/Pet entities have mandatory participation in the *POAttends/PAttends/Owns* relationships, and that a PetOwner may own many pets. Therefore, for any given Appointment we can identify the Owner through the *POAttends* relationship, but we cannot then identify the Pet through the *Owns* relationship. However, for any given Appointment, we can identify the Pet through the *PAttends* relationship and for any given Pet we can identify the PetOwner through the *Owns* relationship, which suggests that the *POAttends* relationship is redundant. In a similar way, through the *PAttends* relationship we can identify the Pet, and through the *Registers* relationship we can identify the Clinic involved in the Appointment, which suggests the *Schedules* relationship is also redundant.

Participation defined in Section 7.5.5

Note that the *IsContactedBy* relationship between Clinic and PetOwner also appears to be redundant. However, *PerfectPets* notes the details of pet owners when they first make contact and only obtains the details of pets at the first appointment, and so the *IsContactedBy* relationship is retained. The revised ER diagram is shown in Figure 17.7.

Step 1.8 Check model supports user transactions

In this step, you check that the logical data model you have developed supports the transactions identified by the users. This involves checking that:

■ the required attributes are present in the data model, and

■ where attributes have to be taken from more than one entity, there is a pathway between the two entities; in other words, there is an identified relationship, either direct or indirect, between the two entities.

The transaction pathway diagram for the query transactions identified in Section 17.1.2 is shown in Figure 17.8, and you can readily check that the required attributes are available from an individual entity or from multiple entities via one or more relationships.

Step 2.1 Create tables

In this step, you create tables from the logical data model to represent the entities and relationships described in the user's view of the practice, using a Database Design Language (DBDL) for relational databases.

DBDL discussed in Step 2.1 in Chapter 10

Figure 17.7

Revised ER diagram for *PerfectPets* with redundant relationships removed.

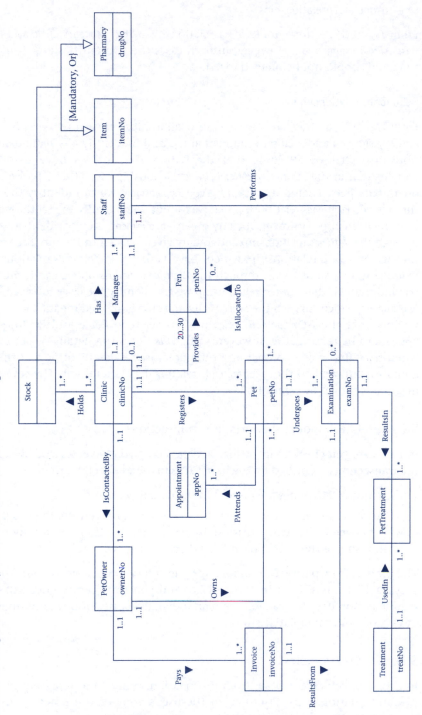

Figure 17.8

Transaction pathway diagram for *PerfectPets*.

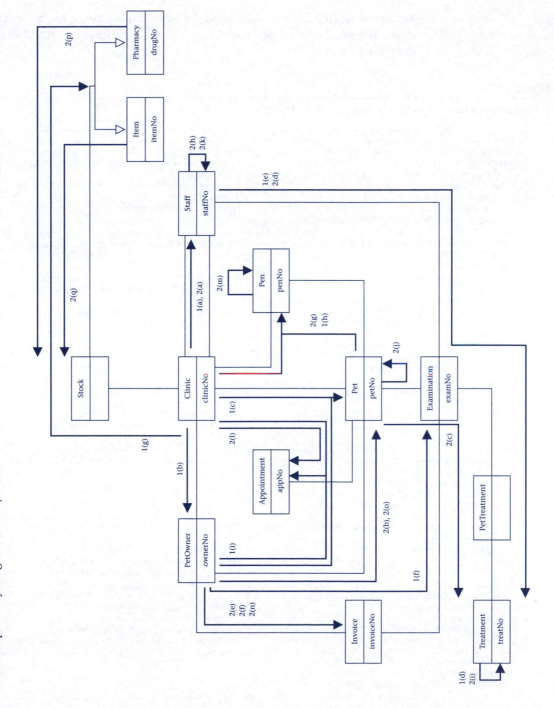

Document tables and foreign key attributes

At the end of Step 2.1, you document the full composition of the tables created from the logical data model. Each table is described using the DBDL, as shown in Figure 17.9.

Figure 17.9

Tables created from logical data model for *PerfectPets*.

Clinic (clinicNo, street, city, state, zipcode, telNo, faxNo, mgrStaffNo) **Primary Key** clinicNo **Alternate Key** zipCode **Alternate Key** telNo **Alternate Key** faxNo **Foreign Key** mgrStaffNo **references** Staff(staffNo)	**Staff** (staffNo, sFName, sLName, sStreet, sCity, sState, sZipCode, sTelNo, DOB, sex, SSN, position, salary, clinicNo) **Primary Key** staffNo **Alternate Key** SSN **Foreign Key** clinicNo **references** Clinic(clinicNo)
PetOwner (ownerNo, oFName, oLName, oState, oZipCode, oTelNo, clinicNo) **Primary Key** ownerNo **Foreign Key** clinicNo **references** Clinic(clinicNo)	**Pet** (petNo, petName, petType, petDescription, pDOB, dateRegistered, petStatus, ownerNo, clinicNo) **Primary Key** petNo **Foreign Key** ownerNo **references** Owner(ownerNo) **Foreign Key** clinicNo **references** Clinic(clinicNo)
Examination (examNo, examDate, examTime, examResults, petNo, staffNo) **Primary Key** examNo **Alternate Key** staffNo, examDate, examTime **Foreign Key** petNo **references** Pet(petNo) **Foreign Key** staffNo **references** Staff(staffNo)	**Treatment** (treatNo, description, cost) **Primary Key** treatNo
Pen (penNo, penCapacity, penStatus, clinicNo) **Primary Key** penNo **Foreign Key** clinicNo **references** Clinic(clinicNo)	**PetPen** (penNo, petNo, dateIn, dataOut, comments) **Primary Key** penNo, petNo, dateIn **Alternate Key** penNo, petNo, dateOut **Foreign Key** penNo **references** Pen(penNo) **Foreign Key** petNo **references** Pet(petNo)
PetTreatment (examNo, treatNo, startDate, endDate, quantity, ptComments) **Primary Key** examNo, treatNo **Foreign Key** examNo **references** Examination(examNo) **Foreign Key** treatNo **references** Treatment(treatNo)	**Item** (itemNo, itemName, itemDescription, itemCost) **Primary Key** itemNo
Pharmacy (drugNo, drugName, drugDescription, dosage, methodAdmin, drugCost) **Primary Key** drugNo	**ItemClinicStock** (itemNo, clinicNo, inStock, reorderLevel, reorderQty) **Primary Key** itemNo, clinicNo **Foreign Key** itemNo **references** Item(itemNo) **Foreign Key** clinicNo **references** Clinic(clinicNo)
PharmClinicStock (drugNo, clinicNo, inStock, reorderLevel, reorderQty) **Primary Key** drugNo, clinicNo **Foreign Key** drugNo **references** Pharmacy(drugNo) **Foreign Key** clinicNo **references** Clinic(clinicNo)	**Invoice** (invoiceNo, invoiceDate, datePaid, paymentMethod, ownerNo, examNo) **Primary Key** invoiceNo **Foreign Key** ownerNo **references** Owner(ownerNo) **Foreign Key** examNo **references** Examination(examNo)
Appointment (appNo, aDate, aTime, petNo) **Primary Key** appNo **Foreign Key** petNo **references** Pet(petNo)	

Step 2.2 Check table structures using normalization

Normalization covered in Chapter 8

In this step, you want to ensure that each table created in the previous step is in at least third normal form (3NF). If you identify tables that are not in 3NF, this may indicate that part of the logical data model is incorrect, or you have introduced an error when deriving the tables from the model. However, you can readily check that the tables identified in Figure 17.9 are in 3NF.

Step 2.3 Check tables support user transactions

This step is similar to Step 1.8, except in this step you're checking that the mapping from entities to tables and the posting of primary keys to act as foreign keys have been undertaken correctly. In this case, you can again readily check the mapping has been performed correctly and the tables do support the user transactions identified in Section 17.1.2.

Step 2.4 Check business rules

Business rules discussed in Section 2.3

Business rules are the constraints that you wish to impose in order to protect the database from becoming inconsistent. Of the six types of business rules, four were identified in previous steps and documented in the data dictionary, namely: required data, column domain constraints, entity integrity, and multiplicity. We consider the remaining two here: referential integrity and other business rules.

Referential integrity

There are two issues to consider here:

Participation defined in Section 7.5.5

(1) *Identify whether nulls are allowed for the foreign key.* In general, if the participation of the child table in the relationship is mandatory, then the strategy is that nulls are not allowed. On the other hand, if the participation of the child table is optional, then nulls should be allowed.

(2) *Identify the existence constraints under which a foreign key may be inserted, updated, or deleted.* In general, this involves specifying two actions for each foreign key: an ON UPDATE action and an ON DELETE action, relating to what should happen to maintain referential integrity if a record in the parent table is updated/deleted. Figure 17.10 shows the necessary actions for the foreign keys identified in Figure 17.9.

Other business rules

Finally, consider whether there are any other types of constraints that *PerfectPets* has defined that have not been covered elsewhere in the data model. Such constraints are more generally called *business rules*.

Figure 17.10

The referential integrity constraints for the *PerfectPets* tables.

Clinic **Foreign Key** mgrStaffNo **references** Staff(staffNo) ON UPDATE CASCADE ON DELETE NO ACTION
Staff **Foreign Key** clinicNo **references** Clinic(clinicNo) ON UPDATE CASCADE ON DELETE NO ACTION
PetOwner **Foreign Key** clinicNo **references** Clinic(clinicNo) ON UPDATE CASCADE ON DELETE NO ACTION
Pet **Foreign Key** ownerNo **references** Owner(ownerNo) ON UPDATE CASCADE ON DELETE CASCADE **Foreign Key** clinicNo **references** Clinic(clinicNo) ON UPDATE CASCADE ON DELETE NO ACTION
Examination **Foreign Key** petNo **references** Pet(petNo) ON UPDATE CASCADE ON DELETE CASCADE **Foreign Key** staffNo **references** Staff(staffNo) ON UPDATE CASCADE ON DELETE NO ACTION
Pen **Foreign Key** clinicNo **references** Clinic(clinicNo) ON UPDATE CASCADE ON DELETE CASCADE
PetPen **Foreign Key** penNo **references** Pen(penNo) ON UPDATE CASCADE ON DELETE CASCADE **Foreign Key** petNo **references** Pet(petNo) ON UPDATE CASCADE ON DELETE CASCADE
PetTreatment **Foreign Key** treatNo **references** Treatment(treatNo) ON UPDATE CASCADE ON DELETE NO ACTION
ItemClinicStock **Foreign Key** itemNo **references** Item(itemNo) ON UPDATE CASCADE ON DELETE NO ACTION **Foreign Key** clinicNo **references** Clinic(clinicNo) ON UPDATE CASCADE ON DELETE NO ACTION
PharmClinicStock **Foreign Key** drugNo **references** Pharmacy(drugNo) ON UPDATE CASCADE ON DELETE NO ACTION **Foreign Key** clinicNo **references** Clinic(clinicNo) ON UPDATE CASCADE ON DELETE NO ACTION
Invoice **Foreign Key** ownerNo **references** Owner(ownerNo) ON UPDATE CASCADE ON DELETE NO ACTION **Foreign Key** examNo **references** Examination(examNo) ON UPDATE CASCADE ON DELETE NO ACTION
Appointment **Foreign Key** petNo **references** Pet(petNo) ON UPDATE CASCADE ON DELETE CASCADE

Document all business rules

All business rules are documented in the data dictionary for consideration during physical database design.

Step 2.5 Review logical database design with users

The logical database design is now complete and fully documented. At this point, you should review the logical data model and supporting documentation with the users. We'll assume that this does not identify any major deficiencies in the design. This completes the logical database design methodology for *PerfectPets*. In the next chapter, we'll proceed to the physical database design phase.

Chapter 18

PerfectPets – Physical database design

In this chapter, we go through the steps of physical database design for the *PerfectPets* case study introduced in the previous chapter. To demonstrate some of the physical implementation aspects we use Oracle 9i. As we mentioned at the start of the last chapter, we recommend that you attempt the steps in the methodology yourself before reading this chapter. You can then check your solution against our sample solution. If you are unfamiliar with file organizations and indexes, read Appendix D first. You may also find the summary of the methodology in Appendix B helpful.

18.1 Using the physical database design methodology

In this section, we work through the steps in the physical database design methodology to produce a suitable physical design for the *PerfectPets* database.

Step 3.1 Design base tables

Base tables defined in Section 2.3.2

During logical database design you produced a design for a number of **base tables** to represent the entities and relationships in the logical data model. This included a description of:

- each table, its attributes, the primary, alternate, and foreign keys, and integrity constraints;
- each attribute, its domain, an optional default value, whether it can hold nulls, and whether it's derived.

DBDL discussed in Step 2.1 in Chapter 10

The design of the base tables also included a definition of domains, default values, and null indicators. For example, for the Pen table of *PerfectPets*, you may produce the design shown in Figure 18.1 using an extended Database Design Language (DBDL). You use this information to determine how to implement the base tables in the target DBMS, which for this case study is Oracle 9i.

Figure 18.1

DBDL for the Pen table.

```
domain Pen_Numbers          fixed length character string length 4
domain Pen_Capacity         integer value, between 1 and 4
domain Pen_Status           one character, indicating whether pen
                            is available (A) or not available (N)
domain Clinic_Numbers       fixed length character string length 5

Pen(    penNo        Pen_Numbers       NOT NULL,
        penCapacity  Pen_Capacity      NOT NULL DEFAULT 2,
        penStatus    Pen_Status        NOT NULL DEFAULT 'A',
        clinicNo     Clinic_Numbers    NOT NULL)
        Primary Key penNo
        Foreign Key clinicNo References Clinic(clinicNo)ON UPDATE CASCADE ON DELETE NO ACTION
```

Creating base tables in Oracle 9i

In some systems that do not fully comply with the 1999 SQL standard (SQL3), there is no support for one or more of the clauses PRIMARY KEY, FOREIGN KEY, DEFAULT. Similarly, many systems do not support domains. However, Oracle 9i supports many of the SQL3 CREATE TABLE clauses, so you can define:

■ primary keys, using the PRIMARY KEY clause;

■ alternate keys, using the UNIQUE keyword;

■ default values, using the DEFAULT clause;

■ not null columns, using the NOT NULL keyword;

■ foreign keys, using the FOREIGN KEY clause;

■ other column or table constraints using the CHECK and CONSTRAINT clauses.

However, there is no facility to create domains, although Oracle 9i does allow user-defined types to be created. In addition, the data types are slightly different from the SQL standard, as shown in Table 18.1 (compare this with Table 12.1).

In Chapter 12, we saw that Microsoft Access had an Autonumber data type that created a new sequential number for a column value whenever a record was inserted. Oracle does not have such a data type but it does have a similar facility through the (non-standard) SQL CREATE SEQUENCE statement. For example, the statement:

CREATE SEQUENCE appNoSeq
    START WITH 1 **INCREMENT BY** 1 **CACHE** 30;

Table 18.1 Partial list of Oracle data types.

Data type	Use	Size
CHAR(size)	Stores fixed length character data (default size is 1).	Up to 2000 bytes
NCHAR(size)	Same as char data type, except the maximum length is determined by the character set of the database (for example, American English, Eastern European, or Korean).	
VARCHAR2(size)	Stores variable length character data.	Up to 4000 bytes
NVARCHAR2(size)	Same as VARCHAR2 with the same caveat as for nchar data type.	
VARCHAR	Currently the same as char. However, use of VARCHAR2 is recommended as varchar might become a separate data type with different comparison semantics in a later release.	Up to 2000 bytes
NUMBER(l, d) 9.99E125	Stores fixed-point or floating-point numbers, where l stands for length and d stands for the number of decimal digits. For example, NUMBER(5,2) could contain nothing larger than 999.99 without an error.	1.0E-130 ..
DECIMAL(l, d), DEC(l, d), or NUMERIC(l, d)	Same as number. Provided for compatibility with SQL standard.	
INTEGER, INT, or SMALLINT	Provided for compatibility with SQL standard. Converted to NUMBER(38).	
DATE	Stores dates from 1 Jan 4712 B.C. to 31 Dec 4712 A.D.	
BLOB	A binary large object.	Up to 4 Gigabytes
CLOB	A character large object.	Up to 4 Gigabytes
RAW(size)	Raw binary data, such as a sequence of graphics characters or a digitized picture.	Up to 2000 bytes

creates a sequence, called appNoSeq, that starts with the initial value one and increases by one each time. The CACHE 30 clause specifies that Oracle should preallocate 30 sequence numbers and keep them in memory for faster access.

Once a sequence has been created, you can access its values in SQL statements with the following pseudocolumns:

CURRVAL   which returns the current value of the sequence;

NEXTVAL   which increments the sequence and returns the new value.

For example, the SQL statement:

INSERT INTO Appointment(appNo, aDate, aTime, petNo)
VALUES (appNoSeq.NEXTVAL, SYSDATE, '12.00', '010090');

inserts a new record into the Appointment table with the value for column appNo (the appointment number) set to the next available number in the sequence.

Creating a blank table in Oracle 9i using SQL*Plus

To illustrate the process of creating a blank table in Oracle, we first use SQL*Plus, which is an interactive, command-line-driven, SQL interface to the Oracle database. Figure 18.2 shows the creation of the Pen table using the Oracle SQL CREATE TABLE statement.

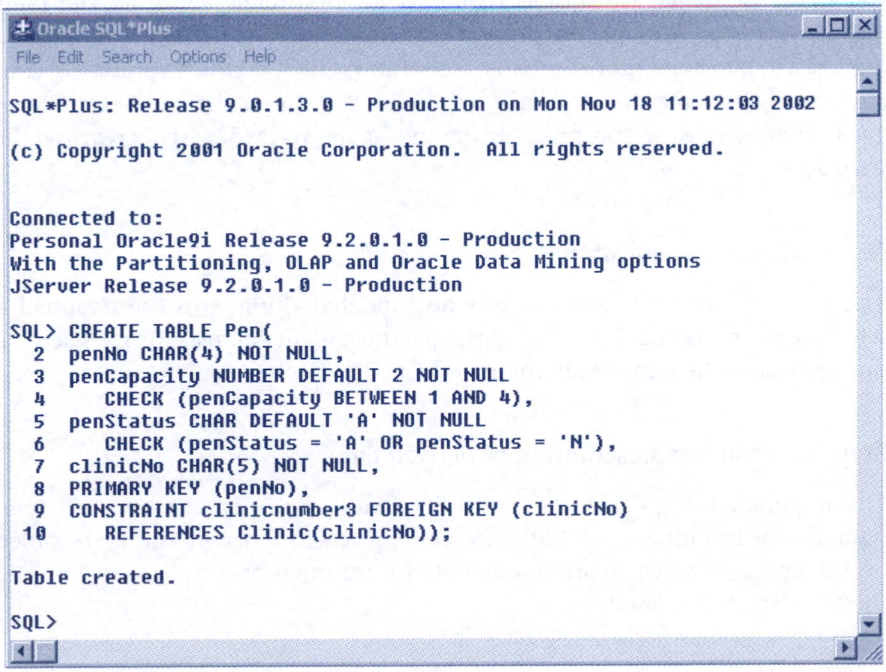

Figure 18.2

Creation of the Pen table using the Oracle SQL CREATE TABLE statement.

```
± Oracle SQL*Plus                                                    _|□|×|
File  Edit  Search  Options  Help

SQL*Plus: Release 9.0.1.3.0 - Production on Mon Nov 18 11:12:03 2002

(c) Copyright 2001 Oracle Corporation.  All rights reserved.


Connected to:
Personal Oracle9i Release 9.2.0.1.0 - Production
With the Partitioning, OLAP and Oracle Data Mining options
JServer Release 9.2.0.1.0 - Production

SQL> CREATE TABLE Pen(
  2  penNo CHAR(4) NOT NULL,
  3  penCapacity NUMBER DEFAULT 2 NOT NULL
  4     CHECK (penCapacity BETWEEN 1 AND 4),
  5  penStatus CHAR DEFAULT 'A' NOT NULL
  6     CHECK (penStatus = 'A' OR penStatus = 'N'),
  7  clinicNo CHAR(5) NOT NULL,
  8  PRIMARY KEY (penNo),
  9  CONSTRAINT clinicnumber3 FOREIGN KEY (clinicNo)
 10     REFERENCES Clinic(clinicNo));

Table created.

SQL>
```

Oracle allows named constraints to be enabled (the default setting) and disabled. In certain situations, it may be desirable to disable constraints temporarily for performance reasons, for example:

■ when loading large amounts of data into a table using SQL*Loader;

■ when performing batch operations that make a significant number of changes to a table;

■ when importing or exporting one table at a time.

Referential actions discussed in Step 2.4 in Chapter 10

By default, Oracle enforces referential integrity on the named foreign keys. Thus, it enforces the referential actions ON DELETE NO ACTION and ON UPDATE NO ACTION. It also allows the additional clauses ON DELETE CASCADE to be specified (to allow deletions from the parent table to cascade to the child table) and ON DELETE SET NULL (to allow deletions from the parent table to cause the corresponding foreign key value to be set to NULL). However, it does not support the ON UPDATE CASCADE action nor the SET DEFAULT action. If any of these actions are required, you will have to consider implementing them as triggers or within the application code. We'll consider this in Step 3.3 shortly.

Creating a table using the Table Wizard

An alternative approach in Oracle 9i is to use the Table Wizard that is part of the Enterprise Manager Console. Using a series of interactive forms, the Table Wizard takes you through the process of defining each of the columns with its associated data type, defining any constraints on the columns and/or constraints on the table that you may require, and defining the key fields. Figure 18.3 shows some of the pages from the Table Wizard when creating the Treatment table.

Document design of base tables

The design of the base tables is fully documented along with the reasons for selecting the proposed design. In particular, document the reasons for selecting one approach where many alternatives exist.

Step 3.2 Design representation of derived data

The requirements given in Section 17.1.1 indicate only one derived item, namely that the total cost of all treatments given to a pet should be recorded on the invoice. The calculation to derive this information can be written using the following SQL statement:

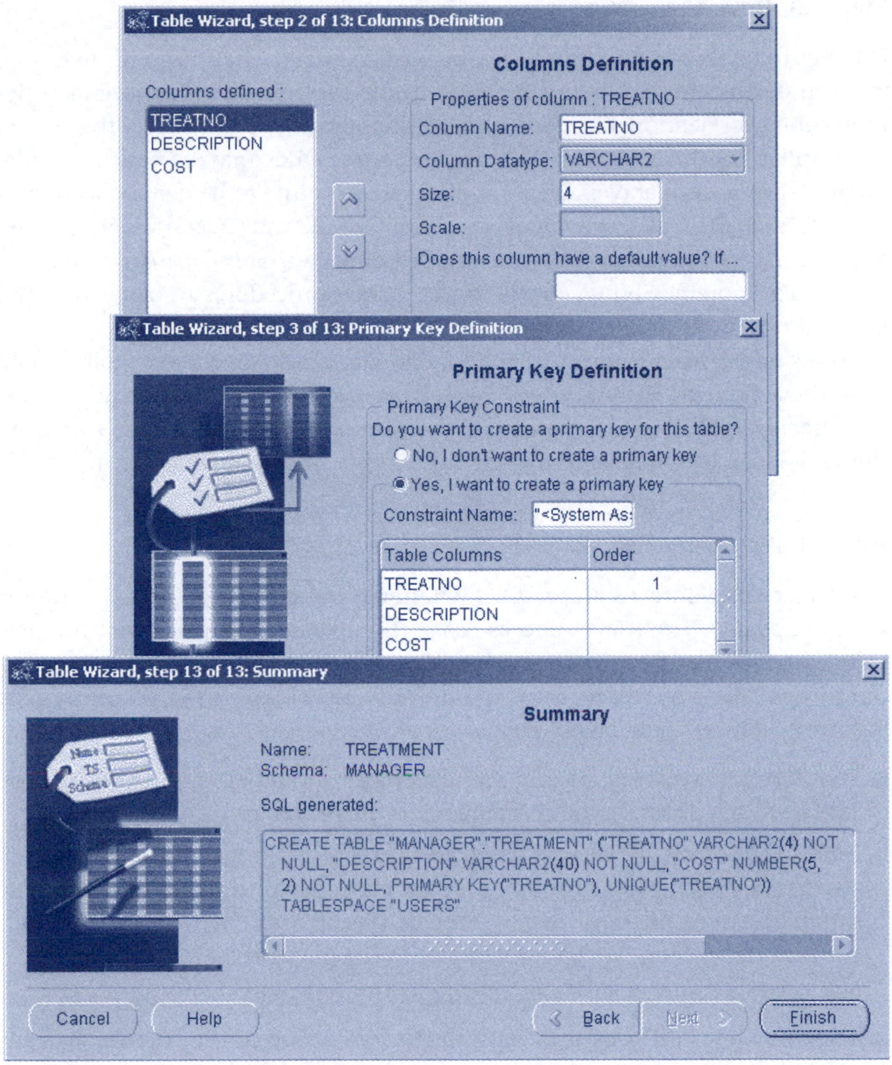

Figure 18.3

Treatment table
created using the
Oracle Table
Wizard.

```
SELECT SUM(pt.quantity*t.cost)
FROM Invoice i, Examination e, PetTreatment pt, Treatment t
WHERE i.examNo = e.examNo AND e.examNo = pt.examNo AND
      pt.treatNo = t.treatNo;
```

If access to the Invoice table is frequent, there may be performance benefits to be gained by storing the total cost in the Invoice table. However, from the expected frequency data (see Table 18.2 later in chapter), you'll see that the access to the Invoice table is not particularly frequent, and so you may decide in this case just to calculate the total whenever it's required.

Step 3.3 Design remaining business rules

Updates to tables may be constrained by business rules. The design of such rules is again dependent on the target DBMS; some systems provide more facilities than others for defining business rules. In Chapter 12, we saw that if the system is compliant with the 1999 SQL standard, some rules may be easy to implement. As we've seen above, Oracle 9i allows constraints to be defined as part of the SQL CREATE TABLE statement using the CHECK and CONSTRAINT clauses, and also allows additional constraints to be defined using *before triggers* and *after triggers*. For more flexibility, Oracle 9i also allows procedures to be created and invoked from SQL.

For example, from Figure 18.1 the foreign key clinicNo in the Pen table should have the action ON UPDATE CASCADE. Unfortunately, as we've already noted, the Oracle CREATE TABLE statement does not support this action. However, this action can be implemented using the triggers shown in Figure 18.4.

Trigger 1 (Pen_Clinic_Check_Before)

The trigger in Figure 18.4(a) is *fired* whenever the clinicNo column in the Pen table is updated. The trigger checks *before* the update takes place that the new value specified exists in the Clinic table. If an Invalid_Clinic exception is raised, the trigger issues an error message and prevents the change from occurring. The following points should be noted:

■ The BEFORE keyword indicates that the trigger should be executed before the update to the clinicNo column is applied to the Pen table.

■ The FOR EACH ROW keyword indicates that this is a row-level trigger, which executes for each row of the Pen table that is updated in the transaction. The alternative type of trigger is a statement-level trigger, which executes once for each transaction. We'll see examples of statement-level triggers shortly.

■ The WHEN clause specifies a condition that must be met for the trigger to fire.

■ The new keyword is used to refer to the new value of the column and the old keyword is used to refer to the old value of the column.

Changes to support triggers on the Clinic table

The three triggers shown in Figure 18.4(b) are fired whenever the clinicNo column in the Clinic table is updated. Before the definition of the triggers, a sequence number updateSequence is created along with a public variable updateSeq (which is accessible to the three triggers through the seqPackage package). In addition, the Pen table is modified to add a column called updateId, which is used to flag whether a record has been updated, to prevent it from being updated more than once during the cascade operation.

Figure 18.4

Oracle triggers to enforce ON UPDATE CASCADE on the foreign key clinicNo in the Pen table when the primary key clinicNo is updated in the Clinic table: (a) trigger for the Pen table.

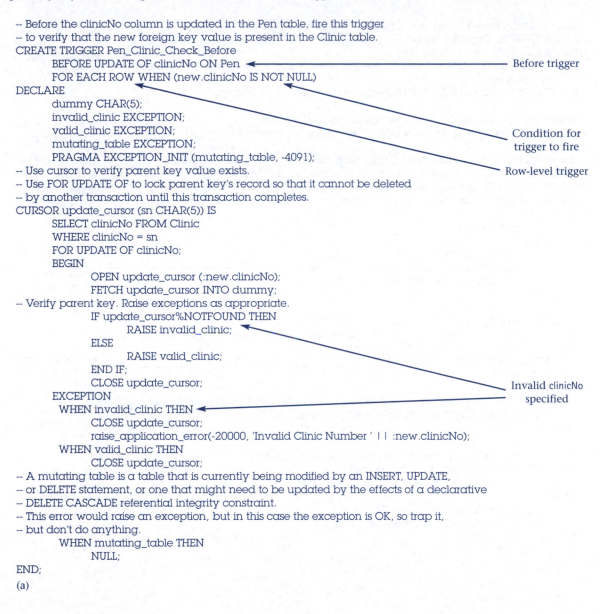

```
-- Before the clinicNo column is updated in the Pen table, fire this trigger
-- to verify that the new foreign key value is present in the Clinic table.
CREATE TRIGGER Pen_Clinic_Check_Before
        BEFORE UPDATE OF clinicNo ON Pen                                        Before trigger
        FOR EACH ROW WHEN (new.clinicNo IS NOT NULL)
DECLARE
        dummy CHAR(5);
        invalid_clinic EXCEPTION;
        valid_clinic EXCEPTION;                                                 Condition for
        mutating_table EXCEPTION;                                               trigger to fire
        PRAGMA EXCEPTION_INIT (mutating_table, -4091);
-- Use cursor to verify parent key value exists.                                Row-level trigger
-- Use FOR UPDATE OF to lock parent key's record so that it cannot be deleted
-- by another transaction until this transaction completes.
CURSOR update_cursor (sn CHAR(5)) IS
        SELECT clinicNo FROM Clinic
        WHERE clinicNo = sn
        FOR UPDATE OF clinicNo;
        BEGIN
                OPEN update_cursor (:new.clinicNo);
                FETCH update_cursor INTO dummy;
-- Verify parent key. Raise exceptions as appropriate.
                IF update_cursor%NOTFOUND THEN
                        RAISE invalid_clinic;
                ELSE
                        RAISE valid_clinic;
                END IF;
                CLOSE update_cursor;
        EXCEPTION                                                               Invalid clinicNo
          WHEN invalid_clinic THEN                                              specified
                CLOSE update_cursor;
                raise_application_error(-20000, 'Invalid Clinic Number ' || :new.clinicNo);
          WHEN valid_clinic THEN
                CLOSE update_cursor;
-- A mutating table is a table that is currently being modified by an INSERT, UPDATE,
-- or DELETE statement, or one that might need to be updated by the effects of a declarative
-- DELETE CASCADE referential integrity constraint.
-- This error would raise an exception, but in this case the exception is OK, so trap it,
-- but don't do anything.
          WHEN mutating_table THEN
                NULL;
END;
```

(a)

Figure 18.4 *Continued*

Oracle triggers to enforce ON UPDATE CASCADE on the foreign key clinicNo in the Pen table when the primary key clinicNo is updated in the Clinic table: (b) triggers for the Clinic table.

```
-- Create a sequence number and a public variable UPDATESEQ.
CREATE SEQUENCE updateSequence INCREMENT BY 1 MAXVALUE 500 CYCLE;
CREATE PACKAGE SeqPackage AS
        updateSeq NUMBER;            ◄─────────────────────────────
END SeqPackage;
CREATE or REPLACE PACKAGE BODY SeqPackage AS END SeqPackage;
```
Package to hold sequence

```
-- Add a new column to the Pen table to flag changed records.
ALTER TABLE Pen ADD updateId NUMBER;  ◄───────────────────────────
```
Add extra column to Pen table

```
-- Before updating the Clinic table using this statement trigger, generate a new
-- sequence number and assign it to the public variable UPDATESEQ.
CREATE TRIGGER Cascade_ClinicNo_Update1
    BEFORE UPDATE OF clinicNo ON Clinic  ◄────────────────────────
    DECLARE
        dummy NUMBER;
        BEGIN
            SELECT updateSequence.NEXTVAL ⎫
            INTO dummy FROM dual;         ⎬◄──────────────────────
            SeqPackage.updateSeq := dummy;⎭
        END;
```
Statement-level before trigger

Set new sequence number for update

```
-- Create a row after-trigger that cascades the update to the Pen table.
-- Only cascade the update if the child row has not already been updated by the trigger.
CREATE TRIGGER Cascade_ClinicNo_Update2
    AFTER UPDATE OF clinicNo ON Clinic ⎫◄─────────────────────────
    FOR EACH ROW                       ⎭
    BEGIN
        UPDATE Pen SET clinicNo = :new.clinicNo, updateId = SeqPackage.updateSeq ⎫
        WHERE Pen.clinicNo = :old.clinicNo AND updateId IS NULL;                 ⎬◄─
    END;
```
Row-level after trigger

Update Pen table and set updated flag for these records

```
-- Create a final statement after-trigger to reset the updateId flags
CREATE TRIGGER Cascade_ClinicNo_Update3
    AFTER UPDATE OF clinicNo ON Clinic  ◄─────────────────────────
    BEGIN
        UPDATE Pen SET updateId = NULL        ⎫
        WHERE updateId = SeqPackage.updateSeq;⎬◄──────────────────
    END;
```
Statement-level after trigger; resets flags for updated records

(b)

Trigger 2 (Cascade_ClinicNo_Update1)

The (statement-level) trigger, Cascade_ClinicNo_Update1, fires before the update to the column clinicNo in the Clinic table to set a new sequence number for the update.

Trigger 3 (Cascade_ClinicNo_Update2)

The (row-level) trigger, Cascade_ClinicNo_Update2, fires to update all records in the Pen table that have the old clinicNo value (:old.clinicNo) to the new value (:new.clinicNo), and to flag the record as having been updated.

Trigger 4 (Cascade_ClinicNo_Update3)

The final (statement-level) trigger, Cascade_ClinicNo_Update3, fires after the update to reset the flagged records back to unflagged.

> Don't worry too much about the details of how these triggers work. What is important to note is the significant amount of programming effort required to implement these actions. Put another way, think how much effort can be saved if the DBMS provides this functionality instead!

Step 4.1 Analyze transactions

Having set up the base tables, integrity constraints, and business rules, the next step is to analyze the transactions to help determine appropriate file organizations and indexes for each base table. Let's assume that the transactions identified in Section 17.1.2 are the most important transactions for *PerfectPets*. To focus on areas that may be problematic, we suggested in Chapter 13 that one way to proceed is to:

(1) Map all transaction paths to tables.

(2) Determine which tables are most frequently accessed by transactions.

(3) Analyze selected transactions that involve these tables.

The first step has already been carried out in Steps 1.8 and 2.3 (see Figure 17.9). To carry out the second step, you need to estimate the frequency with which tables will be accessed. If possible, you could add the frequency information to the transaction path diagram. This sometimes makes the diagram very cluttered and difficult to interpret, and you may prefer to keep the information separate. In discussion with the staff of *PerfectPets*, the frequency information shown in Figure 18.5 is obtained. All this information has to be analyzed to identify those areas that may require special consideration.

Figure 18.5

Logical data model for *PerfectPets* showing expected occurrences.

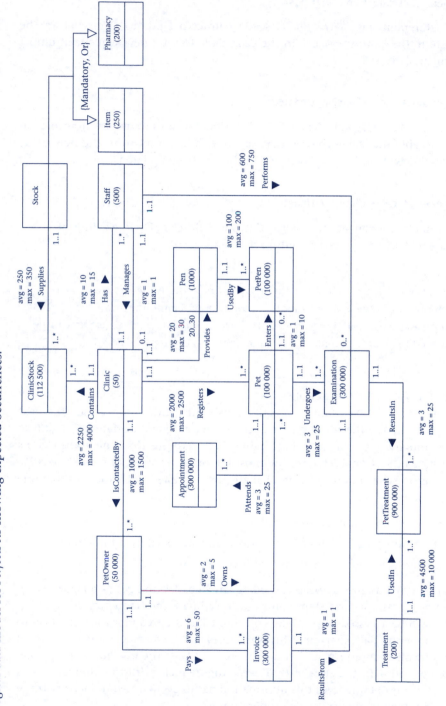

Step 4.2 Choose file organizations

The objective of this step is to choose an optimal file organization for each table, if the target DBMS allows this. To undertake this step, you need to understand how the target DBMS operates at both the logical and physical levels. In this step, we examine how Oracle stores data. The discussion is fairly technical but it should give you a feel for the type of knowledge you need to undertake this step in practice.

Oracle's logical database structure

At the logical level, Oracle maintains tablespaces, schemas, and data blocks and extents/segments, as we now explain.

Tablespaces

An Oracle database is divided into logical storage units called **tablespaces**. A tablespace is used to group related logical structures together. For example, tablespaces commonly group all the application's objects to simplify some administrative operations.

Every Oracle database contains a tablespace named SYSTEM, which is created automatically when the database is created. The SYSTEM tablespace always contains the system catalog tables for the entire database. A small database might need only the SYSTEM tablespace; however, it's recommended that you create at least one additional tablespace to store user data separate from the system catalog, to reduce contention among dictionary objects and schema objects for the same datafiles (see Figure 16.1). Figure 18.6 illustrates an Oracle database consisting of the SYSTEM tablespace and a USERS tablespace.

System catalog defined in Section 1.2.1

A new tablespace can be created using the CREATE TABLESPACE command; for example:

CREATE TABLESPACE USERS
DATAFILE 'DATA3.ORA' **SIZE** 100K;

A table can then be associated with a specific tablespace using the CREATE TABLE or ALTER TABLE statement; for example:

CREATE TABLE Pen (penNo **CHAR**(4) **NOT NULL**, ...)
    TABLESPACE USERS;

If no tablespace is specified when creating a new table, the default tablespace associated with the user when the user account was set up is used. We'll see how this can be specified in Step 6.

Figure 18.6

Relationship
between an Oracle
database,
tablespaces, and
datafiles.

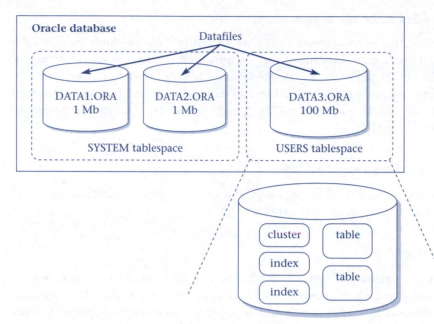

Users, schemas, and schema objects

A *user* (sometimes called a *username*) is a name defined in the database that can
connect to, and access, objects. A *schema* is a named collection of objects, such
as tables, views, clusters, and procedures, associated with a particular user.
Schemas and users help DBAs manage database security.

To access a database, a user must run a database application (such as an
Oracle form or SQL*Plus) and connect using a username defined in the database. When a database user is created, a corresponding schema of the same
name is created for the user. By default, once a user connects to a database, the
user has access to all objects contained in the corresponding schema. As a user
is associated only with the schema of the same name, the terms user and
schema are often used interchangeably.

Note, there is no relationship between a tablespace and a schema; objects in
the same schema can be in different tablespaces, and a tablespace can hold
objects from different schemas.

Data blocks, extents, and segments

The *data block* is the smallest unit of storage that Oracle can use or allocate. One
data block corresponds to a specific number of bytes of physical disk space. You
set the data block size for each Oracle database when you create the database.

This data block size should be a multiple of the operating system's block size (within the system's maximum operating limit) to avoid unnecessary I/O.

The next level of logical database space is called an *extent*. An extent is a specific number of contiguous data blocks allocated for storing a specific type of information. The level above an extent is called a *segment*. A segment is a set of extents allocated for a certain logical structure. For example, each table's data is stored in its own data segment, while each index's data is stored in its own index segment. Figure 18.7 shows the relationship between data blocks, extents, and segments.

Oracle dynamically allocates space when the existing extents of a segment become full. Because extents are allocated as needed, the extents of a segment may or may not be contiguous on disk.

Oracle's physical database structure

The main physical database structures in Oracle are datafiles, redo log files, and control files.

Datafiles

Every Oracle database has one or more physical datafiles. The data of logical database structures (such as tables and indexes) is physically stored in these datafiles. One or more datafiles form a tablespace. The simplest Oracle database would have one tablespace and one datafile. A more complex database might have four tablespaces, each consisting of two datafiles, giving a total of eight datafiles. The architecture for datafiles and tablespaces is shown in Figure 18.6.

Figure 18.7

Relationship between Oracle data blocks, extents, and segments.

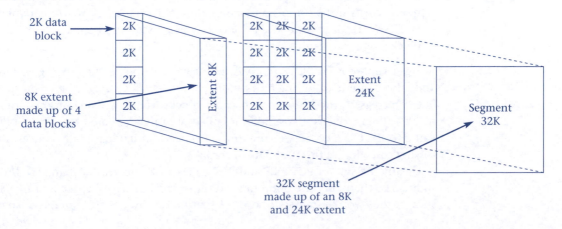

Redo log files

Recovery briefly
discussed in
Section 1.3

Every Oracle database has a set of two or more redo log files, which record all changes made to data for recovery purposes. Should a failure prevent modified data from being permanently written to the datafiles, the changes can be obtained from the redo log, thus preventing work from being lost.

Control files

Every Oracle database has a control file, which contains entries that specify the physical structure of the database, such as:

- the database name;
- the names and locations of a database's datafiles and redo log files;
- the time stamp of database creation.

PCTFREE and PCTUSED

The two space management parameters, PCTFREE and PCTUSED, may also have a significant effect on performance. You specify these parameters when creating or altering a table or cluster (which has its own data segment). You can also specify the storage parameter PCTFREE when creating or altering an index (which has its own index segment). The parameters are used as follows:

- **PCTFREE** sets the minimum percentage of a data block to be reserved as free space for possible updates to records that already exist in that block (default value is 10);
- **PCTUSED** sets the minimum percentage of a block that can be used for record data plus any overhead required by Oracle before new records will be added to the block (default value is 40). After a data block is filled to the limit determined by PCTFREE, Oracle considers the block unavailable for the insertion of new records until the percentage of that block falls below the parameter PCTUSED. Until this value is achieved, Oracle uses the free space of the data block only for updates to records already contained in the data block.

A lower value for PCTFREE reserves less space for updates to existing records, and allows inserts to fill the block more completely. This might save you space but it increases processing costs because blocks frequently need to be reorganized as their free space area becomes filled with new/updated records. A lower value for PCTUSED increases the unused space in a database but reduces processing costs during insert/update operations.

Clearly the sum of PCTFREE and PCTUSED can be no greater than 100. If the sum is less than 100, the optimum setting to balance use of space and I/O is a sum of the two parameters that differs from 100 by the percentage of space occupied by a record. For example, if the block size is 2048 bytes with a 100 byte overhead, and the record size is 390 bytes, which is 20 percent of the available block size, then a good value for the sum of PCTFREE and PCTUSED would be 80 percent to make best use of space. On the other hand, if the sum equals 100, Oracle would attempt to keep no more than PCTFREE free space, which would result in the highest processing costs. The combined use of PCTFREE and PCTUSED is illustrated in Figure 18.8.

The above descriptions of the logical and physical database structures used by Oracle are not intended to be detailed. Rather, they have been included to give you a feel for the type of knowledge of the target DBMS you need to acquire to allow you to successfully undertake some aspects of physical database design. We have also included them to emphasize the differences between systems. For example, having read this step, look back at Step 4.2 in Chapter 13, which dealt with Microsoft Access. You'll see in that step that there was really nothing to do – the file organization in Microsoft Access 2002 is fixed. For PC RDBMSs, this is not unusual. If you were to look now at another multi-user RDBMS, such as Ingres or SQL Server, you'd find that the logical and physical structures used by these systems are different again.

File organizations

Oracle 9i supports *clustered* and *non-clustered* tables. The choice of whether to use a clustered or non-clustered table depends on the analysis of the transactions undertaken previously, but the choice can have an impact on performance. Before considering the appropriateness of clustering, it's a good idea to ignore small tables from further consideration, as small tables can usually be processed in memory. From Figure 18.5, we can see that the small tables in the *PerfectPets* database are Clinic, Staff, Pen, Treatment, Item, and Pharmacy. We

Clustered files discussed in Appendix D.7

Records are inserted until the block is 80 percent full, because PCTFREE specifies that 20 percent of the block must remain available for updates to existing records.

Updates to existing records use the free space reserved in the block. No new records can be inserted into the block until the amount of used space is less than 40 percent.

Figure 18.8

Combined use of PCTFREE and PCTUSED with PCTFREE = 20 percent and PCTUSED = 40 percent.

therefore exclude these tables from further consideration. If we now consider the remaining tables, we produce a summary of interactions between the base tables for the query transactions listed in Section 17.1.2, as shown in Table 18.2. Based on the guidelines provided in Appendix D.7, we decide to create an indexed cluster for the tables PetOwner and Pet based on the join column ownerNo.

Step 4.3 Choose indexes

Indexes
discussed in
Appendix D.5

Oracle automatically adds an index for each primary key. In addition, Oracle recommends that you do not explicitly define unique indexes on tables but instead define UNIQUE integrity constraints on the desired columns. Oracle enforces UNIQUE integrity constraints by automatically defining a unique index on the unique key. Exceptions to this recommendation are usually performance related. For example, using a CREATE TABLE ... AS SELECT with a UNIQUE constraint is slower than creating the table without the constraint and then manually creating a UNIQUE index.

Let's assume that the tables will be created with the identified primary, alternate, and foreign keys specified. What you have to do now is identify whether any additional indexes are required. In Chapter 13, we suggested creating a 'wish-list' and then considering each potential index in the wish-list to deter-

Table 18.2 Interactions between tables and query transactions.

Table	Transaction	Access	Frequency (per day)
Appointment	2(l)	join: Pet on petNo	250
		search condition: aDate	
Examination	2(c), 2(d)	join: Pet on petNo	100
	2(d)	join: Staff on staffNo	
Invoice	2(e), 2(f)	join: PetOwner on ownerNo	10
		search condition: datePaid IS NULL	
	2(n)	join: PetOwner on ownerNo	1 per month
		search condition: invoiceDate	
ItemClinicStock	2(q)	search condition: inStock < reorderLevel	50 per month
Pet	2(b)	join: PetOwner on ownerNo	1 per month
	2(j)	group: petType	1
		order by: petType	
		aggregate: count on petType	
	2(l)	join: Clinic on clinicNo	250
	2(o)	join: PetOwner on ownerNo	1500
PharmClinicStock	2(p)	search condition: inStock < reorderLevel	50 per month

mine whether the increase in query performance outweighs the performance degradation when updates occur. Before creating the wish-list, we again ignore the small tables (Clinic, Staff, Pen, Treatment, Item, and Pharmacy) from further consideration, as small tables can usually be processed in memory without requiring additional indexes. We now consider the remaining tables and their interactions, as shown in Table 18.2. We conclude that there may be performance benefits in adding the indexes shown in Table 18.3.

Table 18.3 Additional indexes for the *PerfectPets* database.

Table	Index
Pet	clinicNo
Appointment	aDate
	petNo
Invoice	ownerNo
	invoiceDate

Note that the search condition used by transaction 2(e) (datePaid **IS NULL**) would suggest creating an index on the datePaid column. However, Oracle does not use an index when the search condition involves an **IS NULL/IS NOT NULL** condition. Further, because transaction 2(j) only runs once a day and there are not many pet types, an index on petType in the Pet table is unwarranted.

Step 5 Design user views

Oracle 9i supports the SQL CREATE VIEW statement, so each user view can be easily created. In addition, using the Oracle Forms Builder, you can create forms based on one or more tables or based on a view. For example, you may decide to create a view for clinic manager details. Figure 18.9(a) illustrates the creation of a view called ClinicManagers using the Enterprise Manager Console, and Figure 18.9(b) shows a form built from this view.

Step 6 Design security measures

As part of the database analysis phase, you need to determine the types of users who'll be working with the system and the levels of access that they must be given to accomplish their designated tasks. As we mentioned in Step 6 in Chapter 14, database security usually involves both system security and data security. One form of system security used by Oracle is the standard username and password

Figure 18.9

Creating and using a user view: (a) creation of a view using the Oracle Enterprise Manager Console; (b) form built from this view.

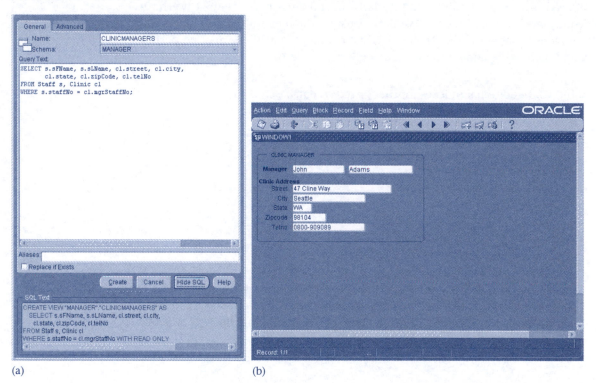

(a)   (b)

mechanism, whereby a user has to provide a valid username and password before access can be gained to the database, although the responsibility to authenticate users can be devolved to the operating system. Figure 18.10 illustrates the creation of a new user called ADAMS with password authentication set. Whenever user ADAMS tries to connect to the database, this user will be presented with a Connect or Log On dialog box similar to the one illustrated in Figure 18.11, prompting for a username and password to access the specified database.

Privileges

A **privilege** is a right to execute a particular type of SQL statement or to access another user's objects. Some examples of privileges include the right to:

■ connect to the database (create a session);

■ create a table;

■ select rows from another user's table.

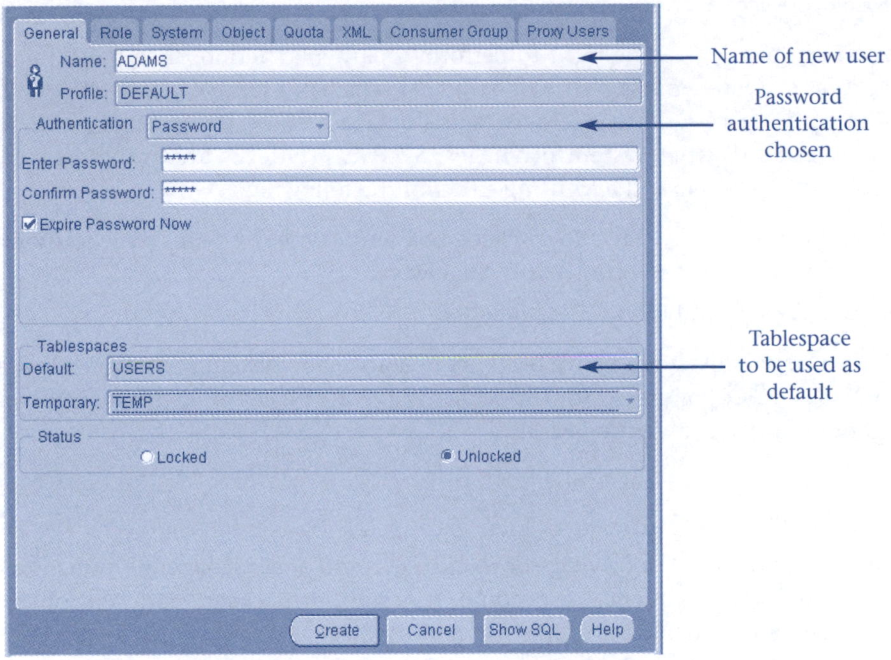

Figure 18.10

Creation of a new user called ADAMS, with password authentication set.

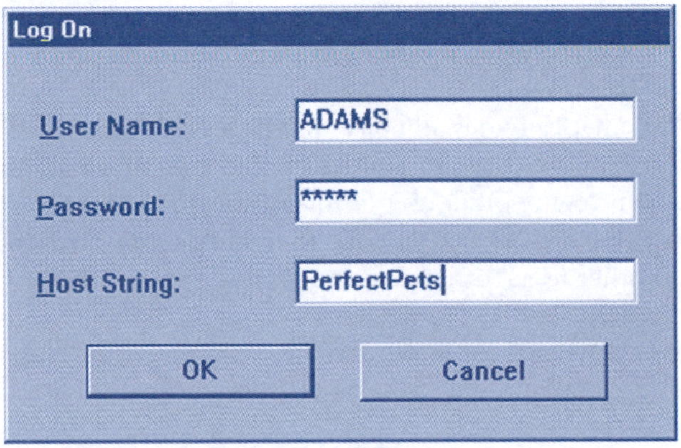

Figure 18.11

Connect dialog box requesting user-name, password, and database to connect to.

You grant privileges to users so these users can accomplish the tasks required for their jobs. As excessive granting of unnecessary privileges can compromise security, you should grant a privilege only to a user who absolutely requires the privilege to accomplish his or her work. In Oracle, there are two distinct categories of privileges:

(a) system privileges

(b) object privileges.

System privileges

A system privilege is the right to perform a particular action or to perform an action on any schema objects of a particular type. For example, the privileges to create tablespaces and to create users in a database are system privileges. There are over 80 distinct system privileges. System privileges are granted to, or revoked from, users and *roles* using either of the following:

Roles discussed shortly

GRANT and REVOKE covered in Chapter 14

- Grant System Privileges/Roles dialog box and Revoke System Privileges/Roles dialog box of the Oracle Security Manager;
- SQL GRANT and REVOKE statements.

However, only users who have been granted a specific system privilege with the ADMIN OPTION or users with the GRANT ANY PRIVILEGE system privilege can grant or revoke system privileges.

Object privileges

An object privilege is a privilege or right to perform a particular action on a specific table, view, sequence, procedure, function, or package. Different object privileges are available for different types of objects. For example, the privilege to delete rows from the table Pen is an object privilege.

Some schema objects (such as clusters, indexes, and triggers) do not have associated object privileges; their use is controlled with system privileges. For example, to alter a cluster, a user must own the cluster or have the ALTER ANY CLUSTER system privilege.

A user automatically has all object privileges for schema objects contained in his or her schema. A user can grant any object privilege on any schema object he or she owns to any other user or role. If the grant includes the WITH GRANT OPTION (of the GRANT statement), the grantee can further grant the object privilege to other users; otherwise, the grantee can use the privilege but cannot grant it to other users.

The object privileges for tables and views are shown in Table 18.4.

Roles

A user can receive a privilege in two different ways:

- You can grant privileges to users explicitly. For example, you can explicitly grant the privilege to insert records into the Clinic table to the user ADAMS using the following SQL statement:

  GRANT INSERT ON Clinic **TO** ADAMS;

Table 18.4 What each object privilege allows a grantee to do with tables and views.

Object/Privilege	Table	View
ALTER	Change the table definition with the ALTER TABLE statement.	N/A
DELETE	Remove rows from the table with the DELETE statement. Note: you must grant the SELECT privilege on the table along with the DELETE privilege.	Remove rows from the view with the DELETE statement.
INDEX	Create an index on the table with the CREATE INDEX statement.	N/A
INSERT	Add new rows to the table with the INSERT statement.	Add new rows to the view with the INSERT statement.
REFERENCES	Create a constraint that refers to the table. You cannot grant this privilege to a role.	N/A
SELECT	Query the table with the SELECT statement.	Query the view with the SELECT statement.
UPDATE	Change data in the table with the UPDATE statement. Note: you must grant the SELECT privilege on the table along with the UPDATE privilege.	Change data in the view with the UPDATE statement.

■ You can also grant privileges to a *role* (a named group of privileges), and then grant the role to one or more users. For example, you can grant the privileges to select, insert, update, and delete records from the Clinic table to the role named DEPUTYMANAGER, which in turn you can grant to the users ADAMS and GLENN. A user can have access to several roles, and several users can be assigned the same roles. Figure 18.12 illustrates the granting of these privileges to the role DEPUTYMANAGER using the Oracle Security Manager.

TIP

Because roles allow for easier and better management of privileges, you should normally grant privileges to roles and not to specific users.

Figure 18.12

Setting the Delete, Insert, Select, and Update privileges on the Clinic table to the role DEPUTYMANAGER.

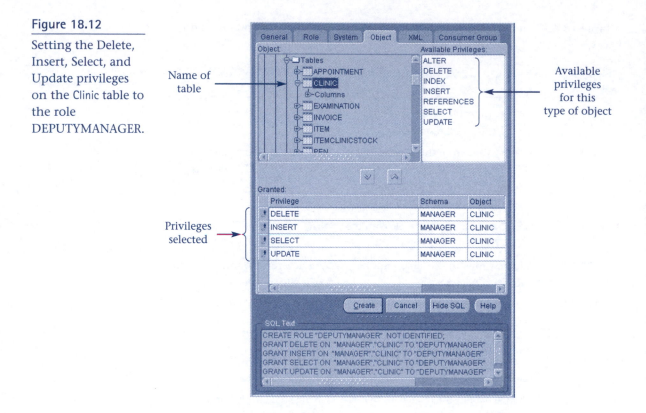

Step 7 Consider the introduction of controlled redundancy

In Step 1.7, the relationship Clinic *Schedules* Appointment was considered to be redundant. However, this causes a potential performance problem. For example, the Pet table has to be accessed just to determine an available time for an appointment at a clinic. In this case, it may be preferable to reinstate the *Schedules* relationship and add the primary key of the Clinic table (clinicNo) to the Appointment table to act as a foreign key.

Consider implications of denormalization

Owing to the addition of the column clinicNo to the Appointment table, it would probably be worthwhile considering the creation of an index on this column to improve the performance of transaction 2(l).

Implementation

You're now in a position to start implementing the base tables, file organizations, indexes, views, and security mechanisms, and thereafter, to start populating the database. However, as discussed in Chapter 16, this is not the end of database design – the ongoing monitoring and tuning of the operational system is a vital activity to achieve continued success for the system. In addition, it's highly likely that once the system goes live, changes will be required as a result of user feedback and changing requirements. In some cases, the changes will be cosmetic, requiring alterations to the user interface, with no impact on the database itself. In others, however, there will be a need to modify the structure of the database, and in these cases, you will have to go through some of the steps in both the logical and physical design methodology again to ensure that the changes are designed and implemented correctly.

Part 6

Current and
emerging trends

Chapter 19

Current and emerging trends

To complete this book, we devote this chapter to examining current and emerging trends in database systems. Many of the topics we consider are significant areas in their own right and we can only provide a brief introduction here. For further information the interested reader is referred to Connolly and Begg (2002). In this chapter we consider:

■ advanced database applications;

■ weaknesses of the current relational DBMSs;

■ distributed DBMSs and replication servers;

■ object-oriented DBMSs and object-relational DBMSs;

- data warehousing;
- OLAP and data mining;
- Web–database integration and XML.

19.1 Advanced database applications

The past decade has seen significant changes in the computer industry. In database systems, we have seen the widespread acceptance of Relational DBMSs (RDBMSs) for traditional business applications, such as order processing, inventory control, banking, and airline reservations. However, existing RDBMSs have proven inadequate for applications with needs that are quite different from those of traditional business database applications. These applications include:

- computer-aided design;
- computer-aided manufacturing;
- office information systems and multimedia systems;
- geographic information systems;
- interactive and dynamic Web sites.

Computer-aided Design (CAD)

A CAD database stores data relating to mechanical and electrical design covering, for example, buildings, aircraft, and integrated circuit chips. Designs of this type have some common characteristics:

- Design data is characterized by a large number of types, each with a small number of instances. Conventional databases are typically the opposite. For example, the *StayHome* database consists of only a dozen or so tables, although tables such as VideoForRent, Member, and RentalAgreement may contain thousands of records.
- Designs may be very large, perhaps consisting of millions of parts, often with many interdependent subsystem designs.
- The design is not static but evolves through time. When a design change occurs, its implications must be propagated through all design representations. The dynamic nature of design may mean that some actions cannot be foreseen at the beginning.
- Updates are far-reaching because of topological or functional relationships, tolerances, and so on. One change is likely to affect a large number of design objects.
- Often, many design alternatives are being considered for each component, and the correct version for each part must be maintained. This involves some form of version control and configuration management.

■ There may be hundreds of staff involved with the design, and they may work in parallel on multiple versions of a large design. Even so, the end product must be consistent and coordinated. This is sometimes referred to as *cooperative engineering*.

Computer-aided Manufacturing (CAM)

A CAM database stores similar data to a CAD system, in addition to data relating to discrete production (such as cars on an assembly line) and continuous production (such as chemical synthesis). For example, in chemical manufacturing, there are applications that monitor information about the state of the system, such as reactor vessel temperatures, flow rates, and yields. There are also applications that control various physical processes, such as opening valves, applying more heat to reactor vessels, and increasing the flow of cooling systems. These applications must respond in real time and be capable of adjusting processes to maintain optimum performance within tight tolerances. In this example, the system has to maintain large volumes of data that is hierarchical in nature and maintain complex relationships between the data. It must also be able to rapidly navigate the data to review and respond to changes.

Office Information Systems (OIS) and multimedia systems

An OIS database stores data relating to the computer control of information in a business, including e-mail, documents, invoices, and so on. To provide better support for this area, we need to handle a wider range of data types other than names, addresses, dates, and currency. Modern systems now handle free-form text, photographs, diagrams, audio, and video sequences. For example, a multimedia document may handle text, photographs, animation, spreadsheets, and voice commentary. The documents may have a specific structure imposed on them, perhaps described using a mark-up language such as SGML (Standardized Generalized Markup Language), HTML (HyperText Markup Language), or XML (eXtensible Markup Language), as we'll discuss in Section 19.8.

Documents may be shared among many users using systems such as e-mail and bulletin boards based on Internet technology.* Again, such applications need to store data that has a much richer structure than records consisting of numbers and text strings. There is also an increasing need to capture handwritten notes using electronic devices. Although many notes can be transcribed into ASCII text using handwriting analysis techniques, most such data cannot. In addition to words, handwritten data can include sketches, diagrams, and so on.

---

* A criticism of database systems, as noted by a number of observers, is that the largest 'database' in the world – the World Wide Web – has developed with little or no use of database technology. We will discuss the integration of the Web and DBMSs in Section 19.8.

Geographic Information Systems (GIS)

A GIS database stores various types of spatial and temporal information, such as that used in land management and underwater exploration. Much of the data in these systems is derived from survey and satellite photographs, and tends to be very large. Searches may involve identifying features based, for example, on shape, color, or texture, using advanced pattern-recognition techniques.

For example, EOS (Earth Observing System) is a collection of satellites launched by NASA in the last decade to gather information that will support scientists concerned with long-term trends regarding the earth's atmosphere, oceans, and land. It's anticipated that these satellites will return over one-third of a petabyte (10^{15} bytes) of data per year. This data will be integrated with other data sources and will be stored in EOSDIS (EOS Data and Information System). EOSDIS will supply the information needs of both scientists and non-scientists. For example, schoolchildren will be able to access EOSDIS to see a simulation of world weather patterns. The immense size of this database and the need to support thousands of users with very heavy volumes of information requests will provide many challenges for DBMSs.

Interactive and dynamic Web sites

Consider a Web site that has an online catalog for selling clothes. The Web site maintains a set of preferences for previous visitors to the site and allows a visitor to:

■ browse through thumbnails of the items in the catalog and select one to obtain a full-size image with supporting details;

■ search for items that match a user-defined set of criteria;

■ obtain a 3D rendering of any item of clothing based on a customized specification (for example, color, size, fabric);

■ select a voiceover commentary giving additional details of the item;

■ view a running total of the bill, with appropriate discounts;

■ conclude the purchase through a secure online transaction.

The requirements for this type of application are not that different from some of the above advanced applications: there is a need to handle multimedia content (text, audio, image, video data, and animation) and to interactively modify the display based on user preferences and user selections. As well as handling complex data, the site also has the added complexity of providing 3D rendering.

As we'll discuss in Section 19.8, the Web now provides a relatively new paradigm for data management, and languages such as XML hold significant promise particularly for the e-commerce market. The Forrester Research Group is predicting that business-to-business transactions will reach $2.1 trillion in

Europe and $7 trillion in the US by 2006. Overall, e-commerce is expected to account for $12.8 trillion in worldwide corporate revenue by 2006 and potentially represent 18 percent of sales in the global economy. As the use of the Internet increases and the technology becomes more sophisticated, then we'll see Web sites and business-to-business transactions handle much more complex and interrelated data.

19.2 Weaknesses of Relational DBMSs (RDBMSs)

In Chapter 2, we mentioned that the relational model has a strong theoretical foundation, based on first-order predicate logic. This theory supported the development of SQL, a declarative language that has now become the standard language for defining and manipulating relational databases. Other strengths of the relational model are its simplicity, its suitability for OnLine Transaction Processing (OLTP), and its support for data independence. However, the relational data model, and RDBMSs in particular, are not without their disadvantages. In this section, we briefly discuss some of the more often-cited disadvantages.

Poor representation of 'real world' entities

Normalization generally leads to the creation of tables that do not correspond to entities in the 'real world'. The fragmentation of a 'real world' entity into many tables, with a physical representation that reflects this structure, is inefficient, leading to many joins during query processing.

Semantic overloading

The relational model has only one construct for representing data and relationships between data, namely the *table*. For example, to represent a many-to-many (*:*) relationship between two entities A and B, we create three tables, one to represent each of the entities A and B, and one to represent the relationship. There is no mechanism to distinguish between entities and relationships, or to distinguish between different kinds of relationship that exist between entities. For example, a 1:* relationship might be *Has*, *Supervises*, *Manages*, and so on. If such distinctions could be made, then it might be possible to build the semantics into the operations. It is said that the relational model is *semantically overloaded*.

Poor support for business rules

In Section 2.3, we introduced the concepts of entity and referential integrity, and in Section 2.2.1 we introduced domains, which are also types of business rules. Unfortunately, many commercial systems do not fully support these rules, and it's necessary to build them into the applications. This, of course, is dangerous and can lead to duplication of effort and, worse still, inconsistencies. Furthermore, there is no support for other types of business rules in the relational model, which again means they have to be built into the DBMS or the application.

Limited operations

The relational model has only a fixed set of operations, such as set and record-oriented operations, operations that are provided in the SQL specification. However, SQL currently does not allow new operations to be specified. Again, this is too restrictive to model the behavior of many 'real world' objects. For example, a GIS application typically uses points, lines, line groups, and polygons, and needs operations for distance, intersection, and containment.

Difficulty handling recursive queries

Atomicity of data means that repeating groups are not allowed in the relational model. As a result, it's extremely difficult to handle recursive queries: that is, queries about relationships that a table has with itself (directly or indirectly). To overcome this problem, SQL can be embedded in a high-level programming language, which provides constructs to facilitate iteration. Additionally, many RDBMSs provide a report writer with similar constructs. In either case, it is the application rather than the inherent capabilities of the system that provides the required functionality.

Impedance mismatch

In Section 3.1.1, we noted that until the most recent version of the standard, SQL lacked *computational completeness*. To overcome this problem and to provide additional flexibility, the SQL standard provides embedded SQL to help develop more complex database applications. However, this approach produces an **impedance mismatch** because we are mixing different programming paradigms:

(1) SQL is a declarative language that handles rows of data, whereas a high-level language such as C is a procedural language that can handle only one row of data at a time.

(2) SQL and 3GLs use different models to represent data. For example, SQL provides the built-in data types Date and Interval, which are not available in traditional programming languages. Thus, it's necessary for the application program to convert between the two representations, which is inefficient, both in programming effort and in the use of runtime resources. Furthermore, since we are using two different type systems, it's not possible to automatically type-check the application as a whole.

The latest release of the SQL standard, SQL3, addresses some of the above deficiencies with the introduction of many new features, such as the ability to define new data types and operations as part of the data definition language, and the addition of new constructs to make the language computationally complete.

19.3 Distributed DBMSs and replication servers

A major motivation behind the development of database systems is the desire to integrate the operational data of an organization and to provide controlled access to the data. Although we may think that integration and controlled access imply centralization, this is not the intention. In fact, the development of computer networks promotes a decentralized mode of work. This decentralized approach mirrors the organizational structure of many companies, which are logically distributed into divisions, departments, projects, and so on, and physically distributed into offices, plants, factories, where each unit maintains its own operational data. The development of a distributed DBMS that reflects this organizational structure, makes the data in all units accessible, and stores data proximate to the location where it's most frequently used should improve our ability to share the data and should improve the efficiency with which we can access the data.

Distributed database

A logically interrelated collection of shared data (and a description of this data), physically distributed over a computer network.

Distributed DBMS

The software system that permits the management of the distributed database and makes the distribution transparent to users.

A **Distributed Database Management System (DDBMS)** consists of a single logical database that is split into a number of **fragments**. Each fragment is stored on one or more computers (**replicas**) under the control of a separate DBMS, with the computers connected by a communications network. Each site is capable of independently processing user requests that require access to local data (that is, each site has some degree of local autonomy) and is also capable of processing data stored on other computers in the network.

Users access the distributed database via applications. Applications are classified as those that do not require data from other sites (**local applications**) and those that do require data from other sites (**global applications**). We require a DDBMS to have at least one global application. A DDBMS therefore has the following characteristics:

- a collection of logically related shared data;
- the data is split into a number of fragments (fragments can be horizontal or vertical, similar to the horizontal and vertical partitions that we discussed in Chapter 15);
- fragments may be replicated;
- fragments/replicas are allocated to sites;
- the sites are linked by a communications network;
- the data at each site is under the control of a DBMS;
- the DBMS at each site can handle local applications, autonomously;
- each DBMS participates in at least one global application.

It's not necessary for every site in the system to have its own local database, as illustrated by the topology of the DDBMS shown in Figure 19.1.

From the definition of the DDBMS, the system is expected to make the distribution *transparent* (invisible) to the user. Thus, the fact that a distributed database is split into fragments that can be stored on different computers, and perhaps replicated, should be hidden from the user. The objective of transparency is to make the distributed system appear like a centralized system. This is sometimes referred to as the *fundamental principle* of distributed DBMSs. This requirement provides significant functionality for the end-user but, unfortunately, creates many additional problems that have to be handled by the DDBMS.

Figure 19.1

Distributed database management system.

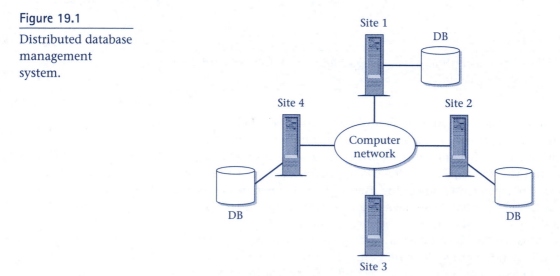

Distributed processing

It's important to make a distinction between a distributed DBMS and distributed processing:

> **Distributed processing**
>
> A centralized database that can be accessed over a computer network.

The key point with the definition of a DDBMS is that the system consists of data that is physically distributed across a number of sites in the network. If the data is centralized, even though other users may be accessing the data over the network, we do not consider this to be a DDBMS, simply distributed processing. We illustrate the topology of distributed processing in Figure 19.2. Compare this figure, which has a central database at site 2, with Figure 19.1, which shows several sites each with their own database.

19.3.1 Advantages and disadvantages of DDBMSs

The distribution of data and applications has potential advantages over traditional centralized database systems. Unfortunately, there are also disadvantages. In this section, we briefly review the advantages and disadvantages of DDBMSs.

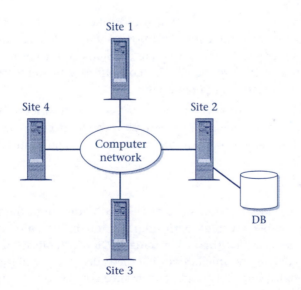

Figure 19.2

Distributed processing.

Advantages

Reflects organizational structure Many organizations are naturally distributed over several locations. It's natural for databases used in such an application to be distributed over these locations.

Improved shareability and local autonomy The geographical distribution of an organization can be reflected in the distribution of the data; users at one site can access data stored at other sites. Data can be placed at the site close to the users who normally use that data. In this way, users have local control of the data, and they can consequently establish and enforce local policies regarding the use of this data.

Improved availability In a centralized DBMS, a computer failure terminates the operations of the DBMS. However, a failure at one site of a DDBMS, or a failure of a communication link making some sites inaccessible, does not make the entire system inoperable.

Improved reliability As data may be replicated so that it exists at more than one site, the failure of a node or a communication link does not necessarily make the data inaccessible.

Improved performance As the data is located near the site of 'greatest demand', and given the inherent parallelism of DDBMSs, it may be easier to improve the speed of database accesses than if we had a remote centralized database. Furthermore, since each site handles only a part of the entire database, there may not be the same contention for CPU and I/O services as characterized by a centralized DBMS.

Economics It's generally accepted that it costs much less to create a system of smaller computers with the equivalent power of a single large computer. This makes it more cost-effective for corporate divisions and departments to obtain separate computers. It's also much more cost-effective to add workstations to a network than to update a mainframe system.

Modular growth In a distributed environment, it's much easier to handle expansion. New sites can be added to the network without affecting the operations of other sites. This flexibility allows an organization to expand relatively easily.

Disadvantages

Complexity A DDBMS that hides the distributed nature from the user and provides an acceptable level of performance, reliability, and availability is inherently more complex than a centralized DBMS. Replication also adds an extra level of complexity which, if not handled adequately, will lead to degradation in availability, reliability, and performance compared with the centralized system, and the advantages we cited above will become disadvantages.

Cost Increased complexity means that we can expect the procurement and maintenance costs for a DDBMS to be higher than those for a centralized DBMS. Furthermore, a DDBMS requires additional hardware to establish a network between sites. There are ongoing communication costs incurred with the use of this network. There are also additional staff costs to manage and maintain the local DBMSs and the underlying network.

Security In a centralized system, access to the data can be easily controlled. However, in a DDBMS not only does access to replicated data have to be controlled in multiple locations, but the network itself has to be made secure. In the past, networks were regarded as an insecure communication medium. Although this is still partially true, significant developments have been made recently to make networks more secure.

Integrity control more difficult Enforcing integrity constraints generally requires access to a large amount of data that defines the constraint, but is not involved in the actual update operation itself. In a DDBMS, the communication and processing costs that are required to enforce integrity constraints may be prohibitive.

Lack of standards Although DDBMSs depend on effective communication, we are only now starting to see the appearance of standard communication and data access protocols. This lack of standards has significantly limited the potential of DDBMSs. There are also no tools or methodologies to help users convert a centralized DBMS into a distributed DBMS.

Lack of experience General-purpose DDBMSs have not been widely accepted, although many of the protocols and problems are well understood. Consequently, we do not yet have the same level of experience in industry as we have with centralized DBMSs. For a prospective adopter of this technology, this may be a significant deterrent.

Database design more complex Besides the normal difficulties of designing a centralized database, the design of a distributed database has to take account of fragmentation of data, allocation of fragments to specific sites, and data replication.

As we mentioned earlier, to date, general-purpose DDBMSs have not been widely accepted, although many of the protocols and problems are well understood. Instead, *data replication*, the copying and maintenance of data on multiple servers, appears to be a more preferred solution. Every major database vendor has a replication solution of one kind or another, and many non-database vendors also offer alternative methods for replicating data. The *replication server* is an alternative, and potentially a more simplified approach to data distribution, as we now discuss.

19.3.2 Replication servers

> **Replication**
>
> The process of generating and reproducing multiple copies of data at one or more sites.

Replication is an important mechanism because it enables organizations to provide users with access to current data where and when they need it. Replication provides a number of benefits, including improved performance when centralized resources get overloaded, increased reliability and data availability, and support for mobile computing and data warehousing. In this section, we discuss several background concepts relating to data replication, including expected functionality and data ownership. We start with a discussion of when replicated data is updated.

Synchronous versus asynchronous replication

Typically protocols for updating replicated data in a DDBMS work on the basis that the replicated data is updated immediately when the source data is updated (that is, as part of the enclosing transaction). This type of replication is called *synchronous replication*. While this mechanism may be appropriate for environments that, by necessity, must keep all replicas fully synchronized (such as financial transactions), it does have several disadvantages. For example, the transaction will be unable to fully complete if one or more of the sites that hold replicas are unavailable. Further, the number of messages required to coordinate the synchronization of data places a significant burden on corporate networks.

Many commercial DBMSs provide an alternative mechanism to synchronous replication, called *asynchronous replication*. With this mechanism, the target database is updated after the source database has been modified. The delay in regaining consistency may range from a few seconds to several hours or even days. However, the data eventually synchronizes to the same value at all replicated sites. Although this violates the principle of distributed data independence, it appears to be a practical compromise between data integrity and availability that may be more appropriate for organizations that are able to work with replicas that do not necessarily have to be synchronized and current.

Functionality

At its basic level, we expect a distributed data replication service to be capable of copying data from one database to another, synchronously or asynchronously. However, there are many other functions that need to be provided, such as:

- *Specification of replication schema* The system should provide a mechanism to allow a privileged user to specify the data and objects to be replicated.

- *Subscription mechanism* The system should provide a mechanism to allow a privileged user to subscribe to the data and objects available for replication.

- *Initialization mechanism* The system should provide a mechanism to allow for the initialization of a target replica.

- *Scalability* The service should be able to handle the replication of both small and large volumes of data.

- *Mapping and transformation* The service should be able to handle replication across different DBMSs and platforms. This may involve mapping and transforming the data from one data model into a different data model, or the data in one data type to a corresponding data type in another DBMS.

- *Object replication* It should be possible to replicate objects other than data. For example, some systems allow indexes and stored procedures (or triggers) to be replicated.

- *Easy administration* It should be easy for the DBA to administer the system and to check the status and monitor the performance of the replication system components.

Data ownership

Ownership relates to which site has the privilege to update the data. The main types of ownership are **master/slave**, **workflow**, and **update-anywhere** (sometimes referred to as *peer-to-peer* or *symmetric replication*).

Master/slave ownership

With master/slave ownership, asynchronously replicated data is owned by one site, the *master* or *primary* site, and can be updated only by that site. Using a *'publish-and-subscribe'* metaphor, the master site (the publisher) makes data available. Other sites 'subscribe' to the data owned by the master site, which means that they receive read-only copies on their local systems. Potentially, each site can be the master site for non-overlapping data sets. However, there can only ever be one site that can update the master copy of a particular data set, and so update conflicts cannot occur between sites.

A master site may own the data in an entire table, in which case other sites subscribe to read-only copies of that table. Alternatively, multiple sites may own distinct fragments of the table, and other sites then subscribe to read-only copies of the fragments. This type of replication is also known as *asymmetric replication*.

Workflow ownership

Like master/slave ownership, this model avoids update conflicts while at the same time providing a more dynamic ownership model. Workflow ownership allows the right to update replicated data to move from site to site. However, at any one moment, there is only ever one site that may update that particular data set. A typical example of workflow ownership is an order processing system, where the processing of orders follows a series of steps, such as order entry, credit approval, invoicing, shipping, and so on. In a centralized DBMS, applications of this nature access and update the data in one integrated database: each application updates the order data in sequence when, and only when, the state of the order indicates that the previous step has been completed.

Update-anywhere (symmetric replication) ownership

The two previous models share a common property: at any given moment, only one site may update the data; all other sites have read-only access to the replicas. In some environments, this is too restrictive. The update-anywhere model creates a peer-to-peer environment where multiple sites have equal rights to update replicated data. This allows local sites to function autonomously, even when other sites are not available.

   Shared ownership can lead to conflict scenarios and the replication architecture has to be able to employ a methodology for conflict detection and resolution. A simple mechanism to detect conflict within a single table is for the source site to send both the old and new values (*before-* and *after-images*) for any records that have been updated since the last refresh. At the target site, the replication server can check each record in the target database that has also been updated against these values. However, consideration has to be given to detecting other types of conflict such as violation of referential integrity between two tables. There have been many mechanisms proposed for conflict resolution, but some of the most common are: earliest/latest timestamps, site priority, and holding for manual resolution.

19.4 Object–oriented DBMSs and object–relational DBMSs

In Section 19.2, we reviewed the weaknesses of the relational model against the requirements for the types of advanced database applications that are emerging. In this section, we briefly introduce two competing approaches that attempt to overcome these perceived weaknesses. Both are based on the concepts of object-orientation, which solve some of the classic problems of software development.

19.4.1 Object–oriented DBMSs (OODBMSs)

One approach to integrating object-oriented concepts with database systems is the **Object-oriented Database Management System (OODBMS)**. The OODBMS started initially in the engineering and design domains, and has also become the favored system for financial and telecommunications applications. There are many different definitions that have been proposed for an object-oriented data model. For example, Kim (1991) defines an Object-oriented Data Model (OODM), Object-oriented Database (OODB), and Object-oriented DBMS (OODBMS) as:

OODM
A (logical) data model that captures the semantics of objects supported in object-oriented programming.

OODB
A persistent and sharable collection of objects defined by an OODM.

OODBMS
The manager of an OODB.

These definitions are very non-descriptive and tend to reflect the fact that there is no one object-oriented data model equivalent to the underlying data model of relational systems. Each system provides its own interpretation of base functionality. Based on some of the current commercial OODBMSs, we can see that the concepts of object-oriented data models are drawn from different areas, as shown in Figure 19.3.

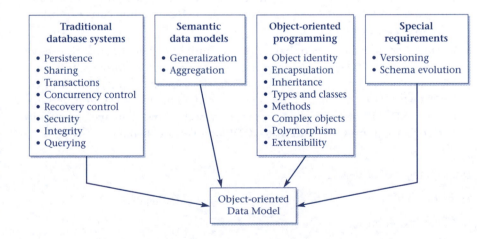

Figure 19.3

Origins of object-oriented data model.

One of the early criticisms often cited about OODBMSs was that they lacked a formal data model. However, within the past decade, several important vendors (including Sun Microsystems, eXcelon Corporation, Objectivity Inc., POET Software, Computer Associates, and Versant Corporation) have formed the Object Data Management Group (ODMG) to define standards for OODBMSs. The ODMG has produced an object model that specifies a standard model for the semantics of database objects. The model is important because it determines the built-in semantics that the OODBMS understands and can enforce. The ODMG also provides an Object Definition Language and an Object Query Language, which together form a superset of SQL.

Advantages of OODBMSs

Many of the advantages of OODBMSs are a result of the incorporation of object-orientation within the system. For example:

■ enriched modeling capabilities;

■ extensibility;

■ removal of impedance mismatch;

■ applicability to advanced database applications.

Others are the result of employing more appropriate protocols. For example:

■ support for schema evolution;

■ support for long-duration transactions.

Two other advantages often cited are:

■ *More expressive query language* OODBMSs generally use *navigational access* to move from one object to the next. This is in contrast to the *associative access* of SQL (that is, declarative statements with selection based on one or more predicates). Navigational access is more suitable for handling parts explosion, recursive queries, and so on.

■ *Improved performance* There have been a number of benchmarks that have suggested OODBMSs provide significant performance improvements over RDBMSs. For example, in 1989 and 1990, the OO1 benchmark was run on the OODBMSs GemStone, Ontos, ObjectStore, Objectivity/DB, and Versant, and the RDBMSs INGRES and Sybase. The results showed an average 30-fold performance improvement for the OODBMS over the RDBMS.

Disadvantages of OODBMSs

Some of the disadvantages often cited about the OODBMS are:

■ lack of experience;

■ lack of standards;

■ competition from RDBMSs;

■ complexity;

■ lack of support for views;

■ lack of support for security.

19.4.2 Object–relational DBMSs (ORDBMSs)

Moving away from the traditional relational data model is sometimes referred to as a *revolutionary approach* to integrating object-oriented concepts with database systems. In contrast, the **Object-relational DBMS (ORDBMS)** is a more *evolutionary approach* to integrating object-oriented concepts with database systems that extends the relational model.

Until recently, the choice of DBMS seemed to be between the RDBMS and the OODBMS. However, many vendors of RDBMS products were conscious of the threat and promise of the OODBMS. They agreed that traditional RDBMSs were not suited to the advanced applications discussed in Section 19.1, and that added functionality was required. However, they rejected the claim that extended RDBMSs will not provide sufficient functionality or will be too slow to cope adequately with the new complexity.

If we examine the advanced database applications that are emerging, we find they make extensive use of many object-oriented features such as a user-extensible type system, encapsulation, inheritance, polymorphism, dynamic binding of methods, complex objects including non-first normal form objects, and object identity (see Figure 19.3). The most obvious way to remedy the shortcomings of the relational model is to extend the model with these types of features. This is the approach that has been taken by many extended RDBMSs, although each has implemented different combinations of features. Thus, there is no single extended relational model; rather, there are a variety of these models, whose characteristics depend upon the way and the degree to which extensions were made. However, all the models do share the same basic relational tables and query language, all incorporate some concept of 'object', and some have the ability to store methods (or procedures or triggers) as well as data in the database.

Three of the leading RDBMS vendors – Oracle, Informix, and IBM – have all extended their systems into ORDBMSs, although the functionality provided by each is slightly different. The concept of the ORDBMS, as a hybrid of the RDBMS and the OODBMS, is very appealing, preserving the wealth of knowledge and experience that has been acquired with the RDBMS. So much so, that some analysts predict the ORDBMS will have a 50 percent larger share of the market than the RDBMS.

As might be expected, the standards activity in this area is based on extensions to the SQL standard. The national standards bodies have been working on object extensions to SQL since 1991. These extensions have become part of the 1999 SQL standard, commonly referred to as SQL3. The SQL3 standard is an ongoing attempt to standardize extensions to the relational model and query language.

Advantages of ORDBMSs

Apart from the advantages of resolving many of the weaknesses cited in Section 19.2, the main advantages of extending the relational data model come from *reuse* and *sharing*. Reuse comes from the ability to extend the DBMS server to perform standard functionality centrally, rather than have it coded in each application. For example, applications may require spatial data types that represent points, lines, and polygons, with associated functions that calculate the distance between two points, the distance between a point and a line, whether a point is contained within a polygon, and whether two polygonal regions overlap, among others. If we can embed this functionality in the server, it saves having to define it in each application that needs it, and consequently allows the functionality to be shared by all applications. These advantages also give rise to increased productivity both for the developer and for the end-user.

Another obvious advantage is that the extended relational approach preserves the significant body of knowledge and experience that has gone into developing relational applications. This is a significant advantage, as many organizations would find it prohibitively expensive to change. If the new functionality is designed appropriately, this approach should allow organizations to take advantage of the new extensions in an evolutionary way without losing the benefits of current database features and functions. Thus, an ORDBMS could be introduced in an integrative fashion, as proof-of-concept projects. The recent SQL3 standard is designed to be upwardly compatible with the SQL2 standard, and so any ORDBMS that complies with SQL3 should provide this capability.

Disadvantages of ORDBMSs

The ORDBMS approach has the obvious disadvantages of complexity and associated increased costs. Further, there are the proponents of the relational approach that believe the essential simplicity and purity of the relational model are lost with these types of extensions. There are also those that believe that the RDBMS is being extended for what will be a minority of applications that do not achieve optimal performance with current relational technology.

In addition, object-oriented purists are not attracted by these extensions either. They argue that the terminology of ORDBMSs is revealing. Instead of discussing object models, terms like user-defined data types are used. The terminology of object-orientation abounds with terms like abstract types, class hierarchies, and object models. However, ORDBMS vendors are attempting to portray object models as extensions to the relational model with some additional complexities. This potentially misses the point of object-orientation, highlighting the large semantic gap between these two technologies. Object applications are simply not as data-centric as relational-based ones. Object-oriented models and programs deeply combine relationships and encapsulated objects to mirror more closely the 'real world'. In fact, objects are fundamentally not extensions of data, but a completely different concept with far greater power to express 'real world' relationships and behaviors.

19.5 Data warehousing

Since the 1970s, organizations have largely focused their investment in new computer systems (called OnLine Transaction Processing (OLTP) systems) that automate business processes. In this way, organizations gained competitive advantage through systems that offered more efficient and cost-effective services to the customer. Throughout this period, organizations accumulated growing amounts of data stored in their operational databases. However, in recent times, where such systems are commonplace, organizations are focusing on ways to use operational data to support decision making, as a means of regaining competitive advantage.

Operational systems were never primarily designed to support business decision making and so using such systems may never be an easy solution. The legacy is that a typical organization may have numerous operational systems with overlapping and sometimes contradictory definitions, such as data types. The challenge for an organization is to turn its archives of data into a source of knowledge, so that a single integrated/consolidated view of the organization's data is presented to the user. The concept of a **data warehouse** was deemed the solution to meet the requirements of a system capable of supporting decision making, receiving data from multiple operational data sources.

Data warehouse

A consolidated/integrated view of corporate data drawn from disparate operational data sources and a range of end-user access tools capable of supporting simple to highly complex queries to support decision making.

The data held in a data warehouse is described as being subject-oriented, integrated, time-variant, and non-volatile (Inmon, 1993):

■ *Subject-oriented* as the warehouse is organized around the major subjects of the organization (such as customers, products, and sales) rather than the major application areas (such as customer invoicing, stock control, and product sales). This is reflected in the need to store decision-support data rather than application-oriented data.

■ *Integrated* because of the coming together of source data from different organization-wide applications systems. The source data is often inconsistent, using, for example, different data types and/or formats. The integrated data source must be made consistent to present a unified view of the data to the users.

■ *Time-variant* because data in the warehouse is only accurate and valid at some point in time or over some time interval. The time-variance of the data warehouse is also shown in the extended time that the data is held, the implicit or explicit association of time with all data, and the fact that the data represents a series of snapshots.

■ *Non-volatile* as the data is not updated in real time but is refreshed from operational systems on a regular basis. New data is always added as a supplement to the database, rather than a replacement. The database continually absorbs this new data, incrementally integrating it with the previous data.

The typical architecture of a data warehouse is shown in Figure 19.4.

Figure 19.4

The typical architecture of a data warehouse.

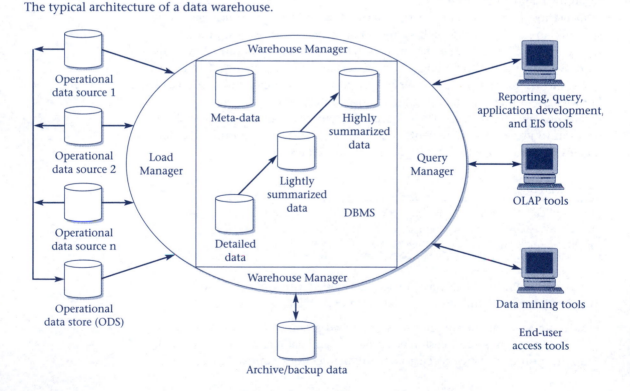

The source of *operational data* for the data warehouse is supplied from mainframes, proprietary file systems, private workstations and servers, and external systems such as the Internet. An *Operational Data Store* (ODS) is a repository of current and integrated operational data used for analysis. It is often structured and supplied with data in the same way as the data warehouse, but may in fact act simply as a staging area for data to be moved into the warehouse. The *load manager* performs all the operations associated with the extraction and loading of data into the warehouse. The *warehouse manager* performs all the operations associated with the management of the data, such as the transformation and merging of source data, creation of indexes and views on base tables, generation of aggregations, and backing up and archiving data. The *query manager* performs all the operations associated with the management of user queries. *Detailed data* is not stored online but is made available by summarizing the data to the next level of detail. However, on a regular basis, detailed data is added to the warehouse to supplement the summarized data. The warehouse stores all the predefined *lightly and highly summarized data* generated by the warehouse manager. The purpose of summary information is to speed up the performance of queries. Although there are increased operational costs associated with initially summarizing the data, this is offset by removing the requirement to continually perform summary operations (such as sorting or grouping) in answering user queries. The summary data is updated continuously as new data is loaded into the warehouse. Detailed and summarized data is stored offline for the purposes of archiving and backup. *Metadata* (data about data) definitions are used by all the processes in the warehouse, including the extraction and loading processes, the warehouse management process, and as part of the query management process.

The principal purpose of data warehousing is to provide information to business users for strategic decision making. These users interact with the warehouse using *end-user access tools*. The data warehouse must efficiently support *ad hoc* and routine analysis as well as more complex data analysis. The types of end-user access tools typically include reporting and query tools, application development tools, Executive Information System (EIS) tools, OnLine Analytical Processing (OLAP) tools, and data mining tools. We discuss OLAP and data mining tools in the following sections.

19.5.1 Data marts

Accompanying the emergence of data warehouses is the related concept of **data marts**.

Data mart
A subset of a data warehouse that supports the decision making requirements of a particular department or business area.

A data mart holds a subset of the data in a data warehouse, normally in the form of summary data relating to a particular department or business area such as Marketing or Customer Services. The data mart can be standalone or linked centrally to the corporate data warehouse. As a data warehouse grows larger, the ability to serve the various needs of the organization may be compromised. The popularity of data marts stems from the fact that corporate data warehouses proved difficult to build and use.

There are several approaches to building data marts. One approach is to build several data marts with a view to the eventual integration into a data warehouse and another approach is to build the infrastructure for a corporate data warehouse while at the same time building one or more data marts to satisfy immediate business needs.

Data mart architectures can be built as two-tier or three-tier database applications. The data warehouse is the optional first tier (if the data warehouse provides the data for the data mart), the data mart is the second tier, and the end-user workstation is the third tier. Data is distributed amongst the tiers. There are many reasons for creating a data mart, which include:

■ To give users access to the data they need to analyze most often.

■ To provide data in a form that matches the collective view of the data by a group of users in a department or business area.

■ To improve end-user response time due to the reduction in the volume of data to be accessed.

■ To provide appropriately structured data as dictated by the requirements of end-user access tools such as OnLine Analytical Processing (OLAP) and data mining tools, which may require their own internal database structures. In practice, these tools often create their own data mart designed to support their specific functionality.

■ Data marts normally use less data so tasks such as data cleansing, loading, transformation, and integration are far easier, and hence implementing and setting up a data mart is simpler compared with establishing a corporate data warehouse.

■ The cost of implementing data marts is normally less than that required to establish a data warehouse.

■ The potential users of a data mart are more clearly defined and can be more easily targeted to obtain support for a data mart project rather than a corporate data warehouse project.

Databases designed to support data warehousing or data mart applications are necessarily different from those that support traditional OLTP applications. Readers interested in learning how to design databases for decision support applications are referred to Connolly and Begg (2002).

19.6 OnLine Analytical Processing (OLAP)

Over the past few decades, we have witnessed the increasing popularity and prevalence of RDBMSs such that we now find a significant proportion of corporate data is housed in such systems. Relational databases have been used primarily to support traditional OLTP systems. To provide appropriate support for OLTP systems, RDBMSs have been developed to enable the highly efficient execution of a large number of relatively simple transactions.

In the past few years, RDBMS vendors have targeted the data warehousing market and have promoted their systems as tools for building data warehouses. A data warehouse stores operational data and is expected to support a wide range of queries from the relatively simple to the highly complex. However, the ability to answer particular queries is dependent on the types of end-user access tools available for use on the data warehouse. General-purpose tools such as reporting and query tools can easily support 'who?' and 'what?' questions about past events. A typical query submitted directly to a data warehouse is: 'What was the total revenue for Seattle in the third quarter of 2003?' However, accessing a data warehouse using a tool called **OnLine Analytical Processing (OLAP)** can allow for far more advanced querying and analysis of the data.

OnLine Analytical Processing (OLAP)
The dynamic synthesis, analysis, and consolidation of large volumes of multi-dimensional data.

OLAP is a term describing a technology that uses a multi-dimensional view of summarized data to provide quick access to strategic information for the purposes of advanced analysis. OLAP enables users to gain a deeper understanding and knowledge about various aspects of their corporate data through fast, consistent, interactive access to a wide variety of possible views of the data. OLAP allows the user to view corporate data in such a way that it is a better model of the true dimensionality of the organization. While OLAP systems can easily answer 'who?' and 'what?' questions, it's their ability to answer 'what if?' and 'why?' questions that distinguishes them from general-purpose query tools. OLAP enables decision making about future actions. A typical OLAP calculation can be more complex than simply summarizing data; for example, 'What would be the effect on property sales in the different regions of the US if legal costs went up by 3.5 percent and government taxes went down by 1.5 percent for properties over $100,000?' Hence, the types of analysis available from OLAP range from basic navigation and browsing (referred to as 'slicing and dicing'), to calculations, to more complex analyses such as time series and complex modeling.

There are many examples of OLAP applications in various business areas, as listed in Table 19.1.

Table 19.1 Examples of OLAP applications in various business areas.

Business area	Examples of OLAP applications
Finance	Budgeting, activity-based costing, financial performance analysis, and financial modeling.
Sales	Sales analysis and sales forecasting.
Marketing	Market research analysis, sales forecasting, promotions analysis, customer analysis, and market/customer segmentation.
Manufacturing	Production planning and defect analysis.

An essential requirement of all OLAP applications is the ability to provide users with Just-in-Time (JIT) information, which is necessary to make effective decisions about an organization's strategic directions. JIT information is computed data that usually reflects complex relationships and is often calculated on the fly. Analyzing and modeling complex relationships are practical only if response times are consistently short. In addition, because the nature of data relationships may not be known in advance, the data model must be flexible. A truly flexible data model ensures that OLAP systems can respond to changing business requirements as required for effective decision making. Although OLAP applications are found in widely divergent business areas, they all require multi-dimensional views of corporate data, support for complex calculations (such as forecasting), and time intelligence. Time intelligence is a key feature of almost any analytical application as performance is almost always judged over time; for example, this month versus last month or this month versus the same month last year.

The benefits that potentially follow the successful implementation of an OLAP application include:

■ More controlled and timely access to strategic information can allow more effective decision making.

■ Reduced backlog of applications development for IT staff by making end-users self-sufficient enough to make their own database changes and build their own models.

■ Retention of organizational control over the integrity of corporate data as OLAP applications are dependent on data warehouses and OLTP systems to refresh their source-level data.

■ Reduced amount of queries and network traffic on OLTP systems or on the data warehouse.

■ Improved potential revenue and profitability by enabling the organization to respond more quickly to market demands.

19.7 Data mining

Simply storing information in a data warehouse does not provide the benefits an organization is seeking. To realize the value of a data warehouse, it's necessary to extract the knowledge hidden within the warehouse. However, as the amount and complexity of the data in a data warehouse grow, it becomes increasingly difficult, if not impossible, for business analysts to identify trends and relationships in the data using simple query and reporting tools. Data mining is one of the best ways to extract meaningful trends and patterns from huge amounts of data. Data mining discovers information within data warehouses that queries and reports cannot effectively reveal.

Data mining

The process of extracting valid, previously unknown, comprehensible, and actionable information from large databases and using it to make crucial business decisions.

Data mining is concerned with the analysis of data and the use of software techniques for finding hidden and unexpected patterns and relationships in sets of data. The focus of data mining is to reveal information that is hidden and unexpected, as there is little value in finding patterns and relationships that are already intuitive. Examining the underlying rules and features in the data identifies the patterns and relationships.

Data mining analysis tends to work from the data up and the techniques that produce the most accurate results normally require large volumes of data to deliver reliable conclusions. The analysis process starts by developing an optimal representation of the structure of sample data, during which time knowledge is acquired. This knowledge is then extended to larger sets of data, working on the assumption that the larger data set has a structure similar to the sample data.

Data mining can provide huge paybacks for companies who have made a significant investment in data warehousing. Although data mining is still a relatively new technology, it's already used in a number of industries. Table 19.2 lists examples of applications of data mining in retail/marketing, banking, insurance, and medicine.

There are four main operations associated with data mining techniques, which include *predictive modeling*, *database segmentation*, *link analysis*, and *deviation detection*. Although any of the four major operations can be used for implementing any of the business applications listed in Table 19.2, there are certain recognized associations between the applications and the corresponding operations. For example, direct marketing strategies are normally implemented using the database segmentation operation, while fraud detection could be

Table 19.2 Examples of data mining applications.

Retail/Marketing

Identifying buying patterns of customers
Finding associations among customer demographic characteristics
Predicting response to mailing campaigns
Market basket analysis

Banking

Detecting patterns of fraudulent credit card use
Identifying loyal customers
Predicting customers likely to change their credit card affiliation
Determining credit card spending by customer groups

Insurance

Claims analysis
Predicting which customers will buy new policies

Medicine

Characterizing patient behavior to predict surgery visits
Identifying successful medical therapies for different illnesses

implemented by any of the four operations. Further, many applications work particularly well when several operations are used. For example, a common approach to customer profiling is to segment the database first and then apply predictive modeling to the resultant data segments.

Techniques are specific implementations of the data mining operations. However, each operation has its own strengths and weaknesses. With this in mind, data mining tools sometimes offer a choice of operations to implement a technique. The selection is often based on the suitability for certain input data types, transparency of the mining output, tolerance of missing variable values, level of accuracy possible, and increasingly, the ability to handle large volumes of data.

19.8 Web–database integration and XML

Just over a decade after its conception in 1989, the World Wide Web (Web for short) is arguably the most popular and powerful networked information system to date. Its growth in the past few years has been near exponential and it has started an information revolution that will continue through the next decade. Now the combination of the Web and databases brings many new opportunities for creating advanced database applications (we cited one example in Section 19.1).

The Web is a compelling platform for the delivery and dissemination of *data-centric*, interactive applications. Organizations are now rapidly building new database applications or re-engineering existing ones to take full advantage of the Web as a strategic platform for implementing innovative business solutions, in effect becoming *Web-centric* organizations.

From initially connecting a handful of nodes with ARPANET, the Internet was estimated to have over 100 million users in January 1997.[†] One year later, the estimate had risen to over 270 million users in over 100 countries, and in early 2001 the revised estimate was over 390 million users, rising to over 600 million in 2003. One projection for expected growth predicts 940 million users by 2004. In addition, some estimate that there are presently about 2.5 billion documents on the Internet, growing at 7.5 million a day. If we include intranets and extranets, the number of documents could be as much as an incredible 800 billion.

19.8.1 Static and dynamic Web pages

An HTML/XML document stored in a file is an example of a static Web page: the content of the document does not change unless the file itself is changed. On the other hand, the content of a dynamic Web page is generated each time it's accessed. As a result, a dynamic Web page can have features that are not found in static pages, such as:

■ It can respond to user input from the browser. For example, returning data requested by the completion of a form or the results of a database query.

■ It can be customized by and for each user. For example, once a user has specified some preferences when accessing a particular site or page (such as area of interest or level of expertise), this information can be retained and information returned appropriate to these preferences.

When the documents to be published are dynamic, such as those resulting from queries to databases, the hypertext needs to be generated by the server. To achieve this, we can write scripts that perform conversions from different data formats into HTML 'on the fly'. These scripts also need to understand the queries performed by clients through HTML forms and the results generated by the applications owning the data (for example, the DBMS). As a database is dynamic, changing as users create, insert, update, and delete data, then generating dynamic Web pages is a much more appropriate approach than creating static ones. We cover some approaches for creating dynamic Web pages shortly.

Many Web sites today are file-based, where each Web document is stored in a separate file. For small Web sites, this approach is not too much of a problem.

[†] In this context, the Internet means the Web, e-mail, FTP, Gopher, and Telnet services.

However, for large sites, this can lead to significant management problems. For example, maintaining current copies of hundreds or thousands of different documents in separate files is difficult enough, but also maintaining links between these files is even more formidable, particularly when the documents are created and maintained by different authors.

A second problem stems from the fact that many Web sites now contain more information of a dynamic nature, such as product and pricing information. Maintaining such information both in a database and in separate HTML/XML files can be an enormous task, and difficult to keep synchronized. For these and other reasons, allowing databases to be accessed directly from the Web is increasingly the approach that is being adopted for the management of dynamic Web content. The storage of Web information in a database can either replace or complement file storage.

19.8.2 Requirements for Web–DBMS integration

While many DBMS vendors are working to provide proprietary database connectivity solutions for the Web, most organizations require a more general solution to prevent them from being tied into one technology. In this section, we briefly list some of the most important requirements for the integration of database applications with the Web. These requirements are ideals and not fully achievable at the present time, and some may need to be traded off against others. Not in any ranked order, the requirements are as follows:

- The ability to access valuable corporate data in a secure manner.
- Data and vendor independent connectivity to allow freedom of choice in the selection of the DBMS now and in the future.
- The ability to interface to the database independent of any proprietary Web browser or Web server.
- A connectivity solution that takes advantage of all the features of an organization's DBMS.
- An open-architecture approach to allow interoperability with a variety of systems and technologies.
- A cost-effective solution that allows for scalability, growth, and changes in strategic directions, and helps reduce the costs of developing and maintaining applications.
- Support for transactions that span multiple HTTP requests.
- Support for session- and application-based authentication.
- Acceptable performance.
- Minimal administration overhead.
- A set of high-level productivity tools to allow applications to be developed, maintained, and deployed with relative ease and speed.

19.8.3 Approaches to integrating the Web and DBMSs

There are many approaches to integrating databases into the Web environment and in such a rapidly changing arena, new approaches are appearing regularly. Some common examples are:

- scripting languages such as JavaScript and VBScript;
- Common Gateway Interface (CGI), one of the early, and possibly one of the most widely used, techniques;
- HTTP cookies;
- extensions to the Web server, such as the Netscape API (NSAPI) and Microsoft's Internet Information Server API (ISAPI);
- Java and JDBC, SQLJ, Servlets, and JavaServer Pages (JSP);
- vendor-specific solutions such as Microsoft's Web Solution Platform with Active Server Pages (ASPs) and ActiveX Data Objects (ADO) and Oracle's Internet Platform with Oracle Portal and Oracle PL/SQL Server Pages (PSP).

19.8.4 XML

Most documents on the Web are currently stored and transmitted in HTML. One of the strengths of HTML is its simplicity, allowing it to be used by a wide variety of users. However, its simplicity is arguably also one of its weaknesses, with the growing need from users who want tags to simplify some tasks and make HTML documents more attractive and dynamic. In an attempt to satisfy this demand, vendors introduced some browser-specific HTML tags, which made it difficult to develop sophisticated, widely viewable Web documents. To prevent this split, the World Wide Web Consortium (W3C) has produced a new standard called XML (eXtensible Markup Language), which could preserve the general application independence that makes HTML portable and powerful. XML is a restricted version of SGML (Standard Generalized Markup Language), designed especially for Web documents. For example, XML supports links that point to multiple documents, as opposed to an HTML link that can reference just one destination document.

> **XML**
> ───
> A meta-language (a language for describing other languages) that enables designers to create their own customized tags to provide functionality not available with HTML.

XML is set to impact every aspect of programming, including graphical interfaces, embedded systems, distributed systems, and from our perspective, database management. For example, since XML describes the structure of data, it could become a useful mechanism for defining the structure of heterogeneous databases and data sources. With the ability to define an entire database schema, XML could potentially be used to take the contents of an Oracle schema, for example, and translate it to an Informix or Sybase schema. It is already becoming the *de facto* standard for data communication within the software industry, and it is quickly replacing EDI (Electronic Data Interchange) systems as the primary medium for data interchange among organizations. Some analysts believe it will become the language in which most documents are created and stored, both on and off the Internet.

XML and databases

As the amount of data in XML format expands, there will be an increasing demand to store, retrieve, and query this data. It's anticipated that there will be two main models that will exist: data-centric and document-centric. In a **data-centric model**, XML is used as the storage and interchange format for data that is structured, appears in a regular order, and is most likely to be machine processed instead of read by a human. In a data-centric model, the fact that the data is stored and transferred as XML is incidental and other formats could also have been used. In this case, the data could be stored in a relational, object-relational, or object-oriented DBMS. For example, Oracle has completely integrated XML into its Oracle 9i system. XML can be stored as entire documents using the data types XMLType or CLOB/BLOB (Character/Binary Large Object) or can be decomposed into its constituent elements and stored that way. The Oracle query language has also been extended to permit searching of XML-based content.

In a **document-centric model**, the documents are designed for human consumption (for example, books, newspapers, and e-mail). Due to the nature of this information, much of the data will be irregular or incomplete, and its structure may change rapidly or unpredictably. Unfortunately, relational, object-relational, and object-oriented DBMSs do not handle data of this nature particularly well. Content management systems are an important tool for handling these types of documents. Underlying such a system, you may now find a *native XML database*:

> **Native XML database**
> _____
> Defines a (logical) data model for an XML document (as opposed to the data in that document) and stores and retrieves documents according to that model. At a minimum, the model must include elements, attributes, PCDATA, and document order. The XML document must be the unit of (logical) storage, although it is not restricted by any underlying physical storage model (so traditional DBMSs are not ruled out).

Query languages

As mentioned above, DBMS vendors have extended SQL to handle the query of XML-based content. A number of companies have joined together to standardize XML extensions to SQL. This effort is known as SQL/XML and the initial work has been submitted to ISO and ANSI. In addition, W3C formed an XML Query Working Group to produce a data model for XML documents, a set of query operators on this model, and a query language based on these query operators (called XQuery). Queries operate on single documents or fixed collections of documents, and they can select entire documents or subtrees of documents that match conditions based on document content and structure. Queries can also construct new documents based on what has been selected. Ultimately, collections of XML documents will be accessed like databases.

The technology surrounding the Web is highly dynamic and it is likely that we will see significant developments in this area over the next few years.

Chapter summary

✓ Advanced database applications include Computer-aided Design (CAD), Computer-aided Manufacturing (CAM), Office Information Systems (OIS) and multimedia systems, Geographic Information Systems (GIS), and interactive and dynamic Websites.

✓ The relational model, and relational systems in particular, have weaknesses such as poor representation of 'real world' entities, semantic overloading, poor support for business rules, limited operations, difficulty handling recursive queries, and impedance mismatch. The limited modeling capabilities of RDBMSs have made them unsuitable for advanced database applications.

✓ A **distributed database** is a collection of logically interrelated, shared data (and a description of this data), physically distributed over a computer network. The **DDBMS** is the software that transparently manages the distributed database. A DDBMS is distinct from **distributed processing**, where a centralized DBMS is accessed over a network.

✓ The advantages of a DDBMS are that it reflects the organizational structure, it makes remote data more sharable, it improves reliability, availability, and performance, it may be more economical, and it provides for modular growth. The major disadvantages are cost, complexity, lack of standards, and experience.

✓ **Replication** is the process of generating and reproducing multiple copies of data at one or more sites. Replication provides a number of benefits, including improved performance when centralized resources get overloaded, increased reliability and data availability, and support for mobile computing and data warehousing facilitating decision support.

✓ An **Object-oriented DBMS (OODBMS)** is a manager of an **OODB**. An OODB is a persistent and sharable repository of objects defined in an OODM. An **OODM** is a data model that captures the semantics of objects supported in object-oriented programming. Advantages of OODBMSs include enriched modeling capabilities, extensibility, removal of impedance mismatch, more expressive query language.

✓ Several important vendors have formed the **Object Data Management Group** (ODMG) to define standards for OODBMSs. The ODMG has produced an Object Model that specifies a standard model for the semantics of database objects. The model is important because it determines the built-in semantics that the OODBMS understands and can enforce. The design of class libraries and applications that use these semantics should be portable across the various OODBMSs that support the Object Model.

✓ There is no single extended relational data model; rather, there are a variety of these models, whose characteristics depend upon the way and the degree to which extensions were made. However, all the models do share the same basic relational tables and query language, all incorporate some concept of 'object', and some have the ability to store methods or procedures/triggers as well as data in the database. These systems are generally referred to now as **Object–relational DBMSs (ORDBMSs).**

✓ **A data warehouse** is a consolidated/integrated view of corporate data drawn from disparate operational data sources and a range of end-user access tools capable of supporting simple to highly complex queries to support decision making. The data held in a data warehouse is described as being subject-oriented, integrated, time-variant, and non-volatile. A **data mart** is a subset of a data warehouse that supports the decision making requirements of a particular department or business area.

✓ OLAP is the dynamic synthesis, analysis, and consolidation of large volumes of multi-dimensional data. OLAP describes a technology that uses a multi-dimensional view of summarized data to provide quick access to strategic information for the purposes of advanced analysis.

✓ **Data mining** is the process of extracting valid, previously unknown, comprehensible, and actionable information from large databases and using it to make crucial business decisions.

✓ The Web is now the most popular and powerful networked information system to date. To prevent storing data redundantly outside the database in static Web pages, it is important to integrate the operational database into the Web environment. There are many different approaches to Web–database integration and the area is likely to see change over the next few years as the technologies mature.

 XML (eXtensible Markup Language) is a meta-language (a language for describing other languages) that enables designers to create their own customized tags to provide functionality not available with HTML. XML is set to impact every aspect of programming, including database management.

Review questions

19.1 Discuss the general characteristics of advanced database applications.

19.2 Discuss why the weaknesses of the relational data model and relational DBMSs may make them unsuitable for advanced database applications.

19.3 Explain what is meant by a DDBMS, and discuss the motivation in providing such a system.

19.4 Compare and contrast a DDBMS with distributed processing. Under what circumstances would you choose a DDBMS over distributed processing?

19.5 Discuss the advantages and disadvantages of a DDBMS.

19.6 Describe the expected functionality of a replication server.

19.7 Compare and contrast the different ownership models for replication. Give examples to illustrate your answer.

19.8 Give a definition of an OODBMS. What are the advantages and disadvantages of an OODBMS?

19.9 Give a definition of an ORDBMS. What are the advantages and disadvantages of an ORDBMS?

19.10 Give a definition of a data warehouse. Discuss the benefits of implementing a data warehouse.

19.11 Describe the characteristics of the data held in a data warehouse.

19.12 Discuss how data marts differ from data warehouses and identify the main reasons for implementing a data mart.

19.13 Discuss what OnLine Analytical Processing (OLAP) is and how OLAP differs from data warehousing.

19.14 Describe OLAP applications and identify the characteristics of such applications.

19.15 Discuss how data mining can realize the value of a data warehouse.

19.16 Why would we want to dynamically generate Web pages from data held in the operational database? List some general requirements for Web–database integration.

19.17 What is XML? Discuss the approaches for managing XML-based data.

Appendices

Alternative data modeling notations

In this chapter you will learn:

Alternative data modeling notations.   ◀

In Chapter 7, you learned how to create an Entity–Relationship (ER) model using an increasingly popular notation called UML (Unified Modeling Language). In this appendix you are shown two additional notations that are often used to create ER models. The first ER notation is called the Chen notation and the second is called the Crow's Feet notation. We demonstrate each by presenting a table that shows the notation used for each of the main concepts of the ER model and then we present the notation using as an example the ER model shown in Figure 9.9.

A.1   ER modeling using the Chen notation

Table A.1 shows the Chen notation for the main concepts of the ER model and Figure A.1 shows the ER model in Figure 9.9 redrawn using the Chen notation.

A.2   ER modeling using the Crow's Feet notation

Table A.2 shows the Crow's Feet notation for the main concepts of the ER model and Figure A.2 shows the ER model in Figure 9.9 redrawn using the Crow's Feet notation.

Table A.1

The Chen notation for ER modeling.

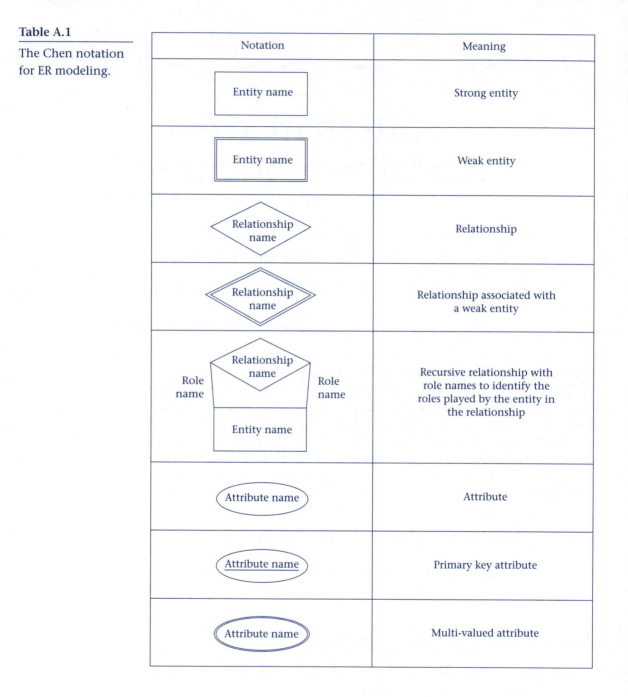

Notation	Meaning
Entity name	Strong entity
Entity name	Weak entity
Relationship name	Relationship
Relationship name	Relationship associated with a weak entity
Relationship name / Role name / Role name / Entity name	Recursive relationship with role names to identify the roles played by the entity in the relationship
Attribute name	Attribute
Attribute name	Primary key attribute
Attribute name	Multi-valued attribute

Table A.1 *Continued*

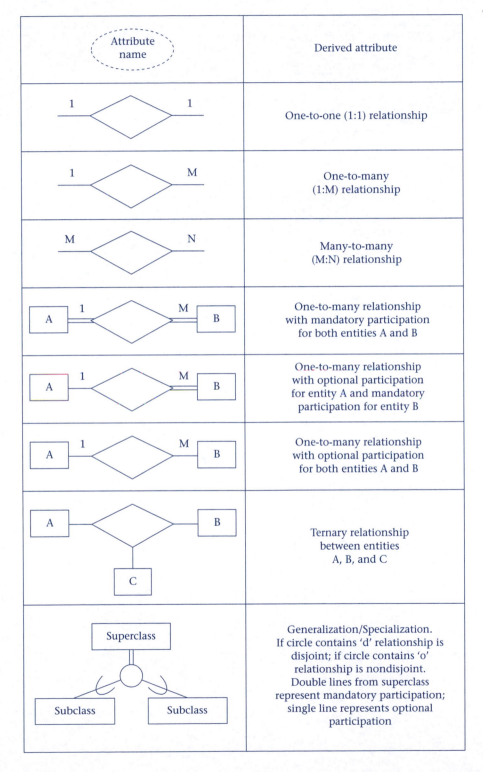

Attribute name	Derived attribute
1 ⟨⟩ 1	One-to-one (1:1) relationship
1 ⟨⟩ M	One-to-many (1:M) relationship
M ⟨⟩ N	Many-to-many (M:N) relationship
A 1 ⟨⟩ M B	One-to-many relationship with mandatory participation for both entities A and B
A 1 ⟨⟩ M B	One-to-many relationship with optional participation for entity A and mandatory participation for entity B
A 1 ⟨⟩ M B	One-to-many relationship with optional participation for both entities A and B
A ⟨⟩ B / C	Ternary relationship between entities A, B, and C
Superclass / Subclass Subclass	Generalization/Specialization. If circle contains 'd' relationship is disjoint; if circle contains 'o' relationship is nondisjoint. Double lines from superclass represent mandatory participation; single line represents optional participation

Figure A.1

The ER model shown in Figure 9.9 redrawn using the Chen notation.

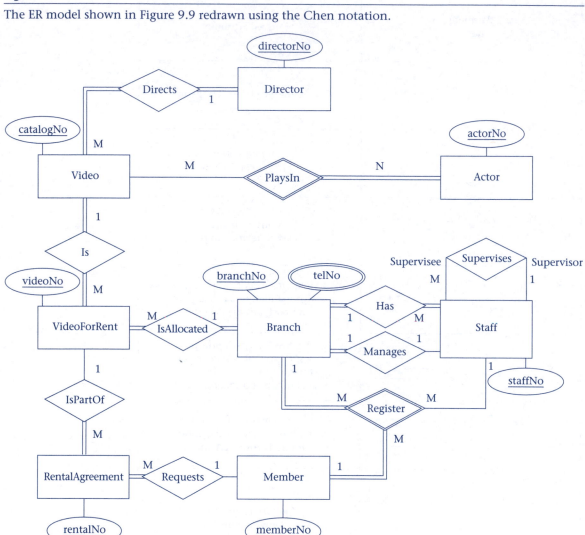

Notation	Meaning
Entity name	Entity
Relationship name	Relationship
Relationship name — Role name — Entity name — Role name	Recursive relationship with role names to identify the roles played by the entity in the relationship
Entity name — Attribute name — Attribute 1 — Attribute 2 — Attribute n	Attributes are listed in the lower section of the entity symbol The primary key attribute is underlined Multi-valued attribute placed in curly brackets { }
Relationship name	One-to-one relationship
Relationship name	One-to-many relationship
Relationship name	Many-to-many relationship

Table A.2

The Crow's Feet notation for ER modeling.

Table A.2

Continued

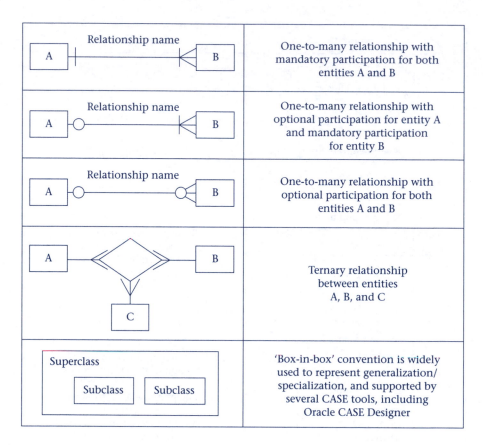

	One-to-many relationship with mandatory participation for both entities A and B
	One-to-many relationship with optional participation for entity A and mandatory participation for entity B
	One-to-many relationship with optional participation for both entities A and B
	Ternary relationship between entities A, B, and C
	'Box-in-box' convention is widely used to represent generalization/specialization, and supported by several CASE tools, including Oracle CASE Designer

Figure A.2

The ER model shown in Figure 9.9 redrawn using the Crow's Feet notation.

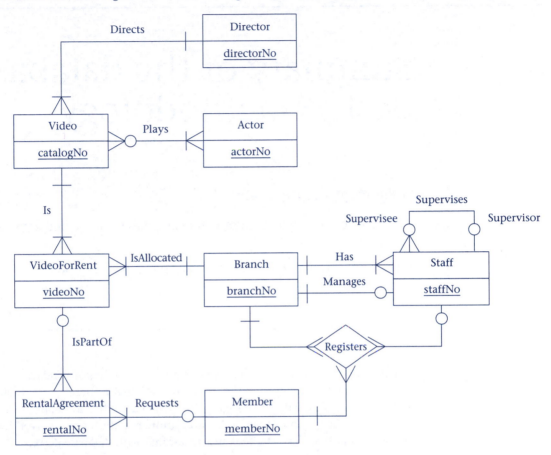

Appendix B

Summary of the database design methodology

In this chapter you will learn:

 Database design is composed of two main phases: logical and physical database design.

 The steps involved in the main phases of the database design methodology.

In this book, we present a database design methodology for relational databases. This methodology is made up of the two main phases logical database design and physical database design, which were described in detail in Chapters 9, 10, and 12 to 16. In this appendix, we summarize the steps involved in these phases for those readers who are already familiar with database design.

Step 1 Create and check ER model

During analysis, you will have identified a number of user views. Depending on the amount of overlap, for manageability you may decide to merge some of these views. The purpose of this step is to build a logical data model of the organization (or part of the organization) for each of these (possibly merged) views.

Step 1.1 Identify entities

Identify and document the main entities in the organization.

Step 1.2 Identify relationships

Identify the important relationships that exist between the entities that you have identified. Determine the multiplicity constraints of the relationships. Document relationships. Use Entity–Relationship (ER) modeling when necessary.

Step 1.3 Identify and associate attributes with entities or relationships

Associate attributes with the appropriate entities or relationships. Identify simple/composite attributes, single-valued/multi-valued attributes, and derived attributes. Document attributes.

Step 1.4 Determine attribute domains

Determine domains for the attributes in the ER model. Document attribute domains.

Step 1.5 Determine candidate, primary key, and alternate attributes

Identify the candidate key(s) for each entity and, if there is more than one candidate key, choose one to be the primary key, the others becoming alternate keys. Document candidate, primary, and alternate keys for each strong entity.

Step 1.6 Specialize/Generalize entities (optional step)

Identify superclass and subclass entities, where appropriate.

Step 1.7 Check model for redundancy

Examine the ER model to ensure there is no redundancy. Specifically, re-examine 1:1 relationships and remove redundant relationships.

Step 1.8 Check model supports user transactions

Ensure that the ER model supports the transactions required by the users.

Step 1.9 Review model with users

Step 2 Map ER model to tables

Map the ER model to a set of tables and check the structure of the tables.

Step 2.1 Map tables

In this step, you produce a set of tables to represent the entities, relationships, attributes, and constraints for the ER model created in Step 1. The structures of the tables are derived from the information that describes the ER model. This information includes the data dictionary, and any other documentation that describes the model. Also, document any new primary or candidate keys that have been formed as a result of the process of creating tables for the ER model.

The basic rules for creating tables are as follows:

(a) For each entity, create a table that includes all the entity's simple attributes.

(b) Relationships can be represented by the primary key/foreign key mechanism. In deciding where to post the foreign key, you must identify the 'parent' and 'child' entities in the relationship. The parent entity then posts a copy of its primary key into the child table, to act as the foreign key.

A summary of the rules for creating tables from an ER model is shown in Table B.1.

Table B.1 Summary of how to represent entities, relationships, and multi-valued attributes as tables.

Entity/Relationship/Attribute	Representation as table(s)
Strong or weak entity	Create table that includes all simple attributes.
1:* binary relationship	Post copy of primary key of entity on 'one' side to table representing entity on 'many' side. Any attributes of relationship are also posted to 'many' side.
1:* recursive relationship	As entity on 'one' and 'many' side is the same, the table representing the entity receives a second copy of the primary key, which is renamed, and also any attributes of the relationship.
1:1 binary relationship:	
Mandatory participation on *both* sides	Combine entities into one table.
Mandatory participation on *one* side	Post copy of primary key of entity with optional participation to table representing entity with mandatory participation. Any attributes of relationship are also posted to table representing entity with mandatory participation.

Table B.1 *Continued*

Entity/Relationship/Attribute	Representation as table(s)
Optional participation on *both* sides	Without further information, post copy of primary key of one entity to the other. However, if information is available, treat entity that is closer to having mandatory participation as being the child entity.
: binary relationship/ complex relationship	Create a table to represent the relationship and include any attributes associated with the relationship. Post a copy of the primary key from each parent entity into the new table to act as foreign keys.
Multi-valued attribute	Create a table to represent the multi-valued attribute and post a copy of the primary key of the parent entity into the new table to act as a foreign key.

You may use Step 1.6 to introduce specialization/generalization into your ER model. For each superclass/subclass relationship, you identify the superclass as the parent entity and the subclass as the child entity. There are various options on how you may best represent such a relationship as one or more tables. The selection of the most appropriate option is dependent on the participation and disjoint constraints on the superclass/subclass relationship. A summary of how to map tables from your EER model is shown in Table B.2.

Table B.2 Options available for the representation of a superclass/subclass relationship based on the participation and disjoint constraints.

Participation constraint	Disjoint constraint	Tables required
Mandatory	Nondisjoint {And}	Single table
Optional	Nondisjoint {And}	Two tables: one table for superclass and one table for all subclasses
Mandatory	Disjoint {Or}	Many tables: one table for each combined superclass/subclass
Optional	Disjoint {Or}	Many tables: one table for superclass and one for each subclass

Step 2.2 Check table structures using normalization

The purpose of this step is to examine the groupings of columns in each table created in Step 2.1. You check the composition of each table using the rules of normalization. Each table should be in at least third normal form (3NF).

Step 2.3 Check tables support user transactions

In this step, you ensure that the tables support the required transactions, which are described in the users' requirements specifications.

Step 2.4 Check business rules

Check that all business rules are represented in the logical database design. These include specifying the required data, attribute domain constraints, entity integrity, multiplicity, referential integrity, and any other business rules. Document all business rules.

Step 2.5 Review logical database design with users

Ensure that the logical database design is a true representation of the data requirements of the organization (or part of the organization) to be supported by the database.

Step 2.6 Build and check global logical data model[*]

Combine the individual local logical data models into a single global logical data model that represents the data requirements of the organization (or part of the organization) to be supported by the database.

Step 2.6.1 Merge local logical data models into global model

Merge the individual local logical data models into a single global logical data model. Some typical tasks of this step are as follows:

(1) Review the names and contents of entities/tables and their primary keys.

(2) Review the names and contents of relationships/foreign keys.

(3) Merge entities/tables from the local data models.

(4) Include (without merging) entities/tables unique to each local data model.

(5) Merge relationships/foreign keys from the local data models.

---

[*] Step 2.6 is only required when creating a multi-user view database, using the view integration approach (described in Appendix C).

(6) Include (without merging) relationships/foreign keys unique to each local data model.

(7) Check for missing entities/tables and relationships/foreign keys.

(8) Check foreign keys.

(9) Check business rules.

(10) Draw the global ER/table diagram.

(11) Update the documentation.

Step 2.6.2 Check global logical data model

This step is equivalent to Steps 2.3 and 2.4, where you check the structure of the tables created for the global data model using normalization and then check that these tables are capable of supporting all user transactions.

Step 2.6.3 Check for future growth

Determine whether there are any significant changes likely in the foreseeable future and assess whether the global logical data model can accommodate these changes.

Step 2.6.4 Review global logical data model with users

Ensure that the global logical data model is a true representation of the data requirements of the organization (or the part of the organization) to be supported by the database.

Step 3 Translate logical database design for target DBMS

Produce a basic working set of tables from the logical data model.

Step 3.1 Design base tables

Decide how to represent the base tables you have identified in the logical data model in the target DBMS. Document design of tables.

Step 3.2 Design representation of derived data

Consider how derived data will be represented. The choice is to calculate derived data each time it's needed or to introduce redundancy and store the derived data as a column in a table. Document design of derived data.

Step 3.3 Design remaining business rules

Design the remaining business rules for the target DBMS. Document design of the remaining business rules.

Step 4 Choose file organizations and indexes

Determine the file organizations that will be used to store the base tables; that is, the way in which tables and records will be held on secondary storage. Consider the addition of indexes to improve performance.

Step 4.1 Analyze transactions

Understand the functionality of the transactions that will run on the database and analyze the important transactions.

Step 4.2 Choose file organizations

Determine an efficient file organization for each base table.

Step 4.3 Choose indexes

Determine whether adding indexes will improve the performance of the system.

Step 5 Design user views

Design the user views that you identified during the requirements collection and analysis stage.

Step 6 Design security mechanisms

Design the security measures for the database implementation as specified by the users during the requirements collection and analysis stage. Document the design of the security measures.

Step 7 Consider the introduction of controlled redundancy

Determine whether introducing redundancy in a controlled manner by relaxing the normalization rules will improve the performance of the system. Consider duplicating columns or joining tables together to achieve improved performance. In particular, consider combining one-to-one (1:1) relationships, duplicating nonkey columns in one-to-many (1:*) relationships to reduce joins, duplicating foreign key columns in one-to-many (1:*) relationships to reduce joins, duplicating columns in many-to-many (*:*) relationships to reduce joins, introducing repeating groups, creating extract tables, and partitioning tables.

Step 8 Monitor and tune the operational system

Monitor the operational system and improve the performance of the system to correct inappropriate design decisions or reflect changing requirements.

Appendix C

Advanced logical database design

In this appendix you will learn:

➤ How to merge local logical data models into a global logical data model of the data requirements of the organization.

➤ How to ensure that the resultant global model is a true and accurate representation of the data requirements of the organization (or part of the organization) being modeled.

Methodology
summarized in
Appendix B

View integration
approach discussed in
Sections 4.5 and 6.4.4

Centralized approach
discussed in Sections
4.5 and 6.4.4

This appendix describes what you should do when you're creating a reasonably complex database system with several user views and you have chosen to manage these user views (wholly or partly) using the **view integration** approach. This appendix assumes that you have created local data models each representing one or more user views using Steps 1 and 2 of the database design methodology described in Chapters 9 and 10.

In Chapter 6, we identified several user views for the *StayHome* database system, namely Director, Manager, Supervisor, Assistant, and Buyer. Following analysis of the requirements for each user view, we decided to manage these user views using a mixture of the centralized and view integration approaches. We used the **centralized approach** to merge the requirements for the Manager, Supervisor, and Assistant user views into a collection of user views called *Branch* and merged the requirements for the Director and Buyer user views into a collection of user views called *Business*. In Chapters 9 and 10, we used the Branch user views to demonstrate the building of a local logical data model using Steps 1 and 2 of the methodology. The ER diagram was shown in Figure 9.9 and a description of the tables was shown in Figure 10.11.

In this appendix, we first present the users' requirements specification for the Business user views of *StayHome*. We don't demonstrate the building of the local logical data model for this collection of user views but instead present important components of the logical model, namely the ER diagram and a description of the tables based on this model. We then use the local logical data models for the Branch and Business user views to demonstrate how to merge data models.

C.1 The Business user views of *StayHome*

In this section, we present the users' requirements specification for the Business user views of *StayHome* and the corresponding local logical data model.

Step 1 was covered in Chapter 9.

> **TIP**
>
> You may find it useful to read the requirements in the following section and then attempt Steps 1 and 2 of the methodology yourself. You can then check your solution against our sample solution.

Step 2 was covered in Chapter 10.

C.1.1 Users' requirements specification

The requirements specification for the Business user views is listed in two sections: the first describes the data used by the Business user views and the second provides examples of how the data is used (that is, the transactions performed on the data).

Data requirements

The details held on a branch of *StayHome* are the branch address and the telephone number. Each branch is given a branch number, which is unique throughout the company.

Each branch of *StayHome* has staff, which includes a Manager. The details held on a member of staff are his or her name, position, and salary. Each member of staff is given a staff number, which is unique throughout the company.

Each branch of *StayHome* is allocated a stock of videos. The details held on a video are the catalog number, video number, title, category, daily rental rate, and purchase price. The catalog number uniquely identifies each video. However, in most cases there are several copies of each video at a branch, and the individual copies are identified using the video number.

Each branch of *StayHome* receives videos from video suppliers. The details held on video suppliers are the supplier number, name, address, telephone number, and status. Orders for videos are placed with these suppliers and the details held on a video order are the order number, supplier number, supplier address, video catalog number, video title, video purchase price, quantity, date order placed, date order received, and the address of the branch receiving the order.

A customer of *StayHome* must first register as a member of a local branch of *StayHome*. The details held on a member are name, address, and the date that the member registered at a branch. Each member is given a member number, which is unique throughout all branches of the company and is used even when a member chooses to register at more than one branch.

The details held on each video rented are the rental number, full name and member number, the video number, title, and daily rental rate, and the dates the video is rented out and returned. The rental number is unique throughout the company.

Transaction requirements

Data entry

(a) Enter the details for a newly released video (such as details of a video called *Return of the King*).

(b) Enter the details of a video supplier (such as a supplier called *WorldView Videos*).

(c) Enter the details of a video order (such as ordering 10 copies of *Return of the King* for branch B002).

Data update/deletion

(d) Update/delete the details of a given video.

(e) Update/delete the details of a given video supplier.

(f) Update/delete the details of a given video order.

Data queries

(g) List the name, position, and salary of staff at all branches, ordered by branch number.

(h) List the name and telephone number of the Manager at a given branch.

(i) List the catalog number and title of all videos at a given branch, ordered by title.

(j) List the number of copies of a given video at a given branch.

(k) List the number of members at each branch, ordered by branch number.

(l) List the number of members who joined this year at each branch, ordered by branch number.

(m) List the number of video rentals at each branch between certain dates, ordered by branch number.

(n) List the number of videos in each category at a given branch, ordered by category.

(o) List the name, address, and telephone number of all video suppliers, ordered by supplier number.

(p) List the name and telephone number of a video supplier.

(q) List the details of all video orders placed with a given supplier, sorted by the date ordered.

(r) List the details of all video orders placed on a certain date.

(s) List the total daily rentals for videos at each branch between certain dates, ordered by branch number.

C.1.2 Local logical data model

As we've just mentioned, rather than go through the process of building the local logical data model for the Business user views of *StayHome*, we assume instead that this model was produced using Steps 1 and 2 of the methodology and present the important components of the logical model, namely:

■ ER diagram, shown in Figure C.1;

■ tables, shown in Figure C.2.

Let's now use the Branch and Business local logical data models to build a global logical data model for *StayHome*. We describe the process of merging the two data models by including additional steps to Step 2 of the logical database design methodology described in Chapter 10.

Step 2.6 Build and check global logical data model

Objective
To combine the individual local logical data models into a single global logical data model that represents the data requirements of the organization (or part of the organization) that is being modeled.

In this continuation of Step 2, you build a global logical data model, which represents all user views by merging together the local logical data models produced for each user view of the database. However, if you're also using the centralized approach for managing multiple user views, a local logical data model represents the merged requirements for two or more user views. Having combined the models together it may be necessary to check that the tables based on the global model are appropriately normalized and still support the

Figure C.1

ER model for the Business user views of *StayHome*.

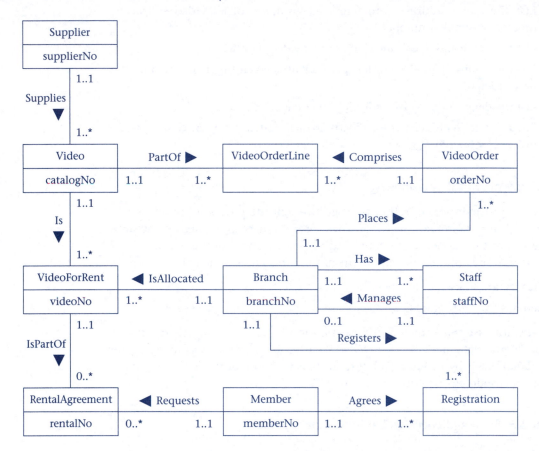

required transactions, as you did in Steps 2.2 and 2.3 of Chapter 10. However, you need only check those areas of the model that resulted in any change during the merging process. In a large system, this will significantly reduce the amount of rechecking that needs to be performed.

Although each local logical data model should be correct, comprehensive, and unambiguous, each model is only a representation of one or more but not all user views of the database. In other words, the model is not strictly a model of the function of the organization, but it's a model of one or more user views and hence may not be complete. This may mean that there may be inconsistencies as well as overlaps when you look at the complete set of user views. Thus, when you merge the local logical data models into a single global model, you must resolve conflicts between the user views and any overlaps that exist.

Figure C.2

Tables for the Business user views of *StayHome*.

Branch (branchNo, address, telNo, mgrStaffNo) **Primary Key** branchNo **Alternate Key** telNo **Foreign Key** mgrStaffNo **references** Staff(staffNo)	**Member** (memberNo, name, address) **Primary Key** memberNo
Registration (branchNo, memberNo, dateJoined) **Primary Key** branchNo, memberNo **Foreign Key** branchNo **references** Branch(branchNo) **Foreign Key** memberNo **references** Member(memberNo)	**RentalAgreement** (rentalNo, dateOut, dateReturn, memberNo, videoNo) **Primary Key** rentalNo **Alternate Key** memberNo, videoNo, dateOut **Foreign Key** memberNo **references** Member(memberNo) **Foreign Key** videoNo **references** Video(videoNo)
Staff (staffNo, name, position, salary, branchNo) **Primary Key** staffNo **Foreign Key** branchNo **references** Branch(branchNo)	**Supplier** (supplierNo, sName, sAddress, sTelNo, status) **Primary Key** supplierNo **Alternate Key** sTelNo
Video (catalogNo, title, category, dailyRental, price, supplierNo) **Primary Key** catalogNo **Foreign Key** supplierNo **references** Supplier(supplierNo)	**VideoForRent** (videoNo, available, catalogNo, branchNo) **Primary Key** videoNo **Foreign Key** catalogNo **references** Video(catalogNo) **Foreign Key** branchNo **references** Branch(branchNo)
VideoOrder (orderNo, dateOrdered, dateReceived, branchNo) **Primary Key** orderNo **Foreign Key** branchNo **references** Branch(branchNo)	**VideoOrderLine** (orderNo, catalogNo, quantity) **Primary Key** orderNo, catalogNo **Foreign Key** orderNo **references** VideoOrder(orderNo) **Foreign Key** catalogNo **references** Video(catalogNo)

The tasks involved in Step 2.6 are:

■ Step 2.6.1 Merge local logical data models into global model

■ Step 2.6.2 Check global logical data model

■ Step 2.6.3 Check for future growth

■ Step 2.6.4 Review global logical data model with users

Step 2.6.1 Merge local logical data models into global model

Objective
To merge the individual local logical data models into a single global logical data model.

Up to this point, for each local logical data model you have produced an ER diagram, a set of tables, a data dictionary, and supporting documentation that describes the constraints on the data. In this step, you use these components to identify the similarities and differences between the models, to help merge them.

For simple database systems with a relatively small number of entities/tables, it's an easy task to compare the local models, merge them together, and resolve any differences that exist. However, in a large system, a more systematic approach must be taken. We present one approach that may be used to merge the local models together and resolve any inconsistencies found. Some typical tasks of this approach are:

(1) Review the names and contents of entities/tables and their primary keys.

(2) Review the names and contents of relationships/foreign keys.

(3) Merge entities/tables from the local data models.

(4) Include (without merging) entities/tables unique to each local data model.

(5) Merge relationships/foreign keys from the local data models.

(6) Include (without merging) relationships/foreign keys unique to each local data model.

(7) Check for missing entities/tables and relationships/foreign keys.

(8) Check foreign keys.

(9) Check integrity constraints.

(10) Draw the global ER/table diagram.

(11) Update the documentation.

In some of the above tasks, we have used the terms 'entities/tables' and 'relationships/foreign keys' because you may prefer to:

■ examine the ER diagrams and their supporting documentation, or

■ examine the tables that have been produced from the ER diagrams and supporting documentation, or

■ use a combination of both sources of information.

> TIP
>
> Perhaps the easiest way to merge several local data models together is to first merge two of the data models to produce a new model, and then to successively merge the remaining local data models until all the local models are represented in the final global data model. This may prove a simpler approach than trying to merge all the local data models at the same time.

To ensure that you are comparing like with like, it's important that each local model has been created following Steps 1 and 2 of the methodology.

Review the names and contents of entities/tables and their primary keys

It may be worthwhile reviewing the names and descriptions of entities/tables that appear in the local data models by inspecting the data dictionary. Problems can arise when two or more entities/tables:

■ have the same name but are, in fact, different (homonyms);

■ are the same but have different names (synonyms).

It may be necessary to compare the data content of each entity/table to resolve these problems. In particular, you may use the primary keys (or candidate keys) to help identify equivalent entities/tables that may be named differently across user views. A comparison of the tables and primary keys in the Branch and Business user views of *StayHome* is shown in Table C.1. The tables that are common to both views are highlighted.

Table C.1 Comparison of tables and primary keys for the Branch and Business user views of *StayHome*.

Branch user views		Business user views	
Table	Primary key	Table	Primary key
Branch	**branchNo**	**Branch**	**branchNo**
Staff	**staffNo**	**Staff**	**staffNo**
Telephone	telNo		
Video	**catalogNo**	**Video**	**catalogNo**
VideoForRent	**videoNo**	**VideoForRent**	**videoNo**
		Supplier	supplierNo
		VideoOrder	orderNo
		VideoOrderLine	orderNo, catalogNo
RentalAgreement	**rentalNo**	**RentalAgreement**	**rentalNo**
Member	**memberNo**	**Member**	**memberNo**
Registration	**branchNo, memberNo**	**Registration**	**branchNo, memberNo**
Actor	actorNo		
Role	catalogNo, actorNo		
Director	directorNo		

Review the names and contents of relationships/foreign keys

This activity is the same as that described for entities/tables. A comparison of the relationships/foreign keys in the Branch and Business user views of *StayHome* is shown in Table C.2. The relationships/foreign keys that are common to both views are again highlighted.

Table C.2 Comparison of relationships/foreign keys for the Branch and Business user views of *StayHome*.

Branch user views			Business user views		
Child table	Foreign key	Parent table	Child table	Foreign key	Parent table
Branch	**MgrStaffNo →**	**Staff(staffNo)**	**Branch**	**MgrStaffNo →**	**Staff(staffNo)**
Telephone	branchNo →	Branch(branchNo)			
Registration	**branchNo →**	**Branch(branchNo)**	**Registration**	**branchNo →**	**Branch(branchNo)**
	memberNo →	**Member(memberNo)**		**memberNo →**	**Member(memberNo)**
	staffNo →	Staff(staffNo)			
Staff	**branchNo →**	**Branch(branchNo)**	**Staff**	**branchNo →**	**Branch(branchNo)**
	supervisorStaffNo →	Staff(staffNo)			
Video	directorNo →	Director(directorNo)	Video	supplierNo →	Supplier(supplierNo)
VideoForRent	**catalogNo →**	**Video(catalogNo)**	**VideoForRent**	**catalogNo →**	**Video(catalogNo)**
	branchNo →	**Branch(branchNo)**		**branchNo →**	**Branch(branchNo)**
RentalAgreement	**memberNo →**	**Member(memberNo)**	**RentalAgreement**	**memberNo →**	**Member(memberNo)**
	videoNo →	**VideoForRent(videoNo)**		**videoNo →**	**VideoForRent(videoNo)**
			VideoOrder	branchNo →	Branch(branchNo)
			VideoOrderLine	orderNo →	VideoOrder(orderNo)
				catalogNo →	Video(catalogNo)
Role	actorNo →	Actor(actorNo)			
	catalogNo →	Video(catalogNo)			

Merge entities/tables from the local data models

You should examine the name and content of each entity/table in the models to be merged to determine whether entities/tables represent the same thing and can therefore be merged. Typical activities involved in this task include:

- Merge entities/tables with the same name and the same primary key.
- Merge entities/tables with the same name using different primary keys.
- Merge entities/tables with different names using the same or different primary keys.

Include (without merging) entities/tables unique to each local data model

The previous tasks should identify all entities/tables that are the same. All remaining entities/tables are included in the global model without change.

Merge relationships/foreign keys from the local data models

In this step, you examine the name and purpose of each relationship/foreign key in the data models. Before merging relationships/foreign keys, it's important to resolve any conflicts between the relationships such as differences in multiplicity constraints. The activities in this step include merging relationships/foreign keys with the same name and the same purpose, and then merging relationships/foreign keys with different names but the same purpose.

Include (without merging) relationships/foreign keys unique to each local data model

Again, the previous task should identify relationships/foreign keys that are the same (by definition, they must be between the same entities/tables, which would have been merged together earlier). All remaining relationships/foreign keys are included in the global model without change.

Check for missing entities/tables and relationships/foreign keys

Perhaps one of the most difficult tasks in producing the global model is identifying missing entities/tables and relationships/foreign keys between different local data models. If a corporate data model exists for the organization, which identifies *all* of the important data used by an organization, this may reveal entities/tables and relationships that do not appear in any local data model. Alternatively, as a preventative measure, when interviewing the users of a specific user view, ask them to pay particular attention to the entities/tables and relationships/foreign keys that also exist in other user views. Otherwise, examine the attributes/columns of each entity/table and look for references to entities/tables in other local data models. You may find that you have an attribute/column associated with an entity/table in one local data model that corresponds to a primary key, alternate key, or even a nonkey attribute/column of an entity/table in another local data model.

Check foreign keys

During this step, entities/tables and relationships may have been merged, primary keys changed, and new relationships identified. Check that the foreign keys in child tables are still correct, and make any necessary modifications that are required. The tables that represent the global logical data model for the *StayHome* database are shown in Figure C.3.

Check integrity constraints and business rules

Check that the integrity constraints and business rules for the global logical data model do not conflict with those originally specified for each user view. If any new relationships have been identified and new foreign keys have been created, ensure that appropriate referential integrity constraints are specified. Any conflicts must be resolved in consultation with the users.

Figure C.3

Table structures for the global logical data model of *StayHome*.

Actor (actorNo, actorName) **Primary Key** actorNo	**Branch** (branchNo, street, city, state, zipCode, mgrStaffNo) **Primary Key** branchNo **Alternate Key** zipCode **Foreign Key** mgrStaffNo **references** Staff(staffNo)
Director (directorNo, directorName) **Primary Key** directorNo	**Member** (memberNo, fName, lName, address) **Primary Key** memberNo
Registration (branchNo, memberNo, staffNo, dateJoined) **Primary Key** branchNo, memberNo **Foreign Key** branchNo **references** Branch(branchNo) **Foreign Key** memberNo **references** Member(memberNo) **Foreign Key** staffNo **references** Staff(staffNo)	**RentalAgreement** (rentalNo, dateOut, dateReturn, memberNo, videoNo) **Primary Key** rentalNo **Alternate Key** memberNo, videoNo, dateOut **Foreign Key** memberNo **references** Member(memberNo) **Foreign Key** videoNo **references** Video(videoNo)
Role (catalogNo, actorNo, character) **Primary Key** catalogNo, actorNo **Foreign Key** catalogNo **references** Video(catalogNo) **Foreign Key** actorNo **references** Actor(actorNo)	**Staff** (staffNo, name, position, salary, branchNo, supervisorStaffNo) **Primary Key** staffNo **Foreign Key** branchNo **references** Branch(branchNo) **Foreign Key** supervisorStaffNo **references** Staff(staffNo)
Supplier (supplierNo, name, address, telNo, status) **Primary Key** supplierNo **Alternate Key** telNo	**Telephone** (telNo, branchNo) **Primary Key** telNo **Foreign Key** branchNo **references** Branch(branchNo)
Video (catalogNo, title, category, dailyRental, price, directorNo, supplierNo) **Primary Key** catalogNo **Foreign Key** directorNo **references** Director(directorNo) **Foreign Key** supplierNo **references** Supplier(supplierNo)	**VideoForRent**(videoNo, available, catalogNo, branchNo) **Primary Key** videoNo **Foreign Key** catalogNo **references** Video(catalogNo) **Foreign Key** branchNo **references** Branch(branchNo)
VideoOrder (orderNo, dateOrdered, dateReceived, branchNo) **Primary Key** orderNo **Foreign Key** branchNo **references** Branch(branchNo)	**VideoOrderLine** (orderNo, catalogNo, quantity) **Primary Key** orderNo, catalogNo **Foreign Key** orderNo **references** VideoOrder(orderNo) **Foreign Key** catalogNo **references** Video(catalogNo)

Draw the global ER/table diagram

You now draw a final diagram that represents all the merged local logical data models. If tables have been used as the basis for merging, we call the resulting diagram a **global table diagram**, which shows primary keys and foreign keys. If local ER diagrams have been used, the resulting diagram is simply a global ER diagram. The global table diagram for the *StayHome* database is shown in Figure C.4.

Figure C.4

The global table diagram for the *StayHome* database system.

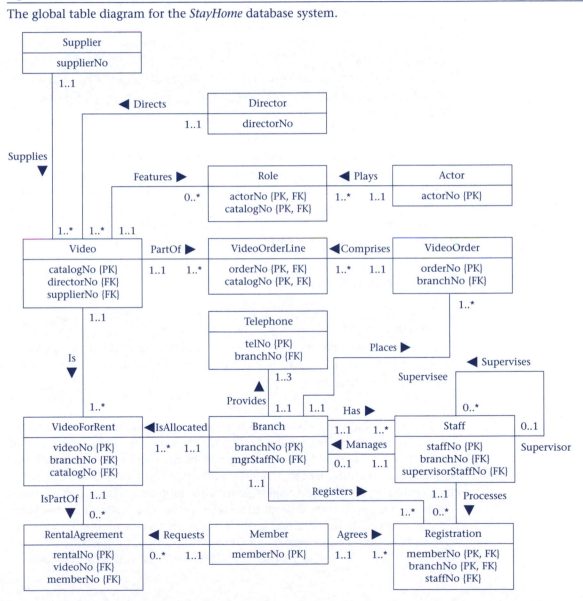

Update the documentation

Update the documentation to reflect any changes made during the development of the global data model. It's very important that the documentation is up to date and reflects the current data model. If changes are made to the model subsequently, either during database implementation or during maintenance, then the documentation should be updated at the same time. Out-of-date information will cause considerable confusion at a later time.

Step 2.6.2 Check global logical data model

> **Objective**
> To check the tables created from the global logical data model are appropriately structured using normalization and support the required transactions, if necessary.

In this step you check the structure of the tables created for the global data model using normalization and also check that these tables are capable of supporting all user transactions, as you did in Steps 2.2 and 2.3 covered in Chapter 10. However, you need only check those areas of the model that resulted in any change during the merging process. In a large system, this will significantly reduce the amount of rechecking that needs to be performed.

Step 2.6.3 Check for future growth

> **Objective**
> To determine whether there are any significant changes likely in the foreseeable future and to assess whether the global logical data model can accommodate these changes.

It's important that the global logical data model can be easily expanded. If the model can sustain current requirements only, then the life of the model may be relatively short and significant reworking may be necessary to accommodate new requirements. It's important to develop a model that is *extensible*, and has the ability to evolve to support new requirements with minimal effect on existing users. Of course, this can be very difficult to achieve, as the organization may not know what it wants to do in the future. Even if it does, it may be prohibitively expensive in both time and money to accommodate possible future enhancements now. Therefore, you may have to be very selective in what you accommodate.

Step 2.6.4 Review global logical data model with users

> **Objective**
> To ensure that the global logical data model is a true representation of the data requirements of the organization.

The global logical data model for the organization should now be complete and accurate. The model and the documentation that describes the model should be reviewed with the users to ensure that it's a true representation of the data requirements of the organization.

You are now ready to translate the logical design into a physical design. This is covered in Steps 3 to 8 of the methodology, which we describe in Chapters 12 to 16.

Appendix summary

✓ Step 2.6 of Step 2 of the logical database design methodology is optional and only required when creating a reasonably complex database system with multiple and varied user views that are to be managed using the **view integration** approach.

Appendix D

File organizations and indexes

In this appendix you will learn:

- The distinction between primary and secondary storage.
- The meanings of file organization and access method.
- How heap files are organized.
- How sequential files are organized.
- How hash files are organized.
- What an index is and how it can be used to speed up database retrievals.
- The distinction between primary, secondary, and clustered indexes.
- How multilevel indexes are organized.
- How B^+-Trees are organized.
- How bitmap indexes are organized.
- How join indexes are organized.
- How to select an appropriate file organization.
- How indexed clusters and hash clusters are organized.

Steps 4.2 and 4.3 of the physical database design methodology presented in Chapter 13 concern the selection of appropriate file organizations and indexes for the base tables that have been created to represent the data requirements of the organization (or the part of the organization) being modeled. In this appendix, we introduce the main concepts regarding the physical storage of the database on **secondary storage** devices such as magnetic disks and optical disks. The computer's **primary storage**, that is main memory, is inappropriate for storing the database. Although the access times for primary storage are much faster than secondary storage, primary storage is not large or reliable enough to store the quantity of data that a typical database might require. As the data stored in primary storage disappears when power is lost, we refer to primary storage as **volatile** storage. In contrast, the data on secondary storage persists through power loss, and is consequently referred to as **non-volatile** storage. Further, the cost of storage per unit of data is an order of magnitude greater for primary storage than for disk.

In the following section we introduce the basic concepts of physical storage and then discuss the main types of file organization, namely heap (unsorted), sequential (sorted), and hash files. In Section D.5, we discuss how indexes can be used to improve the performance of database retrievals. In particular, we look at multilevel indexes, B+-Trees, bitmap indexes, and join indexes. The examples in this appendix are drawn from the *StayHome* case study introduced in Section 6.4.4.

D.1 Basic concepts

The database on secondary storage is organized into one or more *files*, where each file consists of one or more *records* and each record consists of one or more *fields*. Typically, a record corresponds to an entity occurrence and a field to an attribute/column. Consider the Staff table from the *StayHome* case study shown in Figure D.1.

We may expect each record in this table to map onto a record in the operating system file that holds the Staff table. Each field in a record would store one column from the Staff table. When you request a record from the DBMS, for example Staff record S0003, the DBMS maps this *logical record* onto a *physical record* and retrieves the physical record into the DBMS *buffers* in primary storage using the operating system file access routines.

staffNo	name	position	salary	branchNo
S1500	Tom Daniels	Manager	46000	B001
S0003	Sally Adams	Assistant	30000	B001
S0010	Mary Martinez	Manager	50000	B002
S3250	Robert Chin	Supervisor	32000	B002
S2250	Sally Stern	Manager	48000	B004
S0415	Art Peters	Manager	41000	B003

Figure D.1

Staff table from the *StayHome* case study.

The physical record is the unit of transfer between disk and primary storage, and vice versa. Generally, a physical record consists of more than one logical record although, depending on size, a logical record may correspond to one physical record. It is even possible for a large logical record to span more than one physical record. The terms 'block' and 'page' are generally used in place of physical record. In the remainder of this appendix we use the term 'page'. For example, the Staff records in Figure D.1 may be stored on two pages, as shown in Figure D.2.

The order in which records are stored and accessed in the file is dependent on the *file organization*:

File organization

A way of arranging the records in a file when the file is stored on disk.

The main types of file organization are:

- *Heap (unordered) files* Records are placed on disk in no particular order.
- *Sequential (sorted) files* Records are ordered by the value of a specified field.
- *Hash files* Records are placed on disk according to a hash function.

Along with a file organization, there is a set of *access methods*:

Access method

The steps involved in storing and retrieving records from a file.

Since some access methods can be applied only to certain file organizations (for example, we cannot apply an indexed access method to a file without an index), the terms file organization and access method are used interchangeably. In the remainder of this appendix, we discuss the main types of file organization and provide guidelines for choosing appropriate file organizations.

Figure D.2

Storage of the Staff table in pages.

staffNo	name	position	salary	branchNo	Page
S1500	Tom Daniels	Manager	46000	B001	1
S0003	Sally Adams	Assistant	30000	B001	
S0010	Mary Martinez	Manager	50000	B002	
S3250	Robert Chin	Supervisor	32000	B002	
S2250	Sally Stern	Manager	48000	B004	2
S0415	Art Peters	Manager	41000	B003	

D.2 Heap files

An *unordered file*, sometimes called a *heap file*, is the simplest type of file organization. Records are placed in the file in the same order as they are inserted. A new record is inserted in the last page of the file; if there is insufficient space in the last page, a new page is added to the file. This makes insertion very efficient. However, as a heap file has no particular ordering with respect to field values, a *linear search* must be performed to access a record. A linear search involves reading pages from the file until the required record is found. This makes retrievals from heap files that have more than a few pages relatively slow, unless the retrieval involves a large proportion of the records in the file.

To delete a record, the required page first has to be retrieved, the record marked as deleted, and the page written back to disk. The space with deleted records is not reused. Consequently, performance progressively deteriorates as deletions occur. This means that heap files have to be periodically reorganized by the Database Administrator (DBA) to reclaim the unused space of deleted records.

Heap files are one of the best organizations for bulk loading data into a table, as records are inserted at the end of the sequence; there is no overhead incurred in calculating what page the record should go on.

D.3 Ordered files

The records in a file can be sorted on the values of one or more of the fields, forming a key-sequenced data set. The field(s) that the file is sorted on is called the *ordering field*. If the ordering field is also a key field of the file, and therefore guaranteed to have a unique value in each record, the field is also called the *ordering key* for the file. For example, consider the following SQL query:

SELECT *
FROM Staff
ORDER BY staffNo;

If the records of the Staff table are already ordered according to the ordering column staffNo, it should be possible to reduce the execution time for the query, as no sorting is necessary.

Keys defined in
Section 2.2.3

Although in Section 2.2 we stated that records in the relational model are unordered, this applies as an external (logical) property not as an implementational (physical) property. There will always be a first record, second record, and *n*th record.

If the records are ordered on staffNo, under certain conditions we can use a *binary search* to execute queries that involve a search condition based on staffNo. For example, consider the following SQL query:

SELECT *
FROM Staff
WHERE staffNo = 'S1500';

If we use the sample records shown in Figure D.1 and for simplicity assume there is one record per page, we would get the ordered file shown in Figure D.3. The binary search proceeds as follows:

(1) Retrieve the mid-page of the file. Check whether the required record is between the first and last record of this page. If so, the required record lies in this page and no more pages need to be retrieved.

(2) If the value of the key field in the first record on the page is greater than the required value, the required value (if it exists) occurs on an earlier page. Therefore, we repeat the above steps using the lower half of the file as the new search area.

(3) If the value of the key field in the last record on the page is less than the required value, the required value occurs on a later page, and so we repeat the above steps using the top half of the file as the new search area. In this way, half the search space is eliminated from the search with each page retrieved.

In our case, the middle page is page 3, and the record on the retrieved page (S0415) does not equal the one we want (S1500). The value of the key field in page 3 is less than the one we want, so we can discard the first half of the file from the search. We now retrieve the mid-page of the top half of the file, that is page 5. This time the value of the key field (S2250) is greater than S1500, which enables us to discard the top half of this search space. We now retrieve the mid-page of the remaining search space (page 4), which is the record we want.

Figure D.3

Binary search on ordered Staff file.

Page	staffNo	name	position	salary	branchNo
1	S0003	Sally Adams	Assistant	30000	B001
2	S0010	Mary Martinez	Manager	50000	B002
3	S0415	Art Peters	Manager	41000	B003
4	S1500	Tom Daniels	Manager	46000	B001
5	S2250	Sally Stern	Manager	48000	B004
6	S3250	Robert Chin	Supervisor	32000	B002

In general, the binary search is more efficient than a linear search. However, binary search is applied more frequently to data in primary storage than secondary storage.

Inserting and deleting records in a sorted file is problematic because the order of records has to be maintained. To insert a new record, we must find the correct position in the ordering for the record and then find space to insert it. If there is sufficient space in the required page for the new record, then the single page can be reordered and written back to disk. If this is not the case, then it would be necessary to move one or more records onto the next page. Again, the next page may have no free space and the records on this page must be moved, and so on.

Inserting a record near the start of a large file could be very time-consuming. One solution is to create a temporary unsorted file, called an *overflow file*. Insertions are added to the overflow file and, periodically, the overflow file is merged with the main sorted file. This makes insertions very efficient, but has a detrimental effect on retrievals. If the record is not found during the binary search, the overflow file has to be searched linearly. Inversely, to delete a record we must reorganize the records to remove the now free slot.

Ordered files are rarely used for database storage unless a primary index is added to the file (see Section D.5.1).

D.4 Hash files

In a hash file, records do not have to be written sequentially to the file. Instead, a *hash function* calculates the address of the page in which the record is to be stored based on the values of one or more of the fields in the record. The base field is called the *hash field*, or if the field is also a key field of the file, it is called the *hash key*. Records in a hash file will appear to be randomly distributed across the available file space. For this reason, hash files are sometimes called *random*, or *direct*, files.

The hash function is chosen so that records are as evenly distributed as possible throughout the file. One technique, called *division–remainder hashing*, uses the MOD function, which takes the field value, divides it by some predetermined integer value, and uses the remainder of this division as the disk address.

The problem with most hashing functions is that they do not guarantee a unique address because the number of possible values a hash field can take is typically much larger than the number of available addresses for records. Each address generated by a hashing function corresponds to a page, or *bucket*, with *slots* for multiple records. Within a bucket, records are placed in order of arrival. When the same address is generated for two or more records, a *collision* is said to have occurred and we must insert the second record in another position. Collision management complicates hash file management and degrades overall performance.

D.5   Indexes

In this section, we discuss techniques for making the retrieval of data more efficient using **indexes**.

> **Index**
>
> A data structure that allows the DBMS to locate particular records in a file more quickly, and thereby speed up response to user queries.

An index in a database is similar to an index in a book. It is an auxiliary structure associated with a file that can be referred to when searching for an item of information, just like searching the index of a book, in which you look up a keyword and get a list of one of more pages the keyword appears on. An index prevents you from having to scan sequentially through the file each time you want to find the item. In the case of database indexes, the required item will be one or more records in a file. As in the book index analogy, the index is ordered, and each index entry contains the item required and one or more locations (record identifiers) where the item can be found.

While indexes are not strictly necessary to use the DBMS, they can have a significant impact on performance. As with the book index, you could find the desired keyword by looking through the entire book, but this would be tedious and time-consuming. Having an index at the back of the book in alphabetical order of keyword allows you to go directly to the page or pages you want.

An index structure is associated with a particular search key, and contains records consisting of the key value and the address of the logical record in the file containing the key value. The file containing the logical records is called the *datafile* and the file containing the index records is called the *index file*. The values in the index file are ordered according to the *indexing field*, which is usually based on a single column.

D.5.1   Types of indexes

There are different types of indexes, the main ones being:

Primary index   The datafile is sequentially ordered by an ordering key field (see Section D.3), and the indexing field is built on the ordering key field, which is guaranteed to have a unique value in each record.

Clustering index   The datafile is sequentially ordered on a nonkey field, and the indexing field is built on this nonkey field, so that there can be more than one record corresponding to a value of the indexing field. The nonkey field is called a *clustering field*.

Secondary index   An index that is defined on a non-ordering field of the datafile.

A file can have *at most* one primary index or one clustering index, and in addition can have several secondary indexes. In addition, an index can be *sparse* or *dense*: a sparse index has an index record for only some of the search key values in the file; a dense index has an index record for every search key value in the file.

The search key for an index can consist of one or more fields. Figure D.4 looks at four dense indexes on the (reduced) Staff table: one based on the salary column, one based on the branchNo column, one based on the composite index (salary, branchNo), and one based on the composite index (branchNo, salary).

D.5.2 Secondary indexes

A secondary index is also an ordered file similar to a primary index. However, whereas the datafile associated with a primary index is sorted on the index key, the datafile associated with a secondary index may not be sorted on the indexing key. Further, the secondary index key need not contain unique values, unlike a primary index. For example, we may wish to create a secondary index on the branchNo column of the Staff table. From Figure D.1, we can see that the values in the branchNo column are not unique.

Secondary indexes improve the performance of queries that use columns other than the primary key. However, the improvement to queries has to be balanced against the overhead involved in maintaining the indexes while the database is being updated. This is part of physical database design and was discussed in Chapter 13.

Figure D.4

Indexes on the Staff table: (a) (salary, branchNo) and salary; (b) (branchNo, salary) and branchNo.

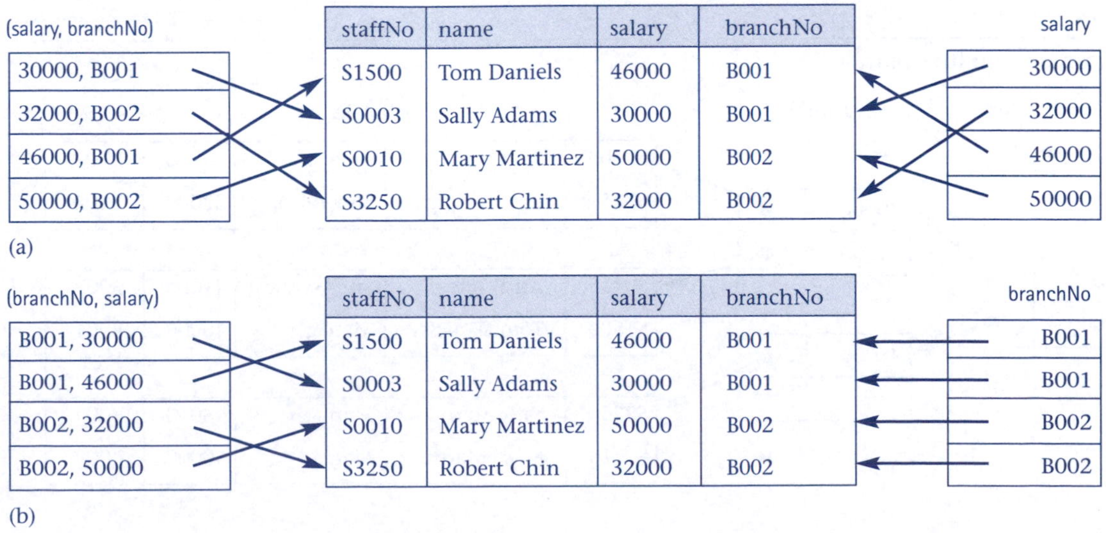

(a)

(b)

D.5.3 Multilevel indexes

Consider again the Staff table, this time sorted on the salary column, and the query 'Find all staff with a salary between $32,000 and $45,000'. We have already noted that if the file is ordered, we can perform a binary search to find the first record and then a sequential scan from that point on to find the remaining qualifying records. However, if the Staff file is large, the initial binary search could be quite slow.

One method to overcome this is to create an index file based on the salary column. If the index contains an entry for the first value of the salary column on each page of the datafile, we could then perform a binary search on the index file to find the page containing the first salary value greater than $32,000.

However, when the index file becomes large and extends over many pages, the search time for the required index increases. A *multilevel index* attempts to overcome this problem by reducing the search range. It does this by treating the index like any other file, splits the index into a number of smaller indexes, and maintains an index to the indexes. Figure D.5 shows an example of a two-level (sparse) index for the Staff table of Figure D.1. Each page in the datafile can store two records. For illustration, there are also two index records per page, although in practice there would be many index records per page. Each index record stores an access key (salary) value and a page address. The stored access key value is the first in the addressed page.

To locate the records we require, we start from the second-level index and search the page for the last access key value that is less than or equal to 32 000, in our case 30 000. This record contains an address to the first-level index page to continue the search. Repeating the above process leads to page 1 in the data-

Figure D.5

Example of multilevel index.

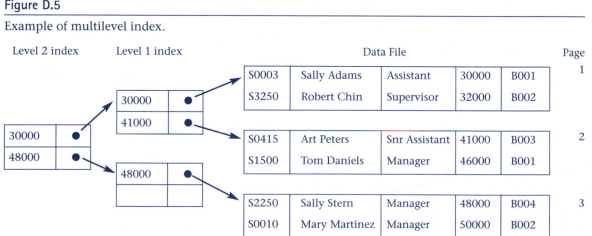

file, where the first record is stored. We can now find the remaining qualifying records by reading serially through the datafile.

IBM's Indexed Sequential Access Method (ISAM) is based on a two-level index structure. Insertion is handled by overflow pages, as discussed in Section D.3. In general, an n-level index can be built, although three levels are common in practice; a file would have to be very large to require more than three levels. In the following section, we discuss a particular type of multilevel dense index called a B+-Tree.

D.5.4   B+–Trees

The major disadvantage of ISAM is that as the database grows, performance deteriorates rapidly due to overflows and so the DBA needs to periodically reorganize the index. Reorganization not only is expensive but makes the file unavailable while it takes place. The B+-Tree structure overcomes this problem by splitting a node whenever it overflows.

A B+-Tree is a special type of multilevel index in which the number of levels from the top of the tree (called the *root node*) to the bottom of the tree (called the *leaf nodes*) are the same; in other words, the tree is *balanced*. The leaf nodes contain pointers to the records of the table, rather than the records themselves.

A B+-Tree always takes approximately the same time to access any data record by ensuring that the same number of nodes is searched: in other words, by ensuring that the tree has a constant depth. Being a dense index, every record is addressed by the index so there is no requirement for the datafile to be sorted. However, balancing can be costly to maintain as the tree contents are updated.

In practice, each node in the tree is actually a page, so we can generally store several key values on the same page. For example, if we assume that a page has 4096 bytes and the key field and its associated pointer requires 4 bytes of storage, and each page has a 4-byte pointer to the next node on the same level, we could store $(4096 - 4)/(4 + 4) = 511$ index records per page. The root can store 511 records and can have 512 children. Each child can also store 511 records, giving a total of 261 632 records. Each child can also have 512 children, giving a total of 262 144 children on level 2 of the tree. Each of these children can have 511 records giving a total of 133 955 584. This gives a theoretical maximum number of index records as:

root:	511
Level 1:	261 632
Level 2:	133 955 584
TOTAL	134 217 727

Thus, we can randomly access one record in the file containing 134 217 727 records within four disk accesses (in fact, the root is normally stored in main memory, so there is one less disk access). In practice, however, the number of records held in each page would be smaller as not all pages would be full.

D.5.5 Bitmap indexes

Another type of index that is becoming increasingly popular, particularly in data warehousing, is the *bitmap index*. Bitmap indexes are generally used on columns that have a sparse domain (that is, the domain contains a relatively low number of possible values). Rather than storing the actual value of the column, the bitmap index stores a *bit vector* for each column indicating which records contain this particular domain value. Each bit that is set to 1 in the bitmap corresponds to a row identifier. If the number of different domain values is small, then bitmap indexes are very space efficient.

For example, consider the Video table shown in Figure D.6(a). Let's assume that the category column can take only one of the values present (that is, Action, Children, Fantasy, or Sci-Fi) and similarly let's assume that the dailyRental column can take only one of the values present (that is, $4.00, $4.50, or $5.00). We could construct bitmap indexes to represent these two columns as shown in Figure D.6(b).

Bitmap indexes provide two important advantages over B+-tree indexes.

Figure D.6:
(a) Video table;
(b) bitmap indexes on the category and dailyRental columns.

catalogNo	title	category	dailyRental	price	directorNo
207132	Die Another Day	Action	5.00	21.99	D1001
902355	Harry Potter	Children	4.50	14.50	D7834
330553	Lord of the Rings	Fantasy	5.00	31.99	D4576
781132	Shrek	Children	4.00	18.50	D0078
445624	Men in Black II	Action	4.00	29.99	D5743
634817	Independence Day	Sci-Fi	4.50	32.99	D3765

(a)

Action	Children	Fantasy	Sci-Fi
1	0	0	0
0	1	0	0
0	0	1	0
0	1	0	0
1	0	0	0
0	0	0	1

4.00	4.50	5.00
0	0	1
0	1	0
0	0	1
1	0	0
1	0	0
0	1	0

(b)

First, they can be more compact than B[+]-tree indexes requiring less storage space and they lend themselves to compression techniques. Second, bitmap indexes can provide significant performance improvements when the query involves multiple predicates each with its own bitmap index. For example, consider the query:

SELECT catalogNo, title
FROM Video
WHERE category = 'Fantasy' **AND** dailyRental = 5.00;

In this case, we can take the third bit vector for category and perform a bitwise AND with third bit vector for dailyRental to obtain a bit vector that has a 1 for every Fantasy video with a daily rental rate of $5.00.

D.5.6 Join indexes

Another type of index that is becoming increasingly popular, again particularly in data warehousing, is the *join index*. A join index is an index on columns from two or more tables that come from the same domain. For example, consider the extended Branch and Member tables shown in Figure D.7(a). We could create a join index on the nonkey city column to generate the index table shown in Figure D.7(b). We've chosen to sort the join index on the BranchRowID but it could have been sorted on any of the three columns. Sometimes two join indexes are created, one as shown and one with the two rowID columns reversed.

This type of query could be common in data warehousing applications where we're attempting to find out facts about related pieces of data (in this case, we're attempting to find how many members come from a city that has an existing branch). The index join precomputes the join of the Branch and Member tables based on the city column, thereby removing the need to perform the join each time the query is run, and improving the performance of the query. This could be particularly important if the query has a high frequency. Oracle combines the bitmap index and the join index to provide a *bitmap join index*.

D.6 Guidelines for selecting file organizations

As an aid to understanding file organizations more fully, in this section we provide guidelines for selecting a file organization based on the following types of files:

■ heap
■ hash
■ Indexed Sequential Access Method (ISAM)
■ B[+]-Tree.

Figure D.7

(a) Branch and Member tables; (b) join index on the nonkey city column.

Branch

rowID	branchNo	street	city	state	zipCode	mgrStaffNo
20001	B001	8 Jefferson Way	Portland	OR	97201	S1500
20002	B002	City Center Plaza	Seattle	WA	98122	S0010
20003	B003	14 – 8th Avenue	New York	NY	10012	S0415
20004	B004	16 – 14th Avenue	Seattle	WA	98128	S2250
20005	...					

Member

rowID	memberNo	fName	lName	street	city	state	zipCode
30001	M250178	Bob	Adams	57 – 11th Avenue	Seattle	WA	98105
30002	M166884	Art	Peters	89 Redmond Rd	Portland	OR	97117
30003	M115656	Serena	Parker	22 W. Capital Way	Portland	OR	97201
30004	M284354	Don	Nelson	123 Suffolk Lane	Seattle	WA	98117
30005	...						

(a)

Join Index

branchRowID	memberRowID	city
20001	30002	Portland
20001	30003	Portland
20002	30001	Seattle
20002	30004	Seattle
20004	30001	Seattle
20004	30004	Seattle
20005	...	

(b)

Heap (unsorted)

Heap is a good storage structure in the following situations:

(1) When data is being bulk-loaded into the table. For example, you may want to insert a batch of records into a table after it has been created. If you choose heap as the initial file organization, it may be more efficient to restructure the file after you've completed the insertions.

(2) The table is only a few pages long. In this case, the time to locate any record is short, even if the entire table has to be searched sequentially.

(3) When every record in the table has to be retrieved (in any order) every time the table is accessed. For example, retrieve the addresses of all members of *StayHome*.

(4) When the table has an additional access structure, such as an index key, heap storage can be used to conserve space.

Heap files are inappropriate when only selected records of a table are to be accessed.

Hash

Hash is a good storage structure when records are retrieved based on an exact match on the hash field value, particularly if the access order is random. For example, if the Member table is hashed on memberNo, retrieval of the record with memberNo equal to M250178 is efficient. However, hash is not a good storage structure in the following situations:

(1) When records are retrieved based on a pattern match of the hash field value. For example, retrieve all members whose member number (memberNo) begins with the characters 'M2'.

(2) When records are retrieved based on a range of values for the hash field. For example, retrieve all members with a member number between 'M200000' and 'M200100'.

(3) When records are retrieved based on a column other than the hash column. For example, if the Member table is hashed on memberNo, then hashing could not be used to search for a record based on the lName column. In this case, it would be necessary to perform a linear search to find the record, or add lName as a secondary index.

(4) When records are retrieved based on only part of the hash field. For example, if the Role table is hashed on catalogNo and actorNo, then hashing could not be used to search for a record based on the catalogNo column alone. Again, it would be necessary to perform a linear search to find the record.

(5) When the hash column is frequently updated. When a hash column is updated, the DBMS must delete the entire record and possibly relocate it to a new address (if the hash function results in a new address). Thus, frequent updating of the hash column impacts performance.

Indexed Sequential Access Method (ISAM)

ISAM is a more versatile storage structure than hash; it supports retrievals based on exact key match, pattern matching, range of values, and part key specification. However, the ISAM index is static, created when the file is created. Thus, you'll find that the performance of an ISAM file deteriorates as the table is updated. Updates also cause an ISAM file to lose the access key sequence, so that retrievals in order of the access key will become slower. These two problems are overcome by the B⁺-Tree file organization.

B⁺-Tree

Again, B⁺-Tree is a more versatile storage structure than hashing. It supports retrievals based on exact key match, pattern matching, range of values, and part key specification. The B⁺-Tree index is dynamic, growing as the table grows. Thus, unlike ISAM, the performance of a B⁺-Tree file does not deteriorate as the table is updated. The B⁺-Tree also maintains the order of the access key even when the file is updated, so retrieval of records in the order of the access key is more efficient than ISAM. However, if the table is not frequently updated, the ISAM structure may be more efficient as it has one less level of index than the B⁺-Tree, whose leaf nodes contain pointers to the actual records of the table rather than the actual records themselves.

D.7   Clustered and non–clustered tables

Some DBMSs, such as Oracle, support *clustered* and *non-clustered* tables. The choice of whether to use a clustered or non-clustered table depends on the analysis of the transactions undertaken previously, but the choice can have an impact on performance. In this section, we briefly examine both types of structures and provide guidelines for the use of clustered tables.

Clusters are groups of one or more tables physically stored together because they share common columns and are often used together. With related records being physically stored together, disk access time is improved. The related columns of the tables in a cluster are called the *cluster key*. The cluster key is stored only once, and so clusters store a set of tables more efficiently than if the tables were stored individually (not clustered).

Figure D.8 illustrates how the Branch and Staff tables would be stored if we clustered the tables based on the column branchNo. When these two tables are clustered, each unique branchNo value is stored only once, in the cluster key. To each branchNo value are attached the columns from both these tables.

As we now discuss, Oracle supports two types of clusters: indexed clusters and hash clusters.

D.7.1 Indexed clusters

In an indexed cluster, records with the same cluster key are stored together. Oracle suggests using indexed clusters when:

- queries retrieve records over a range of cluster key values;
- clustered tables may grow unpredictably.

Clusters can improve performance of data retrieval, depending on the data distribution and what SQL operations are most often performed on the data. In particular, tables that are joined in a query benefit from the use of clusters because the records common to the joined tables are retrieved with the same I/O operation.

To create an indexed cluster in Oracle called BranchIndexedCluster with the cluster key column branchNo, we could use the following SQL statement:

CREATE CLUSTER BranchIndexedCluster
    (branchNo **CHAR**(4))
SIZE 512
STORAGE (INITIAL 100K **NEXT** 50K **PCTINCREASE** 10);

Figure D.8

How the Branch and Staff tables would be stored clustered on branchNo.

street	city	state	zipCode	mgrStaffNo	branchNo	staffNo	name	position	salary
8 Jefferson Way	Portland	OR	97201	S1500	B001	S1500	Tom Daniels	Manager	46000
						S0003	Sally Adams	Assistant	30000
City Center Plaza	Seattle	WA	98122	S0010	B002	S0010	Mary Martinez	Manager	50000
						S3250	Robert Chin	Supervisor	32000
...									

Branch table   Cluster key   Staff table

The SIZE parameter specifies the amount of space (in bytes) to store all records with the same cluster key value. The size is optional and, if omitted, Oracle reserves one data block for each cluster key value. The INITIAL parameter specifies the size (in bytes) of the cluster's first extent, and the NEXT parameter specifies the size (in bytes) of the next extent to be allocated. The PCTIN-CREASE parameter specifies the percentage by which the third and subsequent extents grow over the preceding extent (default 50). In our example, we have specified that each subsequent extent should be 10 percent larger than the preceding extent.

Once the hash cluster has been created, we can create the tables that will be part of the structure. For example:

CREATE TABLE Branch
(branchNo **CHAR**(4) **PRIMARY KEY**,
...)
CLUSTER BranchIndexedCluster (branchNo);

Guidelines for using indexed clusters

You may find the following guidelines helpful when deciding whether to cluster tables:

- Consider clustering tables that are often accessed in join statements.

- Do not cluster tables if they are joined only occasionally or their common column values are modified frequently. (Modifying a record's cluster key value takes longer than modifying the value in an unclustered table, because Oracle may have to migrate the modified record to another block to maintain the cluster.)

- Do not cluster tables if a full search of one of the tables is often required. (A full search of a clustered table can take longer than a full search of an unclustered table. Oracle is likely to read more blocks because the tables are stored together.)

1:* relationships defined in Section 7.5.2

- Consider clustering tables involved in one-to-many (1:*) relationships if you often select a record from the parent table and then the corresponding records from the child table. (Child records are stored in the same data block(s) as the parent record, so they are likely to be in memory when you select them, requiring Oracle to perform less I/O.)

- Consider storing a child table alone in a cluster if you often select many child records of the same parent. (This measure improves the performance of queries that select child records of the same parent but does not decrease the performance of a full search of the parent table.)

■ Do not cluster tables if the data from all tables with the same cluster key value exceeds more than one or two Oracle blocks. (To access a record in a clustered table, Oracle reads all blocks containing records with that value. If these records occupy multiple blocks, accessing a single record could require more reads than accessing the same record in an unclustered table.)

D.7.2 Hash clusters

Hash clusters also cluster table data in a manner similar to index clusters. However, a record is stored in a hash cluster based on the result of applying a hash function to the record's cluster key value. All records with the same hash key value are stored together on disk. Oracle suggests using hash clusters when:

■ queries retrieve records based on equality conditions involving all cluster key columns (for example, return all records for branch B001);

■ clustered tables are static or we can determine the maximum number of records and the maximum amount of space required by the cluster when it is created.

To create a hash cluster in Oracle called BranchHashCluster clustered by the column branchNo, we could use the following SQL statement:

```
CREATE CLUSTER BranchHashCluster
  (branchNo CHAR(4))
  HASH IS branchNo HASHKEYS 5000;
```

Guidelines for using hash clusters

You may find the following guidelines helpful when deciding whether to use hash clusters:

■ Consider using hash clusters to store tables that are frequently accessed using a search clause containing equality conditions with the same column(s). Designate these column(s) as the cluster key.

■ Store a table in a hash cluster if you can determine how much space is required to hold all records with a given cluster key value, both now and in the future.

■ Do not use hash clusters if space is scarce and you cannot afford to allocate additional space for records to be inserted in the future.

■ Do not use a hash cluster to store a constantly growing table if the process of occasionally creating a new, larger hash cluster to hold that table is impractical.

■ Do not store a table in a hash cluster if a search of the entire table is often required and you must allocate a significant amount of space to the hash cluster in anticipation of the table growing. (Such full searches must read all blocks allocated to the hash cluster, even though some blocks may contain few records. Storing the table alone would reduce the number of blocks read by a full table search.)

■ Do not store a table in a hash cluster if your application frequently modifies the cluster key values.

■ Storing a single table in a hash cluster can be useful, regardless of whether the table is often joined with other tables, provided that hashing is appropriate for the table based on the previous guidelines.

Appendix summary

✓ **Heap** files are good for inserting a large number of records into the file. They are inappropriate when only selected records are to be retrieved.

✓ **Hash** files are good when retrieval is based on an exact key match. They are not good when retrieval is based on pattern matching, range of values, part keys, or when retrieval is based on a column other than the hash field.

✓ **ISAM** is more versatile than hashing, supporting retrievals based on exact key match, pattern matching, range of values, and part key specification. However, the ISAM index is static and so performance deteriorates as the table is updated. Updates also cause the ISAM file to lose the access key sequence, so that retrievals in order of the access key become slower.

✓ These two problems are overcome by the **B$^+$-Tree** file organization, which has a dynamic index. If a table is not frequently updated or not very large nor likely to be, the ISAM structure may be more efficient as it has one less level of index than the B$^+$-Tree, whose leaf nodes contain record pointers.

✓ **Secondary indexes** provide a mechanism for specifying an additional key for a base table that can be used to retrieve data more efficiently. However, there is an overhead involved in the maintenance and use of secondary indexes that has to be balanced against the performance improvement gained when retrieving data.

✓ **Clusters** are groups of one or more tables physically stored together because they share common columns and are often used together. With related records being physically stored together, disk access time is improved. The related columns of the tables in a cluster are called the

cluster key. The cluster key is stored only once, and so clusters store a set of tables more efficiently than if the tables were stored individually (not clustered). Oracle supports two types of clusters: indexed clusters and hash clusters.

Appendix E

Common data models

In this appendix you will learn:

➤ More about building logical data models.

➤ About common logical data models.

In this appendix, we introduce some common data models that you may find useful. In fact, it has been estimated that one-third of a data model consists of common constructs that are applicable to most companies and the remaining two-thirds are either industry-specific or company-specific. Thus, most data modeling work is re-creating constructs that have already been produced many times before in other companies.

The two mains aims of this appendix therefore are to provide you with:

(1) additional knowledge of building data models;

(2) data model templates that you may find useful in your business. The models featured here may not represent your company exactly, but they may provide a starting point from which you can develop a more suitable model that matches your company's specific requirements.

We provide models for the following common business areas:

■ Customer order entry

■ Inventory control

■ Asset management

■ Project management

■ Course management

■ Human resource management

■ Payroll management.

We also provide the following data models which are less common but may still be useful from both a business perspective and a learning perspective:

■ Vehicle rentals

■ Student accommodation

■ Client transportation

■ Publisher printing

■ County library

■ Real estate rentals

■ Travel agent

■ Student results.

In each case, we provide a short description of the requirements, and show an example of a typical logical data model and the mapping of the model to a set of tables. We assume that you are familiar with the modeling notation used throughout this book. If you are not, look at Chapter 7 on ER modeling, which introduces the main concepts and notations we use in this appendix. You will also find a summary of the database design methodology in Appendix B.

E.1 Customer order entry

A company wishes to create a database for its order entry activities. A customer can place one or more orders, with each order for one or more products. Each order gives rise to one invoice, which can be paid by a number of methods, such as check, credit card, or cash. The name of the employee who initially processes the customer order is recorded.

An employee in the Shipping Department is responsible for packaging the order and sending it to the customer. If an ordered product is not in stock, Shipping send out what is in stock, so more than one shipment may be required to fulfill the order. The logical data model is shown in Figure E.1 and the associated tables in Figure E.2.

Figure E.1

Logical data model for customer order entry.

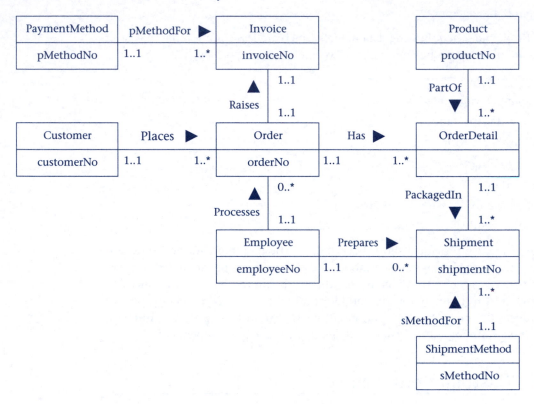

Figure E.2

Tables for customer order entry.

Customer	(<u>customerNo</u>, customerName, customerStreet, customerCity, customerState, customerZipCode, custTelNo, custFaxNo, DOB, maritalStatus, creditRating) Primary Key customerNo Alternate Key custTelNo Alternate Key custFaxNo
Employee	(<u>employeeNo</u>, title, firstName, middleName, lastName, address, workTelExt, homeTelNo, empEmailAddress, socialSecurityNumber, DOB, position, sex, salary, dateStarted) Primary Key employeeNo Alternate Key socialSecurityNumber
Invoice	(<u>invoiceNo</u>, dateRaised, datePaid, creditCardNo, holdersName, expiryDate, orderNo, pMethodNo) Primary Key invoiceNo Foreign Key orderNo references Order(orderNo) Foreign Key pMethodNo references PaymentMethod(pMethodNo)
Order	(<u>orderNo</u>, orderDate, billingStreet, billingCity, billingState, billingZipCode, promisedDate, status, customerNo, employeeNo) Primary Key orderNo Foreign Key customerNo references Customer(customerNo) Foreign Key employeeNo references Employee(employeeNo)
OrderDetail	(<u>orderNo</u>, <u>productNo</u>, quantityOrdered) Primary Key orderNo, productNo Foreign Key orderNo references Order(orderNo) Foreign Key productNo references Product(productNo)
PaymentMethod	(<u>pMethodNo</u>, paymentMethod) Primary Key pMethodNo
Product	(<u>productNo</u>, productName, serialNo, unitPrice, quantityOnHand, reorderLevel, reorderQuantity, reorderLeadTime) Primary Key productNo Alternate Key serialNo
Shipment	(<u>shipmentNo</u>, quantity, shipmentDate, completeStatus, orderNo, productNo, employeeNo, sMethodNo) Primary Key shipmentNo Foreign Key orderNo, productNo references OrderDetail(orderNo, productNo) Foreign Key employeeNo references Employee(employeeNo) Foreign Key sMethodNo references ShipmentMethod(sMethodNo)
ShipmentMethod	(<u>sMethodNo</u>, shipmentMethod) Primary Key sMethodNo

E.2   Inventory control

A company wishes to create a database to control its inventory, which consists of a number of products divided into a number of categories, such as clothing, food, and stationery. An employee raises a purchase order when a product has to be reordered from the supplier. The tracking records supplies received, units sold, and any wastage. The logical data model is shown in Figure E.3 and the associated tables in Figure E.4.

Figure E.3

Logical data model for inventory control.

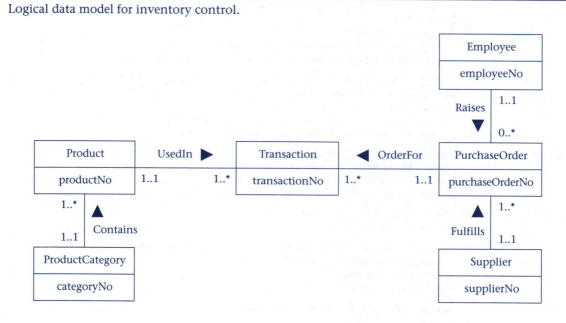

Figure E.4

Tables for inventory control.

Employee	As defined in Section D.1.2
Product	(<u>productNo</u>, productName, serialNo, unitPrice, quantityOnHand, reorderLevel, reorderQuantity, reorderLeadTime, categoryNo) Primary Key productNo Alternate Key serialNo Foreign Key categoryNo references ProductCategory(categoryNo)
ProductCategory	(<u>categoryNo</u>, categoryDescription) Primary Key categoryNo
PurchaseOrder	(<u>purchaseOrderNo</u>, purchaseOrderDescription, orderDate, dateRequired, shippedDate, freightCharge, supplierNo, employeeNo) Primary Key purchaseOrderNo Foreign Key supplierNo references Supplier(supplierNo) Foreign Key employeeNo references Employee(employeeNo)
Supplier	(<u>supplierNo</u>, supplierName, supplierStreet, supplierCity, supplierState, supplierZipCode, suppTelNo, suppFaxNo, suppEmailAddress, suppWebAddress, contactName, contactTelNo, contactFaxNo, contactEmailAddress, paymentTerms) Primary Key supplierNo Alternate Key supplierName Alternate Key suppTelNo Alternate Key suppFaxNo
Transaction	(<u>transactionNo</u>, transactionDate, transactionDescription, unitPrice, unitsOrdered, unitsReceived, unitsSold, unitsWastage, productNo, purchaseOrderNo) Primary Key transactionNo Foreign Key productNo references Product(productNo) Foreign Key purchaseOrderNo references PurchaseOrder(purchaseOrderNo)

E.3   Asset management

A company wishes to create a database to monitor each of its assets (such as PCs, printers, cars, desks, chairs). Assets are divided into a number of categories, such as computers and furniture. An asset is assigned to an employee. On a regular basis, an employee in the Finance Department checks each asset to determine its current market value, and records the date and the current value of the asset. As a result of the assessment, the company may decide to sell the asset. Also on a regular basis, maintenance is carried out on each asset. In some cases, the maintenance is carried out by an employee, but in others, the asset has to be sent to an external company for maintenance. The logical data model is shown in Figure E.5 and the associated tables in Figure E.6.

Figure E.5

Logical data model for asset management.

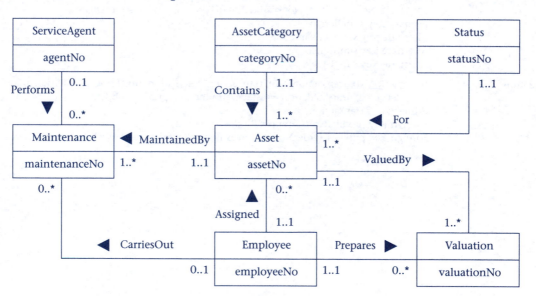

Figure E.6

Tables for asset management.

Employee	As defined in Section D.1.2
Asset	(<u>assetNo</u>, assetDescription, serialNo, dateAcquired, purchasePrice, currentValue, dateSold, nextMaintenanceDate, employeeNo, assetCategoryNo, statusNo) Primary Key assetNo Alternate Key serialNo Foreign Key employeeNo references Employee(employeeNo) Foreign Key assetCategoryNo references AssetCategory(assetCategoryNo) Foreign Key statusNo references Status(statusNo)
AssetCategory	(<u>assetCategoryNo</u>, assetCategoryDescription) Primary Key assetCategoryNo
Maintenance	(<u>maintenanceNo</u>, maintenanceDate, maintenanceDescription, maintenanceCost, assetNo, employeeNo, agentNo) Primary Key maintenanceNo Foreign Key assetNo references Asset(assetNo) Foreign Key employeeNo references Employee(employeeNo) Foreign Key agentNo references ServiceAgent(agentNo)
ServiceAgent	(<u>agentNo</u>, agentName, agentStreet, agentCity, agentState, agentZipCode, agentTelNo, agentFaxNo, agentEmailAddress, agentWebAddress, contactName, contactTelNo, contactFaxNo, contactEmailAddress) Primary Key agentNo Alternate Key agentName Alternate Key agentTelNo Alternate Key agentFaxNo
Status	(<u>statusNo</u>, statusDescription) Primary Key statusNo
Valuation	(<u>valuationNo</u>, valuationDate, valuationPrice, assetNo, employeeNo) Primary Key valuationNo Foreign Key assetNo references Asset(assetNo) Foreign Key employeeNo references Employee(employeeNo)

E.4 Project management

A consultancy company wishes to create a database to help manage its projects. Each project is for a specific client and has a nominated project manager. The project is divided into a number of work packages and employees bill their time and expenses against a work package. Each employee has a specific role, which defines the charging rate for the client. Over time, an employee can work on several work packages associated with the same project. In addition, most, but not all, work packages have a number of associated documents as deliverables, each of which may be written by more than one employee. The logical data model is shown in Figure E.7 and the associated tables in Figure E.8.

Figure E.7

Logical data model for project management.

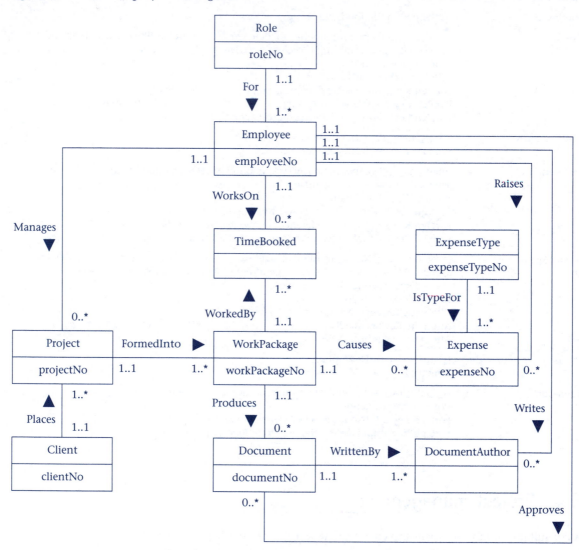

Figure E.8

Tables for project management.

Client	(<u>clientNo</u>, clientName, clientStreet, clientCity, clientState, clientZipCode, clientTelNo, clientFaxNo, clientWebAddress, contactName, contactTelNo, contactFaxNo, contactEmailAddress) Primary Key clientNo Alternate Key clientName Alternate Key clientTelNo Alternate Key clientFaxNo
Document	(<u>documentNo</u>, documentTitle, documentDate, versionNo, workPackageNo, approvedByEmployeeNo) Primary Key documentNo Foreign Key workPackageNo references WorkPackage(workPackageNo) Foreign Key approvedByEmployeeNo references Employee(employeeNo)
DocumentAuthor	(<u>documentNo</u>, <u>employeeNo</u>) Primary Key documentNo, employeeNo Foreign Key documentNo references Document(documentNo) Foreign Key employeeNo references Employee(employeeNo)
Employee	(<u>employeeNo</u>, dateStartRole, firstName, middleName, lastName, address, workTelExt, homeTelNo, empEmailAddress, socialSecurityNumber, DOB, position, sex, salary, dateStarted, roleNo) Primary Key employeeNo Alternate Key socialSecurityNumber Foreign Key roleNo references Role(roleNo)
Expense	(<u>expenseNo</u>, expenseDate, expenseDescription, expenseAmount, workPackageNo, employeeNo, expenseTypeNo) Primary Key expenseNo Alternate Key workPackageNo, employeeNo, expenseDate Foreign Key workPackageNo references WorkPackage(workPackageNo) Foreign Key employeeNo references Employee(employeeNo) Foreign Key expenseTypeNo reference ExpenseType(expenseTypeNo)
ExpenseType	(<u>expenseTypeNo</u>, expenseTypeDescription) Primary Key expenseTypeNo
Project	(<u>projectNo</u>, projectName, plannedStartDate, plannedEndDate, actualStartDate, actualEndDate, projectedCost, actualCost, clientNo, managerEmployeeNo) Primary Key projectNo Foreign Key clientNo references Client(clientNo) Foreign Key managerEmployeeNo references Employee(employeeNo)
Role	(<u>roleNo</u>, roleDescription, billingRate) Primary Key roleNo
TimeBooked	(<u>workPackageNo</u>, <u>employeeNo</u>, dateStartWork, dateStopWork, timeWorked) Primary Key workPackageNo, employeeNo Foreign Key workPackageNo references WorkPackage(workPackageNo) Foreign Key employeeNo references Employee(employeeNo)
WorkPackage	(<u>workPackageNo</u>, plannedStartDate, plannedEndDate, actualStartDate, actualEndDate, projectedCost, actualCost, projectNo) Primary Key workPackageNo Foreign Key projectNo references Project(projectNo)

E.5 Course management

A training company wishes to create a database of its course information. The company delivers a number of seminars and training courses. Each course is delivered by one member of staff at some location (such as internal seminar room S10, Hilton Hotel Suite 100). The fees vary for each course and on the number of delegates a company sends. For example, if a company sends one person, the charge may be $1000. If the company sends two people, the first may be charged $1000, but the second may be charged $750. The course can be attended by a number of delegates, subject to some upper limit for the course. A delegate can register as an individual or through his or her company. The name of the employee who registers the delegate is recorded. An invoice is sent either to the delegate or to his or her company. The logical data model is shown in Figure E.9 and the associated tables in Figure E.10.

Figure E.9

Logical data model for course management.

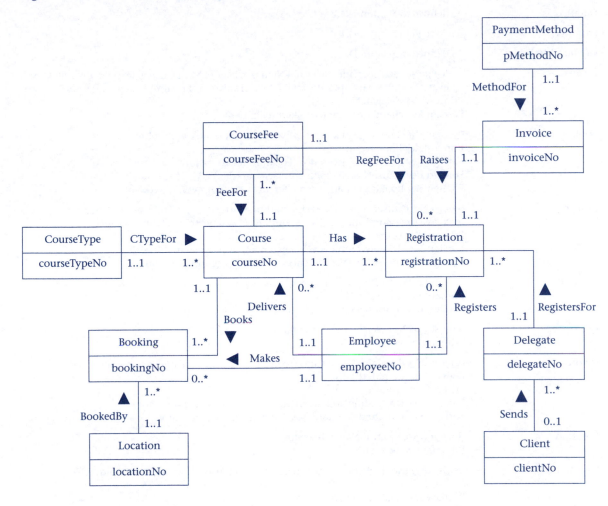

Figure E.10

Tables for course management.

Client	As defined in Section D.4.2
Employee	As defined in Section D.1.2
PaymentMethod	As defined in Section D.1.2
Delegate	(<u>delegateNo</u>, delegateTitle, delegateFName, delegateLName, delegateStreet, delegateCity, delegateState, delegateZipCode, attTelNo, attFaxNo, attEmailAddress, clientNo) Primary Key delegateNo Foreign Key clientNo references Client(clientNo)
Booking	(<u>bookingNo</u>, bookingDate, locationNo, courseNo, bookingEmployeeNo) Primary Key bookingNo Foreign Key locationNo references Location(locationNo) Foreign Key courseNo references Course(courseNo) Foreign Key bookingEmployeeNo references Employee(employeeNo)
Course	(<u>courseNo</u>, courseName, courseDescription, startDate, startTime, endDate, endTime, maxDelegates, confirmed, delivererEmployeeNo, courseTypeNo) Primary Key courseNo Foreign Key delivererEmployeeNo references Employee(employeeNo) Foreign Key courseTypeNo references CourseType(courseTypeNo)
CourseFee	(<u>courseFeeNo</u>, feeDescription, fee, courseNo) Primary Key courseFeeNo Foreign Key courseNo references Course(courseNo)
CourseType	(<u>courseTypeNo</u>, courseTypeDescription) Primary Key courseTypeNo
Invoice	(<u>invoiceNo</u>, dateRaised, datePaid, creditCardNo, holdersName, expiryDate, registrationNo, pMethodNo) Primary Key invoiceNo Foreign Key registrationNo references Registration(registrationNo) Foreign Key pMethodNo references PaymentMethod(pMethodNo)
Location	(<u>locationNo</u>, locationName, maxSize) Primary Key locationNo
Registration	(<u>registrationNo</u>, registrationDate, delegateNo, courseFeeNo, registerEmployeeNo, courseNo) Primary Key registrationNo Foreign Key delegateNo references Delegate(delegateNo) Foreign Key courseFeeNo references CourseFee(courseFeeNo) Foreign Key registerEmployeeNo references Employee(employeeNo) Foreign Key courseNo references Course(courseNo)

E.6 Human resource management

An HRM Department wishes to create a database to monitor its employees. The company is divided into a number of departments, and employees are assigned to one department. The department has a designated Manager who has overall responsibility for the department and the employees in the department. However, to help manage the department, a number of employees are nominated to supervise groups of staff. When a new employee joins the company, information on previous work history and qualifications is required. On a regular basis, each employee is required to undergo a review, which is normally carried out by the Manager, but may be delegated to a nominated representative.

The company has defined a number of position types, such as Manager, Business Analyst, Salesperson, Secretary, and each type has a number of grades associated with it, which for most non-senior positions determines the employee's salary. At a senior level, salary is negotiable. Posts are allocated to a department depending on its workload. For example, a department may be allocated two new Business Analyst posts. A post will be filled by one employee, although over time, employees will fill a number of different posts.

The logical data model is shown in Figure E.11 and the associated tables in Figure E.12.

Figure E.11

Logical data model for human resource management.

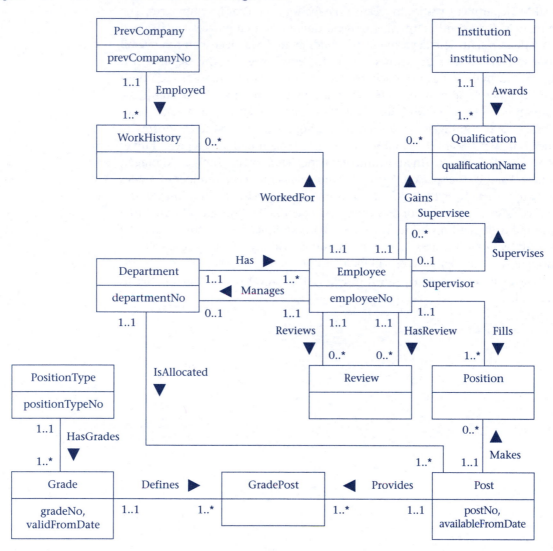

Figure E.12

Tables for human resource management.

Department	(<u>departmentNo</u>, departmentName, deptLocation, managerEmployeeNo) Primary Key departmentNo Foreign Key managerEmployeeNo references Employee(employeeNo)
Employee	(<u>employeeNo</u>, title, firstName, middleName, lastName, address, workTelExt, homeTelNo, empEmailAddress, socialSecurityNumber, DOB, position, sex, salary, dateStarted, dateLeft, departmentNo, supervisorEmployeeNo) Primary Key employeeNo Alternate Key socialSecurityNumber Foreign Key departmentNo references Department(departmentNo) Foreign Key supervisorEmployeeNo references Employee(employeeNo)
Grade	(<u>gradeNo</u>, <u>validFromDate</u>, validToDate, gradeDescription, gradeSalary, noDaysLeaveEntitlement, positionTypeNo) Primary Key gradeNo, validFromDate Foreign Key positionTypeNo references PositionType(positionTypeNo)
GradePost	(<u>gradeNo</u>, <u>validFromDate</u>, <u>postNo</u>, <u>availableFromDate</u>) Primary Key gradeNo, validFromDate, postNo, availableFromDate Foreign Key gradeNo, validFromDate references Grade(gradeNo, validFromDate) Foreign Key postNo, availableFromDate references Post(postNo, availableFromDate)
Institution	(<u>institutionNo</u>, institutionName, instAddress, instTelNo, instFaxNo, instWebAddress, contactName, contactTelNo, contactFaxNo, contactEmailAddress) Primary Key institutionNo Alternate Key institutionName Alternate Key instTelNo Alternate Key instFaxNo
Position	(<u>employeeNo</u>, <u>postNo</u>, <u>startDate</u>, endDate) Primary Key employeeNo, postNo, startDate Foreign Key employeeNo references Employee(employeeNo) Foreign Key postNo, startDate references Post(postNo, availableFromDate)
PositionType	(<u>positionTypeNo</u>, positionTypeDescription) Primary Key positionTypeNo
Post	(<u>postNo</u>, <u>availableFromDate</u>, availableToDate, postDescription, salariedHourly, fullPartTime, temporaryPermanent, freeLaborStandardsActExempt, departmentNo) Primary Key postNo, availableFromDate Foreign Key departmentNo references Department(departmentNo)
PrevCompany	(<u>prevCompanyNo</u>, pCompanyName, pCompanyStreet, pCompanyCity, pCompanyState, pCompanyZipCode, pCompanyTelNo, pCompanyFaxNo, pCompanyWebAddress, contactName, contactTelNo, contactFaxNo, contactEmailAddress) Primary Key prevCompanyNo Alternate Key pCompanyName Alternate Key pCompanyTelNo Alternate Key pCompanyFaxNo
Qualification	(<u>qualificationName</u>, <u>employeeNo</u>, gradeObtained, startQualDate, endQualDate, gpa, institutionNo) Primary Key qualificationName, employeeNo Foreign Key employeeNo references Employee(employeeNo) Foreign Key institutionNo references Institution(institutionNo)

Figure E.12

Continued

Review

(<u>revieweeEmployeeNo</u>, <u>reviewerEmployeeNo</u>, <u>reviewDate</u>, comments)
Primary Key revieweeEmployeeNo,
reviewerEmployeeNo, reviewDate
Foreign Key revieweeEmployeeNo references Employee(employeeNo)
Foreign Key reviewerEmployeeNo references Employee(employeeNo)

WorkHistory

(<u>prevCompanyNo</u>, <u>employeeNo</u>, prevPosition, prevGrade, prevSalary, prevLocation,
prevResponsibilities)
Primary Key prevCompanyNo, employeeNo
Foreign Key prevCompanyNo references PrevCompany(prevCompanyNo)
Foreign Key employeeNo references Employee(employeeNo)

E.7 Payroll management

The Payroll Department wishes to create a database to monitor employees' salary payments. To calculate an employee's salary, Payroll need to take into consideration holidays taken against holiday entitlement, number of days' sick leave in pay period, bonuses, and deductions. An employee must specify how his or her salary should be paid, although this may change over time. Most employees are paid by electronic bank transfer, but some types of employees may be paid by cash or check. If payment is electronic, then a routing number and account type are required. Payment can be made by only one method. There are various reasons for deductions being made; for example, federal tax, state tax, medical plan, retirement plan, or cash advance.

The logical data model is shown in Figure E.13 and the associated tables in Figure E.14.

Figure E.13

Logical data model for payroll management.

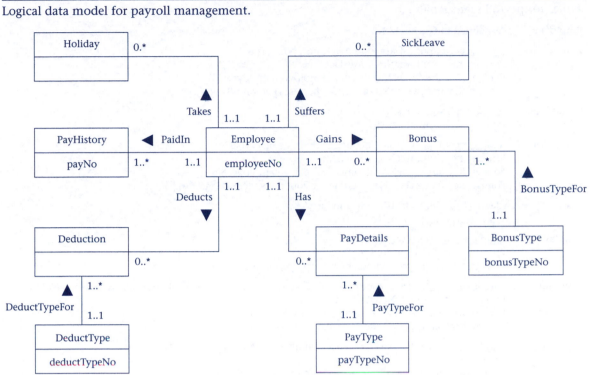

Figure E.14

Tables for payroll management.

Employee	As defined in Section D.1.2
Bonus	(employeeNo, bonusDate, bonusAmount, bonusTypeNo) Primary Key employeeNo, bonusDate Foreign Key employeeNo references Employee(employeeNo) Foreign Key bonusTypeNo references BonusType(bonusTypeNo)
BonusType	(bonusTypeNo, bonusDescription) Primary Key bonusTypeNo
Deduction	(employeeNo, deductDate, deductAmount, deductTypeNo) Primary Key employeeNo, deductDate Foreign Key employeeNo references Employee(employeeNo) Foreign Key deductTypeNo references DeductType(deductTypeNo)
DeductType	(deductTypeNo, deductDescription) Primary Key deductTypeNo
Holiday	(employeeNo, startDate, endDate) Primary Key employeeNo, startDate Foreign Key employeeNo references Employee(employeeNo)
PayDetails	(employeeNo, startDate, routingNumber, accountType, bankName, bankAddress, payTypeNo) Primary Key employeeNo, startDate Foreign Key employeeNo references Employee(employeeNo) Foreign Key payTypeNo references PayType(payTypeNo)
PayHistory	(payNo, employeeNo, payDate, checkNumber, payAmount) Primary Key payNo Foreign Key employeeNo references Employee(employeeNo)
PayType	(payTypeNo, payTypeDescription) Primary Key payTypeNo
SickLeave	(employeeNo, startDate, endDate, reason) Primary Key employeeNo, startDate Foreign Key employeeNo references Employee(employeeNo)

E.8   Vehicle rentals

A vehicle rental company wishes to create a database to monitor the renting of vehicles to clients. The company has various outlets and each outlet has staff including a Manager and several Senior Mechanics who are responsible for supervising the work of allocated groups of Mechanics. Each outlet has a stock of vehicles for rent that may be rented by clients for various periods of time, from a minimum of four hours to a maximum of six months. Each rental agreement between a client and the company is uniquely identified using a rental number. A client must take out insurance cover for each vehicle rental period. Each vehicle is checked for faults after each rental. The logical data model is shown in Figure E.15 and the associated tables in Figure E.16.

Figure E.15

Logical data model for vehicle rentals.

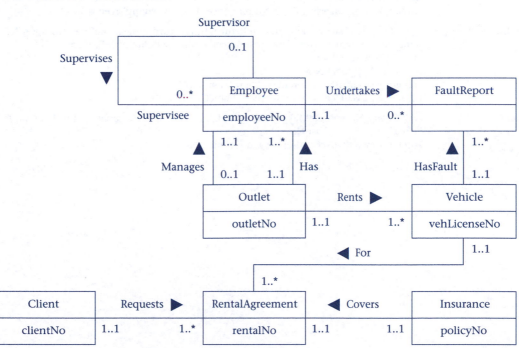

Figure E.16

Tables for vehicle rentals.

Client	As defined in Section D.4.2
Employee	(<u>employeeNo</u>, title, firstName, middleName, lastName, address, workTelExt, homeTelNo, empEmailAddress, socialSecurityNumber, DOB, position, sex, salary, dateStarted, outletNo, supervisorEmployeeNo) Primary Key employeeNo Alternate Key socialSecurityNumber Foreign Key outletNo references Outlet(outletNo) Foreign Key supervisorEmployeeNo references Employee(employeeNo)
FaultReport	(<u>vehLicenseNo</u>, <u>dateChecked</u>, timeChecked, comments, employeeNo) Primary Key vehLicenseNo, dateChecked Foreign Key vehLicenseNo references Vehicle(vehLicenseNo) Foreign Key employeeNo references Employee(employeeNo)
Outlet	(<u>outletNo</u>, outletStreet, outletCity, outletState, outletZipCode, outletTelNo, outletFaxNo, managerEmployeeNo) Primary Key outletNo Alternate Key outletTelNo Alternate Key outletFaxNo Foreign Key managerEmployeeNo references Employee(employeeNo)
RentalAgreement	(<u>rentalNo</u>, dateStart, timeStart, dateReturn, timeReturn, mileageBefore, mileageAfter, policyNo, insuranceCoverType, insurancePremium, clientNo, vehLicenseNo) Primary Key rentalNo Alternate Key policyNo Foreign Key clientNo references Client(clientNo) Foreign Key vehLicenseNo references Vehicle(vehLicenseNo)
Vehicle	(<u>vehLicenseNo</u>, vehicleMake, vehicleModel, color, noDoors, capacity, hireRate, outletNo) Primary Key vehLicenseNo Foreign Key outletNo references Outlet(outletNo)

E.9 Student accommodation

The Accommodation Office of a university wishes to create a database to monitor the allocation of accommodation to students. Each student requiring accommodation fills out an application form, which holds the student's details and an indication of the type of accommodation required and the duration. Students may rent a room in a hall of residence or student apartment. The halls provide only single rooms, which have a room number, place number, and monthly rental rate. The place number uniquely identifies each room in all the halls controlled by the Accommodation Office and is used when renting a room to a student. Each hall is managed by a member of the Accommodation Office.

The Accommodation Office also offers student apartments, each identified by a unique apartment number. These apartments are fully furnished and provide single room accommodation for groups of three, four, or five students. Each bedroom in an apartment has a monthly rental rate, a room number, and a place number. The place number uniquely identifies each room available in all student apartments and is used when renting a room to a student. Apartments are inspected by members of the Accommodation Office on a regular basis to ensure that the accommodation is well maintained.

New lease agreements are negotiated at the start of each academic year with a minimum rental period of one semester and a maximum rental period of one year. The students pay for their accommodation throughout the academic year and are sent an invoice at the start of each semester. If a student does not pay by a certain date, two reminder letters are sent. The logical data model is shown in Figure E.17 and the associated tables in Figure E.18.

Figure E.17

Logical data model for student accommodation.

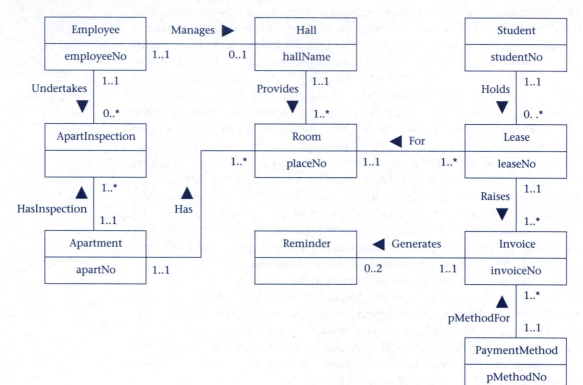

Figure E.18

Tables for student accommodation.

Employee	As defined in Section D.1.2
PaymentMethod	As defined in Section D.1.2
Apartment	(<u>apartNo</u>, apartAddress, noOfRoomsInApart) Primary Key apartNo
ApartInspection	(<u>apartNo</u>, <u>dateOfInspection</u>, comments, status, employeeNo) Primary Key apartNo, dateOfInspection Foreign Key apartNo references Apartment(apartNo) Foreign Key employeeNo references Employee(employeeNo)
Hall	(<u>hallName</u>, hallAddress, hallTelNo, hallFaxNo, noOfRoomsInHall, managerEmployeeNo) Primary Key hallName Alternate Key hallTelNo Alternate Key hallFaxNo Foreign Key managerEmployeeNo references Employee(employeeNo)
Invoice	(<u>invoiceNo</u>, semester, dateDue, datePaid, leaseNo, pMethodNo) Primary Key invoiceNo Foreign Key leaseNo references Lease(leaseNo) Foreign Key pMethodNo references PaymentMethod(pMethodNo)
Reminder	(<u>invoiceNo</u>, dateReminder1sent, dateReminder2sent, dateInterview, comments) Primary Key invoiceNo Foreign Key invoiceNo references Invoice(invoiceNo)
Lease	(<u>leaseNo</u>, duration, dateStart, dateLeave, studentNo, placeNo) Primary Key leaseNo Alternate Key placeNo, dateStart Alternate Key studentNo, dateStart Foreign Key studentNo references Student(studentNo) Foreign Key placeNo references Room(placeNo)
Room	(<u>placeNo</u>, roomNo, rentPerSemester, hallName, apartNo) Primary Key placeNo Alternate Key roomNo, hallName Alternate Key roomNo, apartNo Foreign Key hallName references Hall(hallName) Foreign Key apartNo references Apartment(apartNo)
Student	(<u>studentNo</u>, studentFirstName, studentMiddleInitial, studentLastName, studentHomeStreet, studentHomeCity, studentHomeState, studentHomeZipCode, studentHomeTelNo, studentSex, studentDOB, studentType, studentStatus, accommodationTypeRequired, accommodationDuration) Primary Key studentNo

E.10 Client transportation

A haulage company that specializes in the transportation of loads throughout the US wishes to create a database to control client orders for transportation. The company has many offices throughout the US to process client orders. A client registers with an office and can place one or more orders. Each order describes the load to be transported along with the collection address and the delivery address. The transportation requirements for each order are then calculated. The transport requirements describe the number of units and trailers required to transport the load. Each office is allocated several units and trailers. One unit can pull one or two trailers. The logical data model is shown in Figure E.19 and the associated tables in Figure E.20.

Figure E.19

Logical data model for client transportation.

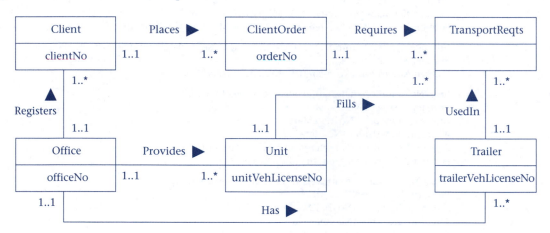

Figure E.20

Tables for client transportation.

Client	(<u>clientNo</u>, clientName, clientStreet, clientCity, clientState, clientZipCode, clientTelNo, clientFaxNo, clientWebAddress, contactName, contactTelNo, contactFaxNo, contactEmailAddress, officeNo) Primary Key clientNo Alternate Key clientTelNo Alternate Key clientFaxNo Foreign Key officeNo references Office(officeNo)
Office	(<u>officeNo</u>, officeAddress, officeTelNo, officeFaxNo) Primary Key officeNo Alternate Key officeTelNo Alternate Key officeFaxNo
ClientOrder	(<u>orderNo</u>, dateOrder, collectionDate, collectionAddress, deliveryDate, deliveryAddress, loadWeight, loadDescription, clientNo) Primary Key orderNo Foreign Key clientNo references Client(clientNo)
Trailer	(<u>trailerVehLicenseNo</u>, trailerDescription, trailerLength, maxCarryingWeight, officeNo) Primary Key trailerVehLicenseNo Foreign Key officeNo references Office(officeNo)
TransportReqts	(<u>orderNo</u>, <u>transportReqPartNo</u>, unitVehLicenseNo, trailerVehLicenseNo1, trailerVehLicenseNo2) Primary Key orderNo, transportReqPartNo Foreign Key unitVehLicenseNo references Unit(unitVehLicenseNo) Foreign Key trailerVehLicenseNo1 references Trailer(trailerVehLicenseNo) Foreign Key trailerVehLicenseNo2 references Trailer(trailerVehLicenseNo)
Unit	(<u>unitVehLicenseNo</u>, unitDescription, maxPayLoad, officeNo) Primary Key unitVehLicenseNo Foreign Key officeNo references Office(officeNo)

E.11 Publisher printing

A printing company that handles print jobs for book publishers wishes to create a database to control client requests for printing. A book publisher submits an order that describes the printing job. A print job requires the use of materials, such as paper and ink, which are assigned to a job through one or more purchase orders. Each print job is assigned to a Print Manager, who has the responsibility to ensure that the job is carried out correctly. For larger print jobs, additional employees are normally allocated to help with the printing. The logical data model is shown in Figure E.21 and the associated tables in Figure E.22.

Figure E.21

Logical data model for publisher printing.

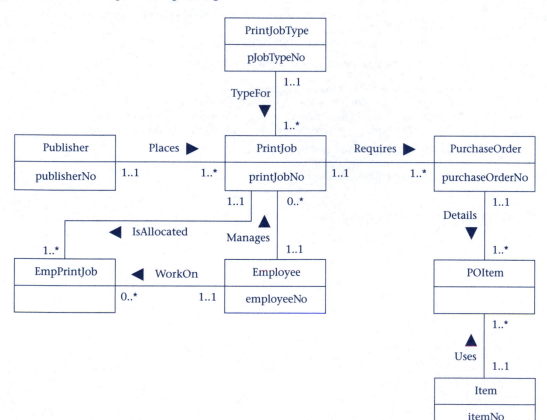

Figure E.22

Tables for publisher printing.

Employee	As defined in Section D.1.2
EmpPrintJob	(<u>employeeNo</u>, <u>printJobNo</u>, jobDate) Primary Key employeeNo, printJobNo Foreign Key employeeNo references Employee(employeeNo) Foreign Key printJobNo references PrintJob(printJobNo)
Item	(<u>itemNo</u>, itemDescription, itemPrice, itemQuantityInStock, itemReorderLevel, itemReorderQuantity, itemReorderLeadTime) Primary Key itemNo
PrintJob	(<u>printJobNo</u>, printJobDescription, printJobDateReceived, printJobDateCompleted, managerEmployeeNo, publisherNo, printJobTypeNo) Primary Key printJobNo Foreign Key managerEmployeeNo references Employee(employeeNo) Foreign Key publisherNo references Publisher(publisherNo) Foreign Key printJobTypeNo references PrintJobType(printJobTypeNo)
Publisher	(<u>publisherNo</u>, publisherName, publisherStreet, publisherCity, publisherState, publisherZipCode, pubTelNo, pubFaxNo, pubWebAddress, contactName, contactTelNo, contactFaxNo, contactEmailAddress, creditRating) Primary Key publisherNo Alternate Key publisherName Alternate Key pubTelNo Alternate Key pubFaxNo
POItem	(<u>purchaseOrderNo</u>, <u>itemNo</u>, quantity) Primary Key purchaseOrderNo, itemNo Foreign Key purchaseOrderNo references PurchaseOrder (purchaseOrderNo) Foreign Key itemNo references Item(itemNo)
PrintJobType	(<u>printJobTypeNo</u>, printJobTypeDescription) Primary key printJobTypeNo
PurchaseOrder	(<u>purchaseOrderNo</u>, <u>printJobNo</u>, purchaseOrderDate) Primary Key purchaseOrderNo Foreign Key printJobNo references PrintJob(printJobNo)

E.12 County library

A county wishes to create a database to control its local libraries. Each library has a number of employees, one of whom is designated as the manager of the library and is responsible for supervising employees and the general day-to-day management of the library. Each library stores a number of books and CDs. A citizen has to become a member of a library before he or she is allowed to borrow any books, but thereafter can borrow books from any county library. Books are stored on shelves and CDs are stored in a number of racks in the center of the library. Generally, a library stocks a number of copies of each book title and each CD. Details of book publishers are maintained but not CD publishers. To find an item, searches can be performed based on the book/CD title, the author/artist's name, the category of the book/CD, or the publisher's name. The logical data model is shown in Figure E.23 and the associated tables in Figure E.24.

Figure E.23

Logical data model for county library.

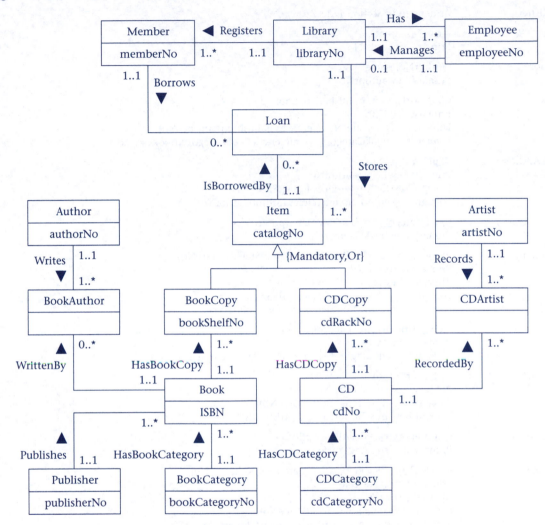

Figure E.24

Tables for county library.

Publisher	As defined in Section D.11.2
Artist	(artistNo, name) Primary Key artistNo
Author	(authorNo, name) Primary Key authorNo
Book	(ISBN, title, year, publisherNo, bookCategoryNo) Primary Key ISBN Foreign Key publisherNo references Publisher(publisherNo) Foreign Key bookCategoryNo references BookCategory(bookCategoryNo)
BookAuthor	(ISBN, authorNo) Primary Key ISBN, authorNo Foreign Key ISBN references Book(ISBN) Foreign Key authorNo references Author(authorNo)
BookCategory	(bookCategoryNo, bookCatDescription) Primary Key bookCategoryNo
BookCopy	(catalogNo, bookShelfNo, ISBN, dateInStock, libraryNo) Primary Key catalogNo Alternate Key bookShelfNo Foreign Key ISBN references Book(ISBN) Foreign Key libraryNo references Library(libraryNo)
CD	(cdNo, title, releaseDate, cdCategoryNo) Primary Key cdNo Foreign Key cdCategoryNo references CDCategory(cdCategoryNo)
CDArtist	(cdNo, artistNo) Primary Key cdNo, artistNo Foreign Key cdNo references CD(cdNo) Foreign Key artistNo references Artist(artistNo)
CDCategory	(cdCategoryNo, cdCatDescription) Primary Key cdCategoryNo
CDCopy	(catalogNo, cdRackNo, cdNo, dateInStock, libraryNo) Primary Key catalogNo Alternate Key cdRackNo Foreign Key cdNo references CD(cdNo) Foreign Key libraryNo references Library(libraryNo)
Employee	(employeeNo, title, firstName, middleName, lastName, address, workTelExt, homeTelNo, empEmailAddress, socialSecurityNumber, DOB, position, sex, salary, dateStarted, libraryNo) Primary Key employeeNo Alternate Key socialSecurityNumber Foreign Key libraryNo references Library(libraryNo)
Library	(libraryNo, libStreet, libCity, libState, libZipCode, libTelNo, libFaxNo, libWebAddress, managerEmployeeNo) Primary Key libraryNo Alternate Key libTelNo Alternate Key libFaxNo

Figure E.24

Continued

Foreign Key managerEmployeeNo references Employee(employeeNo)

Loan   (catalogNo, memberNo, dateOut, dateReturn)
Primary Key catalogNo, memberNo
Foreign Key catalogNo references BookCopy(catalogNo) and CDCopy(catalogNo)
Foreign Key memberNo references Member(memberNo)

Member   (memberNo, memTitle, memFirstName, memMiddleName, memLastName, memAddress,
memWorkTelExt, memHomeTelNo, memDOB, memSex, dateJoined, libraryNo)
Primary Key memberNo
Foreign Key libraryNo references Library(libraryNo)

E.13 Real estate rentals

A real estate agency with branches throughout the US wishes to create a database to control the properties it rents out on behalf of owners, who are classified as Business and Private owners. Within each branch, staff oversee the rental of properties, and are responsible for handling property viewings and lease agreements. Some staff are also given the role Supervisor, responsible for overseeing a group of staff and ensuring the efficient management of the branch. The administrative work of each group of staff is supported by a Secretary. The logical data model is shown in Figure E.25 and the associated tables in Figure E.26.

Figure E.25

Logical data model for real estate agency.

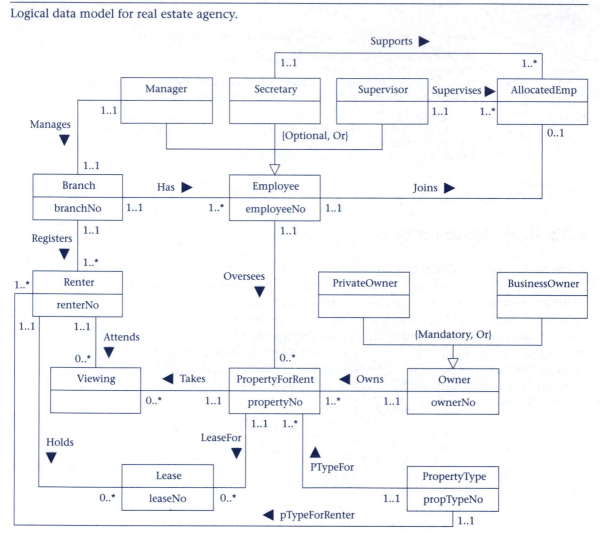

Figure E.26

Tables for real estate agency.

AllocatedEmp	(<u>superviseeEmployeeNo</u>, supervisorEmployeeNo, secretaryEmployeeNo) Primary Key superviseeEmployeeNo Foreign Key superviseeEmployeeNo references Employee(employeeNo) Foreign Key supervisorEmployeeNo references Employee(employeeNo) Foreign Key secretaryEmployeeNo references Employee(employeeNo)
Branch	(<u>branchNo</u>, branchStreet, branchCity, branchState, branchZipCode, branchTelNo, branchFaxNo, managerEmployeeNo) Primary Key branchNo Alternate Key branchTelNo Alternate Key branchFaxNo Foreign Key managerEmployeeNo references Employee(employeeNo)
BusinessOwner	(<u>ownerNo</u>, businessName, businessAddress, businessTelNo, businessFaxNo, contactName, contactTelNo, contactFaxNo, contactEmailAddress) Primary Key ownerNo Alternate Key businessName Alternate Key businessTelNo Alternate Key businessFaxNo
Employee	(<u>employeeNo</u>, title, firstName, middleName, lastName, address, workTelExt, homeTelNo, empEmailAddress, socialSecurityNumber, DOB, position, sex, salary, typingSpeed, dateStarted, branchNo) Primary Key employeeNo Alternate Key socialSecurityNumber Foreign Key branchNo references Branch(branchNo)
Lease	(<u>leaseNo</u>, rentStart, rentFinish, depositPaid, renterNo, propertyNo) Primary Key leaseNo Foreign Key renterNo references Renter(renterNo) Foreign Key propertyNo references PropertyForRent(propertyNo)
PrivateOwner	(<u>ownerNo</u>, ownerName, ownerAddress, ownerTelNo) Primary Key ownerNo
PropertyForRent	(<u>propertyNo</u>, propStreet, propCity, propState, propZipCode, noRooms, rent, propTypeNo, ownerNo, employeeNo, branchNo) Primary Key propertyNo Foreign Key propTypeNo references PropertyType(propTypeNo) Foreign Key ownerNo references PrivateOwner(ownerNo) and BusinessOwner(ownerNo) Foreign Key employeeNo references Employee(employeeNo) Foreign Key branchNo references Branch(branchNo)
PropertyType	(<u>propTypeNo</u>, propTypeDescription) Primary Key propTypeNo
Renter	(<u>renterNo</u>, rFName, rLName, rAddress, rTelNo, maxRent, prefTypeNo) Primary Key renterNo Foreign Key prefTypeNo references PropertyType(propTypeNo)
Viewing	(<u>propertyNo</u>, <u>renterNo</u>, <u>dateView</u>, comments) Primary Key propertyNo, renterNo, dateView Foreign Key propertyNo references PropertyForRent(propertyNo) Foreign Key renterNo references Renter(renterNo)

E.14 Travel agent

A travel agent wishes to create a database for its customer holiday booking activities. The travel agent has numerous branches spread through the major cities in the US. A customer can call into, or contact by telephone, any branch and book a holiday. A holiday normally includes a flight and accommodation, although sometimes customers require only a flight or only accommodation. Once the travel agent has found a suitable holiday for a customer, the flight and accommodation requirements are reserved for the customer. However, the reservation can only be held for up to 24 hours by which time the customer must accept or decline the booking. Once the booking is accepted, the customer is invoiced for the holiday and must pay the invoice in full, a minimum of four weeks before the departure date. The name of the employee who initially processes the customer booking is recorded. The ER model is shown in Figure E.27 and the associated tables in Figure E.28.

Figure E.27

ER model for travel agent.

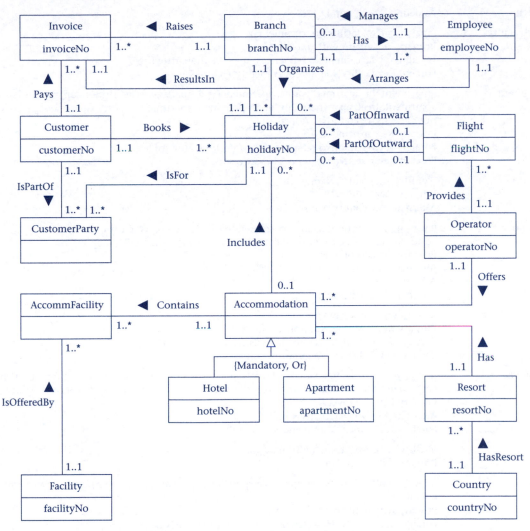

Figure E.28

Tables for travel agent.

Branch	As defined in Section D.13.2
ApartFacility	(<u>apartmentNo</u>, <u>facilityNo</u>, comments) Primary Key apartmentNo, facilityNo Foreign Key apartmentNo references Apartment(apartmentNo) Foreign Key facilityNo references Facility(facilityNo)
Apartment	(<u>apartmentNo</u>, apartmentName, apartmentType, apartmentDescription, apartmentRating, apartmentStreet, apartmentCity, apartmentState, apartmentCountry, apartmentZipCode, noOfRooms, operatorNo, resortNo) Primary Key apartmentNo Foreign Key operatorNo references Operator(operatorNo) Foreign Key resortNo references Resort(resortNo)
Country	(<u>countryNo</u>, countryName) Primary Key countryNo Alternate Key countryName
Customer	(<u>customerNo</u>, customerName, customerStreet, customerCity, customerState, customerZipCode, custTelNo, custFaxNo, nationality, sex, DOB, passportNo) Primary Key customerNo Alternate Key custTelNo Alternate Key custFaxNo Alternate Key passportNo
CustomerParty	(<u>customerNo</u>, <u>holidayNo</u>) Primary Key customerNo, holidayNo Foreign Key customerNo references Customer(customerNo) Foreign Key holidayNo references Holiday(holidayNo)
Employee	(<u>employeeNo</u>, title, firstName, middleName, lastName, address, workTelExt, homeTelNo, empEmailAddress, socialSecurityNumber, DOB, position, sex, salary, dateStarted, branchNo) Primary Key employeeNo Alternate Key socialSecurityNumber Foreign Key branchNo references Branch(branchNo)
Facility	(<u>facilityNo</u>, description, additionalCharge) Primary Key facilityNo
Flight	(<u>flightNo</u>, planeType, seatCapacity, airportDepart, departTime, airportArrive, arriveTime, operatorNo) Primary Key flightNo Foreign Key operatorNo references Operator(operatorNo)
Hotel	(<u>hotelNo</u>, hotelName, hotelStreet, hotelCity, hotelState, hotelCountry, hotelZipCode, hotelTelNo, hotelFaxNo, hotelType, hotelDescription, hotelRating, hotelManagerName, operatorNo, resortNo) Primary Key hotelNo Foreign Key operatorNo references Operator(operatorNo) Foreign Key resortNo references Resort(resortNo)
HotelFacility	(<u>hotelNo</u>, <u>facilityNo</u>, comments) Primary Key hotelNo, facilityNo Foreign Key hotelNo references Hotel(hotelNo) Foreign Key facilityNo references Facility(facilityNo)

Figure E.28

Continued

Holiday	(holidayNo, status, dateBooked, cateringType, startDate, finishDate, invoiceNo, totalCost, dateSent, datePaid, bookCustomerNo, hotelNo, apartmentNo, inwardFlightNo, inwardNoOfSeats, outwardFlightNo, outwardNoOfSeats, employeeNo, branchNo) Primary Key holidayNo Foreign Key bookCustomerNo references Customer(customerNo) Foreign Key hotelNo references Hotel(hotelNo) Foreign Key apartmentNo references Apartment(apartmentNo) Foreign Key inwardFlightNo references Flight(flightNo) Foreign Key outwardFlightNo references Flight(flightNo) Foreign Key employeeNo references Employee(employeeNo) ForeignKey branchNo references Branch(branchNo)
Operator	(operatorNo, operatorName, operatorType, operatorStreet, operatorCity, operatorState, operatorZipCode, operTelNo, operFaxNo, contactName, contactTelNo, contactFaxNo, contactEmailAddress) Primary Key operatorNo Alternate Key operTelNo Alternate Key operFaxNo
Resort	(resortNo, resortName, distanceFromAirport, timeFromAirport, countryNo) Primary Key resortNo Foreign Key countryNo references Country(countryNo)

E.15 Student results

A university wishes to create a database for recording the results of students. When a student joins the university he or she registers with a particular course. Each student is also assigned an Advisor of Studies. Each year of each course is made up of modules. The minimum and maximum number of modules that make up a year of a course is 6 and 8, respectively. A student must take and pass each module in a given year before he or she is allowed to move into the next year of the course or to graduate. A student is normally allowed three attempts to pass a module; however, additional attempts are allowed at the discretion of the university. A particular module can be offered as part of one or more courses.

The university has several departments, each of which offers a portfolio of courses. Each department has a Head of Department (HOD) and each course has a Course Leader. Each module is assigned to a member of staff called a Module Coordinator, who has the responsibility to oversee the teaching and the assessment of the module. The ER model is shown in Figure E.29 and the associated tables in Figure E.30.

Figure E.29

ER model for student results.

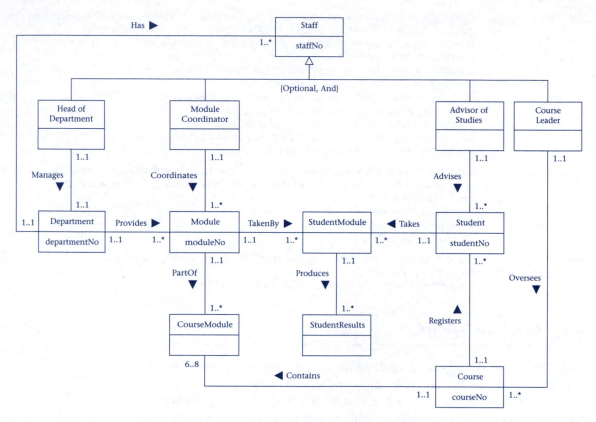

Figure E.30

Tables for student results.

Course (<u>courseNo</u>, courseName, level, entranceRequirements, maxNumber, courseLeaderNo)
Primary Key courseNo
Alternate Key courseName
Foreign Key courseLeaderNo references Staff(staffNo)

CourseModule (<u>courseNo</u>, <u>moduleNo</u>)
Primary Key courseNo, moduleNo
Foreign Key courseNo references Course(courseNo)
Foreign Key moduleNo references Module(moduleNo)

Department (<u>departmentNo</u>, departmentName, location, HODstaffNo)
Primary Key departmentNo
Alternate Key departmentName
Foreign Key HODstaffNo references Staff(staffNo)

Module (<u>moduleNo</u>, moduleName, semesterDelivered, moduleAims, moduleObjectives,
moduleSyllabus, moduleResources, moduleModeOfAssessment, moduleCoordinatorStaffNo,
departmentNo)
Primary Key moduleNo
Alternate Key moduleName
Foreign Key moduleCoordinatorStaffNo references Staff(staffNo)
Foreign Key departmentNo references Department(departmentNo)

Staff (<u>staffNo</u>, title, firstName, lastName, address, homeTelNo, workTelExt, empEmailAddress,
socialSecurityNumber, DOB, position, sex, salary, dateStarted, departmentNo)
Primary Key staffNo
Alternate Key socialSecurityNumber
Foreign Key departmentNo references Department(departmentNo)

Student (<u>studentNo</u>, studentFirstName, studentMiddleName, studentLastName, studentHomeStreet,
studentHomeCity, studentHomeState, studentHomeZipCode, studentHomeTelNo,
familyHomeStreet, familyHomeCity, familyHomeState, familyHomeZipCode,
familyHomeTelNo, studentDOB, studentSex, nationality, courseNo, advisorStaffNo)
Primary Key studentNo
Foreign Key courseNo references Course(courseNo)
Foreign Key advisorStaffNo references Staff(staffNo)

StudentModule (<u>studentNo</u>, <u>moduleNo</u>)
Primary key studentNo, moduleNo
Foreign Key studentNo references Student(studentNo)
Foreign Key moduleNo references Module(moduleNo)

StudentResult (<u>studentNo</u>, <u>moduleNo</u>, <u>attempt</u>, attemptDate, mark,
proposal, additionalComments)
Primary key studentNo, moduleNo, attempt
Foreign Key studentNo, moduleNo references StudentModule(studentNo, moduleNo)

Glossary

Access method. The steps involved in storing and retrieving records from a file.

Alias. An alternative name given to an attribute. In SQL, you may substitute an alias for a table name.

Alternate keys (ER/relational model). The candidate keys that are not selected as the primary key of the entity/table.

Anomalies. See *Update anomalies*.

Application design. A stage of the database system development lifecycle that involves designing the user interface and the application programs that use and process the database.

Application server. Handles the business logic and data processing layer in a three-tier client–server architecture.

Attribute (ER model). A property of an entity or a relationship.

Attribute (relational model). An attribute is a named column of a relation.

Attribute inheritance. The process by which a member of a subclass may possess subclass-specific attributes, and inherit those attributes associated with the superclass.

Authentication. A mechanism that determines whether a user is who he or she claims to be.

Authorization. The granting of a right or privilege that enables a subject to have legitimate access to a database system or a database system's object.

Backup. The process of periodically taking a copy of the database and log file (and possibly programs) onto offline storage media.

Base table. A named table whose records are physically stored in the database.

Binary relationship. An ER term used to describe a relationship between *two* entities. For example, Branch *Has* Staff.

Bottom-up approach (to database design). A design philosophy that begins by identifying individual design components and then aggregates these components into larger units. In database design, you start at the bottom level by identifying the attributes, and then group the attributes together to form tables that represent entities and relationships.

Business rules. Rules that define or constrain some aspect of the organization.

Candidate key (ER/relational model). A superkey that contains only the minimum number of attributes/columns necessary for unique identification.

Cardinality. Describes the number of possible relationships for each participating entity.

Centralized approach (to database design). Requirements for each user view are merged into a single set of requirements for the new database application.

Chasm trap. Suggests the existence of a relationship between entities, but the pathway does not exist between certain entity occurrences.

Client. A software application that requests services from one or more servers. See also *Two-tier/Three-tier client–server architecture*.

Clustering field. Any nonkey field in a record that is used to cluster (group together) the rows that have a common value for this field.

Clustering index. An index defined on a clustering field of a file. A file can have at most one primary index or one clustering index.

Column (relational model). Same as *attribute*.

Complex relationship. A relationship where the degree is higher than binary.

Composite attribute. An attribute composed of multiple single components.

Composite key. A primary key that contains more than one column.

Concurrency control. A DBMS service that coordinates the simultaneous execution of transactions in a multi-user environment while preserving data integrity.

Constraint. A consistency rule that the database is not permitted to violate.

Data administration. The management and control of the company data, including database planning, development and maintenance of standards, policies and procedures, and conceptual and logical database design.

Data conversion and loading. A stage of the database system development lifecycle that involves transferring any existing data into the new database and converting any existing applications to run on the new database.

Data dictionary. See *System catalog*.

Data independence. The separation of data descriptions from the applications that use the data. This means that if new data structures are added to the database or existing structures in the database are modified then the application programs that use the database are unaffected, provided they don't directly depend upon what has been modified.

Data mart. A subset of a data warehouse that supports the requirements of a particular department or business area.

Data mining. The process of extracting valid, previously unknown, comprehensible, and actionable information from large databases and using it to make crucial business decisions.

Data model. An integrated collection of concepts for describing data, relationships between data, and constraints on the data used by an organization.

Data redundancy. Same as *redundant data*.

Data security. Covers access and use of database objects (such as tables and views) and the actions that users can have on the objects.

Data warehouse. A consolidated/integrated view of corporate data drawn from disparate operational data sources and a range of end-user access tools capable of supporting simple to highly complex queries to support decision making.

Database. A shared collection of logically related data (and a description of this data), designed to meet the information needs of an organization.

Database administration. The management and control of the physical realization of a database application, including physical database design and implementation, setting security and integrity controls, monitoring system performance, and reorganizing the database as necessary.

(Database) application program. A computer program that interacts with the database by issuing an appropriate request (typically an SQL statement) to the DBMS.

Database design. A stage of the database system development lifecycle that involves creating a design for a database that will support the organization's mission statement and mission objectives for the required database.

Database integrity. Refers to the correctness and consistency of stored data. Integrity is usually expressed in terms of constraints.

Database Management System (DBMS). A software system that enables users to define, create, and maintain the database, and provides controlled access to this database.

Database planning. The management activities that allow the stages of the database system development lifecycle to be realized as efficiently and effectively as possible.

Database security. The mechanisms that protect the database against intentional or accidental threats. RDBMSs generally provide two types of security: *data security* and *system security*.

Database server. Same as server (see *Two-tier/Three-tier client–server architecture*).

DBMS engine. Same as server (see *Two-tier client–server architecture*).

DBMS selection. A stage of the database system development lifecycle that involves the selection of an appropriate DBMS to support the database system.

Degree of a relationship. The number of participating entities in a relationship.

Denormalization. Formally, the term refers to a change to the structure of a base table, such that the new table is in a lower normal form than the original table. However, the term is also used more loosely to refer to situations where we combine two tables into one new table, where the new table is in the same normal form but contains more nulls than the original tables.

Derived attribute. An attribute that represents a value that is derivable from the value of a related attribute, or a set of attributes, not necessarily in the same entity.

Design methodology. A structured approach that uses procedures, techniques, tools, and documentation aids to support and facilitate the process of design.

Disjoint constraint. Describes the relationship between members of the subclasses and indicates whether it's possible for a member of a superclass to be a member of one, or more than one, subclass.

Distributed database. A collection of multiple, logically interrelated, shared data (and a description of this data), physically distributed over a computer network.

Distributed DBMS (DDBMS). The software that transparently manages the distributed database.

Domain. The set of allowable values for one or more attributes.

Encryption. The encoding of the data by a special algorithm that renders the data unreadable by any program without the decryption key.

Entity. A set of objects with the same properties that are identified by a user or organization as having an independent existence.

Entity integrity. In a base table, no column of a primary key can be null.

Entity occurrence. A uniquely identifiable object in an entity.

Entity–Relationship model. A detailed logical representation of entities, attributes, and relationships for an organization.

Fact-finding. The formal process of using techniques such as interviews and questionnaires to collect facts about systems, requirements, and preferences.

Fan trap. Occurs when two entities have a 1:* relationship that fan out from a third entity, but the two entities should have a direct relationship between them to provide the necessary information.

Field (relational model). Same as *tuple*.

File. A named collection of related records stored on secondary storage.

File-based system. A collection of programs designed to manage (create, insert, delete, update, and retrieve) data in one or more files and to produce applications (usually reports) based on the data in these files.

File organization. A way of arranging the records in a file when the file is stored on disk.

First normal form (1NF). A table in which the intersection of every column and record contains only one value.

Foreign key. A column, or set of columns, within one table that matches the candidate key of some (possibly the same) table.

4GL (Fourth-Generation Language). A nonprocedural language, such as SQL, that only requires the user to define *what* must be done; the 4GL translates the *what* into details of *how* this should be executed.

Full functional dependency. A condition in which a column is functionally dependent on a composite key but not on any subset of that key.

Functional dependency. A property of the meaning of the columns in a table indicating how columns relate to one another. It describes the relationship between columns in a table. For example, if A and B are columns of a table, B is functionally dependent on A (denoted $A \rightarrow B$), if each value of A is associated with exactly one value of B. (A and B may each consist of one or more columns.)

Generalization. The process of minimizing the differences between entities by identifying their common features.

Generalization hierarchy. Same as *type hierarchy*.

Global logical data model. A data model that represents the data requirements of all user views of an organization.

Implementation. A stage of the database system development lifecycle that involves the physical realization of the database and application designs.

Index. A data structure that allows the DBMS to locate particular records in a file more quickly, and thereby speed up response to user queries.

Information system. The resources that enable the collection, management, control, and dissemination of data/information throughout an organization.

Inheritance. See *Attribute inheritance*.

Integrity constraints. Constraints imposed to prevent the database from becoming inconsistent.

IS-A hierarchy. Same as *type hierarchy*.

Journaling. The process of keeping and maintaining a log file (or journal) of all changes made to the database to enable recovery to be undertaken effectively in the event of a failure.

Local logical data model. A data model that represents the data requirements of one or more, but not all, user views of an organization.

Logical database design. The process of constructing a model of the data used in an organization based on a specific data model, but independent of a particular DBMS and other physical considerations.

Meta-data. Data about data; see *System catalog*.

Mission objective. Identifies a particular task that the database system must support.

Mission statement. Defines the major aims of the database system.

Multiplicity. Defines the number of occurrences of one entity that may relate to a single occurrence of an associated entity.

Multi-valued attribute. An attribute that holds multiple values for an entity occurrence.

Nonkey attribute/column. An attribute/column that is not part of a key.

Normal forms. Stages in the normalization process. The first three normal forms are called *first normal form (1NF)*, *second normal form (2NF)*, and *third normal form (3NF)*.

Normalization. A technique for producing a set of tables with desirable properties that supports the requirements of a user or organization.

Null. Represents a value for a column that is currently unknown or is not applicable for this record.

Object-oriented Data Model (OODM). A data model that captures the semantics of objects supported in object-oriented programming.

Object-oriented Database (OODB). A persistent and sharable repository of objects defined in an object-oriented data model.

Object-oriented DBMS (OODBMS). A manager of an object-oriented database.

Object-relational DBMS (ORDBMS). An extension to the relational DBMS to incorporate some concept of 'object'. There is no single ORDBMS, rather a number of such systems, whose characteristics depend upon the way and the degree to which the extension has been made.

OnLine Analytical Processing (OLAP). The dynamic synthesis, analysis, and consolidation of large volumes of multi-dimensional data. OLAP describes a technology that uses a multi-dimensional view of summarized data to provide quick access to strategic information for the purposes of advanced analysis.

Operational maintenance. A stage of the database system development lifecycle that involves monitoring and maintaining the system following installation.

Participation constraint (EER model). Determines whether every occurrence in the superclass must participate as a member of a subclass.

Participation constraint (ER model). Determines whether all or only some entity occurrences participate in a relationship.

Physical database design. The process of producing a description of the implementation of the database on secondary storage; it describes the base tables, file organizations, and indexes used to achieve efficient access to the data, and any associated integrity constraints and security restrictions.

Primary index. An index built on the ordering key field of the file. A file can have at most one primary index or one clustering index. The ordering key is guaranteed to have a unique value in each record.

Primary key (ER model). The candidate key that is selected to identify each entity occurrence.

Primary key (relational model). The candidate key that is selected to identify records uniquely within the table.

Privileges. The actions that a user is permitted to carry out on a given base table or view.

Prototyping. A stage of the database system development lifecycle that involves building a working model of a database application.

QBE (Query-by-Example). A nonprocedural database language for relational DBMSs. QBE is a graphical 'point-and-click' way of querying the database.

RDBMS. Relational DBMS.

Record (relational model). Same as *tuple*.

Recovery control. The process of restoring the database to a correct state in the event of a failure.

Recursive relationship. A relationship where the same entity participates more than once in *different* roles. For example, Staff *Supervises* Staff.

Redundant data. Duplicated data that is stored in more than one table.

Referential integrity. If a foreign key exists in a table, either the foreign key value must match a candidate key value of some record in its home table or the foreign key value must be wholly null.

Relation. A relation is a table with columns and rows.

Relational database. A collection of normalized tables.

Relational model. A data model that represents data in the form of tables (or relations).

Relationship. A meaningful association among entities.

Relationship occurrence. A uniquely identifiable association between two entities.

Replication. The process of generating and reproducing multiple copies of data at one or more sites.

Requirements collection and analysis. A stage of the database system development lifecycle that involves collecting and analyzing information about the organization to be supported by the database system, and using this information to identify the requirements for the new database system.

Row (relational model). Same as *tuple*.

Second normal form (2NF). A table that is already in 1NF and in which the values in each non-primary-key column can be worked out from the values in all the columns that make up the primary key.

Secondary index. An index that is defined on a non-ordering field of the datafile.

Security. Same as *database security*.

Server. A software application that provides services to requesting clients. See also *Two-tier/Three-tier client–server architecture*.

Simple attribute. An attribute composed of a single component.

Single-valued attribute. An attribute that holds a single value for an entity occurrence.

Specialization. The process of maximizing the differences between members of an entity by identifying their distinguishing characteristics.

Specialization hierarchy. Same as *type hierarchy*.

SQL (Structured Query Language). A nonprocedural database language for RDBMSs. In other words, you specify *what* information you require, rather than *how* to get it. SQL has been standardized by the International Organization for Standardization (ISO), making it both the formal and *de facto* standard language for defining and manipulating RDBMSs.

Strong entity. An entity that is not dependent on the existence of another entity for its primary key.

Subclass. A distinct grouping of occurrences of an entity, which require to be represented in a data model. See also *Specialization* and *Generalization*.

Superclass. An entity that includes one or more distinct groupings of its occurrences, which require to be represented in a data model. See also *Specialization* and *Generalization*.

Superkey (ER model). An attribute, or set of attributes, that uniquely identifies each entity occurrence.

Superkey (relational model). A column, or set of columns, that uniquely identifies a record within a table.

System catalog. Holds data about the structure of the database, users, applications, and so on.

System definition. A stage of the database system development lifecycle that involves defining the scope and boundary of the database system, including its major user views.

System security. Covers access and use of the database at the system level, such as a username and password.

Table (relational model). Same as *relation*.

Table diagram. A diagrammatic representation of the tables in a database (including primary and foreign keys).

Ternary relationship. A relationship between *three* entities. For example, the relationship *Registers* between Branch, Staff, and Member.

Testing. A stage of the database system development lifecycle that involves executing the application programs with the intent of finding errors.

Third normal form (3NF). A table that is already in 1NF and 2NF, and in which the values in all non-primary-key columns can be worked out from *only* the primary key column(s) and no other columns.

3GL (Third-Generation Language). A procedural language such as COBOL, C, C++, that requires the user (usually a programmer) to specify *what* must be done and also *how* it must be done.

Threat. Any situation or event, whether intentional or unintentional, that may adversely affect a system and consequently the organization.

Three-tier client–server architecture. Consists of a *client* that handles the user interface, an *application server* that handles the business logic and data processing layer, and a *database server* that runs the DBMS.

Top-down approach (to database design). A design philosophy that begins by defining the main structures of the system and then moves to smaller units within those structures. In database design, you start at the top level by identifying the entities and relationships between the data, then you add more details, such as the information you want to hold about the entities and relationships (called attributes) and any constraints on the entities, relationships, and attributes.

Transaction. An action, or series of actions, carried out by a single user or application program, which accesses or changes the contents of the database.

Transaction Processing Monitor (TPM). A program that controls data transfer between clients and servers in order to provide a consistent environment for OnLine Transaction Processing (OLTP).

Transitive dependency. A condition where A, B, C are columns of a table, such that if B is functionally dependent on A (A → B) and C is functionally dependent on B (B → C), then C is transitively dependent on A via B (provided that A is not functionally dependent on B or C). If a transitive dependency exists on the primary key, the table is not in 3NF. The transitive dependency must be removed for a table to achieve 3NF.

Tuple (relational model). A record of a *relation*.

Two-tier client–server architecture. Consists of a *client* program that handles the main business and data processing logic and interfaces with the user, and a *server* program that manages and controls access to the database.

Type hierarchy. The collection of an entity and its subclasses and their subclasses, and so on.

UML (Unified Modeling Language). The successor to a number of object-oriented analysis and design methods introduced in the 1980s and 1990s.

Update anomalies. Inconsistencies that may arise when a user attempts to update a table that contains redundant data. There are three types of anomalies: insertion, deletion, and modification.

User view. Defines what is required of a database application from the perspective of a particular job (such as Manager or Supervisor) or business application area (such as marketing, personnel, or stock control).

View. A 'virtual table' that does not actually exist in the database but is generated by the DBMS from the underlying base tables whenever it's accessed.

View integration approach (to database design). Requirements for each user view are used to build a separate data model to represent that user view. The resulting data models are merged at a later stage in database design.

Weak entity. An entity that is partially or wholly dependent on the existence of some other entity (or entities) for its primary key.

XML (eXtensible Markup Language). A meta-language (a language for describing other languages) that enables designers to create their own customized tags to provide functionality not available with HTML.

References

Chen P.P (1976). The Entity-Relationship model – Toward a unified view of data. *ACM Transactions on Database Systems*, **1**(1), 9–36

Codd E.F. (1970). A relational model of data for large shared data banks. *Communications of the ACM*, **13**(6), 377–387

Connolly T.M. and Begg C.E. (2002). *Database Systems: A Practical Approach to Design, Implementation, and Management*, 3rd edn. Harlow, England: Addison-Wesley

Inmon W.H. (1993). *Building the Data Warehouse*. New York: John Wiley & Sons

Kim W. (1991). Object-oriented database systems: strengths and weaknesses. *Journal of Object-Oriented Programming*, **4**(4), 21–29

OASIG (1996). Research report. Available at *http://www.comlab.ox.ac.uk/oucl/users/john.nicholls/oas-sum.html*

Shneiderman D. (1992). *Design the User Interface: Strategies for Effective Human–Computer Interaction*, 2nd edn. Reading, MA: Addison-Wesley

Sommerville I. (2000). *Software Engineering*, 6th edn. Harlow, England: Addison-Wesley

Index

secondary index 287, 448, 449, 509
  choosing 288–9, 289–90
  removing 291
secondary storage 443
security 101, 505, 509
  countermeasures 103–10
    authentication 106
    authorization 105
    backup and recovery 108
    encryption 110 109
    integrity 109
    journaling 108
    privileges 106–7
    view 108
  of data 299, 504
  mechanisms in physical database
      design 298–303, 426
  in Microsoft Access 300–3
  in Oracle 367–72
  in *PerfectPets* case study 367–72
  in *StayHome* case study 298–303
  threats 102–3
  user-level 301–2
    documentation of 303
segment in Oracle 363
semantic overloading in RDBMS 381
SEQUEL 38
server 10
simple attribute 151, 509
  in logical database design 204–8
simple join operation 59–60, 72
single-value attribute 152, 509
single-valued per group 53
slots 447
software 10
software crisis 78–9
Sommerville, I. 93
sort key 51
  major 51
  minor 51
space management in Oracle 364–5
specialization 509
  in EER model 247–54
    attribute inheritance 249
    process of 249–50
    specialization process 249–50
    superclasses and subclasses 247

superclass/subclass relationships
    247–9, 252–4
  tables representing 254–6
  in logical database design 211–12,
    421
  in *PerfectPets* case study 341
specialization hierarchy 249, 509
Standardized Generalized Mark-up
    Language (SGML) 379
static web pages 403–4
StayHome case study 123–43
  business user views
    global model 431–41
    local model 431
    user requirements specification
      429–31
  database design 143
  database planning 126–32
  file organizations 292–3
  indexes for 293–4
  new requirements from 325–6
  overview 123–6
  requirements collection and analysis
    135–43
    data requirements 139
    legal issues 143
    system requirements 136–7
    transaction requirements 140–3,
      430–1
    on user views 135–6, 138–9
  system definition 133–4
  systems boundary 133
  tables required 236–8
  user views 133–4
storage
  volatile *vs* non-volatile 443
  structures *see* file organization;
      indexes
striping unit 323
strong entity 155, 210, 509
structured interviews 120
Structured Query Language (SQL) 8,
    34, 37–40, 509
  aggregate functions 51–3
  AVG function 51–3